The German Federal Constitutional Court

The German Federal Constitutional Court

The Court Without Limits

MATTHIAS JESTAEDT
OLIVER LEPSIUS
CHRISTOPH MÖLLERS
CHRISTOPH SCHÖNBERGER

OXFORD
UNIVERSITY PRESS

OXFORD
UNIVERSITY PRESS

Great Clarendon Street, Oxford, OX2 6DP,
United Kingdom

Oxford University Press is a department of the University of Oxford.
It furthers the University's objective of excellence in research, scholarship,
and education by publishing worldwide. Oxford is a registered trade mark of
Oxford University Press in the UK and in certain other countries

This translation of the book published as
Matthias Jestaedt, Oliver Lepsius, Christoph Möllers, Christoph Schönberger,
Das entgrenzte Gericht. Eine kritische Bilanz nach sechzig Jahren Bundesverfassungsgericht,
is published under licence from Suhrkamp Verlag Berlin

The translation of this work was funded by Geisteswissenschaften International—Translation Funding for Humanities and Social Sciences from Germany, a joint initiative of the Fritz Thyssen Foundation, the German Federal Foreign Office, the collecting society VG WORT, and the Börsenverein des Deutschen Buchhandels (German Publishers & Booksellers Association).

First Edition published in 2020

Published in the United States of America by Oxford University Press
198 Madison Avenue, New York, NY 10016, United States of America

British Library Cataloguing in Publication Data
Data available

Library of Congress Control Number: 2019916872

ISBN 978–0–19–879354–0

Contents

Table of Cases

Note on tables: For the benefit of digital users, table entries that span two pages (e.g., 52–53) may, on occasion, appear on only one of those pages.

BVERFG (FEDERAL CONSTITUTIONAL COURT)

BVERFGE (DECISIONS OF THE FEDERAL CONSTITUTIONAL COURT)

BVERFGK (CHAMBER DECISIONS OF THE FEDERAL CONSTITUTIONAL COURT)

BVERWGE (DECISIONS OF THE FEDERAL ADMINISTRATIVE COURT)

US CASES

Table of Legislation

EUROPEAN LEGISLATION

INTERNATIONAL LEGISLATION

Introduction

Justin Collings

Few blessings compare with the gift of good teachers. As a law student and as a graduate student, I had some of the best of them. A few of my professors, moreover, were truly cosmopolitan, and they occasionally made passing comments about constitutions and constitutionalism in other parts of the world. I found this fascinating, especially when they spoke of a court that some of them rated the most influential in the world. It was enough to drive a busy graduate student to drop just about everything and learn German. The language, you see, was my passport to the German Constitutional Court.

I later tried, in a doctoral dissertation, to write that Court's history. Later still, I turned that dissertation into a book. In the process, I read countless Court decisions and newspaper articles about Court decisions. I examined the archives of important judges and of politicians who clashed with those judges. I read a lot of German history. Most of this material was in German. Sometimes it made for rough going. But nothing I read was as rebarbatively difficult, as impenetrably dense, or as mystifyingly foreign as the imposing citadel of German constitutional scholarship.

Here was something wholly different—a tradition, as far as I could tell, with no Anglo-American counterpart; a systematizing, conceptualizing, categorizing, refining, and purifying project of evidently boundless horizons. I had never seen anything like it. These scholars described their enterprise in terms I could dimly understand and barely translate. It was unquestionably impressive work. There was even an aesthetic lure in the nuanced precision of its taxonomical exactitude. But it was not, as the English say, my cup of tea. And it was not, as the Germans say, my *Fragestellung*.

I sensed almost immediately that these scholars' enterprise was qualitatively different from my own. I was interested in the German Constitutional Court as an agent *in* history and *of* history—a tribunal that both shaped and was shaped by Germany's postwar development. Much of this scholarship, by contrast, seemed timeless. It took the Court and its jurisprudence for granted. It operated, I thought, in a kind of eternity. There were many exceptions, of course—some of them marvelous exceptions. But for the most part, as I wrote my history of the German Court, I kept a respectful distance from much of its scholarly commentary.

And then, rather late in the game, I found the book you are about to read.

The German Federal Constitutional Court: The Court Without Limits. Matthias Jestaedt, Oliver Lepsius, Christoph Möllers, and Christoph Schönberger, published by Oxford University Press under licence (2020).
DOI: 10.1093/oso/9780198793540.001.0001

I can hardly describe its impact. Here were writers after my own heart, addressing with intelligence and insight the questions that drove my own research. They wrote with stylistic verve and substantive panache. They were deeply familiar with the dogmatic, systematizing tradition, but wrote outside that tradition and against it. They wrote about the Court with profound knowledge, enormous authority, and the critical detachment of a loyal opposition. They asked all the right questions. They offered scintillating answers. They probed, and provoked, and pushed the quest further. My book was much better because I read theirs. I didn't know any of the authors, but I owed them a big debt. I still do. Introducing this English version of their landmark volume is only partial payment. It is an even greater pleasure.

But before I can properly introduce the book, I must first introduce its protagonist. And so, as the nineteenth-century novelists liked to put it: Reader, meet Court—or *Bundesverfassungsgericht* for short.

* * *

December 1952. The chancellor was angry. Very angry. He was also genuinely perplexed. Just who did these judges think they were? How dared they stall his treasured treaty by invoking a constitution at whose creation he had presided? How dare they question his assessment of the national interest or reasons of state? Whatever Adenauer and his fellow framers had in mind when they established a constitutional court for the neophyte nation, it surely wasn't this. Perhaps the chancellor never really said, in a bewildered dialect, "*Dat ham wir uns so nicht vorjestellt!*"[1], but he should have. The phrase captures a deep truth for Adenauer and for everybody else. In virtually all matters related to the Federal Constitutional Court, nobody saw it coming.

* * *

The Court's creation was largely uncontroversial. Both major parties had reasons to welcome judicial review of legislation and judicial resolution of intergovernmental conflicts. Opposition was scattered and slight. In any case, the framers had larger fish to fry. Founding a new state in Germany's western occupation zones raised scores of burning, divisive questions. Constitutional justice seemed, by comparison, a minor concern.

The framers called their work a "Basic Law" (*Grundgesetz*) rather than a "constitution" (*Verfassung*). They meant it to be a transitory charter for a temporary state. Germany, they hoped, would soon reunite. The German people could then adopt a

[1] Roughly, "We never imagined that!"

constitution all their own. The framers did not, however, shun the term "constitution" altogether. They embedded it in the title of a newfangled court—the Federal *Constitutional* Court (*Bundesverfassungsgericht*).

That Court would wield impressive powers—alarming powers, critics thought.[2] It would have final say on whether to strip the fundamental rights of those who abused fundamental rights,[3] and whether to ban anti-constitutional political parties.[4] It would field challenges to parliamentary elections[5] and presidential acts.[6] Most momentously, it would resolve conflicts among constitutional organs and assess the constitutionality of state and federal laws.[7]

Impressive as these powers were, they gave little inkling of the role the Court would come to play. That role became clearer with the Federal Constitutional Court Act (FCCA) of March 1951. This Act, the Court's organic statute, proved more contentious than the underlying constitutional provisions. The law took a year-and-a-half to pass. It remains one of postwar Germany's most consequential statutes.

The FCCA provided for a bicameral Court with a dozen justices in each "Senate."[8] Half the justices would be appointed by the Bundestag, Parliament's national arm, and half by the Bundesrat, its federalist arm. The Court would announce its judgments "in the name of the People."[9] These judgments—including those declaring statutes null and void—would have the force of law.[10] The Court would have little power to avoid this responsibility. The FCCA all but precluded any American-style political question doctrine.[11] Whatever cases came before the Court, the justices would decide. And the cases came in droves.

Constitutional appeals could reach the Court in three main ways: by judicial referral, by official petition, and by citizen complaint.

The referral system followed the Austrian model. If, during a judicial proceeding, a judge concluded that a pertinent law was unconstitutional, the judge must stay the proceedings, refer the matter to the Constitutional Court, and decide the case in accordance with the high Court's answer.[12] Such referrals triggered "concrete" constitutional review.

[2] See, e.g., Werner Weber, *Weimarer Verfassung und Bonner Grundgesetz* (Fleischer 1949).

[3] Art. 18 GG. Following the German practice, I shall cite to the Basic Law as "GG" (for *Grundgesetz*), to the Federal Constitutional Court Act (for *Bundesverfassungsgerichtsgesetz*), and to the Court's official decisions as "BVerfGE" (for *Entscheidungen des Bundesverfassungsgerichts*).

[4] Art. 21(2) GG.

[5] Art. 41(2) GG.

[6] Art. 61 GG.

[7] Art. 93(1), 100(1) GG.

[8] The number was later reduced to ten, and later still to eight, where it has remained.

[9] BVerfGG s. 25(4).

[10] BVerfGG s. 31(2), 78.

[11] As one early commentator put it, "The theory of *justizfreie Hoheitsakte*, or 'political questions' beyond the jurisdiction of the courts, has been explicitly eliminated by the Law on the Federal Constitutional Court." Richard J. Barnet, 'The Protection of Constitutional Rights in Germany' (1959) 45 *Virginia Law Review* 1139, 1164.

[12] BVerfGG ss. 80–2.

Only the federal cabinet, state governments, and qualified (federal) parliamentary minorities could challenge laws directly.[13] Such challenges were not subject to a case-or-controversy requirement, and involved the Court in "norm control" (*Normenkontrolle*), or abstract review. Although the number of such appeals has always been small, they have launched many of the Court's most explosive cases.

Most cases begin through citizen complaints (*Verfassungsbeschwerden*). The idea that individual citizens might invoke the Court's jurisdiction faced hostility and scorn in the Parliamentary Council.[14] Many framers thought such complaints would overwhelm the Court and serve little practical purpose. But the first postwar Parliament embraced them,[15] and the individual complaint soon became the Court's chief source of business and the principal basis of its enduring popularity. Citizen complaints helped bind West Germans to a constitution and a Court they had no hand in creating. To be sure, citizen complaints were subject to exhaustion requirements. But a citizen who thought herself deprived of a constitutional right might, after disappointment in the ordinary courts, bring her cause to Karlsruhe. Thousands did, many to challenge lower court decisions. The individual complaint was later enshrined in the constitution itself.[16]

The Court's first members were an impressive group. They wielded a rich array of legal, political, economic, and academic experience. They had less experience as judges. This was by design. Christian Democrats wanted politically-sensitive justices, and Social Democrats wanted justices untarred by the judiciary's complicity with Nazism. On the whole, the founding justices had impeccable anti-Nazi credentials. Many had been persecuted by the regime. Some lost jobs or spouses. Others went into exile. Some were of Jewish descent—the highest-ranking Jews in the new West German state.

During the Bundestag debates over the FCCA, one MP called the Court "the final step in building a state based upon the rule of law (*Rechtsstaat*)."[17] Clearly, West Germany's legislators thought they had done something significant. But no one foresaw how far their work would reach.

* * *

The Court began with a bang. In their very first judgment, the justices rejected the strong positivism that allegedly had fueled judges' capitulation to Nazism. They also invalidated parts of an important federal law and recognized the possibility of "unconstitutional constitutional amendments."[18] Heady stuff, but the

[13] BVerfGG s. 13(6).
[14] Barnet (n 11) 1155.
[15] BVerfGG ss. 90–6.
[16] See GG s. 93(1)(4).
[17] Quoted in Arthur von Mehren, 'Constitutionalism in Germany—The First Decision of the New Constitutional Court' (1952) 1 *American Journal of Comparative Law* 78.
[18] 1 BVerfGE 14 (1951).

Court was only getting started. In the months and years ahead, it moved from strength to strength.

In 1952 and 1953, the Court fought a three-front war for institutional independence and constitutional supremacy: against the Federal Government, against the ordinary judiciary, and against the public law academy. The justices triumphed on all sides.[19] During the 1950s, the Court also banned two political parties—the communists on the Left and the neo-Nazis on the Right. In a pair of landmark judgments, the justices told the legislature that the Basic Law meant what it said when it promised gender equality.[20] Above all, there was the trio of 1957–1958 judgments that founded the Court's rights jurisprudence. In *Elfes*, the Court held that fundamental rights reach every human activity; in *Lüth*, that they reach every legal relationship; and in *Pharmacy*, that they may be limited only in proportional ways.[21] The influence of these three judgments, in Germany itself and abroad, can hardly be measured.

There were, of course, many less-famous cases. Some decisions disappointed contemporaries and appalled posterity—one banning non-binding anti-nuclear plebiscites,[22] for instance, and another approving criminal sanctions for male gay sex.[23] Taken together, however, it was, by any standard, a remarkable first decade.

The Court's second decade was quieter but still striking. The Court secured a reputation as a catalyst of liberalism and democracy. In 1962, in a tartly-worded judgment widely hailed as a triumph for federalism and free speech, the justices quashed Adenauer's effort to launch a government-controlled television network.[24] Four years later, an evenly split Senate technically upheld a police raid of *Der Spiegel*, the country's most popular weekly. But the Court also took the unusual step of publishing the dissenters' views as well, including their passionate defense of press freedom.[25] The Court aggressively regulated party finance,[26] and continued to refine its rights jurisprudence.[27] By decade's end, one scholar observed that "[t]he jurisprudence of the Federal Constitutional Court has, as we all know, fostered the development of a true democratic understanding in the Federal Republic—not least in the sphere of public opinion. There are decisions of the Federal Constitutional Court," this scholar concluded, "that, as harbingers of the free *Rechtsstaat* and of democracy, were years ahead of public opinion."[28]

19 For more on these exchanges, see the essay by Matthias Jestaedt in this volume.

20 3 BVerfGE 225 (1953); 10 BVerfGE 59 (1959).

21 See 6 BVerfGE 32 (1957) (Elfes); 7 BVerfGE 198 (1958) (Lüth); 7 BVerfGE 377 (Pharmacy). The *Pharmacy* judgment contained the seeds of, but did not fully articulate, the famous proportionality principle that has since then swept the world.

22 8 BVerfGE 104 (1958); 8 BVerfGE 122 (1958).

23 6 BVerfGE 389 (1957).

24 12 BVerfGE 205 (1961).

25 20 BVerfGE 162 (1966). Dissents were not formally allowed until 1970.

26 See 8 BVerfGE 51 (1958); 20 BVerfGE 56 (1966).

27 See, e.g., 16 BVerfGE 194 (1963); 25 BVerfGE 256 (1969); 30 BVerfGE 173 (1971).

28 Wilhelm Karl Geck, 'Diskussionsbeitrag' in *Veröffentlichungen der Vereinigung der Deutschen Staatsrechtslehrer* 29th vol. (Walter de Gruyter GmbH & Co. KG, 1970) 113.

This statement coincided with dramatic political change. In September 1969, Willy Brandt became chancellor at the head of a Social–Liberal coalition. Christian Democrats left power for the first time. On taking office, Brandt vowed to "dare more democracy." He called on his compatriots to emerge from their adolescence, to engage more actively as citizens, and to make the Federal Republic, at long last, a full democracy. The new government promised reforms across the board. They came in swift succession. Many collided with the Constitutional Court.

That collision was stupendous. The Court squelched or hobbled reforms dealing with abortion,[29] university governance,[30] college admissions,[31] conscientious objection,[32] and more. In foreign affairs, the Court upheld the Basic Treaty with East Germany, but saddled it with an interpretation that, critics said, would cripple negotiations for decades.[33] The Court also curbed European integration. The justices promised to review Community law's compatibility with the Basic Law, at least until the EEC developed its own effective rights regime.[34]

Many of these judgments sparked raucous critiques—some from foremost politicians. The unprecedented criticism stirred talk of a constitutional crisis. But the Court had defenders as well as critics. Its apologists, by and large, adduced its historic contributions.

Two factors finally defused the confrontation. First, the pace of reform slackened—especially after 1974, when the pragmatic Helmut Schmidt replaced a battered Willy Brandt as chancellor. Second, the Court became more deferential, most prominently in 1979 when it approved a landmark labor law.[35] In the end, the Court emerged from the crisis relatively unscathed. Indeed, the alarm with which many observers reacted to the criticism confirmed the Court's centrality to the constitutional order. As Christoph Schönberger observes later in these pages, crises are not necessarily signs of weakness. This crisis revealed the Court's strength.

Conservatives regained power in 1982 and kept it a long time. During the 1980s, the Court clashed with the government only rarely. On some hot-button issues—nuclear armament,[36] for instance, or the government's power to fake a no-confidence vote to trigger a snap election[37]—the justices proved quite compliant. Elsewhere, such as with the rights of protesters or parliamentary minorities, the Court was sometimes more aggressive.[38] In 1983, the justices delighted the public by inventing and enforcing a right to "personal data self-determination."[39]

[29] 39 BVerfGE 1 (1975).
[30] 35 BVerfGE 79 (1973).
[31] 33 BVerfGE 303 (1972).
[32] 48 BVerfGE 127 (1978).
[33] 36 BVerfGE 1 (1973).
[34] 37 BVerfGE 271 (1974).
[35] 50 BVerfGE 290 (1979).
[36] See 68 BVerfGE 1 (1984).
[37] See 62 BVerfGE 1 (1983).
[38] See, e.g., 69 BVerfGE 315 (1985); 80 BVerfGE 188 (1989).
[39] 65 BVerfGE 1 (1985).

In hindsight, the judgment and the notion look prescient. An accident of the calendar (the judgment came down on the threshold of 1984, the "Orwell Year") made the judges look like heroes.

* * *

All along, the Court continued to articulate a rights jurisprudence of sophistication and daring. The justices refined the proportionality test into a work of art—a methodological masterpiece that became their most successful export.[40] They also expanded rights' objective reach, imposing on the state a generalized "duty to protect" (*Schutzpflicht*) along with other affirmative obligations.[41] The Court's judgments grew ever longer as the justices elaborated ever more governing standards.[42]

In the process, there developed a dialogic relationship—indeed, a *symbiotic* relationship—between the Court and its scholarly commentariat. By the end of the 1980s, prominent academics complained that public lawyers had abandoned independent theory for dutiful, dogmatic, systematizing exegesis of Constitutional Court decisions. One critic bemoaned the "dethroning" of state theory by "Constitutional Court positivism."[43] It was clear, however, that both sides were benefiting. On the one hand, the Court gained prestige and an aura of expertise from the lavish attention of dedicated scholars; on the other hand, the Court's power and prominence raised constitutional law to the summit of legal science. Many scholars became justices. Some were extraordinarily influential justices. Retired justices returned to the academy as mini-celebrities. This became constitutional law's revolving door. The pattern accelerated over time. It shows little sign of abating.[44]

* * *

The Court's role changed after German reunification. For starters, the Basic Law's permanence, long assumed in practice, was now enshrined in law. Reunification did not produce a new, pan-German constitution. Instead, the Eastern states simply acceded to the Basic Law. The constitution, the Court, and its seven dozen volumes of decisions thus lost any lingering trace of transience. At the same time, reunification marked the end of an era. It closed the Court's heroic age—the era of epochal judgments and jurisgenerative landmarks. The Court continued to decide

[40] See, e.g., Alec Stone Sweet and Jud Mathews, 'Proportionality Balancing and Global Constitutionalism' (2008) 47 *Columbia Journal of Transnational Law* 72.

[41] See, e.g., 39 BVerfGE 1, 42–44 (1975) (duty to protect unborn human life); 33 BVerfGE 303, 329–338 (1972) (duty to provide higher education).

[42] On this development, see Oliver Lepsius' essay in this volume.

[43] Bernhard Schlinck, 'Die Entthronung der Staatsrechtswissenschaft durch die Verfassungsgerichtsbarkeit' (1989) 28 *Der Staat* 161.

[44] For more on this development, see the essay by Matthias Jestaedt in this volume.

important cases, some of them quite controversial. But it did so within frameworks constructed long since. Unlike parliament and the Federal Government, the Court never moved after reunification. Instead it stayed in Karlsruhe—the site and symbol of its ancient glories, the antonomastic emblem of its constitutional identity.[45]

* * *

After 1990, the Court helped mediate between Germany's reuniting halves. Eastern interests found a stronger advocate in Karlsruhe than in Bonn or, later, Berlin. In the middle of the 1990s, the Court triggered another bidecadal crisis[46] in a trio of judgments dealing with rights of assembly, speech, and negative religious freedom. In the speech case, the Court seemed to recognize a constitutional right to call soldiers murderers.[47] Critics railed against what they saw as untrammeled license to slander the armed forces. Even more controversial was a judgment that said Bavaria could not require crucifixes on public classroom walls.[48] The outcry in Bavaria—but not only in Bavaria—was extraordinary. Thousands marched in protest. Politicians breathed defiance. Criticism of the judgment smoldered into denunciations of the Court. Many wondered aloud what purpose the Court still served.

The crisis passed, but the question didn't. The Court that made its mark and earned its fame as the guardian of postwar liberalization and democratization faced a crisis of identity. Reunited Germany was widely hailed as one of the world's most stable, prosperous, and liberal democracies. The self-proclaimed guardian of the postwar constitution now faced a new conundrum: mature individuals don't need guardians. The Court was also losing influence to powerful supranational rivals—the European Court of Justice and the European Court of Human Rights. Karlsruhe's *raison d'être* was thus doubly in doubt. Its achievements lay in the past; its present function seemed redundant.

The Court responded as embattled institutions often do—by redoubling its efforts in what it had always done well. The justices continued to expand and refine doctrine. They discharged, as never before, their role as what Oliver Lepsius calls "the standard-setting authority." The Court's judgments grew longer and longer. The legislature's leeway shrank smaller and smaller. The Court even took to reviewing both substantive laws and legislative procedures for objective reasonableness. To some, the Court seemed to be doing more and more, even as the country needed it less and less.

And then there was European integration. In 1993, the Court approved Germany's accession to the Maastricht Treaty,[49] but did so in a long judgment that

[45] For more on this point, see Christoph Schönberger's essay in this volume.

[46] The Court's three crises have come in the 1950s, the 1970s, and the 1990s. Another was due in the 2010s, but it appears to be late in coming.

[47] 93 BVerfGE 266 (1995).

[48] 93 BVerfGE 1 (1995).

[49] 89 BVerfGE 155 (1993).

chided the EU for its democratic deficiencies and warned that European integration must not undermine democracy in Germany. Specifically, integration must not sap individual Germans' right to vote by draining Parliament of meaningful powers. In 2009, the Court approved the Lisbon Treaty, again with caveats. This time the justices' reservations ran deeper.[50] The Court held explicitly that Germany could never, while the Basic Law remained in force, be part of a European federal state (*Bundesstaat*). The Basic Law, the justices explained, both established and guaranteed a particular constitutional *identity*—a term they repeated, as in mystical incantation, some three dozen times.[51] The Court thus proclaimed itself the guardian of German constitutional identity against the menace of supranational encroachment.

Reviews of the judgment were mixed. The authors of this book were largely critical, sometimes trenchantly so. Some critics saw in the judgment the floundering of a Court that had lost its way—a Court imprisoned in its own past, uncertain of its role in an altered world. Others sighed at the fool's errand of defending German constitutional identity against a European project that formed part of that identity's essential core. The Court, it seemed, was spending past capital to erect levies against the wave of the future.

* * *

This book first appeared when *Lisbon* was still recent. Its publication honored the Court's sixtieth birthday in September 2011. As its subtitle suggested, it was meant to take stock—to provide a "critical balance" after decades of constitutional justice in Germany. Each author grappled with what the Court had achieved, what it had become, and whither it seemed to be going. Each sensed that somehow the Court had transgressed important boundaries and that, partly as a result, it faced new and pressing tests.

The authors engage their common topic from very different angles. Christoph Schönberger charts the Court's historical development, with a nuanced attention to the motley preconditions—and the irreducible contingency—of its remarkable rise. Matthias Jestaedt also stresses that nothing in the Court's growth was preordained, but his approach is more institutional. Jestaedt limns the Court's initially fraught relations with political actors, ordinary judges, and legal academics, and he scrutinizes the institutional peculiarities that have made the Court what it is. Schönberger and Jestaedt end their assessments on strikingly different notes, with Schönberger extolling the "art of retreat" and Jestaedt rejecting "premature swan songs."

[50] 123 BVerfGE 267 (2009).

[51] See Gary Jacobsohn, 'Anchoring and Sailing: Contrasting Imperatives of Constitutional Revolution' in Gary Jacobsohn and Miguel Schor (eds.), *Comparative Constitutional Theory* (Edward Elgar, 2018) 334, 338–42.

The approach of Oliver Lepsius is more doctrinal, but in a distinctive way. Lepsius argues that the Court's great landmarks were all products of their time, but that subsequent scholars—and the justices themselves—have ignored this context in their subsequent efforts to harmonize the Court's case law in a systematic way. Lepsius chronicles the proliferation of doctrinal standards over time, underscores the bizarre lengths to which that proliferation has recently extended, and warns that the era of bold new standards is probably gone for good.

Lastly, Christoph Möllers takes up the daunting question that hovers over all four essays: the question of the Court's legitimacy. Möllers investigates the possible bases of such legitimacy, carefully assesses each one, and shows them all to be problematic. There are, Möllers insists, no easy answers. And although he rejects facile Yes/No answers to the question of the Court's legitimacy, he poses that question in a penetrating, inescapable form.

* * *

Each essay succeeds brilliantly in its appointed task. Each is a masterpiece of its kind. Collectively, the authors' achievement is enormous. It is surely the most important book on the German Constitutional Court to appear in the twenty-first century. One might even hazard grander claims. The book's importance can hardly be overstated. Until now, it has been available only in German, and its usefulness to the global constitutional community has been limited accordingly. Oxford University Press have done a great service by making it available in English. It deserves the widest imaginable readership.

1
Karlsruhe

Notes on a Court

Christoph Schönberger

I. Rise

It was new. It lacked tradition. The scarlet robes of its judges were borrowed from the Florentine Renaissance. In the Karlsruhe palace gardens, it occupied five flat cubes made out of concrete, steel, and, most striking, glass. This court was not, and did not intend to be, like typical German courts.

Also lacking in tradition was the state that the Federal Constitutional Court served. The Federal Republic salvaged what it could from the bankruptcy of Nazi Germany and the uncertainties of the emerging conflict between East and West. It unified the three Western occupation zones, provisionally as West Germans and their politicians wanted to believe. The "natives of Trizonia," as a Rhenish carnival song called them with desperate postwar humor, became citizens of a makeshift West German state, a state which was governed and administered from Bonn on the Rhine without any pomp or pageantry.

This improvised political system needed a legal foundation. Since the revolutions in the United States and France at the end of the eighteenth century, we call such legal founding documents constitutions. But this word seemed too elevated, solemn, and conclusive for the modest state of Bonn, which organized only a part of an increasingly divided country and still operated under Allied supervision. The Parliamentary Council, which created the West German founding statute in the few months from the fall of 1948 to the spring of 1949 at the pedagogical academy in Bonn, chose an unassuming appellation: the Basic Law. Older traditions resonated faintly in this designation, for in the Holy Roman Empire [12] of the German Nation, which had organized what was then Germany until 1806, one had already recognized fundamental laws (leges fundamentales). But in the situation of the year 1949 this name signaled primarily the unfinished and provisional nature of the entire document. And still today a glance at the final section of the Basic Law reveals a varied potpourri of provisions ranging from nationality law to the churches to the status of the South German Notary. The Parliamentary Council had to hurriedly see to these matters without ordering them conclusively, because the document was not considered permanent.

The German Federal Constitutional Court: The Court Without Limits. Matthias Jestaedt, Oliver Lepsius, Christoph Möllers, and Christoph Schönberger, published by Oxford University Press under licence (2020).
DOI: 10.1093/oso/9780198793540.001.0001

This Basic Law was not called a constitution and was not intended to fully serve as one. But the Court empowered to interpret the Basic Law was called the Federal Constitutional Court and thus carried the term constitution in its name. The Parliamentary Council was only marginally interested in the Court (Fronz 1971; Niclauß 2006). Too many other matters had to be debated and decided, from federal problems to financial issues. Besides, the main parties agreed on the fundamentals of constitutional justice. The novel power of the Federal Constitutional Court to declare a statute null and void for violations of the Basic Law generated no controversy (Laufer 1968, 52 f.). Among several European neighbors, the situation was entirely different after the Second World War. Constitutional review remained unthinkable in the French Fourth Republic, and it was introduced in Italy only after bitter political strife. The left-leaning parties especially feared a limitation of the democratic powers of parliament and wanted the popular assembly to have complete legislative freedom for the transformation of society (Pasquino 1998, 44 ff.). In the Parliamentary Council, however, even the Social Democrats advocated precisely this type of control. Only the [13] Communists were opposed (Kau 2008, 91 ff.). While in the Weimar Republic the advantages and disadvantages of constitutional adjudication had been hotly debated (Wendenburg 1984; Beaud/Pasquino 2007; Baumert 2009; on older roots see Scheuner 1976), there were no longer any such fundamental controversies during the drafting of the Basic Law.

On the other hand, the Parliamentary Council experienced great difficulties in the general *organization of the highest courts*. In contrast to Switzerland or the United States, Germany had no unified high court at the federal level since the founding of the German Empire. There was no German Supreme Court with a final say over all legal questions from private law to criminal law or even administrative law. To a certain extent, the Reichsgericht in Leipzig exercised this authority for civil and criminal law issues before 1945. If the Parliamentary Council concerned itself with the establishment of a Federal Constitutional Court, it did so above all with respect to the general organization of the future German high courts. The main question for the Council was whether the Federal Constitutional Court would be a German Supreme Court or a special institution alongside the other specialized high courts. The issue was not merely a narrow, technical one. On the contrary, it was about the very nature of constitutional justice. For in a unified Federal High Court along the lines of the U.S. Supreme Court, routine everyday legal questions are decided as well as the constitutional questions that frequently have important political implications. Above all, the representatives of the traditional German judiciary opposed the establishment of such a court. They believed that ordinary law was nonpolitical while constitutional law was inevitably political by nature. Therefore, they feared that the entire judiciary would lose authority if a German Supreme Court [14] could decide both types of questions (Laufer 1968, 52 ff.; Sörgel 1969, 142 ff.; Otto 1971, 177 ff.). This perspective won out. The Basic Law set the Federal Constitutional Court alongside the other courts of the Federation and the states. A unified Federal High Court was still envisioned in the constitutional text, but was never realized afterwards. Yet the debate in the Parliamentary Council did not provide a very convincing account of the problem of constitutional courts, for the image of there being an opposition between "legal" and "political" is often merely an ideology of judges. Even ordinary court decisions have a political dimension, especially those of the highest courts. When the Federal Labor Court decides on the permissibility of strikes and lockouts, or when the Federal High Court of Justice decides on the appropriateness of criminal sanctions for preimplantation diagnoses, then those are decisions with a political dimension. But the political element becomes especially prominent when a court must decide whether the Federal President can dissolve the Bundestag before its term ends or whether the amount of the statutorily set social aid does not satisfy constitutional requirements. If these types of decisions are assigned to courts, then the question arises whether one should trust them to the regular courts in addition to their usual caseload or create special courts, which by their composition and organization are better suited to handle cases with more directly political implications. The question becomes more pressing when politicians do not fully trust the traditional judiciary to carry out constitutional review. In Austria after the First World War, Hans Kelsen produced the practical design for the first independent constitutional court and then provided it with a theoretical justification (Kelsen 1929a; Haller 1979, 45 ff.). This form of a specialized constitutional control that is separate from [15] the regular judiciary was more appropriate for the continental European states, because their legal culture, in contrast to the Anglo-American one, is traditionally oriented toward systematic legislation and its career judges are accustomed to interpreting and applying specific statutory law instead of broad and vague constitutional provisions (Capelletti/Ritterspach 1971, 89 ff.; Beyme 2006, 521 f.).

The problem took on special significance in postwar Germany, because the personnel of the highest courts had overwhelmingly served in the Nazi court system before 1945. Indirectly, therefore, the problem of a possible German Supreme Court also raised the question whether the Federal Constitutional Court would share in this tainted legacy.[1] The Parliamentary Council did not commit itself on this issue. Indeed, it opted for a separate constitutional court, thereby deciding in favor of a more directly political institution in the tradition of Kelsen. The Basic Law thus provided that the Bundestag and the Federal Council each select one half of the judges. But in contrast to the proposal of the constitutional convention at

[1] A prominent example makes the problem evident. During the very partisan debate over the selection of the first President of the Federal Constitutional Court, Federal Chancellor Adenauer advised Hermann Höpker-Aschoff, who subsequently became the Court's first President, to renounce his candidacy in the interim, because he had been a leading staff member of the "Main Trusteeship Office East" between 1943 and 1945. This was the German occupation authority responsible for the seizure and administration of Polish state and private property among the so-called "incorporated Eastern areas." As justification, Adenauer referred to the danger of a corresponding public criticism. (Wengst 1984, 237 with FN 67; Aders 1994, 304 f.)[16].

Herrenchiemsee, the Basic Law did not devote a separate section to the Federal Constitutional Court. Rather, the Federal Constitutional Court is included in the section on the federal judiciary, though certainly at the very top (Laufer 1968, 57 ff.). A close interweaving of the Court's personnel with the proposed Federal High Court was considered obvious. But the Basic Law only provided that some members of the Federal Constitutional Court must be professional judges, in other words, selected from the career judges of the federal courts. Finally, the Parliamentary Council left many fundamental issues regarding the Federal Constitutional Court to future legislation. Its members had more pressing concerns. The Federal Republic thus emerged in 1949 with a constitutional court that still existed only on paper. Federal President Theodor Heuss and Federal Chancellor Konrad Adenauer had been in office two years when they participated in the official opening of the Federal Constitutional Court in the Karlsruhe playhouse on September 28, 1951.

Adolf Arndt, the legal expert of the main opposition party, the Social Democrats, spearheaded the actual establishment of the Court after 1949. By contrast, the Adenauer government and its parliamentary majority were not in a hurry to see this unknown player emerge (Laufer 1968, 97 ff.; Gosewinkel 1991, 181 ff.). A central issue became evident, which accounts for the subsequent significance of the Court. With astounding speed after 1949, the Federal Republic developed something that Germany had never had in its constitutional history until then: a parliamentary system of government along the lines of Great Britain with a clear counterpoise between government and opposition (Lehmbruch 1998, 37 ff.). In 1949, many politicians from the two main parties considered a "grand coalition" between the Christian Democrats (CDU) and the Social Democrats (SPD) as a necessity of the times. But Konrad Adenauer was firmly opposed and succeeded in establishing a coalition government with a small conservative majority, while the Social Democrats had to remain on the opposition benches for many years (Schwarz 1986, 619 ff.). The Federal Republic was on its way toward Adenauer's "chancellor democracy," which made the weak chancellors and unstable parliaments of the Weimar Republic a distant memory. It quickly became apparent that with a reliable parliamentary majority, a Federal Government was very strong. This novel experience [17] prompted a search for a counterpoise to the Federal Government. The Federal Constitutional Court seemed to offer the balance needed (Dreher 1951, 381).

The Federal Constitutional Court Act, adopted in 1951, finally provided for the organization of the Court and for the selection of its judges. The Bundestag decided on a system with two Senates, each with twelve members. Both Senates were composed of four federal judges and eight additional members. The federal judges became judges of the Constitutional Court for the remainder of their period of office as members of a Federal Court, that is, until they retired officially, whereas the other members had eight-year terms with the possibility of reelection. Subsequent reforms reduced the number of judges on the Court. These changes produced the current composition, in which each Senate has eight members, three of which must come from the Federal High Courts. Since 1970, the term of office of all Constitutional Court judges is a single term of twelve years without the option for reelection. In the debates of the early 1950s, the SPD advocated that the members of the Court from outside the federal judiciary would not need formal legal qualifications, but only "experience in public life." The Social Democrats wanted lay judges to stress the connection of the Court with the political system and society. The governing majority, however, adopted the requirement that the nonjudicial appointees have the formal legal qualification for assuming a judicial post (Gosewinkel 1991, 197 f., 203). In effect, this means that all Constitutional Court judges must be fully qualified jurists. Thus, the Federal Constitutional Court from its inception was a pure jurists' court.

The *system of twin Senates* is a German peculiarity. Each Senate renders its judgments as "the Federal Constitutional Court," without needing the consent of its judicial colleagues from [18] the other Senate. That is not typical of other countries. The Supreme Court in Washington, for example, decides all cases in its full nine-member plenum. The bipartite structure of the Karlsruhe Court reflects a compromise between the government's draft bill and that of the SPD group of the Bundestag. The government's draft followed the German tradition of anonymous judicial decision-making by interchangeable judges. Out of the total of twenty-four judges, panels of nine members were supposed to conduct business in turn. By contrast, the SPD wanted the Court to be composed of judges who had high public profiles, as is the case in America. Hence, they envisioned a Court with ten members, who always convened as a full plenum. The current twin Senate system occupies the middle ground between these two models (Kralewski/Neunreither 1963, 187, 190 f., 194, 196; Schiffers 1984, XVI, 282 ff.). There were a couple of reasons for the adoption of this twin Senate solution. German high courts are traditionally composed of several separate panels. The German emphasis on professional specialization also plays a role in this, just as it does in German administration (Gross 1967, 195). Initially, one also viewed the First Senate, responsible for fundamental rights questions, as bearing the imprint of the traditional German judiciary, and the Second Senate, responsible for the relations between the branches of government, as reflecting the tradition of Staatsgerichtsbarkeit from the Weimar period (Kommers 1976, 86 f.). In addition, the drafters anticipated a great workload for the Court, which could not be entrusted to a unified chamber (Arndt 1951, 297). [19]

A peculiarly *German preference for proportional representation and parity* also played a role in the decision for a twin chambered court. This can already be seen in the even number of eight judges allocated to each Senate. This even number makes four-to-four split decisions an ever present possibility, which would mean that a violation of a constitutional provision could not be found by the Court.[2]

[2] The rule rests indirectly on the Basic Law stipulation that the Bundestag and the Federal Council choose the same number of judges. This federal parity is an obvious consequence of the

The practice of the two largest political parties to choose judges equally according to party proposals reinforces this strict parity. Because a two-thirds majority is required for any election of a new judge, this means in practice that any new member of the Court needs to be agreed on by the Christian Democrats and the Social Democrats. In fact, the seats on the Court are informally distributed between the main parties, and the Bundestag and the Federal Council do in fact regularly accept the proposition of the party to which the seat is informally allotted.[3] Such parity is not possible in the U.S. Supreme Court, because of the uneven number of nine Justices. The fully equal Senates stand in a long German tradition, where stalemate was not uncommon. In the Holy Roman Empire of the German Nation, a decision of the Imperial Diet that had great religious significance could only be made when the protestant and catholic sections consented. A decision of the Diet could be stymied at any time by the separation of the political groups along religious lines according to a procedure called *itio in partes*. The highest courts of the Holy Roman Empire, Imperial Chamber Court and Imperial Council, had similar parity rules. In the land of the Reformation, the confessional division between Catholics and Protestants produced a dogged psychological barrier to the majority principle, whose effects can still be felt (Gross 1967, 38; Lehmbruch 1996, 30 ff.; Schönberger 2001, 37 ff.). One cares much less for majority decisions than for maintaining a balance among participants, whether they are Protestants and Catholics, federal and state governments, or "red" and "black" parties. The Federal Constitutional Court fits well into this cultural pattern of consensual agreements.

It all started in September 1951. After the passage of the Federal Constitutional Court Act, the first twenty-four judges were elected and took up their work. The former capital of the south-western state of Baden, Karlsruhe, was selected as seat of the Court. The Federal Ministry of Justice finally decided the issue, while the SPD had advocated settling the Court in Berlin. This was due to the fact that the Federal High Court of Justice, which holds supreme jurisdiction on civil and criminal cases, was already seated in Karlsruhe. The Federal Ministry of Justice considered the novel Federal Constitutional Court a mere adjunct of this court, all the more so as the establishment of a new Federal Supreme Court was still being considered at the time. These courts should somehow be combined in Karlsruhe

decision for two equally empowered Senates, where each Senate would have an equal number of judges. On the problems associated with Paragraph 15, Section 4, Sentence 3 of the Federal Constitutional Court Act according to which a constitutional violation cannot be found by a tie vote, see Lortz 2003.

[3] On this, see Bettermann 1981, 725 ff. This practice developed as a consequence of the Federal Constitutional Court Act, which since 1956 stipulated a two-thirds majority in the Bundestag and Federal Council for the election of judges. In effect, the election of judges is divided between the two large parties ("ancestral fiefdoms"), and the smaller coalition partners are regularly granted one seat (Schlaich/Korioth 2010, RN 44f). However, this practice is beginning to change as the voter share of the big parties diminishes continually and two-thirds majorities can no longer be reached without the support of smaller parties like the Green party.

(Laufer 1968, 99, 137 ff.; Roellecke 2003, 553 f.). Through the choice of location, the young Federal Constitutional Court came under the shadow of a powerful high court, successor to the tradition-rich Reichsgericht in Leipzig, which embodied the German high judiciary before 1945. The administrative office of the newly born Constitutional Court even had to borrow its first inventory from this mighty neighbor. In a certain sense, the Federal Constitutional Court was not yet itself. The first President of the Court was very aware of that. Hermann Höpker-Aschoff, the former Prussian finance minister, was also disturbed by the spatial distance from metropolitan city life and the political centers of power. The urbane patrician, not dissimilar to Adenauer in stature and bearing, complained in an official letter that the legislature had "exiled the [21] Federal Constitutional Court to the provincial solitude of a former minor capital."[4]

Hardly a few days old, the Federal Constitutional Court was immediately embroiled in its first, most difficult crisis. It became involved in the fierce *controversies over the rearmament of Germany*. After the outbreak of the Korean War, the United States and the Adenauer government pressed for the establishment of a West German military under the auspices of a European defense community. Just a few years after the end of the Second World War, this intention set off one of the most intense domestic political controversies in the entire history of the Federal Republic. It was also a debate about constitutional law. The constitutional issue was whether the Basic Law permitted rearmament without a constitutional amendment (Laufer 1968, 379 ff.; Baring 1969, 378 ff.; Häußler 1994, 28 ff.). The debate among lawyers on the issue was just as bitter as that which occurred in the general public. It produced a thriller with many twists and turns in the Federal Constitutional Court, casting the Court's twin Senate system in a bad light for the first time. At the time, the Court's two Senates had markedly contrary political profiles. The First Senate, empowered to address questions of fundamental rights, was composed primarily of jurists aligned with the SPD, while the Second Senate, concerned with the relations between the branches of government, was mainly composed of CDU aligned judges.[5] There was talk of a "red" and a "black" Senate (Baring 1969, 380). The Social Democrats, therefore, attempted [22] to bring the case before the First Senate, while the Christian Democrats tried to bring it before the Second Senate. The Court rejected both petitions on procedural grounds. Complete confusion set in when, at the urging of the Federal Government, the Federal President Heuss requested an advisory opinion from the full plenum of the Court, which was still legally permitted then. By this maneuver, the Federal Government wanted to

[4] Letter of the President of the Federal Constitutional Court to the Federal Ministry of Justice of October 13, 1952, published in: Leibholz 1957b, 149–56 (156).

[5] This was because during the first election of judges, the Christian Democrats, following the tradition of Staatsgerichtsbarkeit, considered the Second Senate more important. The SPD, by contrast, viewed the First Senate, with its jurisdiction on fundamental rights, as more significant. On this, see Wengst 1984, 241, 243.

prevent a decision on the merits by the First Senate, while at the same time reducing the Federal Constitutional Court to the role of mere advisor. To protect its authority and prevent putting its Senates in conflict with one another, the Court reacted with a procedural ruling, which boldly claimed that advisory opinions of the Court's plenum would be legally binding on both Senates.[6] Again pressured by Adenauer, Theodor Heuss then withdrew his request for an advisory opinion. The Federal Government sharply criticized the Court's decision. The Federal Minister of Justice, Thomas Dehler, even declared publicly that the Court had "shockingly deviated from the path of the law" and "thereby created a severe crisis" (Baring 1969, 423). But the young Federal Constitutional Court gained support from public opinion, which prompted Adenauer to distance himself from Dehler. In the election of September 1953, Adenauer won an overwhelming victory. His government now had a two-thirds majority at its disposal in the Bundestag, which it used to amend the Basic Law and thereby secure the constitutional basis for rearmament. But the project of an integrated European army failed nevertheless, because France could not be won over to the idea of the Europeanization of its armed forces. In 1954, a proposal for an integrated European army was conclusively defeated in the French Parliament. The political times had changed. A [23] decision of the Federal Constitutional Court on the merits never came about.

The Court survived a dramatic test. It skillfully played for time and did not allow itself to be drawn into the political fray. At the same time, its limitations became clear. The fundamental foreign policy decision on rearmament had to be made in Bonn, not Karlsruhe. But the involvement of the Court made the decision more bearable for the parliamentary minority. Subsequent decisions of the Court on fundamental foreign policy questions, such as the Basic Treaty with East Germany (1973), the Maastricht Treaty with the founding of the European currency union (1993), and most recently the Lisbon Treaty (2009), all followed this pattern.[7] The Federal Constitutional Court was not an insuperable obstacle for the parliamentary majority. However, by setting up certain interpretive limitations, the Court made those political majority decisions more bearable for the parliamentary opposition or for critics from civil society.

In the midst of the fierce conflicts on the rearmament issue, the Court also initiated a *struggle over its institutional status* (Laufer 1968, 278 ff.; Lembcke 2007, 91 ff.). The Court did not accept the position intended for it in the general organization of the administration of justice. Initially, the Court's position vis-à-vis the Federal Government was no different than that of other high courts, such as its neighbor in Karlsruhe, the Federal High Court of Justice. It stood under the administrative supervision of the Federal Justice Ministry, [23] which also administered its budget

[6] BVerfGE 2, 79—Plenary on Rearmament (1952). On this, see Wild 2011.

[7] BVerfGE 36, 1—The Basic Treaty (1973); BVerfGE 89, 155—Maastricht (1993); BVerfGE 123, 267—Lisbon (2009).

and personnel. Written communications with the Federal Government were only possible through official channels via the Justice Ministry. During the cumbersome inaugural year of 1951/52, the building renovations and personnel hiring in Karlsruhe were approved in Bonn only after long delays (Häußler 1994, 23 f.) The Court considered this general situation to be incompatible with its pre-eminent constitutional role. One of the first judges, the Göttingen law professor Gerhard Leibholz, therefore composed a groundbreaking report on the status of the Federal Constitutional Court (Leibholz 1957a). In doing so, Leibholz was influenced by the example of Anglo-American judges, with which he had become acquainted during his emigration to Great Britain in the Nazi era (Zweigert 1971, 117; Wiegandt 1995, 303). His Status Report provided the basis for a Memorandum, which the Court submitted in June 1952 to the Federal President, the Bundestag, the Federal Council, and the Federal Government. The Memorandum affirmed that the Federal Constitutional Court was an "independent High Court of Justice empowered with the full guarantees of judicial independence" and "at the same time, being called to be Guardian of the Constitution, a constitutional organ endowed with supreme authority." As such it stood, according to the Memorandum, "as an equal alongside the Bundestag, Federal Council, and Federal Government" (Bundesverfassungsgericht 1957, 145). With this bold reasoning, the Court pulled out all the stops. It claimed simultaneously all the privileges of a court of law and all the prerogatives of a constitutional organ. By its self-designation as a "constitutional organ," it raised itself to the same level as the major political institutions. The Court thereby presented itself as a powerful player who belonged to both the judicial and the political domain. That was a very daring move. The Court showed a degree of chutzpah, which caused even its own President to be taken aback.[8] The Status Report [24] and the Memorandum amounted to a seminal self-authorization of the Federal Constitutional Court.[9] On one point, however, the Court could not be contradicted: the Constitutional Court is not a mere court like the others, as is already clear from its highly politicized appointment procedure. But it is precisely this closeness to the political realm which renders the position of the Court precarious. The Status Report was a stroke of genius, because it made institutional virtue out of political necessity.

To be sure, the Court had to face withering criticism from outside as well as many disagreements within the Court itself.[10] But the Constitutional Court came

8 In a letter to the Federal Ministry of Justice (see n. 4), Höpker-Aschoff distanced himself to a great extent from the Memorandum of his own Court. On the Court's internal conflicts, see Laufer 1968, 282, 309 ff.; Spieker 2004, 207 ff.

9 For stimulating comparative reflections on this issue with a view to the American Supreme Court and the French Constitutional Council, see Herrmann 2006.

10 The sharpest criticism came from an expert opinion written by the aging law professor Richard Thoma, which was commissioned by the Ministry of Justice. The esteemed elder of Weimar Republic legal positivism was particularly critical with respect to a sentence in the Status Report according to which the Constitutional Court had to take into account the political effects of its decisions. This tenet, he wrote, reminds one "embarrassingly of the 'situational interpretation' invented by Carl Schmitt,

through all of this. Authority is never merely conferred, but always also taken. The Federal Government proved pliable, because it did not want to squander the Court's goodwill in the ongoing rearmament debate (Wesel 2004, 79). The administrative supervision by the Justice Ministry ended. The Court obtained its own budget and personnel. From that point on it interacted with the other branches of government as an equal. Its judges wereno longer submitted to the general rules governing the status of federal civil servants and judges. [26] In a highly symbolic decision a few years later, in 1963, the members of the Court even gave up the traditional robes of German high court judges. They donned scarlet gowns of operatic opulence, which the tailors of the Baden state theater in Karlsruhe designed for them based on models from fifteenth-century Florence. The judges informally advised the journalists accredited to cover the Court against any snickering (Wesel 2004, 80; Lembcke 2007, 359 f.; Felz 2008, 249). As a consequence of this development, it seems natural today that the President of the Federal Constitutional Court appears next to the Federal Chancellor and Federal President at official ceremonies. But this positioning is not at all obvious or self-evident. It is the long-term result of deft self-promotion by the Court in 1952. In a short, conflict-filled period, the Court had established itself. "That is not how we thought it would be." Adenauer's statement, whether true or not, expressed an unwilling recognition of the new player in Karlsruhe. No doubt, the young Federal Republic would hear far more from this Court in the years to come. [27]

II. Achievements

The Federal Constitutional Court became the midwife of the second German democracy. That remains its central achievement. From the beginning, it decidedly distanced itself from the poisoned legacy of the Nazi era, worked toward a fundamental liberalization of the German legal system, and shook up the traditional judiciary.

The fundamental rights, as formulated in the Basic Law, were the central instrument in this process. From its inception, the Court was, above all, a fundamental rights court. In reaction to National Socialism, the Parliamentary Council began the Basic Law with a fundamental rights' catalogue, at the pinnacle of which stood the then still novel guarantee of human dignity. The Basic Law made clear from the outset that these fundamental rights were applicable not merely against the administration, but also even against the legislature (Art. 1, 3 GG). Traditionally in Europe, there was no such limitation on and control of the legislature. Statutory law could not be reviewed, and the election and position of the popular assembly was considered

which allowed such a smooth transition to the situation created by the victorious Nazi party." (Thoma 1957, 171; on this critique and the countercriticism of the Court, see Lembcke 2007, 95 ff.).

the guarantor of freedom. One guaranteed freedom through parliament, not against it (Schönberger 2011). Several European countries like the United Kingdom and the Netherlands still see it this way today.

The tradition on the other side of the Atlantic was quite different. In the United States, the troubled history of the former colonies with the distant parliament in London produced a readiness to submit even statutory law to judicial review. In 1803, the Supreme Court in its famous opinion *Marbury v. Madison* had already claimed for the first time the authority not to apply statutes that infringed on the U.S. Constitution. [28] From the beginning of the twentieth century, the Supreme Court took up in earnest the judicial protection of the first ten amendments of the Constitution. It did this, undoubtedly, inside the legal culture of the *common law*, which accorded judges a stronger position than was traditionally accepted for their counterparts in continental Europe. And it undertook this judicial protection of fundamental rights not as a separate constitutional court, but rather as part of its general duties as a supreme jurisdiction applying federal law in concrete cases (Zweigert 1976, 64 ff.; Helms 2006, 53 ff.).

In Europe, the postwar change, in regard to courts, started in Germany and Italy. Both countries reacted to their totalitarian experiences under National Socialism and Fascism by establishing separate constitutional courts and binding their elected assemblies to basic rights. Older democracies like Great Britain or France did not see the need for such a limitation of parliament's freedom of action (Ferejohn/Pasquino 2004, 1674). Although the Members of the Parliamentary Council agreed in principle on the establishment of judicial review, they had no clear idea how the constitutional control of the legislature could work in practice (Bumke 1998, 124 ff.). Even the question whether there should be a constitutional complaint, a right of individuals to challenge violations of fundamental rights directly before the Federal Constitutional Court, had not been answered yet in the Basic Law. Especially controversial was the possibility of challenging court decisions before the Federal Constitutional Court, because it reached deeply into the sphere of the traditional judiciary. Eventually, government and opposition found a consensus on the question in the parliamentary deliberations on the Federal Constitutional Court Act. They introduced the current constitutional complaint procedure.[29] This was due to an understanding between two outstanding jurists of the time, Willi Geiger on the right and Adolf Arndt on the left. Willi Geiger was a multifaceted career judge, who served as a young attorney under the German occupation in Poland and became a representative of catholic natural law ideas after the war. He served as a high official in the Justice Ministry at the time, prepared the Federal Constitutional Court Act, and saw it through Parliament. Shortly thereafter, he became a Constitutional Court judge for a record twenty-seven years. Geiger was convinced that the introduction of the constitutional complaint was indispensable for the rule of law (Geiger 1952, 272 ff.; on Geiger, see Godau-Schüttke 2008, 203 ff.). Adolf Arndt was the foremost legal expert of the Social Democratic parliamentary opposition in the Bundestag of the 1950s. He had already contributed to the introduction of a similar complaint before the constitutional court of the state of Hesse under the Hessian postwar constitution (Gosewinkel 1991, 200) and also favored its introduction at the federal level. Since 1951, therefore, any citizen has been able to introduce a constitutional complaint against any act of public authority. The new court was immediately overwhelmed by such petitions and began to complain about its overburdening (Zweigert 1952). Nothing has changed since then. The "Gang nach Karlsruhe," the path to Karlsruhe to petition the Court, quickly became proverbial (Wesel 2004). Court President Höpker-Aschoff had already anticipated such problems in his speech on the opening of the Court in September 1951: "Not only will those who believe their fundamental rights are violated turn to us, but also those who in their need seek assistance or relief and pardon. Disappointments will be unavoidable" (Höpker-Aschoff 1951, 20).

Through its fundamental rights jurisprudence, the Court contributed to a thoroughgoing *liberalization of German society* (Bryde 2006, 322 ff.; Herbert 2006, 96 ff.). By the 1950s, it reached decisions that profoundly reconfigured the German legal system. This liberalizing effect extended also to traditional German public law scholarship, which initially had deep reservations with respect to the new Basic Law (Günther 2006, 135). One of the most important questions was coming to terms with the legacy of the Nazi past. While most German elites of the postwar decades were tainted by their prior involvement in Nazi Germany, the Court opted for an unambiguous break with the Nazi period. [30] This clear stance by the young Court was possible because of its lack of tradition. There was a remarkably high number of opponents of the National Socialist regime in its ranks, who had gone into exile, joined resistance movements, or outlasted the Third Reich in standby positions (Ley 1982, 532; Wengst 1984, 243 f.). The large number of Nazi opponents among its judges distinguished the Court from the regular judiciary, where most of the judges had already held judgeships under Hitler (Godau-Schüttke 2008) and were often still under the influence of conservative cultural traditions dating back to the times of the monarchy. The decision of the Parliamentary Council for a separate constitutional court produced a notable gulf between the Court and the legal elites in the high administration, the regular judiciary, and the universities, especially in the early years. Much more so than today, the Federal Constitutional Court stood then at a striking distance from the personnel and the cultural attitudes of the traditional German judiciary.

That was already evident in the Court's seminal decision on fundamental rights, the 1958 Lüth Decision (Henne/Riedlinger 2005; Harlan 2011).[11] At issue was the boycott call of Hamburg Senate's director, Erich Lüth, against a postwar romantic movie by Veit Harlan, who had directed the film Jud Süß, an anti-Semitic

[11] BVerfGE 7, 198—Lüth (1958).

propaganda film, in the National Socialist period. The civil courts had granted an injunction against Lüth in favor of the distributor of the Harlan film. The Federal Constitutional Court struck it down on the grounds that Lüth's boycott call was protected as freedom of speech under the Basic Law. The reasoning of the decision extended beyond the traditional view that fundamental rights only applied to the relationship between state and citizen and emphasized instead their applicability [31] to the entire legal system, including private law. Partly in line with contemporary natural law ideas, the Court reasoned that the fundamental rights of the Basic Law had established a "system of values," which must be given expression throughout the law. That was a difficult proposition, prompting the Court to interpret the fragmentary text of the Basic Law as a closed system.[12] The problem was that such an interpretation could quickly become paternalistic.[13] Already, in the 1950s, the use of similar formulas in Court judgments prohibiting unconstitutional parties—1952 against the right-wing radical SRP and 1956 against the German Communist Party[14]—made evident this potential, if the Court's "system of values" approach were followed. However, the main thrust of the Court decisions remained roundly liberal. Invoking the fundamental rights enshrined in the new Basic Law, the Court reinterpreted existing statutes, which mostly stemmed from the times of Imperial Germany, in a liberal vein. The newly found high regard for freedom of opinion and sharp public debate expressed by the Court broke clearly with authoritarian traditions (Herbert 2006, 98 f.). Not coincidentally, the Court confirmed its arguments in the Lüth Decision with a citation of a significant American Supreme Court Justice [32] quoted in English. It affirmed that the fundamental right of freedom of speech was "the foundation of any freedom whatsoever, the matrix, the indispensable condition of nearly every other form of freedom' (Cardozo)."[15] Though full of pathos, the Court thus introduced a little American casualness into German legal prose. The guarantee of a free public debate remained a guiding concern of the Court's up until its spectacular rejection of the Adenauer government's plan for a German Television Corporation (1961) and its Spiegel Decision (1966).[16]

12 Compare the early defense of this approach by one of the first Constitutional Court judges in 1954:

> Created in haste under difficult conditions and intended to offer intermediary solutions to contradictory positions, the Basic Law unavoidably contains gaps and ambiguities. Therefore, a broad and creative interpretation is required, which, alongside the express language, takes into account the sense and purpose of the individual provision, the spirit and system of the Basic Law, the historical development of the constitutional principles and institutions, and the comparable order of other constitutions. (Federer 1954, 18)

13 Contemporary criticism ironically came primarily from the representatives of a traditional statist outlook, who were tainted by their Nazi past (Günther 2004, 192 ff.; Möllers 2008a, 38 ff.).

14 BVerfGE 2, 1—SRP-Prohibition (1952); BVerfGE 5, 85—German Communist Party Prohibition (1956).

15 BVerfGE 7, 198 at 208—Lüth (1958).

16 BVerfGE 12, 205—Deutschland-Fernsehen GmbH (German Television Corporation) (1961); 20, 162—Spiegel (1966).

The Court also quickly developed standards for a substantive review of statutes with respect to fundamental rights, standards that were bolstered by reliance on the principle of proportionality. German administrative courts originally developed this principle for the judicial review of administrative action under police law. The Court transferred this standard to the judicial review of legislation. So, in the 1958 Pharmacy Decision, the Court derived standards to protect against economic statism and protectionism from the Basic Law's guarantee of freedom of profession.[17] German administrative law for economic matters at that time recognized various so-called licensing clauses. These clauses required an administrative permit for the exercise of particular professions in order to discourage excessive competition in certain professional fields. They stood in a long line of German authoritarian paternalism, which the national-liberal historian Heinrich von Treitschke had already mocked in the nineteenth century as the "patriarcal, patronizing overintrusiveness of German administrations" (Treitschke 1864 (1921), 83). The Federal Constitutional Court declared this type of licensing clause invalid in the Bavarian Pharmacy Law. In its view, this requirement typically infringed upon the constitutional guarantee of [33] professional freedom, because the licensing clause protected those already active in a profession from competition.[18] The liberalization achieved via fundamental rights jurisprudence thereby took on not only a cultural but also an economic dimension. Building on these fundamental decisions from the late 1950s, the Court continued to set the tone in the area of fundamental rights in a way that sometimes entered the general consciousness of the German public. Among these judgments was the 1983 Census Decision,[19] in which the Court, confronted with the privacy issues raised by a comprehensive population census, developed a new "right to informational self-determination." It thereby adapted its privacy jurisprudence to the age of data processing in a way that proved prophetic in light of later technical developments.

Along with questions of freedom, *equality* concerns were especially important. In the socially conservative times of the 1950s, the new Federal Constitutional Court pressed ahead with the enforcement of equal rights for men and women. The only woman on the Court, Erna Scheffler, played a significant role (Henne 2006; Waldhoff 2008a). The Constitutional Court prevailed in this even against the vehement resistance of the Federal High Court of Justice, which remained committed to a natural law laden view of the traditional family.[20] [34] Thus, in a 1959 decision,

[17] BVerfGE 7, 377—Pharmacy (1958).

[18] The equally new Federal Administrative Court had already preceded the Constitutional Court on this path as it could autonomously strike down older statutes which had been adopted before 1949 without prior recourse to the Constitutional Court (Schönberger 2006, 69 ff.).

[19] BVerfGE 65, 1—Census (1983); on this, Peilert 2000.

[20] The relationship of the Constitutional Court to the assertive Federal High Court of Justice under its first President Hermann Weinkauff remained very tense throughout the 1950s. The procedure of concrete judicial review initially enhanced the Federal High Court's self-confidence. This procedure allows lower courts to submit statutes to the Constitutional Court, if they believe the statute at issue in a case is incompatible with the Basic Law. Concrete judicial review concentrates constitutional review

the Court rejected the deciding vote of the husband, which the Civil Code had provided in child-rearing disputes between husband and wife. In doing so, the Court declared the natural law framework of the postwar era irrelevant in constitutional matters.[21]

But occasionally the Court's judicial activism regarding fundamental rights had more ambiguous consequences. The 1957 "Elfes Decision" is a case in point.[22] It is one of the Court's most important judgments, because under its interpretation of Art. 2, 1 GG, every human behavior, even those not protected by specific fundamental rights, enjoys fundamental rights protection under Art. 2 and can be made the subject of a constitutional complaint. Wilhelm Elfes was a politician of the Catholic Center Party under the Weimar Republic and mayor of Mönchengladbach after the war. Within the CDU, he was an opponent of Adenauer's policy of Western integration and rearmament, which he saw as a turning away from the goal of German unity. Elfes stayed in contact with the SED, the ruling Communist party of East Germany, and voiced his pacifist critique of Adenauer's policy publicly, both at home and abroad. The reissuance of his passport was denied in 1953, because he allegedly endangered important concerns of the Federal Republic. Courts all the way up to the Federal Administrative Court confirmed the denial. When Elfes lodged a constitutional complaint against those decisions, the Federal Constitutional Court rejected it as well. But it still made use of the occasion to extend [35] its interpretation of Art. 2, 1 GG, such that every human action, including even travelling out of the country, was covered. Nonetheless, it confirmed the denial of the passport renewal in the case of Elfes. This was certainly a decision in the spirit of the Cold War (Fiedler 2000, 83). It remains striking that one of the most fundamental Court judgments regarding personal freedom resulted in a German citizen being prevented by German authorities and courts from traveling abroad to express his opinion, all with the blessing of the Federal Constitutional Court.

The Court's seminal 1953 opinion on the *continuation of civil servants' legal status* under Art. 131 holds a distinctive place in this grand panorama of a gradual liberalization of German law and society via constitutional judicial activism.[23] The Court had to decide on the constitutional complaints of former civil servants who

in the Constitutional Court. Initially, the legislation provided that lower courts had to refer the case via the Federal High Court in its jurisdictional area. The Federal High Court of Justice used this referral power to add an advisory opinion of its own on the constitutional questions at issue in the case. Sometimes, these advisory opinions were published in the High Court's official reports before the Constitutional Court had even considered the issue. In 1955, the Federal Constitutional Court finally declared this practice of adding advisory opinions [34] unconstitutional in the face of vehement protest by the highest federal courts (BVerfGE 4, 358). On this controversy, see Bachof 1956; Faller 1990, 187 ff.; Baldus 2005, 243 ff.

21 BVerfGE 10, 59—Casting Vote (1959).

22 BVerfGE 6, 32—Elfes (1957).

23 BVerfGE 3, 58—Civil Servants (1953); continued and confirmed in BVerfGE 6, 132—Gestapo (1957). On this, see Kirn 1972; Grigoleit 2004, 184 ff.; Menzel 2005.

had not been reinstated after denazification. Their complaint was directed against the statute implementing Art. 131 GG, which laid down the rights of persons who had been expelled from public service after May 8, 1945. The statute in question was the result of a rather generous compromise, which largely guaranteed former civil servants a claim to reinstatement and transitional salaries. But, of course, it did not satisfy all the wishes and needs of former civil servants, who mostly considered their dismissal due to Nazi Party membership illegal [36] and demanded full back pay and corresponding pension benefits. Supporting their cause, the Federal High Court of Justice considered the statute unconstitutional, because it saw the rights of civil servants as part of a supra-positive, natural law guarantee of property rights. The Federal Constitutional Court's reaction was both coolly and provocatively radical. The Court justified the constitutionality of the statute under Art. 131 GG with the thesis that the former legal status of all German civil servants had ceased to exist with the collapse on May 8, 1945. National Socialism, in the view of the Court, had destroyed the former neutral and nonpartisan civil service. Therefore, the existing legal status of all civil servants had been established from scratch after the Second World War. In view of the Court's radical discontinuity thesis, there was no room for making good on constitutional claims based on the former legal status of civil servants. This judgment unleashed a storm of angry responses, not least among professors of public law (Forsthoff 1954; Naumann and Spanner 1955; Günther 2004, 107 ff.). The Court antagonized the German elites in the administration, the courts, and the universities. Its decision destroyed the myth of a purely state oriented administration and judiciary, which were supposed to have survived the Third Reich despite the radical politicization of all public institutions by the National Socialists.[24] The new Federal Constitutional Court thus drew a sharp line of separation with respect to National Socialism long before the general public started to engage with this past again at the end of the 1950s.

Beyond the questions of fundamental rights, the Federal Constitutional Court also made an important contribution to the *protection of the democratic process* generally (Bryde 2006, 324 ff.). It insisted over and over [37] on the fundamental significance of the multiparty system and of an organized opposition.[25] Its jurisprudence turned with special intensity toward the Bundestag's minority parties and their opportunities to challenge and review government actions. That extended from the boundaries of the Government's public relations activity during election periods[26] to the rights of parliamentary investigative committees[27] and to

[24] On the politics of history contained in the judgment, see Frei 1996, 69 ff., 93 ff.

[25] Not without a bit of irony, the 1956 decision on the Prohibition of the Communist Party (BVerfGE 5, 85 at 198 f.) was especially clear on this point.

[26] BVerfGE 44, 125—Public Relations (1977), addressing public relations of the Federal Government during federal parliamentary campaigns.

[27] BVerfGE 67, 100—Flick Investigative Committee (1984), concerning boundaries of the subpoena powers of the investigative committee on the Flick party donation scandal.

the parliamentary supervision of the secret services.[28] The Court also strengthened the rights of individual Members of the Bundestag who were not affiliated with a party group. This clarification was prompted by the departure of the former police official Wüppesahl from the parliamentary group of the Green Party.[29]

The Court also contributed to a better understanding of the important position of political parties for a constitutional democracy. Its doctrine of the so-called "Party State," adopted under the influence of Gerhard Leibholz (Wiegandt 1995, 170 ff.), placed such value on political parties that it effectively declared them institutions with constitutional status. This doctrine had problematical historical models, reflecting the young Leibholz's ambiguous fascination for Italian fascism in the 1920s. It was also too much of a good thing as this jurisprudence tended to constitutionally enshrine a complete party monopoly on the democratic institutions. However, with the traditional German skepticism about parties still looming in the background, the Court's doctrine made clear that a liberal democracy could not function without political parties and anchored them in the consciousness of the legal elites and the general public. [38]

One of the Court's most important achievements with respect to the establishment of a liberal democracy in West Germany is its contribution to the acceptance of the majority principle in German political culture. The Court permitted Germans first to tolerate and then to adopt as their own the principle of majority rule in the context of a parliamentary system of government. Acceptance of majority rule was never very deep in Germany, because of a long history of profound regional, religious, and social divisions (Schönberger 2001, 629 ff.). There was no parliamentary system of government during the long period of constitutional monarchy. Legislation then was the product of complex compromises between the monarchical government and the popular assembly. The short-lived Weimar Republic did not fully alter this view. The situation only changed in the Federal Republic. To be sure, first-past-the-post voting and a Westminster-type two-party system was still inconceivable. Even the religious divide, which was the most important historical cause of the German distance from the majority principle, remained very pronounced (Bösch 2001, 21 ff., 109 ff.). Not surprisingly, the efforts of the Christian Democrats and the Social Democrats to introduce first-past-the-post voting during their "Grand Coalition" at the end of the 1960s came to nothing. But the concentration of the party system since the 1950s produced for the first time a clear juxtaposition between the governing coalition and the opposition in the Bundestag. In view of the deeply rooted skepticism toward majority rule, the acceptance of parliamentary government was only possible and viable when it

28 BVerfGE 70, 134—Budgetary Review of the Secret Services (1986), considering exclusion of Members of Parliament of the Green parliamentary group from the subcommittee for the budgetary review of the secret services.

29 BVerfGE 80, 188—Wüppesahl (1989).

could be hemmed in and moderated by other institutions. In the federal tradition, the Federal Council remained one such counterweight. Another was the Federal Constitutional Court, which could at any time show the majority in the Bundestag [39] the constitutional limits to its power. In this way, the Federal Republic warmed up to the principle of majority rule in parliament, although a certain disposition to question the democratic legitimacy of majority rule on important, controversial or long-range decisions keeps resurfacing from time to time in the general public (Guggenberger/Offe 1984). [40]

III. Success

The success of the Federal Constitutional Court was and is astonishing. It was never self-evident. It is only with the benefit of hindsight that this success seems inevitable. However, German commentators quite readily assume the perspective of the philosophy of history where developments follow a necessary course. Countless ceremonial addresses celebrate the Court as the full perfection of the German Rechtsstaat, part of a collective coming of age story, in which the Germans made various missteps and endured numerous troubles along the way from constitutional monarchy to parliamentary democracy. The typical praise for the Court could almost be formulated adapting a verse from Goethe about tiny Weimar:[30]

> Karlsruhe, thine was a wonderful fate:
> Like Judah's Bethlehem, small and great!

This sense of triumphant relief is more than understandable in psychological terms in view of Germany's history during the first half of the twentieth century. Around the globe too, constitutional courts have become a regular feature of modern constitutional democracies in the second half of the twentieth century (Ginsburg 2008). Constitutional courts sometimes no longer appear as artificial innovations, but as natural elements of the constitutional landscape. That conceals from view the fact that the success of the Federal Constitutional Court rests on very special conditions, which the Court encountered and made use of in the Federal Republic. On closer consideration, the successful assertion of the Court turns out to be quite ambiguous.

Its success rested above all on the Tabula rasa left behind by National Socialism and the war, the partition of the country, and the displacement of millions of people.

[30] The original verse comes from Goethe's poem "On the Death of Mieding" from 1782 (Goethe 1966, 76):

> 'O Weimar! Thine was a wonderful fate:
> Like Judah´s Bethlehem, small and great!

Although there never was a clean slate after 1945, in postwar Germany many traditions were partly discredited, severed, or weakened. That was particularly true with respect to the public institutions, the administration, and the legal system. When tradition was invoked in postwar Germany, this did not express self-confident continuity, but, on the contrary, deep anxiety and disorientation. In this sense, the fact that the Federal High Court of Justice defended a supposedly natural image of the family in the 1950s or many professors of public law held onto an apparently timeless view of the state, indicated uncertainty and shock. Tradition is emphatically invoked only if it is already half lost. This postwar vacuum opened the space for the Federal Constitutional Court to find its place as a new, unburdened, modern institution. The Court also profited from the weakening of the federal system. National Socialism, the war, and the occupation by the Allies destroyed many peculiarities of German federalism, especially with respect to the administration of the states and administrative law. German federalism had become so unitary that it no longer presented an obstacle to the Federal Constitutional Court's penetrating reconfiguration of the entire legal system. That would have been inconceivable under the Weimar Republic (Schönberger 2006, 61 ff.).

The Court also profited from the disrepute of other institutions. Traditional antiparliamentary resentments were still widely held in the general population and among the elites [42]. The bureaucracy was caught up in a painstaking rebuilding and had lost its former self-confidence. The early critics of the Court among public law scholars (Weber 1951, 31 ff.; Günther 2004, 139 f.) defended the traditional administrative state against the danger of an encroaching "judicial state" so intensely, because they were acutely aware of the weakening of the bureaucracy. Unlike the Staatsgerichtshof in the Weimar Republic, the Federal Constitutional Court was not confronted with an established system of public institutions. Its daring self-empowerment during the 1950s took advantage of the vague openness, which generally characterized the early Federal Republic. Under these circumstances, the Court was not even put at a disadvantage by the fact that it entered the political scene belatedly in 1951, when the other actors had already started performing the play two years before.

A painful finding makes evident an even more ambiguous aspect of the Court's success. The reconfiguration of the German legal system, inspired by the guiding principles of the new constitution and vigorously pursued by the Federal Constitutional Court, used interpretive techniques that were characteristic of the transformation after 1933. Many actors in the early Federal Republic's legal system were not entirely unfamiliar with the experience of ordinary law being realigned according to textually vague ideological standards. Then, it was the National Socialist ideology; now, it was the fundamental principles of the democratic and social Rechtsstaat (Stolleis 1994, 240; Schönberger 2006, 61). In substantive terms, the redirection of the law after 1949/51 obviously had nothing in common with the establishment of National Socialist law. What is at issue here is the [43] form of the process, not its content. It is remarkable to see the resemblance among the techniques of reorientation after 1933 and after 1949/51, such as the new interpretation of general clauses, vague legal terms, discretionary powers, and assessment clauses. Where the law was once brittle, it was again rendered malleable with remarkable swiftness. The Federal Constitutional Court's success benefited willy-nilly from the poisoned heritage of the legal transformation after 1933. The business-like transformation of the entire legal system that occurred in Germany twice during a short period of time must foster doubts about the general stability of the law, which is exactly what a constitutional court is supposed to guarantee.

Another ambiguous element of the Court's success is the fact that it profited from a *pre-democratic political culture that worshipped authority* (Bryde 1999, 200 ff.; Helms 2006, 68). This political culture did not trace its roots to the short, discredited National Socialist period, but rather to the long epoch of the monarchical authoritarian state, which had just come to an end in 1918 and continued to resonate in the mentality of Germans (Ellwein 1954; Almond/Verba 1963, 428 ff.). The deeply felt need for authority was still alive, but somehow lost in the early Federal Republic. Politics and parties were held in low esteem shortly after the collapse of the National Socialist one-party state. The old German reverence for the law, which had always been stronger than the parliamentary and democratic tradition, renewed itself. West Germans held the judiciary in higher esteem than the parties. The Federal Constitutional Court benefited from this. It became the benevolently strict custodian of a democracy that did not yet fully trust itself. The Court stabilized the young Federal Republic [44] by exploiting the still prevailing authoritarian mentality. In its own modern way, it acted akin to the first federal chancellor Konrad Adenauer, the old patriarch, who gradually reconciled the Germans to the new democracy even though, or rather because, he acted in accord with autocratic manners inherited from monarchical times.[31] Similar processes occurred later on in the 1970s in southern Europe and then again in central and eastern Europe after 1989. Constitutional courts were founded again after the collapse of dictatorships and could become powerful precisely on the basis of political cultures that worshipped authority. Constitutional court judges were perceived as neutral experts for the new order, which somehow filled the void left behind by discredited elites (Bryde 2006, 323). The Federal Constitutional Court took advantage of this opportunity. It borrowed its claim to authority from the pre-democratic political culture and used it to educate the Germans toward democracy. Especially pronounced were its effects on the judiciary, where it succeeded against mighty opposition to capture for itself the traditional respect for the high courts inside the court system.[32]

[31] See the incisive portrait of Adenauer by Sebastian Haffner (1976, 289 ff.).

[32] The paradigmatic case is the Court's establishment of primacy over the Federal High Court of Justice, a frequent opponent (Faller 1990; Baldus 2005, 243 ff.; Henne 2006). The situation was different in regard to the Federal Administrative Court, with which it did not have comparable conflicts

The great success in exporting German constitutional law and constitutional review since the 1970s, extending from Spain to South Africa, was due not least of all to similarly complex relationships with a nondemocratic, dictatorial past. [45] In forms of integrated judicial review as exist in the United States, all courts can consider constitutional questions in the course of their normal duties, and this is not viewed as remarkable. Separate constitutional courts, on the contrary, often give expression to the break with a dictatorial past and to the mistrust felt for the old elites in the administration and the courts (Ferejohn/Pasquino 2004; Beyme 2006). It was not any different in regard to the world's most powerful constitutional court in Karlsruhe. But the difficulty of such a role as educator and preceptor is obvious. It is destined to render itself obsolete (Haltern 1997, 80). At some point, the child grows up, the pupils spread their wings. The Court's role as preceptor no longer fits the democratic maturity of state and society. It may resemble helicopter parents, who do not wish to acknowledge the fact that their child has grown up or who obstruct their child's transition to adulthood through overprotection. The Court itself thus becomes a cause of the disenchantment with politics, which it is often supposed to counteract (Abromeit 1995, 61).

Ultimately, the Court's success was based on its capacity to resonate in German civil society. It profited from the rising esteem of the Basic Law among the general public, the thoroughly unique phenomenon of *constitutional patriotism* (Grimm 2009b, 605 ff.). The Basic Law was not born to this privileged position. In the self-effacing Federal Republic, there was no magnificent revolutionary beginning to remember, as there was in France or the United States. West Germany's postwar start was spartan at best and met with indifference by the general public. In his 1962 address [46] given in the Federal Constitutional Court on its ten-year anniversary, Rudolf Smend dryly stated that "a people unaccustomed to a democratic order and now weary of its history and politics" had just "put up with the Basic Law." In his words, the Basic Law had "not become a banner under which a novel form of state consciousness, a different, strong will to new historical life shaped by the Constitution could coalesce" (Smend 1971, 20). That was true not only for the man on the street, but also for the jurists. At the same time, the President of the Federal Administrative Court, Fritz Werner, confirmed that in legal circles there was "a certain disbelief in regard to questions of constitutional law," which he explained by the fact that the Basic Law was still perceived as provisional (Werner 1959, 527).

The social resonance initially lagged behind the judicial activation of the Basic Law with a considerable delay. But the economic success and political stability of the Federal Republic over time proved advantageous for the appreciation of the

and struggles for position. The Federal Administrative Court was just as unprecedented as the Federal Constitutional Court. It did not possess its own independent tradition and had a comparable institutional interest in activating arguments rooted in the Basic Law, because this would enable it to extend its jurisdiction over state law (Schönberger 2006, 62 ff.).

new constitution, especially because of the perceived contrast with the failure of the strife-torn Weimar Republic (Grimm 2009b, 605 ff.). Whether the achievements of the Federal Republic rested on the Basic Law or not, they were increasingly ascribed to it. The liberal conservative political writer Dolf Sternberger coined the new term "constitutional patriotism" at the thirtieth anniversary of the Basic Law in 1979, and Jürgen Habermas adopted it a little later for the political left, giving it a more strongly universalistic accent (Müller 2010, 31 ff.). This constitutional patriotism was a special phenomenon of the Western part of the divided Germany, as Sternberger pointed out succinctly (Sternberger 1990, 13; on this see Kinkela 2001, 285 ff.)[47]:

> The constitution has emerged from the shadows, in which it arose. As it came to life, as strong actors and actions came from its mere provisions, as organs took form that had been outlined there, as we ourselves used the freedoms that were guaranteed there, as we learned to move in and with this state, a new, second type of patriotism arose imperceptibly based solely on the constitution. The national sentiment remains wounded; we do not live in a united Germany. But we live in a complete constitution, in a complete constitutional state, and that itself is a form of fatherland.

If that was the curious case of patriotism without patria, it corresponded to the West German world before reunification. In no other Western democracy does the constitution serve as the foundation of patriotism. France, for example, has gone through too many constitutions since the Revolution to make national identity contingent on such a document. Certainly, the United States might be considered a case in point, as it holds its 1787 Constitution in especially high esteem. Yet the American Constitution is not an isolated document, but an element of a public festival culture, which includes other symbols like the Declaration of Independence, the flag, and the national anthem (Heideking 2002, 124). The Basic Law, by contrast, could not count on such a nurturing, symbolic environment. The typical elements of integration in Western democracies, such as history, nation, or culture could hardly come into play in West Germany, because the National Socialist past and the division of the country made recourse to these difficult or impossible. The Basic Law filled this void. It became the symbol of the break with the Nazi past, of the return to the circle of civilized peoples, of democratic success especially in contrast to East Germany (Ackerman 1997, 778; Grimm 2009b, 614). To be sure, the legal impact of the Basic Law, [48] which the Federal Constitutional Court facilitated, did not merge completely with this constitutional patriotism. But the Court's profane, everyday application of constitutional law benefited from the increasing popularity of the Basic Law. The legal thrust of constitutional law, which anyone could activate at any time by means of the constitutional complaint, and the symbolic promise of the constitution strengthened one another reciprocally.

This particular linkage between symbolism and institution surely contributes to the fact that the Federal Constitutional Court still enjoys the highest public trust of all German institutions (Vorländer/Schaal 2002; Patzelt 2005; Vorländer/Bordocz 2006). Since reunification, however, the peculiar constellation of the former West Germany has disappeared, and it is uncertain whether the constitutional patriotism, which arose under the exceptional circumstances of a divided country, will be retained and renewed in a united Germany. [49]

IV. Weaknesses

Crises are not weaknesses. That is sometimes missed in the discussion on the Federal Constitutional Court, where there is disagreement over whether *crises of the Court* have impaired or do impair its authority. There have been three great crises in the history of the Court. The first was the controversy over rearmament right at the outset. The second was the conflict over a series of decisions in the 1970s, such as those rejecting first trimester abortions and conscientious objection to military service via "postcard,"[33] which were understood as a conservative affront against the reform policies of the SPD/FDP coalition at the time (Vogel 1978; Häußler 1994, 52 ff.; Wesel 2004, 223 ff.). The final one was the public debate over the crucifix decision[34] and other controversial judgments, such as the decision on the decriminalization of the expression "soldiers are murderers" in the 1990s[35] (from the discussion then: Isensee 1996; Wahl 1998). In all these controversies, politicians and parts of the public accused the Court of taking political sides or abandoning a basic political consensus. On the politicians' side, Adenauer's minister of justice, Thomas Dehler, initiated the scolding of the Constitutional Court in the Federal Republic early on with his hot-tempered attacks during the rearmament controversies. But the Court [50] has not suffered recognizably from any of these crises in the long term. Certainly, its judgments were not always persuasive, and they could time and again be interpreted as judicial equivalents of the controversies between the large political camps. But often the rejection of an authority indirectly implies the recognition and confirmation of this very authority. That is not dialectical sophistry. For the very act of rebellion against an institution shows its importance in the eyes of the rebels and the high expectations they hold for it. The disappointment of such expectations by individual decisions, however bitterly they may be received, need not endanger the institution itself as such or put it into question. It can even strengthen it.

[33] Especially controversial were BVerfGE 36, 1—Basic Treaty (1973); BVerfGE 39, 1—Abortion (1975); BVerfGE 48, 127—Alternative Service (1978).

[34] BVerfGE 93, 1—Crucifix (1995).

[35] BVerfGE 93, 266—Soldiers are Murderers (1995).

The weaknesses of the Federal Constitutional Court lie elsewhere and deeper. These weaknesses rest on the fact that the Court is *Janus-faced*, that in many respects it is a Court that wants to run with the hare and hunt with the hounds. The matrix of all these doublings was formulated by Gerhard Leibholz in the Court's seminal self-description in the Status Report, where he pointed out that the Court is simultaneously a court of law and a constitutional organ. The Court's duplex nature is the constitutional law equivalent of the protestant teaching "simul iustus et peccator," the fundamental principle that the believer is at once justified and a sinner. Accordingly, the Federal Constitutional Court blends into the sinful sphere of political institutions and remains nonetheless still an immaculate court of law. Another instance of doubling can be found in the Court's internal division into two Senates, its twin structure, which in terms of its historical origins corresponds to its dual role as a court of basic rights and as a Staatsgerichtshof.[36] [51] According to their modes of election, the Senates are in turn divided to ensure federal as well as partisan parity. [17–20] Moreover, there is a factual division of the Court into one Court producing few elaborate Senate opinions and another one churning out plentiful Chamber decisions. The Federal Constitutional Court is never one, never at one with itself, but always split. The one-headed German eagle that hangs above the judges in their courtroom does not seem to fit their Court well. Much more fitting would be an eagle with two heads, which look in different directions.

The dual nature of the Federal Constitutional Court means above all that it is torn between utterly different institutional logics. As a court, the Federal Constitutional Court moves in the context of the judiciary with its specific legal ties and rules of social behavior. As a constitutional organ, it stands among the other constitutional institutions like the Federal Government or Bundestag and contends with them for power and significance. An individual can deal with such different social roles by adapting her behavior to the different contexts. A devoted husband, for example, can at the same time operate a gambling hall. Typically, there is no difficulty telling one role from the other. But the Federal Constitutional Court cannot vary its roles according to context. It has no choice but to speak the language of the judiciary on the stage of politics and the language of politics on the stage of the judiciary. In the best case, this will benefit both. The Constitutional Court then sometimes makes politics see constitutional reason, and it shakes up the everyday routines of the regular court system through its provocative interventions. [52] In the worst case scenario, it goes wrong for both: the Court stifles politics with its demands of legal coherence,[37] and it deprives the judiciary of its institutional rationality. In the best

[36] Occasionally, this inner division comes to light in vehement conflicts between the Senates. The possibility of balancing divergent decisions through the Court Plenum is hardly used in practice. BVerfGE 96, 375, 409—Child as Harm (1997) is an astonishing example of an open conflict between the Senates at the boundaries of the legal process. On this, see Sangmeister 1999.

[37] This is demonstrated vividly in the more recent attempts by the Court to require the legislature to adhere to a particular type of consistency and procedural rationality (cf. Bumke 2010 and Dann 2010;

of cases, the Federal Constitutional Court combines both judicial familiarity with legal ties and procedures and political sense and tact. If all goes wrong, the Court displays the disadvantages of the judiciary without its merits and the disadvantages of politics without its assets. The Federal Constitutional Court then plays on its capacity as a constitutional organ to loosen the legal restraints and procedural standards that characterize a court,[38] and it takes advantage of its position as a court of law to make political decisions without the public advocacy, campaigning, and responsibility that the political process normally requires. Playing both sides in this way is quite advantageous for the Court. Stressing its character as a court, it can shield itself from political expectations, and it can downplay the demands of the judicial system by emphasizing its position as a constitutional organ. But this comes at a price.

The dual nature of the Federal Constitutional Court creates an urgent *need for self-display and self-justification*. There is no court and [53] no constitutional organ so permanently occupied with demonstrating the meaningfulness of its own existence. When the Federal High Court of Justice renders a judgment, it is merely a judgment. The Federal High Court does not want to prove to the world at the same time that it really needs this court. When the Bundestag passes a bill, it does not simultaneously attempt to demonstrate the magnificence of parliamentary government. Federal Constitutional Court decisions, by contrast, always implicitly resonate with the justification of the Court's existence. The hymns of praise, which have been intoned since the 1950s, especially by the members of the Court themselves,[39] are surely due to this need. Among the other constitutional institutions, only the largely ceremonial office of the Federal President is exposed to a similar pressure to justify its own existence (pointedly on this, see Isensee 1994). However, in the case of the Federal President, this pressure results from a lack of powers in the ordinary political process, whereas the Federal Constitutional Court feels this need despite its extensive jurisdiction. The Federal Constitutional Court is lonesome among the courts and lonesome as well among the constitutional institutions. The Court's dual nature does not open up its world, but rather isolates the institution from both

generally on this problem, see Stone Sweet 2010, 204, with the laconic finding: "In the end, governing with judges means also governing like judges.").

38 Occasionally, it even bumps up against its own statutory foundations, as in the case of permission for live television broadcasts from the courtroom in Karlsruhe (Schulze-Fielitz 2000, 124 f.).

39 According to an insightful observation by Donald Kommers (1976, 271), the (underworked) judges of the Second Senate essentially spent the 1950s publicly praising the First Senate, which was overwhelmed by constitutional complaints, and the Constitutional Court generally:

> They drummed away at the notion that the Court and they, the Justices, were the ultimate guardians of German liberty and democracy. They unceasingly reminded their countrymen, the bar, fellow judges, and Bonn politicians that the Court was not only the nation's highest tribunal but also a constitutional organ coequal in status with the Bundestag, the Bundesrat, the Federal President, and the Federal Government, and was supreme in constitutional matters.

its natural partners in the judiciary and in politics, which makes compensatory (self)-praise necessary or at least understandable.

This also shows the extent to which the Constitutional Court, in contrast to ordinary courts, depends on the political and social *recognition and acceptance* of each of its judgments. Its decisions always come with a self-promotional dimension. That explains the sweeping character of its style of judicial reasoning, which is distinct from traditional court judgments and not seldom shifts back and forth between scholarly treatise, political theory, and magisterial encyclical (cf. Isensee 1996, 1085; Roellecke 2003, 559; Robertson 2010). Unlike the ordinary judiciary, the constitutional court is not institutionally embedded in an ongoing, mundane discursive legal practice and therefore seeks acceptance in other ways (Preuß 1987, 6). This contrast between the Federal Constitutional Court and the regular judiciary is also reflected in their different organizational features (Roellecke 2005a, RN 16; 2005b, RN 2). The Federal Constitutional Court further widens the gap by its highly original use of the general elements of legal procedure, such as the rarity of and the unclear scheduling criteria for oral arguments or its gracious handling of conflict-of-interest provisions (on this, see Wahl 1998, 103 f.; Schulze-Fielitz 2000, 124 ff.; Schlaich/Korioth 2010, RN 69, 72 ff.).

The particular challenges the Court faces are also showing up in its difficult communication with the public (Kranenpohl 2010, 253 ff.). Unlike ordinary courts, to gain general acceptance, the Federal Constitutional Court goes to great lengths to justify its decisions by extensive legal reasoning [55]. But this remains expert legal communication, which can hardly appeal to the general public and can only be understood and assessed by an expert audience (Schulze-Fielitz 2000). This problem may explain the fact that individual judges of the Federal Constitutional Court have a large media presence, while judges of the regular judiciary tend to avoid the media (for a critical view on this, see Wahl 1998, 101 ff.). This public presence can be understood as an attempt to meet head-on the Court's communication problems through "extra-procedural self-interpretation" (Isensee 1996, 1091).

The weaknesses of the Court are for the most part unavoidable. It wavers structurally between judicial bureaucracy and constitutional charisma, between banalization and dramatization of constitutional law. Under the Weimar Republic, Carl Schmitt predicted the inevitable failure of constitutional justice. According to Schmitt, politics has little to gain from its judicialization and justice everything to lose from it (Schmitt 1931, 293 f.; for an early counter-critique in the Federal Republic, see Scheuner 1952, 293 f.). But this Schmittian quip does not really explain the position of constitutional courts, because it rests on a radical juxtaposition of politics and law. The decision for a separate constitutional court, however, is one for an institution that from the outset inseparably blends together justice and politics, so that it does not make sense to criticize its judicial function from the perspective of politics or its political function from the perspective of the judiciary. It should come as no surprise that the Constitutional Court displays multiple idiosyncrasies compared to the regular judiciary, which are, indeed, theatrically underscored by the fancy robes chosen by its judges. The Court is caught in a tragic bind: its legitimacy derives above all from its scrupulous adherence to judicial forms, from which it departs again and again due to its political nature. In this sense, it is a waste of time and effort to demand of the Court to be just a court and only a court (see, e.g., Isensee 1996, 1091; Schlaich/Korioth 2010, RN 35 f.) One should expect from the Court, however, that [55] it notices its own deviations from traditional judicial standards and that it tries not to conceal them from others and itself. The Federal Constitutional Court needs to meet the paradoxical requirement that it take special care of its formal judicial character precisely because of its political nature. [57]

V. Fading

Important institutions do not just disappear. But history does not grant them a grandfather right either. Some institutions of the Federal Republic, which were influential and highly esteemed over decades, have lost a great deal of their significance recently. This is the case, for example, with the German Federal Bank. For a long time, it enjoyed just as high public esteem as the Federal Constitutional Court (Gross 1997, 34 f.), but since the introduction of the common European currency it has lost its old role to a great extent. The Federal Constitutional Court is still far from this type of decrease in importance. Yet there are increasing indications that the Karlsruhe Court has passed its zenith.

This is due, first of all, to the highly welcome stability and prosperity of the Federal Republic over decades, to which the Court itself greatly contributed. A liberal society with a solidified democratic culture is less dependent on initiatives from Karlsruhe than was the case in the early Federal Republic. The old model of a provident custodian has become obsolete. The Court is a victim of its own success. It also suffers from a loss of charisma through routinization. The more the Court gets caught up in the mundane management of a complex legal system because of the plethora of constitutional complaints and chamber decisions, the less it is able to produce transformative judgments. In the early decades of the Federal Republic, the Court innovated by making constitutional law into a means for supervising the entire legal system, which permitted novel forms of systematization (Röhl 2008). But this [58] type of innovation has mostly run its course.

Following their self-image that stems from the early years of the Federal Republic, the judges of the Court like to see themselves as judicial trendspotters for new social developments, to which they answer with creative constitutional interpretation, especially of fundamental rights. It is, however, increasingly doubtful whether constitutional law can master such a task at all. The directive capacity of the constitution has been challenged for a long time in all Western democracies.

Constitutional law could never shape the welfare state of the twentieth century in the same way that it had shaped the state of the liberal era (Tushnet 2008). More recent developments such as the threats to freedom emanating from private actors, the new task of risk management, and the turn from repressive to preventive steering tools have further impaired the ability of constitutional law to shape social developments (Grimm 1991, 408 ff.). The constitution's regulative capacity is eroding. Forcefully activating constitutional law, the defining inheritance of the Federal Constitutional Court from its early years, appears less and less possible. In this respect, the experience of today's judges mirrors that of French Presidents after Charles de Gaulle. They cannot free themselves from the example of an incomparable origin, though they are less and less able to follow the lead.

The fundamental *transformation of the German party system* also calls into question the role of the Court. Until recently, the Federal Constitutional Court formed a counterweight to the compact and stable parliamentary majorities, which formed quickly in the Federal Republic from the 1950s despite the proportional system of representation. [59] The Court put these majorities in their place, but also presupposed their existence as a matter of course when it frequently required the legislature to adopt new legislation. But the German party system is in a state of flux and no longer produces the compact parliamentary majorities of the past. The voter share of the once dominant parties, CDU/CSU and SPD, is decreasing, and new smaller parties like the Greens and the Left have entered the Bundestag. Future parliaments will probably be even more complex, diverse, and unpredictable. In addition, the federal system obliges the parliamentary majority to achieve compromises with the Federal Council, the composition of which is also ever more varied. In the future, parliamentary governance may become even more difficult and drawn-out than it already is today. We witness the disappearance of the strong-willed parliamentary majorities of the past, against which the Federal Constitutional Court could serve as a counterbalance to the left or to the right of the political system. Such a counterweight will become ever less necessary in the future and perhaps only accentuate the political system's tendency toward paralysis.

The Court finds its star waning above all due to the increasing *Europeanization and internationalization* of the German legal system. In hindsight, it becomes clear that the ascent and success of the Federal Constitutional Court expressed a certain introversion of the former Federal Republic. The understanding of constitutional law as a systematic unity based on fundamental rights and constitutional principles, which the Court had developed since the 1950s, was implicitly grounded on the uniform political framework of a nation state. Constitutional interpretation became a mighty factor in the unification of the country, all the more so because traditional federal plurality had largely disappeared (Schönberger 2006, 61 ff.). This national introversion could go unnoticed, because it was paradoxically accompanied by a [60] forceful postwar rejection of the statist tradition by important parts of German public law scholarship, where the grand semantics of public law shifted increasingly from "state" to "constitution" (on this reorientation, see Günther 2004 and Möllers 2008a). The unacknowledged premise of this development was that the entire German legal system could be understood and guided from the Basic Law. This was above all the result of the fact that the Federal Constitutional Court is a separate Court detached from the ordinary judiciary. Constitutional law is the only currency accepted in this Court. Its ascent, therefore, necessarily required it to put the entire German legal system into the horizon of the Basic Law.

Yet the consolidation of European integration and the growing importance of international law have increased the amount of applicable law in Germany that did not originate within this introverted legal world and cannot be made to fit into its framework. The authoritative interpreters of this law do not reside in Karlsruhe, but rather in Luxemburg with the European Court of Justice or in Strasbourg with the European Court of Human Rights. The Federal Constitutional Court has gotten some competition, and since the 1990s this competition has become ever more pronounced (Oeter 2007). In the former Federal Republic, since the 1950s, the Court had finally got the entire judiciary to fall into line behind it. But it will not be able to do so with its new external competitors, which are not by any means its subordinates. The very existence of that type of competitive environment lessens the authority of the Court, as it opens up new opportunities for comparison (cf. generally Sofsky/Paris 1994, 152).[61]

To be sure, this competition is disconcerting for the Federal Constitutional Court, because fundamental questions with respect to the law applicable in Germany are being decided by courts that are at least fully equal to it in terms of legal authority, if not superior. This is all the more troubling for the Court, because the judgments of its European counterparts, in terms of their style of judicial reasoning, lag behind the explanatory standards prevailing in Karlsruhe. Less apparent, but almost more difficult to digest for the Court, is the *loss of the unifying function*, which the Court fulfilled for decades by its interpretation of the Basic Law. This unification is ever less feasible through constitutional law. Yet the success of the Court in the past rested on the possibility that it could reformulate and answer all important questions of the German legal system as constitutional questions. That time is past. The Court is no longer even the master of its former showpiece, fundamental rights. Data protection is a case in point. In 1983, the Court could bring down the Federal Census Act, developing a novel fundamental right to informational privacy from the Basic Law. Confronted with the European Data Retention Directive in 2010, by contrast, it could no longer answer the substantive problem independently and comprehensively with reference to the Basic Law. Its jurisdiction was now limited to filling the leeway European Union law left for national implementation.[40] The room for a sweeping jurisprudence in this field had disappeared.

The more the different legal layers at the international, European, national, and subnational levels come to interpenetrate one another, the less these layers can still be interpreted and integrated [62] on the basis of German constitutional law. The role of exploration and impulse which constitutional law had played for German legal development is increasingly fulfilled, though more sectorally and selectively, at other normative levels such as European and international law.

The Federal Republic's increasing European and international integration even raises the question whether the model of a separate constitutional court, which Hans Kelsen developed and the Federal Republic elaborated to its fullest, is not especially ill-suited for coping with this interweaving of different legal layers. While Germany's ordinary courts routinely process and apply European and international law, the Federal Constitutional Court only touches on these areas of law on an exceptional basis, and only within the framework of the Basic Law. While at the outset of the Federal Republic, the constitution was the foundation of the expansive conquest of all law by the Karlsruhe Court, so is it now becoming more and more an isolated area of retreat. That is especially evident in the Court's 2009 decision on the Lisbon Treaty, which declares in a defensive tone that the "identity" of the German constitutional order is inviolable at its core.[41] Certainly, the Court joins a broader trend here,[63] for even in constitutional law around the world, national peculiarities are being emphasized more strongly as part of a backlash to globalization (Tushnet 1999, 1269 ff.). But the contrast to the hopeful awakening and advance of the Court's early decades is still very remarkable. German constitutional law as expressed in the case law of the Court is in danger of being transformed from a luminous city on a hill to a dark fortress. The Court's glass buildings from the 1960s with their promise of openness (Bürklin 2006; Kranenpohl 2010, 254 ff.) appear to embody the hopes of the past more than those of the present. Whereas, during its heroic decades, the Court conquered the entire legal world for the young Basic Law, it is now often reduced to a halfhearted defense of the aging German *acquis constitutionnel*.

[40] BVerfGE 65, 1—Census (1983); BVerfGE 125, 260—Data Retention (2010); on this, Durner 2010, 394.

[41] BVerfGE 123, 267 (at 353 ff.)—Lisbon (2009). The Court's increasing retreat into the supposedly special "identity" of the German constitution is also displayed in another 2009 decision on the compatibility of a criminal law norm directed against the glorification of the National Socialist dictatorship (Paragraph 130, Section 4 StGB) with the constitutionally guaranteed freedom of speech (BVerfGE 124, 300—Rudolf Heß Commemoration (2009)). The opinion stated that the National Socialist regime has an "antithetical significance characterizing the identity of the Federal Republic of Germany." It is peculiar that this type of constitutional law category would first appear in the jurisprudence of the Court [63] over sixty years after the end of National Socialism. Today's Court looks back and not forward as did the first generation of judges who knew enough about National Socialism from their own experience not to invoke it with ringing pathos.

The Federal Constitutional Court winds up in a peripheral position. Its seat in Karlsruhe alone removes the Court much more from the centers of political power than in the former West Germany. Far from the capital, its judges do not enjoy an informal familiarity with the political elite, as is the case for their colleagues in Rome, Paris, Vienna, or Washington. Since Berlin has reassumed its role as capital and the government moved its headquarters from Bonn to Berlin, this lack of familiarity is more noticeable in united Germany. The Federal Constitutional Court is the only constitutional institution still seated in the same location it held in the former Federal Republic. But the country, which still sees justice dispensed from the Karlsruhe palace gardens, is no longer the same, and it is an open question whether [64] the Court is a match for the Berlin Republic in the same way as it was in the former West Germany. Unlike the Federal Government or even the Federal Bank, the Court is not even compensated for the growing European and international integration of the Federal Republic by participation in supranational councils. Courts are excluded from this typical path of international integration. Intensifying dialogue among high court judges (Slaughter 2003 and Limbach 2008) and the pilgrimages by delegations of foreign judicial officials to Karlsruhe are no substitute for this enhanced cooperation of governments and administrations.

Those are all gradual changes. The Court still draws from its institutional and symbolic capital accumulated over decades. The wider public is hardly aware how much the national constitution's importance has declined (Grimm 2009b, 616) and how much European and international integration has reduced the Court's leeway. Without doubt, the Federal Constitutional Court will preserve important duties. But it will probably be submerged even more into the grey humdrum of Chamber decisions and only seldom find the opportunity for the grand gesture, the shining moment, the constitutional thunderbolt, with which it surprised the public in decades gone by. The real difficulty for the Court lies in coping with its increasing banalization without concealing it through self-important posturing (Schönberger 2009, 557 f.). The Federal Constitutional Court must practice one of the most difficult arts: the art of retreat (Enzensberger 1989). Yet its history so far has hardly prepared it for this exercise. Humility and renunciation were not prominent among the qualities displayed by the Court in the [65] past six decades. Its habitus is determined by the unlikely occurrence that the modest founding statute of a fragile political entity acquired charismatic forces. Leaving behind this legacy cannot come easily to the Federal Constitutional Court, and anyone familiar with its achievements cannot help but feel some melancholy about it. Yet the admonition of Paul's First Letter to the Corinthians, which one of the early judges of the Court repeated to his colleagues (Zweigert 1976, 75), has always provided a lesson for this Court in particular: "To have as though one did not have." [66]

2

The Karlsruhe Phenomenon

What Makes the Court What It Is

Matthias Jestaedt

I. He Who Sows Constitutional Law, Reaps Constitutional Justice

Perhaps no other institution has done as much to shape or symbolize the free democratic Germany that rose from the ruins of the National Socialist regime as has the Federal Constitutional Court (FCC). Anyone who wishes to fashion a reliable image of how the clock ticks in postwar Germany must take a thorough look at the influence of the Court that sits in the Karlsruhe castle district. Some even claim—probably with a wink—that one should not speak of the Bonn or the Berlin Republic, but of the Karlsruhe Republic. Even Ernst-Wolfgang Böckenförde's anxious diagnosis that a "smooth transition occurred from the parliamentary legislative state to a constitution-executing judicial state" (Böckenförde 1981, 402) can be understood as an expression of the extraordinary position and significance of the Federal Constitutional Court in the constitutional order of the Basic Law. The top scores that the Court consistently receives in ratings of public popularity further attest to its singular position (Vorländer/Brodocz 2006).

The fact that this success story seems so unquestionable today should not, however, blind us into thinking that the development was predestined, inevitable, or normatively compelled. Quite the contrary. The Federal Constitutional Court has with good reason been termed a "belated constitutional organ" (Schiffers 1984, VII). The Court opened its doors only on September 7, 1951—half a year after the promulgation of the Federal Constitutional Court Act (Bundesverfassungsgerichtsgesetz, BVerfGG), its organic statute, [80] and two years after the establishment or election of the other federal constitutional organs (the Bundestag: August 14, 1949/September 7, 1949; the Bundesrat: September 7, 1949; the Federal President: September 12, 1949; the Federal Chancellor: September 15, 1949; the Federal Government: September 20, 1949). Whether because the Parliamentary Council consciously wished to delegate the questions to the ordinary legislature (or to the Court's internal administration), or because future demands and developments were simply unforeseeable, the Basic Law's original version of May 23,

The German Federal Constitutional Court: The Court Without Limits. Matthias Jestaedt, Oliver Lepsius, Christoph Möllers, and Christoph Schönberger, published by Oxford University Press under licence (2020).
DOI: 10.1093/oso/9780198793540.001.0001

1949 said nothing about several of what today are central characteristics of the Court's jurisdictional claims and practical operation. Thus, to take four very diverse examples: (1) the question of the Court's status as a constitutional organ was not clarified by the Basic Law;[1] (2) its distinctive configuration as a "twin court"—a court with two coequal senates, each of which decides cases as the Federal Constitutional Court—was first established by the BVerfGG; (3) even the procedural form, which, more than any other, shaped the Court's workload and its reputation—namely, the individual constitutional complaint—was first introduced by ordinary law in 1951 and first adopted in the Basic Law itself in 1969; and (4) only gradually, in response to the Court's growing workload, did the Court establish three-judge screening panels with unique procedures of review (formerly preliminary review committees) that dispose of more than ninety percent [81] of all petitions to the Court, and law clerks for each justice (one each in the 1950s; four each, on average, today).

That the manner and direction in which the Court would develop was only dimly visible when the framers decided to establish an autonomous constitutional court, powerful in the range and weight of its competences, was due, moreover, to the Court's unprecedented nature—unprecedented both in terms of constitutional history and of comparative constitutional development. True, there were repeated references to the Weimar *Reichsstaatsgerichtshof* and the U.S. Supreme Court (though surprisingly not to the Austrian Constitutional Court) during the deliberations about the Basic Law and the FCC. But both in numerous distinctive details and in its overall conception, the Basic Law's constitutional court was an original creation—a novelty *sui generis*—for whose efficacy and impact one could not draw upon the experiences of other tribunals in earlier times or foreign jurisdictions.

It has been widely observed that the *law in action* develops differently from what the *law in the books* portends—that (constitutional) legislative intent and constitutional reality often emphatically part paths. This applies especially to supreme courts—such as constitutional courts—which, because their decisions are not reviewable by any other tribunal, possess the power of speaking the final word. Probably with no other constitutional court, past [82] or present, can one so impressively and convincingly demonstrate the proposition that the power of the last word, once liberated from those who created it and those who determine its legal continuance, can be controlled only to a very limited degree. This is so because the power to make binding constitutional interpretations necessarily comprises the power to define authoritatively—i.e. with legal effect for and against all rivals—the foundations of one's own jurisdiction.

Just as later developments could barely be fathomed during the FCC's founding (1949–1951), so the texts of the Basic Law and of the BVerfGG gave little hint of the factors and causes that would later allow the Court to become what it has become.

[1] It was the Federal Constitutional Court Act that first established, in a slightly elliptical way, in Section 1, paragraph 1: "The Federal Constitutional Court is federal court, autonomous and independent vis-à-vis all other federal constitutional organs."

One can identify, instead, a diverse array of complex, mutually reinforcing developmental conditions. Among these, observers have especially highlighted, along with the Court's ample jurisdiction, the persuasiveness of its jurisprudence and the personal authority of its individual justices (Vorländer 2006, 9 ff.). A gradual historicization of the Karlsruhe Court's influence has helped to illuminate the concrete social, economic, political, and intellectual contexts of the Court's first sixty years and to assess the significance of those contexts for the Court's doctrinal development. But although these four factors are indispensable to any explanation of the Karlsruhe phenomenon, [83] they do not constitute an exhaustive list of ingredients for the Court's formula for success. On the other hand, it is equally clear that, even if one thinks only of psychological and motivational factors that are difficult to grasp and measure, the elements of success and their interdependence cannot really be exhaustively identified (Brodocz 2006; Kranenpohl 2010). The following reflections seek to locate and limn the pronouncedly juridical factors and moments—those developmental conditions, that is, that can be ascertained and assessed with the tools of the legal scholar. [84]

II. The Basic Law and the Federal Constitutional Court—An Asymmetric Partnership

A. The constitution and its mouthpiece

Anyone who seeks the secret of the FCC's success in the sixty years since its founding will soon encounter another success story running parallel to—and, on closer inspection, intimately interwoven with—the Court's own. It is the success story of the Basic Law itself. Without exaggeration one may speak of a mutually reinforcing interdependence. For the paramount importance of the Basic Law in postwar Germany cannot be explained without the influence of the Federal Constitutional Court; and, on the other hand, the Court's resonance and power would have been unthinkable without the Constitution. The one success story, then, cannot be related or understood without the other. The Basic Law and the FCC are linked in their success or, rather, in their destiny (Voßkuhle 2009, 917 ff.).

Of course, this community of success or fate is not symmetrical. It is the Federal Constitutional Court that is empowered to provide the authoritative (if not the exclusive) interpretation of the Basic Law. In other words, whenever called upon, it is "Karlsruhe" that must render binding judgments on how the Basic Law's provisions must be interpreted and applied. In the final analysis, the Basic Law speaks through the Federal Constitutional Court. The Court, therefore, is the Basic Law's ultimate mouthpiece. And yet it is the Basic Law that gives the Court its special position [85] and grants its binding, interpretive power. What the Basic Law gives, it can take away, though the Court's powers of persistence—more or less juristically veiled—cannot be underestimated.

Similarly striking is the similarity of the two strategies of success, if one may call them that. As novices, both the Basic Law and the Federal Constitutional Court entered the domestic arena of the struggle for attention and the power to implement one's will—in short, the struggle for authority in the state. Though they were novices well-equipped to cut a fine figure, both lacked, on the one hand, a clear outlook for the future and, on the other hand, any guarantee of whether and how long they would be able to play the role that had been assigned to them. Despite all this, both of them—armed with their hegemonic claims to leadership and control—prevailed against their older, battle-tested rivals, who initially—and almost reflexively—branded them as upstarts devoid of tradition.

B. Implementing the constitution against competing concepts: Thinking from the perspective of the constitution

In both synchronic and diachronic comparison, the orientation toward (not to say the fixation with) the Basic Law in contemporary Germany is striking. No German constitution before the Basic Law (and no state [*Land*] constitution contemporary to it) was of such immense practical legal (i.e. "juristic" in the narrow sense) significance or of such preeminent importance for Germans' core political sensibilities. In perhaps no other country and [86] in no other period does the resolution of ordinary legal cases make recourse so frequently and intensely to the constitution as in Germany under the Basic Law. This is true whether the legal issue is between private individuals, between a citizen and the state, or between branches or levels of government. The constitution does not serve merely as special law for politics, but aspires rather to be an all-encompassing system of values that penetrates and encompasses every legal relationship. The orientation of other law, especially of statutory law, toward the Basic Law is so pervasive and complete that ten years after its inception, the President of the Federal Administrative Court characterized administrative law as "concrete constitutional law" (*konkretisiertes Verfassungsrecht*) (Werner 1959). Today, there is increasing talk of the constitutionalization of the entire legal order. Some point to this development with pleasure as evidence of a maturing constitutional state. Others view it with concern as evidence of a constitutional state that has lost its way. On the positive side, the orientation of the rest of the legal order toward the Basic Law is portrayed as a process of rendering the constitution more concrete and thereby realizing the values of the free, democratic order. The more critical perspective regards these developments as the forfeiture of statutory law's autonomy (and, with it, that of the political realm as well) and the dwindling of political competition into mere constitutional implementation. The very German concept of constitutional patriotism was coined and elaborated (Sternberger 1979 (1990); Müller 2010) in order to capture and interpret the non-juridical (in the narrow sense) significance of the Basic Law. The Basic Law has grown from the fundamental framework for creating domestic law, to the supreme order of legal values, to the framework for integrating the polity in much more than a legal sense, and finally to a (partial) substitute for the nation (Isensee 1986). [87]

The extent to which the Basic Law prevailed against rival alternatives as a framework for ordering and orienting political action is evident in how decisively the idea of the primacy of the political, which earlier and elsewhere was so much more powerfully pronounced, has yielded to the primacy of the constitution. Few political questions are publicly discussed and resolved today in which the answer is not based—at least in significant part—on the Constitution. This is so in realms as disparate as the foreign deployment of German soldiers (BVerfGE 90, 286 ff. (1994)), commuters' allowances (BVerfGE 122, 210 (2008)), and the rate and calculation of welfare benefits (BVerfGE 125, 175 (2010)). Here the constitution provides the political agenda. True to the motto *quod non est in constitutione, non est in mundo*, there are perennial efforts to amend the Basic Law to encompass all kinds of state goals. To put the point baldly: in Germany under the Basic Law a pattern has taken root of thinking from the perspective of the Constitution. And it seems that, the longer the pattern lasts, the deeper the roots run.

C. The Constitutional Court's triumph over its rivals: *Karlsruhe locuta, causa finita*

As an unprecedented invention of the Basic Law, the Federal Constitutional Court had to find, assert, and defend its position and role, its function and operation amidst and against traditional bearers of state power. On the whole, the Court emerged from these institutional and functional struggles for hierarchical primacy with resounding success. In the process—because the Parliamentary Council contented itself with establishing a few guideposts, and even the [88] legislature that passed the BVerfGG in 1951 punted on important questions—the Court had largely to find its own way, inventing itself as it went along. The Court asserted itself with two claims in particular: first, the claim that the Court was not merely *one* guardian of the constitution (however elevated) among many, but that it was, in the truest sense of the word, the ultimate guardian of quotidian law. True, as Article 20, 3 and Article 1, 3 GG make emphatically clear, all state authorities are bound by the Basic Law and obligated to protect it and work toward its realization. Nevertheless, in the final analysis, all efforts in this regard coalesce in *one* organ, the Federal Constitutional Court. Accordingly, the Court's practical interpretive authority cannot be adequately explained by reference to the binding effect of its decisions as established by statute (Section 31 BVerfGG). For entirely independent of its connection to a concrete case, or of its legally binding force—statutory or otherwise—no interpretation or application of the Basic Law can take root or spread its influence in opposition to—or even merely without the blessing of—the Karlsruhe Court. On the other hand, the Court succeeds to the greatest extent when its claims relate to its own position in the institutional and functional framework of organized state authority. As watchwords for this phenomenon, the following must here suffice: the Court's status as a constitutional organ, and its budgetary and procedural autonomy.

Of course, these processes—which I have somewhat provocatively termed power struggles—did not yield decisive and unambiguous outcomes, either individually or collectively. Instead, the processes are complex, inconclusive, and ongoing—played out on many levels and in regard to countless issues. [89] Even so, a few spectacular historical highlights shed light on the Karlsruhe Court's powers of self-assertion. They concern the Court's relationship to the Federal Republic's other constitutional organs, on the one hand (i.e. the Federal Government, the legislature, and the constituent authority), and to the ordinary, specialized judiciary, on the other.

1. A constitutional organ among constitutional organs

In its first year of existence, the neophyte Court had already set itself on a collision course with governing state institutions that the Basic Law unambiguously designated as constitutional organs. This was true most dramatically with the Federal Government in general, and with the Federal Minister of Justice, Thomas Dehler, in particular. In its now-famous memo of June 27, 1952, "The Position of the Federal Constitutional Court," as well as in its subsequent jurisprudence, the Court claimed (with little basis in the constitutional text) that its constitutional position was not comparable to that of the other federal supreme courts—the Federal Court of Justice, the Federal Administrative Court, the Federal Labor Court, the Federal Social Court, and the Federal Financial Court. Instead, the Basic Law established it both "as a court" and "at the same time a supreme constitutional organ" (BVerfGE 7, 1 (14) (1957)). On this basis the Court founded its claims, not only to independence from the institutional supervision of the Federal Ministry of Justice—with which the Court had clashed swords over various questions both of constitutional interpretation as well as of institutional relationships and organizational hierarchy—but also to equal stature with (and, if necessary, the right to confront) the other federal constitutional [90] organs—the Federal President, the Bundestag, the Bundesrat, and the Federal Government. The Federal Government experienced what this could look like in 1961 during its dispute with the states (*Länder*) over establishing a second German public television station. In that case, the Court rejected the constitutional interpretation put forth by Konrad Adenauer's government across the board and with a wide-ranging legal justification—and, at times, in a tart and summary fashion.[2] The Court concluded by declaring Adenauer's signature project of a federal television network unconstitutional (BVerfGE 12, 205 (220–3, 223–64) (1961)). Especially in the 1970s, in the early years of the social–liberal coalition, the federal legislature learned what it meant for the polity's foundations to be spelled out in binding terms not by its leading democratic organs—the Federal Government, the Bundestag, and the Bundesrat—but by a court ensconced in the idyll of the Karlsruhe castle grounds. Whether the issue was the democratization of the polity by introducing co-determination in the context of the so-called "group university" (*Gruppenuniversität*); the liberalization of society by amending Section 218 of the criminal code to allow abortions during the first trimester of pregnancy; or the new *Ostpolitik* rearranging affairs with East Germany through the Basic Treaty—in the core areas of social–liberal reform policy, the FCC placed irritating obstacles in the path of politicians, imposed insuperable limits, and thereby put the brakes on the new democratic establishment's impulse for reform (BVerfGE 35, 79 ff. (1973); BVerfGE 36, 1 ff. (1973); BVerfGE 39, 1 ff. (1975)). Even the [91] constitution-amending legislature had to learn that the twin court in Karlsruhe played its guardian role very self-consciously, even vis-à-vis the master of the constitution. So it was in 1996, when the Second Senate narrowly approved the Asylum reform introduced by Article 16a GG (BVerfGE 94, 49 ff.), and again in 2004, when the First Senate narrowly approved the electronic eavesdropping authorized by an amendment to Article 13 GG (BVerfGE 109, 279 ff.). How narrowly the constitution-amending legislature escaped humiliation is evident in the dissenting opinions of two justices, who declared the new constitutional provision of Article 13, 3 GG—which was central to the eavesdropping case—to be unconstitutional constitutional law (*verfassungswidriges Verfassungsrecht*). It is telling, for the relationship between the constitutional legislature and Constitutional Court, that a possible "correction" of a Karlsruhe judgment by amending the relevant provision of the Basic Law would be overwhelmingly perceived and denounced as illegitimately undermining the Court's authority.

2. A court among courts

The Federal Constitutional Court asserted itself relative to and in comparison with its rivals for authority and (interpretive) power—not only among the supreme political organs. As a judicial body—indeed as a novel court whose jurisdiction comprises areas of substantive law that had traditionally been separated among specialized courts—the Constitutional Court also needed to position and define itself vis-à-vis the other (so-called specialized) courts.

The Court overcame what might, at first blush, have seemed its most dangerous rival without [92] a struggle and without scars. In its original version, the Basic Law

[2] Thus the Court's discussion of the competency provision of Article 73, 7 GG ("Postal and Television System") begins with the phrase: "The federal government's interpretation of Article 73, 7 GG is not correct."

had provided for the establishment of a supreme federal court.[3] The Parliamentary Council had thus furnished the judiciary with twin summits, so to speak, with the Federal Constitutional Court (under Articles 93 and 94 GG) deciding (federal) constitutional questions, on the one hand, and the Supreme Federal Court (under Article 95 GG) as guarantor of legal unity within the specialized federal judiciary, on the other.[4] But the legislature did not fulfill its charge; in 1968, the provisions regarding the Supreme Federal Court were deleted from the Basic Law and replaced by the stupendously less important joint senate of the federal high courts. Thereafter, the five quondam "federal high courts" (*obere Bundesgerichte*) signed off as "federal supreme courts" (*oberste Bundesgerichte*), or even as the "supreme courts of the federation" (*oberste Gerichtshöfe des Bundes*).[5] They never, however, became the peers of the Federal Constitutional Court.

All more serious conflicts between the Constitutional Court and the specialized courts were decided by the former in its own favor. Four particular turf wars may be taken as representative: (1) From the early- to mid-1950s, the relationship between the FCC, on the one hand, and the federal supreme courts, on the other, was shaped by the so-called "advisory opinion controversy" (*Gutachten-Streit*) (Baldus 2005, 237 ff.). [93] Ostensibly, the issue was whether a federal supreme court—which, according to the BVerfGG's original version, had to refer any constitutional question raised by a trial court to the FCC via the concrete norm control procedure (Article 110, 1 GG) —was allowed to append to the referral its own position (i.e. an "advisory opinion") on the relevant constitutional matter. At a deeper level, the issue was whether and to what extent the federal supreme courts could participate in constitutional interpretation and thereby enter into interpretive competition with the Federal Constitutional Court. The federal legislature decided the "advisory opinion controversy" in favor of the FCC by empowering trial courts to refer questions to the FCC directly (Section 80, 1 BVerfGG). Probably the FCC's most famous decision, the Lüth judgment of January 15, 1958 (BVerfGE 7, 198), which introduced epoch-making doctrine on the impact of fundamental rights on private law, should be considered in this context. In Lüth, the First Senate successfully opposed the interpretive claims, rooted in the Basic Law, of the civil courts in general and of the Federal Court of Justice and of the Federal Labor Court in particular. Moreover, with the dual doctrine of an "objective order of values" and of the "radiating effect" of fundamental rights on the totality of sub-constitutional law, the FCC arrogated to itself the procedural possibility of reviewing in full every

3 Article 95, 1 GG of the original 1949 version read: "To preserve the unity of federal law, a supreme federal court will be established."

4 The dual-summit solution was also clearly expressed in the original version of Article 92 GG: "The judicial authority is entrusted to judges; this authority will be exercised *by the Federal Constitutional Court, the Federal Supreme Court,* the federal courts envisioned in this Basic Law, and the Land courts" (italics added).

5 Compare the Statute on the Preservation of Jurisprudential Unity among the Supreme Courts of the Federation of 19 June 1968, BGBl. I, p. 661.

ordinary-court decision for its conformity with fundamental rights (Brodocz 2005, 271 ff.; Wahl 2005, 371 ff.). All together, the specialized courts surrendered *nolens volens*—and they continue to yield—to the FCC's claims of constitutional supremacy. Exceptions to this rule—such as the early-twenty-first-century dispute over [94] the assembly rights of demonstrators with Neo-Nazi backgrounds, and the dispute over compliance with judgments of the European Court of Human Rights ("Görgülü")—have been rare, and have stirred considerable controversy—even if ultimately neither the Superior Administrative Court for the state of North-Rhine-Westphalia, in the first case, nor the Naumburg Superior State Court (*Oberlandesgericht*), in the second case, was able to oppose successfully the orders from Karlsruhe. No other judicial herb has grown as an antidote to the FCC. *Karlsruhe locuta, causa finita.* The Court thus established its unchallenged jurisprudential supremacy—probably at least as early as the Lüth judgment. The Court's supremacy vis-à-vis the ordinary judiciary is evident and indisputable not only—and not even most powerfully—in the few spectacular *hard cases*, but especially and most enduringly in the roughly 160,000 routine cases in which a constitutional complaint has challenged the decision of an ordinary court. Generally, however, the relationship between the FCC and the other courts is far less fraught than the pertinent publications suggest (Jestaedt 2001). The exaggeration arises because the perception of FCC decisions with respect to the specialized courts gets distorted. What comes into view tends to be only the spectacular Senate decisions and a few of the more prominent chamber decisions (of course, only *prominent* chamber decisions are ever published). Senate decisions, however, are in three respects unrepresentative. First, they make up less than one percent of all FCC decisions involving concrete constitutional review. Second, the success rate [95] in Senate decisions is some fifteen to thirty times greater than it is in chamber decisions. And third, the Senate regularly decides only novel questions of fundamental principle; all other disputes are settled by the chambers without much fanfare. [96]

III. Three Momentous Turning Points

From a juristic perspective, three institutional and functional turning points stand out among the plethora of developmental factors and conditions that, taken together, enabled the FCC to emerge—in both diachronic and synchronic legal comparison—as the third archetype of constitutional justice, alongside the two older models, the U.S. Supreme Court and the Austrian Constitutional Court: first, the decision in favor of constitutional justice in the narrow sense (see **III.A.** below); second, the adoption of a concentrated and isolated constitutional court (see III.B. below); and finally, third, the embrace of a comprehensive form of constitutional adjudication, with the constitutional court superior to all other courts (see III.C. below). All three choices regarding the whether and how of constitutional justice comprise far-reaching preconditions as well as consequences for our understanding of the constitution.

A. Opting for a judicial guardian of the Constitution

A court that resolves disputes between member states of the federation (*Bund*) or between constitutional organs of a single state (either the central state or one of the member states) is known in German as a *Staatsgerichtsbarkeit.* It represents a centuries-old tradition, one that also includes the Weimar Staatsgerichtshof (Geiger 1952, XI ff.; Voßkuhle 2010a, Article 93 RN 2 ff.). By contrast, constitutional justice [97]—i.e. judicial resolution of conflicts on the basis of the constitution as the supreme source of law—is a product of the period following the Second World War. Already during the Weimar era, there was a multi-pronged row over who could and should serve as guardian of the constitution. The Reichsgericht experimented timidly and tentatively (RGZ 111, 320 ff. (1925); RGZ 124, 173 ff. (1929)) with judicial review—i.e. the power of courts to review laws and regulations for their constitutionality and, when needed, to invalidate them. Opponents of judicial review argued that—because of the uniqueness of the constitution, on the one hand, and the strict limitation of courts to deciding legal questions, on the other—the constitutional review of Acts of Parliament was not a proper job for judges, but would embroil judges in crafting constitutional legislation in a manner alien to the judicial role (Schmitt 1931 (2015)). On this view, a constitutional court endowed with the powers of constitutional judicial review was out of the question. This corresponded with the widely-held view, rooted in democratic theory, that a legislature with direct democratic legitimacy must not be subordinated to the vote of a panel of judges with dubious democratic credentials. The few opponents of this view (Kelsen 1931 (2015)) stressed the political character of ordinary adjudication, denied that the special character of constitutional law immunized it against adjudication, and defended the democratic legitimacy of judicial review. But their brief in favor of a genuine constitutional court fell on deaf ears.

After the collapse of the National Socialist regime, the legal and intellectual landscape changed dramatically and enduringly—even without [98] a preparatory or accompanying scholarly discourse. Not least under the likely influence of the victorious Western powers, the state constitutions established in 1946 and 1947—i.e. before the Basic Law—in the French and American occupation zones (Baden, Bavaria, Bremen, Hessen, North Rhine-Westphalia, the Saar region, Baden-Württemberg, and Württemberg-Hohenzollern) introduced constitutional courts with powers of judicial review. The deliberations over the Basic Law during 1948 and 1949 followed in these tracks. No matter how heated the debates over the position and organization of the Federal Constitutional Court became, both in the preliminary constitutional convention at Herrenchiemsee and in the Parliamentary Council itself, a consensus prevailed from the outset that the new federal court would wield the power of judicial review—and this not only as a Staatsgerichtshof in the narrow sense (i.e. a successor to the Weimar *Reichsstaatsgerichtshof*), but as a full-fledged constitutional court. The guardian of the new constitution—not the only guardian, but the supreme one—would be a court of law (Geiger 1952, XIX ff.).

The framers had two preconditions: first, that the constitution would furnish a workable legal standard (see **III.A.1.**); and second, that legislation could be regarded as a justiciable exercise of state power (see **III.A.2.**). Both conditions combine in a peculiar coupling of law and politics (below **III.A.3.**). [99]

1. The "law-ness" of the Constitution

If constitutional questions are to be justiciable—and it is the core contention of all constitutional justice that they should be—if they are to be answerable, that is, by judges in the course of deciding cases, then it must be possible to conceptualize constitutional questions as regular and genuine questions *of law*. Put differently, if the body entrusted with the task is to be considered a court in the traditional sense, and if its activity is to be regarded as adjudication, the standard used to decide the conflict must be a legal standard. Constitutional adjudication thus presupposes at the outset that the constitution is law (Voßkuhle 2010a, Article 93 RN 24 ff.). As banal as that may sound today, it is far from obvious from the perspective of constitutional history. For a long time it was anything but clear whether constitutions enjoyed the character of law and, if they did, what sort of character they enjoyed. Were they, for instance, anything more than a prominent form of the self-imposed limitations of rulers vis-à-vis their subjects, a gentleman's agreement among the powerful, a code of conduct enforced by political sanctions, a soft law for questions concerning sovereignty, or a set of programmatic principles and regulatory ideals? There were few clear answers to these questions. But as long as (and precisely because) there was no true constitutional court, these questions could go unanswered. As late as the Weimar period, leading opponents of judicial review contested the constitution's legal character. Carl Schmitt, for instance, on the basis of a dual conception of the constitution, saw the constitutional statute (*Verfassungsgesetz*—i.e. the constitution in terms of positive law) as dependent in both content and validity on the constitution as the pre- and extra-legal "complete decision over the type and [100] form of political decision" (Schmitt 1928, 20 ff.), the constitution in the positive sense. On this view, the positive-law constitution—like positive law generally—lacks normative autonomy. Constitutional adjudication, by contrast, implies that the constitution as decision-making standard is autonomous by virtue of its normativity and positivity—in other words, that one can isolate, present, discuss, and decide constitutional questions as questions of positive law (Böckenförde 1999a). It is precisely this latter capacity that permits delegating the decision to courts (Lembcke 2007).

Thus, the Basic Law understands itself as extraordinary law in terms of its rank and its regulative object, but as ordinary—i.e. positive—law in terms of its structure and texture. Notwithstanding its distinct origins and amendment procedures (Article 79 GG), and notwithstanding its status as a standard for all other law (i.e. the supremacy of the constitution, Article 1, 3 and Article 20, 3 GG), the Basic Law is, like all other positive law, positive law itself. According to its legal source, the federal constitution is, like the constitutions of the *Länder*, statutory law. Although subject to special quorum and certification requirements not applicable to ordinary statutes (Article 79, 1–2 GG), the Basic Law is produced and modified in the form of a statute through statutory procedures. A primary condition of the Basic Law's efficacy lies in its status as ordinary law in this sense. On the one hand, it forfeits thus the character of something sacred and eternal and is thereby disenchanted. As positive law created by mortals and therefore, in principle, amendable by mortals, it is contingent and disposable. On the other hand, through its [101] integration into positive law—and as the supreme norm in the normative pyramid of domestic positive law—the constitution acquires the distinctive position from which it is able, in a legally (and judicially) comprehensible way, to shape, steer, and guide all other positive law within the domestic legal sphere. Only in this way does the constitution become an instrument for resolving conflicts through judicial power.

2. The justiciability of legislation: Norm control

But constitutional adjudication does not merely presuppose that the constitution possesses the character of ordinary law. Its defining structural feature is judicial review. And judicial review presupposes a legal order conceived as a hierarchy comprising all norms, in which legislation too is integrated and embedded. In this hierarchical order, the legislature is no longer "self-ruling," as the Reichsgericht said of the Weimar legislature in the late 1920s: "The legislature is self-ruling [*selbstherrlich*] and bound by no other limitations except those that it imposes upon itself through the constitution or ordinary law" (RGZ 118, 325, 327 (1927)). Legislation is no longer the sole source of all law, and the legislature no longer enjoys free rein over the law and its limits. Rather, the legislative authority now takes its place as merely one actor among many in the hierarchical process of concretizing and individualizing the law, though it makes a particularly important contribution to law creation. Ordinary law (as it was tellingly termed) was now [102] strictly distinguished from constitutional law because of the differing preconditions for their creation and their differing hierarchical priority. The one is created by the legislative authority (*Gesetzgeber*), the other by the constituent authority (*Verfassungsgesetzgeber*). The fact that these bodies comprise the same individuals in the Bundestag and the Bundesrat must not obscure this crucial distinction. Under the Basic Law, the legislature is no longer "self-ruling," but rather, as Article 1, 3 and Article 20, 3 GG make unmistakably clear, an authority bound by and subject to the constitution. Legislation, accordingly, is no longer a free-floating law creation binding only on itself, but rather—depending on one's preferred formulation—the concretization, actualization, or implementation of the constitution. This is not to say anything, as yet, about the scope and detail, the degree and intensity with which constitutional law shapes statutory law. It is "only" to say that legislation—like all other sub-constitutional lawmaking—takes place under the limitations and within the framework imposed by the constitution. But this is the decisive point for subordinating legislation to judicial oversight. For the legislature's compliance with its obligation to law—and the obligation to the constitution is nothing more than a special form of the obligation to law—can be subject to judicial review (Böckenförde 1999a, 161 f.). In this respect, legislation becomes justiciable. The difficulties that arise, from the perspective of democratic theory, when judges annul acts of legislatures and thus function as a "negative legislature" (Kelsen 1929a, 56) can be mitigated, at least superficially, by invoking the constitution's supremacy as a matter of positive law.

If one considers the integration of both the constitution and statutes within the hierarchical legal [103] order, the balance of power shifts beyond the relationship between the constitutional court and the legislature. For the logical extension of the idea of comprehensive constitutional regulation of all state authority is that all official acts are amenable to review by the constitutional court. This entails a shift in the relationship between the constitutional court and the specialized courts (as well as the executive) on the one hand, and in the status of the constitution within the structure of legal sources, on the other (see also III.B. and III.C.).

3. Linking law and politics

With the constitution's "becoming law" on the one hand, and the justiciability of legislation on the other, the foundations were laid for the Basic Law's distinctive coupling of law and politics. No political question is exempt *per se* from the constitution—or from review by the Constitutional Court. The establishment of constitutional justice via the FCC simultaneously fulfils and belies the dual admonition against a politicization of the judiciary and a juridification of politics. It fulfills the warning because the Constitutional Court is drawn into the political conflicts that pass through its gates, and because everything the Court decides is considered and interpreted by the light of constitutional law. But at the same time it belies the warning because it prepares the ground for a more nuanced classification of law and politics—an alternative to the traditional, stark differentiation. In the first place, every lawmaker is informed by its own political values. And, secondly, a political principle or a political rule does not [104] stop being political when it takes a positive form—when, that is, it becomes law. The principle or the rule remains political within the particular, self-regulating aggregation that we call law. Constitutional law, and with it the Constitutional Court, claim decision-making power "only" for this particular aggregation. The description—usually with a negative connotation—of constitutional law as "political law" needs to be reconsidered against this background (Isensee 1992; Böckenförde 1999a, 163 f.).

The Parliamentary Council already saw the FCC this way—as a court, yes, but as a special court imbued "with a certain political accent" (Doemming et al 1951, 665, 668, and 673). The FCC accounted for this particularity with its hybrid self-characterization as a constitutional organ, on the one hand, and as a court, on the other. In its "Status Memo," the FCC added that a constitutional court, unlike all other courts, "deals with a particular from of legal dispute, namely with 'political' disputes. Political disputes are to be understood as those in which political law is being contested and in which the political itself, in light of existing norms, becomes the object of judicial decision-making" (Bundesverfassungsgericht 1957, 144 f.). As a court, the FCC is limited to deciding legal questions. But in doing so it uses certain instruments unavailable to other courts. It can, for instance, decide questions concerning its own procedures, or concerning the nature of interpreting benchmark law—i.e. the Basic Law itself. (It can also refer to official practice or consider the political consequences of its decisions.) (Roellecke 2005a, section 67 RN 16). [105]

B. Opting for an isolated constitutional tribunal

The decision to complement the skeletal *Staatsgerichtsbarkeit* with a full-fledged constitutional tribunal did not settle the question of what form constitutional adjudication would take. In this respect, there were three basic models. The first was the supreme court model, in which the highest ordinary court assumes the additional duties of a constitutional court. This model unites institutionally the highest specialized court and the constitutional court. The United States Supreme Court, which handed down its first decisions in 1791, is the prototypical example of an integrated constitutional tribunal. In the second model, specialized and constitutional adjudication are institutionally separated. This model embraces an institutionally autonomous constitutional court that stands apart from the specialized courts. The historical prototype of this second model of isolated constitutional adjudication is the Austrian Constitutional Court (*Verfassungsgerichtshof*), established by the Federal Constitutional Law of October 1, 1920, which stood as a third supreme court alongside the Supreme Court of Justice (*Oberster Gerichtshof*, with jurisdiction over civil and criminal matters) and the Administrative Court of Justice (*Verwaltungsgerichtshof*, with jurisdiction over administrative law). Under the third model, constitutional adjudication is not concentrated in a single court, but entrusted to several or even all courts. But even in such cases of diffuse constitutional adjudication, jurisdiction over the law of the state (*Staatsgerichtsbarkeit*) is usually confined to a single, specialized court. Today, constitutional justice forms part of the basic equipment of a constitutional state. The overwhelming majority of states [106] have opted either for the American model or for the Austrian model of a specialized constitutional court with a monopoly over declarations of unconstitutionality. Among the European states, most have preferred the Austrian model. The Federal Republic of Germany is part of this group, with the Federal Constitutional Court conforming to the model of a concentrated and isolated constitutional tribunal (Böckenförde 1999a, 170 ff.). This choice has entailed a number of consequences.

1. Exceptional adjudication

One of the advantages of concentrated and isolated constitutional adjudication lies in the greater structural visibility, awareness, and dignity that it brings to the judicial protection of the constitution. This model elevates and distinguishes the constitution and its protection from the realm of ordinary adjudication by entrusting them to a specialized court with exclusive jurisdiction over these extraordinary duties. This underscores the special character of the constitution. The court's institutional autonomy highlights its special status as the branch of the judiciary to whose judgments the other constitutional organs—including the legislature—are subject. Without this institutional distinctiveness, it would be implausible to claim that the constitutional court enjoys the status of a constitutional organ. Concentrating judicial review—i.e. monopolizing the power to quash norms—within a single supreme court has two additional charms: first, it does not grant to every court, however insignificant, the power to annul parliamentary laws, and [107] second, it does not allow divergent decisions from different courts with attendant uncertainty over a law's validity.

But the establishment of a single constitutional court, isolated from the rest of the judiciary, carries risks as well as opportunities—and those risks stem precisely from the isolation of constitutional protection. The greatest risk is an institutional one: rivalries can arise in which ordinary courts feel threatened by the special "political" court responsible for constitutional questions (Roellecke 2005b). There then arises what in France has been called the *concurrence des juges*: the constitutional court contends with the supreme specialized courts for procedural and interpretive supremacy. This competition can become especially precarious for the constitutional court if—as a result of its judicial recruitment, its infrequent activity, and the corresponding lack of juristic-professional quality in its decisions—the court fares unfavorably in comparison with the time-honored professional judges of the specialized courts of final appeal. The French Conseil constitutionnel provides an example of this. As already noted, the FCC in its early history had to overcome several hierarchical struggles with the other federal courts (on this, see II.C.2.). That it withstood these challenges, on the whole, successfully was due not least to the fact that it possessed effective instruments for securing judicial professionalism. Among these, the selection of justices, the support of scholarly assistants, and the establishment of the chamber system were especially important. [108]

The selection of justices has—despite repeated criticism of the venerable system of partisan proportion in the parliamentary selection committees—been marked overwhelmingly by moderation and skill. In this respect, the legislature intended to ensure a minimum of professionalism among FCC judges. Thus, in the beginning, each twelve-member Senate had to include at least four federal judges. Today, at least three of the eight justices in each Senate must be federal judges (Section 2, 3 BVerfGG). But the other justices—among whom professors of public law have for some time predominated—must meet the qualifications required of ordinary judges. As a result, today's FCC is exclusively a jurists' court. Only extraordinarily rarely have FCC justices abandoned their judicial role for an openly partisan one. Apart from exceptions barely worth mentioning, the justices, once installed, feel more obligated toward their Senate than to those who nominated them in the Bundestag or the Bundesrat. The contribution to the quality and authority of the Court's jurisprudence of this Karlsruhe *esprit de corps*—fostered by the fact that the court deliberates and decides year-round, rather than in limited sessions—should not be underestimated.

Another important means of ensuring judicial professionalism has been the creation of a "third Senate." Though not supplied at first, scholarly assistants were assigned to the First Senate in 1952, and the Second in 1956. Initially, each justice had one assistant. Their number rose steadily with the swelling number of cases. Now, each [109] justice has, on average, four scholarly assistants, who usually work at the FCC for two-and-a-half to three years. Although there are no legally prescribed qualifications for scholarly assistants, they are almost without exception qualified to serve as judges themselves. The largest group consists of ordinary or administrative judges assigned to the FCC. The next largest group comprises government attorneys and assistant university professors, who work overwhelmingly for the academic justices (Gehle 2005, RN 19 ff., section 93a ff.; Zuck 2006, 283 ff.). Scholarly assistants are indispensable both for landmark cases and for the vast number of small, unspectacular ones. Through their number and competence, they contribute decisively to the juridical quality and professionalism of the FCC's decisions.

The chambers, formerly known as three-member screening committees, were introduced in 1956 and have been reformed many times since then. They provide "an outlet against the possible inundation of the Federal Constitutional Court" (Rupp-von Brünneck, in: BVerfGE 42, 143, 154 (1976)) through constitutional complaints. These committees, which conduct the so-called acceptance procedure (*Annahmeverfahren*) (Sections 93a et passim BVerfGG), have also helped to deal with the mountain of constitutional complaints and, more recently, petitions for abstract review as well (Section 81a, 1 BVerfGG). In principle, both Senates have three chambers with three justices each. The chambers, which currently dispose of more than ninety-nine percent of the Court's approximately 6,500 cases every year, must decide cases unanimously (Section 93d, 3, 1 BVerfGG). Not only do they decide whether to admit complaints, they also decide, in cases of obvious merit, whether to grant them (Section 93c, 1, 1 BVerfGG). [110] The sheer quantitative demands on the Court virtually require this decision-making routine, which shapes and strengthens the judicial and professional character of Karlsruhe's jurisprudence.

But, of course, from the perspective of the specialized courts, the acceptance and authority of the FCC's jurisprudence does not depend exclusively on institutional factors. No less important is the justificatory quality of the decisions. In this regard, the FCC benefits from its well-known symbiotic relationship with public law scholarship. On this point, more anon (see section IV. below).

2. Broad standards as jurisdictional boundary

What is true for every other court is true for the Constitutional Court as well: its powers of review cannot reach beyond the scope of the standards it is authorized to interpret. With respect to institutionalizing a specialized court exclusively concerned with constitutional questions, this means that this tribunal is only authorized to decide cases that involve disputes of constitutional law. Accordingly, the FCC can decide only those cases whose object—whether a law, a judgment, a treaty, or some measure taken by another constitutional organ—can be measured against the provisions of the Basic Law. (Cases assessing the conformity of state and federal law at the sub-constitutional level are an exception.) Where such standards of constitutional law are lacking, a legal dispute can be decided by another court: the FCC [111] may not reach the merits in the matter. The First Senate made this generalizable point in response to a constitutional complaint invoking the freedom of opinion: the Court's commission was only to "ensure respect for the requirements of constitutional law. On the other hand, it is not the Federal Constitutional Court's job to decide for itself the relevant legal dispute, which, despite the influence of fundamental rights, has its own character as a civil or criminal case. Accordingly, the [FCC's] power of review does not reach beyond the demands that fundamental rights impose upon the interpretation of the relevant statements." (BVerfGE 94, 1, 9 f. (1996)). Where there is no *constitutional* complaint, there can be no *constitutional* justice.

This distinguishes the Federal Constitutional Court in particular from the U.S. Supreme Court, which in addition to its capacity as a constitutional court also—and, from the perspective of its procedural design, *especially*—fulfills the role of federal court of appeal. In principle, the Supreme Court can decide a case on the basis of any of its legal aspects, so long as it presents a reviewable issue. It need not decide on the basis of a specifically constitutional issue. In those cases in which its decision can be based on either ordinary federal law or on the federal constitution, the Supreme Court can even choose among the relevant standards to justify its decision. By contrast, limitation to a single standard—the constitution— tends to lead a decision-happy court like the FCC to make this standard bear immense interpretive weight. But as the standard (i.e. the content of the constitution) stretches, so too does the power—though limited in comparison to a Supreme Court—of the [112] institutionally autonomous constitutional court. In this respect, one must not overlook the risk that, *in practice*, the constitutionally imposed limitation, "Where there is no constitutional law, there can be no constitutional court," will be inverted: "Where there is a constitutional court, there will also be constitutional law."

C. Opting for a pyramid model of constitutional adjudication

If the FCC shares with the Austrian Constitutional Court the character of a concentrated and isolated constitutional court, it departs from its Austrian model in one essential detail that greatly influences its efficacy and operation. While the Austrian Constitutional Court is merely one high court among three, none of which possess adjudicative authority over the others, the FCC is, thanks to a unique procedural form, superior to all other branches of the judiciary. The adoption of the so-called "judgment complaint" (*Urteilsverfassungsbeschwerde*)—a complaint alleging that an ordinary-court judgment has violated the complainant's constitutional rights—endows the FCC with the legal authority to nullify, as a violation of a fundamental rights, any ordinary-court judgment brought before it, and to return the case thereafter to the court *a quo*. Terminologically imprecise, though not substantively incorrect, some say the FCC has assumed the role of a "super court of appeal." [113] In this regard, the German model—which was based originally on the Austrian model of an isolated constitutional court—approximates the American model of integrated constitutional adjudication. For the U.S. Supreme Court also serves as a kind of super court of appeal. In contrast to the pure Austrian model, the conception of constitutional justice realized by the Basic Law and the BVerfGG has been characterized as a pyramid model. Thus, constitutional complaints against lower-court judgments represent one of the distinguishing features—if not *the* distinguishing feature—of the German model of constitutional justice.

It should be added, by way of clarification, that there is another form of procedure, which also brings together decisions of the specialized courts and of the FCC, but which does result in a hierarchical relationship between constitutional justice and ordinary justice as posited by the pyramid model. This is the so-called judicial referral, or concrete judicial review, envisioned in Article 100, 1 GG. Most states with an institutionally autonomous constitutional tribunal (Austria, for example, or France since 2009) recognize this type of procedure, even if they typically do not allow judgment complaints. The law of the European Union allows something similar in the procedure for a preliminary ruling (Article 267 TFEU). But EU law does not recognize judgment complaints either. In the procedure for concrete judicial review, the specialized court suspends the case before it and refers to the Constitutional Court the question whether the statutory norm, on whose validity the outcome [114] of the case depends, is constitutional (and can thus furnish the basis for decision) or unconstitutional, null, and void (and hence to be ignored when deciding the case). However the FCC decides the constitutional question, it does not resolve the underlying dispute, and does not, therefore, interfere with the judicial power of the referring court.

1. The court that fields complaint against other courts

It is truly astounding: a procedural form embraced in neither the deliberations of the Herrenchiemsee convention nor those of the Parliamentary Council; a form introduced by ordinary legislation in the 1951 Federal Constitutional Court Act (Sections 90 et passim BVerfGG) and given constitutional status only in 1969, twenty years after the Basic Law entered into force—such a form has dominated the Court's jurisprudence, both quantitatively and qualitatively, since the day it opened its doors (Löwer 2005, section 70 RN 163). In the early 1950s, the number of constitutional complaints hovered between 400 and 900 a year. After 1958, it never fell below the 1,000-mark. After 1976, there were no fewer than 2,000 complaints annually, and after 1979, the tally increased to more than 3,000. After reunification, the number of complaints accelerated dramatically. For fifteen years, it ranged between 4,000 and 6,000 per year. Since 2006, it has always been greater than 6,000.[6] The judgment complaint is a sub-category [115] of the individual complaint under Article 93, 1, 4a GG. It comprises those constitutional complaints directed against ordinary-court decisions. These constitute the lion's share (approximately ninety-three percent) of all constitutional complaints because an individual complaint is admissible only after exhaustion of all ordinary-court remedies (Section 90, 2 BVerfGG, principle of subsidiarity). If one further considers that roughly ninety-eight percent of all the FCC decisions that settled a case between 1951 and 2010—i.e. 161,000 decisions out of a total of 164,500—involved a judgment complaint, it is easy to see the extent to which the FCC has become a "complaint-judgment court." This assessment is modified only slightly when one subtracts chamber decisions (which now constitute fully ninety-nine percent of all resolutions of constitutional complaints) and plenum decisions (which one can count on the fingers of a hand). Even if one looks only at cases resolved by a Senate decision, nearly three-fourths of the cases involve individual complaints. Even in this calculation, the spectacular

[6] The statistical data cited here and hereafter is taken or derived from the Court-produced annual statistics of the Federal Constitutional Court for the business year 2010, which may be accessed at https://www.bundesverfassungsgericht.de/DE/Verfahren/Jahresstatistiken/Archiv/2010/statistik_2010_node.html (retrieval date: June 6, 2019). For several years, the Court has given a heading to its yearly statistical compilation; the 2010 statistics bear the motto "full capacity" (*Vollbeschäftigung*).

cases—disputes between constitutional organs, petitions for abstract review, or disputes between the Federal Government and the states—amount to only a small fraction of the cases decided (see Table 2.1). [116]

If the embrace of isolated constitutional adjudication brought the FCC into competition with the other federal supreme courts (the Federal Court of Justice and the Federal Administrative Court, for instance), the embrace of a pyramid model of constitutional adjudication placed the FCC in a position superior to all other courts, the federal supreme courts included. That this breeds tension was discussed earlier (above II.C.2.). On the other hand, one must not overlook the fact that the pyramid model intensifies contacts and exchanges, both [117] quantitatively and qualitatively, beyond what would be possible in a system in which the only direct contact between the constitutional court and specialized courts came through judicial referrals or preliminary rulings. Of course, more frequent and intensive contact entails the risk of more frequent and serious confrontation. But the statistics of the FCC attest notably that such confrontations are not inevitable and need not define relationships between courts.

Table 2.1 Cases Resolved by Decision, 1951–2010

	Plenum, Senate, chamber 1951–2010		Senate 1951–2010	
Procedure type (selection)	**absolute number**	**%**	**absolute number**	**%**
Party ban	5	0.003	5	0.090
Election examination complaint	158	0.096	158	2.836
Dispute between governmental bodies	95	0.058	95	1.705
"Abstract" review of statutes	108	0.066	108	1.938
Dispute between Federation and Land	26	0.016	26	0.467
"Concrete" review of statutes	1,253	0.762	1,042	18.701
Preliminary injunction	1,752	1.065	*	*
Constitutional complaint	160,995	97.862	4,018	72.111
Plenary decision	4	0.002	–	–
All procedures	164,512	100.000	5,572	100.000

* Regarding applications for preliminary injunctions, the statistics of the Federal Constitutional Court do not distinguish between Senate and chamber decisions; these, accordingly, are omitted here.

The success rate of constitutional complaints across the entire sixty years of Karlsruhe adjudication is a paltry 2.4% (of 179,528 constitutional complaints the Court has granted 4,308), and the trend is falling rather than rising (2006: 2.31%; 2007: 2.45%; 2008: 1.90%; 2009: 1.88%; 2010: 1.71%). The numbers are similar if one subtracts other individual complaints and looks only at the success rate of judgment complaints. In the last twenty years (1991–2010), only 2,522 out of 97,093 judgment complaints were successful, a success rate of just 2.6%. Tellingly, for the most interesting relationships of institutional cooperation or confrontation—those between the FCC and the federal supreme courts—the success rate is significantly lower. Between 1991 and 2010, the FCC considered 18,170 complaints against judgments of the five federal supreme courts (the Federal Court of Justice, the Federal Administrative Court, the Federal Welfare Court, the Federal Labor Court, and the Federal Court of Finance). [118] It granted only 313 of them—a success rate of 1.72%. If one looks at the branches of the ordinary judiciary separately, some figures are even lower—a result explained by the fact that the overall success rate is inflated by the relatively high success rate of complaints against decisions of the Federal Administrative Court in asylum cases (Federal Court of Justice: 1.52%; Federal Administrative Court: 4.01%; Federal Welfare Court: 0.91%; Federal Labor Court: 0.98%; Federal Finance Court: 1.24%). A few spectacular cases notwithstanding, the federal supreme courts have little to complain of in the 313 decisions struck down by the FCC in the last twenty years—a fact confirmed by an interesting numerical comparison. In an almost identical period (1992–2010), the FCC quashed as unconstitutional 213 norms of federal and state law. On the other hand, the low success rate of judgment complaints may be read and interpreted as an encouraging sign that the specialized courts offer, on the whole, reliable protection of fundamental rights, and that they have accepted and take seriously their once unfamiliar role as guardians of the constitution. Moreover, the still-rising number of individual complaints (despite sinking odds of success) suggests that the individual complaint, through which a private citizen can challenge a fundamental-rights violation by the state, plays a large and undiminished role as an outlet for legal protection. This, together with the fact that a partial or total abolition of judgment complaints would inevitably and seriously change the character [119] of the Federal Constitutional Court, should be kept in mind when considering (with good reason) how to contain or reduce the Court's overburdened docket.

2. The omnipresence of fundamental rights—and of the Federal Constitutional Court

The individual (judgment) complaint demonstrates more simply and profoundly than any other procedural form how closely the success of the Basic Law—in the form of fundamental rights—depends on the success of the Federal Constitutional Court. In addition to its role as High Court of Individual (Judgment) Complaints, the FCC can just as appropriately be called the Specialized Court of Fundamental Rights.

In the first place, this is true simply and strikingly because under Article 93, 1, 4a GG, individual complaints—which constitute, as noted earlier, roughly ninety-eight percent of all cases that come before the FCC—can only challenge violations of fundamental rights or other rights of similar stature. By contrast, violations of other legal rights of constitutional rank cannot be challenged in individual complaints. It is thus in the interest of every complainant that fundamental rights be interpreted as expansively as possible. If the FCC wishes to reach the merits of a complaint, it must either be sure that fundamental rights suffice as the exclusive grounds of decision, or it must interpret fundamental rights expansively. Moreover, the quantity and variety of [120] cases that come before the Court via individual complaint fosters a form of fundamental rights interpretation and application that is increasingly detailed and oriented toward the individual case.

On the other hand, individual complaints open an ever-wider field of application for the FCC's fundamental rights jurisprudence. Two lines of decision are especially prominent in this respect. These are Elfes and Lüth and their respective progeny, whose doctrines were developed in the Court's early years and, taken together, form the lead melody of Karlsruhe's fundamental rights jurisprudence—a melody extended, refined, and expanded in later years, but ultimately, at its core, unaltered. Two path-breaking propositions for fundamental rights protection and individual complaint procedure stem from the Elfes decision of January 16, 1957 (BVerfGE 6, 32, 52 ff.). One is that the protection of fundamental rights is essentially free from gaps; the other is that conformity with fundamental rights presupposes that the statutory basis for an infringement of fundamental rights must also be in harmony with the constitution. The upshot of the first proposition is that every private act is, at bottom, the object of fundamental rights protection and that any state restriction on such acts (at least any infringement of the general freedom of action protected by Article 2, 1 GG) can be regarded as a rights infringement triggering constitutional justification requirements. The second proposition expands, in practice, the protection of fundamental rights beyond the circle of rights that expressly define private persons as rights-bearers by stipulating that a rights infringement is justified only when its statutory basis complies with fundamental rights [121] *and* fulfills all other constitutional requirements (e.g. that the lawmaker possessed the relevant authority and followed the relevant procedures). In this way, principles of objective constitutional law are made subjective—i.e. a rights-bearer can challenge the failure to observe such principles in a constitutional complaint, even if he himself neither benefits from nor is bound by the relevant constitutional provisions, legislative competence, or legislative procedures. Both propositions herald an enormous expansion of fundamental rights protection—and of the field of application for individual constitutional complaints. The Lüth decision of January 15, 1958 (BVerfGE 7, 198 ff.) went one step further, declaring that not only do fundamental rights defend individual liberty against state encroachment, but that the Basic Law's fundamental rights catalogue established "an objective system of values," which radiates throughout the entire legal order and affects every legal relationship, such that none can stand in opposition to it and all must be interpreted and applied in accordance with its spirit. The Court thus embraced the very principle that had been so vehemently opposed by private-law courts and private-law scholars—namely, the application of fundamental rights to private law, or the influence of fundamental rights on the legal relationships of private parties. Fundamental rights are thus interpreted and implemented as all-embracing norms. Accordingly, no legal relationship is immune per se to the influence of fundamental rights. Put differently, any legal relationship involving a bearer of fundamental rights may be re-characterized as a fundamental-rights relationship. [122] Every violation of law is also potentially a violation of fundamental rights—and may be challenged as such in an individual constitutional complaint (Wahl 2005, 371 ff.). The dual process of expanding both the scope of fundamental rights and the extent of the Court's jurisdiction was strengthened and deepened by the principle—never expressly mentioned in the Basic Law—of proportionality. The so-called Pharmacy judgment of June 11, 1958 (BVerfGE 7, 377 ff.) is commonly considered the fountainhead of proportionality jurisprudence. The proportionality principle does more than enable the structuring of balancing procedures. Because it allows the Court to assess the scope and salience of all factors relevant to balancing in the individual case, it also enables the FCC to place its constitutional imprint on every legal relationship all the way down to the factual level. Thanks to the near-ubiquity of fundamental rights, this confronts the ordinary courts with the specter (at least potentially) of a nearly ubiquitous Constitutional Court. The proportionality principle leaves the ordinary courts with no jurisdictional reserve secure against the oversight and influence of the Constitutional Court.

In order to channel the flood of constitutional complaints opened by this strategy of expansive interpretation and application of fundamental rights into a manageable course, a series of sluices and filtering strategies were soon devised, beginning with the statutory establishment of an admission procedure before three-judge chambers (Section 93a et passim BVerfGG) and extending to extremely flexible adjudicative formulas, each calibrated to meet the FCC's needs. An example is the so-called "Heck formula," [123] according to which the FCC can "intervene in response to a constitutional complaint only when it involves the violation by courts of a specific constitutional right" (BVerfGE 18, 85, 92 (1964)). [124]

IV. Symbiosis with Public Law Scholarship

A. Academically oriented constitutional jurisprudence

Both in comparison with the specialized courts at home and with other constitutional courts abroad, the FCC stands out in its adjudicative and justificatory style—in other words, in its unusual approach to making and justifying its decisions (Lerche 2001). If one wished to give a name to the unique style, manner of expression, and level of reflection of Karlsruhe's jurisprudence, one might characterize it as unusually academically oriented.

Even on the surface, when compared with the judgments of similar courts within the same judicial culture of justification, FCC judgments remind one of scholarly tractates. FCC judgments are roughly three times the length of those of the Federal Court of Justice and the Federal Administrative Court, to take only the two most prominent of the federal supreme courts.[7] While the latter two courts make do, on average, with nine printed pages [125] per judgment, the FCC requires on average a full thirty printed pages (this is without taking into account any relevant differences in length between the decisions of the First and Second Senates). Even excluding the captions, headnotes, and statements of facts—if one looks only at the grounds of decision in the narrow sense: the Court's observations about admissibility and the merits—FCC judgments still average seventeen printed pages. The longest decision of the past ten years was the Second Senate's Lisbon judgment of June 30, 2009 (BVerfGE 123, 267–437)—a sensational judgment, in many respects, which numbered 171 printed pages—followed by the First Senate's Data Retention judgment of March 2, 2010 (BVerfGE 125, 260–385), which totaled 125 printed pages. By far the longest decision ever handed down by the Federal Constitutional Court was the First Senate's Judgment of August 17, 1956, which banned the German Communist Party (BVerfGE 5, 85). Monographic in more than just the quantitative sense, with its unusual tripartite framework and section headings, the judgment's 309 pages filled nearly an entire volume of the Court's official reports. Even chamber decisions, which by definition should address only legal questions already decided by the Senate (Sections 93a, 2, lit. a and 93c, 1, 1 BVerfGG), are on average a solid seven pages long—nearly as long, that is, as the Senate judgments of the federal supreme courts. The record for the longest chamber decision belongs to the second chamber of the Second Senate, whose decision of October 17, 2007 took

[7] The comparison is based on the decisions of the three courts as reported in recent years in their respective official collections—specifically, in BVerwGE 119 to 128, in BGHZ 165 to 174, and in BVerfGE 100 to 125. Strictly speaking, the values are admittedly comparable only with caveats. For in the collections of decisions of the Federal Court of Justice and the Federal Administrative Court, the decisions are not always reproduced in their entirety, but are sometimes abridged. This is not the case with the FCC's official reports. On the other hand, the official reports of the other courts only include (again in contrast to those of the FCC) selected judgments—judgments taken to be especially significant.

thirty-three pages to declare that a question of ecclesiastical self-determination was inadmissible [126] (BVerfGK 12, 308–340).

There are, of course, constitutional courts whose decisions trump those of Karlsruhe in average page length. Of these, the U.S. Supreme Court—which, as of April 2011, had published 563 proud and hefty volumes—comes first to mind. But one must always be aware of differences in the underlying justificatory culture. Judged by Continental European standards, for example, the American Court's style is highly colloquial, frequently featuring an opinion of the court alongside various dissenting and concurring opinions. American decisions also devote considerable attention to the underlying facts, and to the questions of whether and to what extent the decision fits in with previous judgments. All of this is typically absent from FCC decisions, which are devoted instead to a style of thinking and reasoning characteristic of legal dogmatics (*Rechtsdogmatik*), an especially scholarly format typical of German-language jurisprudence. This underscores the FCC's unique—not to say, exclusive—kinship with its academic counterpart: public law scholarship. Constitutional dogmatics provides a common language for both the practitioners (i.e. FCC justices) and the scholars of constitutional law. We will return to this shortly (see **IV.B.** below).

First, however, one should highlight the almost symbiotic link between the FCC and public law scholarship. This began with the fact that, from the very outset, [127] public law scholarship under the Basic Law stood generally—and, after the first two decades, completely and without reservation—behind the Basic Law and its eloquent guardian, the Federal Constitutional Court. In contrast to the public law scholarship of the Weimar era, whose most brilliant minds exerted influence far beyond Germany's borders, there is in the public law scholarship of the Federal Republic no serious effort to delegitimize the Basic Law and the FCC or to advance alternative concepts. Quite the contrary: a basic position has developed (it grows stronger with time) that has been characterized as "Constitutional Court positivism," and that contents itself essentially with the dogmatics (in the sense both of *genitivus subiectivus* and of *genitivus obiectivus*) of Constitutional Court jurisprudence (Schlink 1989; Schlink 2007; Jestaedt 2002). Fifty years ago, on the occasion of the FCC's tenth anniversary celebration, Rudolf Smend could already utter the famous words: "as a practical matter, the Basic Law now applies as it is interpreted by the Federal Constitutional Court, and the scholarly literature comments on it in this sense" (Smend 1962 (1968), 582). The diagnosis remains current. For more than a few public law scholars, the Karlsruhe constitutional oracle serves as a substitute for theory. And nearly as many would look upon the summons to serve on the Constitutional Court as the crowning achievement of their professional career. Individual decisions are, of course, subject to scholarly criticism—sometimes sharp and cutting. But, to all appearances, the basically affirming stance toward the Court is never in serious danger [128] (Isensee 1996, 1085 ff.; Schulze-Fielitz 1997,

1 ff.). This should, perhaps, be unsurprising: constitutional scholarship seems to be the natural ally of constitutional jurisprudence. Constitutional scholarship is, alongside the FCC itself, the chief beneficiary of the postwar pattern of thinking from the perspective of the constitution. The reorientation of legal thinking toward the constitution rewards public law scholarship with an unprecedented increase in significance, impact, and renown among the disciplines of legal scholarship. It has even been anointed a kind of king among juristic disciplines. Accordingly, and unlike the other constitutional organs or the specialized courts, public law scholarship never challenged, frontally or fundamentally, the FCC's leadership claims (on this, see above **II.B.** and **II.C.**). Indeed, practically from the very outset, public law scholarship proved itself a not uncritical, but nevertheless unfailingly loyal companion—and, within the scope of its possibilities as a scholarly discipline, a powerful partner.

This is in no way to suggest a one-sided, asymmetrical, principal–agent relationship (Günther 2006). Unless appearances deceive, it is the criticism of constitutional scholars that the Court, for better or worse, takes most seriously and that, at least in the medium and long run, has the greatest impact. From the Court's perspective, public law scholars constitute the FCC's "primary expert audience" (Lembcke 2007, 216). One misconstrues, then, the complex and subtle reciprocal relationship between the Court and the scholars if one assumes that constitutional scholarship is always oriented toward constitutional jurisprudence and not vice versa. The FCC's proclivity toward scholarship is fostered by the fact that, [129] over time, it became a court of professors, shaped by the personalities of justices who, in addition to their judicial post in Karlsruhe, held professorships in law—and particularly in public law—at German universities. Of the justices who have exerted a formative influence on the Court's doctrine, a disproportionate number were prominent professors of public law. Think, for instance (to name only a few earlier professor-judges and their years of tenure), of Ernst Friesenhahn (1951–1963), Gerhard Leibholz (1951–1971), Konrad Hesse (1975–1987), Ernst-Wolfgang Böckenförde (1983–1986), Dieter Grimm (1987–1999), Paul Kirchhof (1987–1999), and Wolfgang Hoffmann-Riem (1999–2008). As of 2011, from the eight justices in each Senate, five in the First Senate and four in the Second are practicing professors of public law—a total of nine out of sixteen.[8] This, too, naturally shapes ways of thinking and styles of reasoning by and within the Court.

[8] First Senate: Ferdinand Kirchhof (Vice President and Senate Chair; University of Tübingen), Johannes Masing (University of Freiburg), Andreas Paulus (University of Göttingen), Susanne Baer (Humboldt University in Berlin), Gabriele Britz (University of Gießen). Second Senate: Andreas Voßkuhle (President and Senate Chair: University of Freiburg), Udo Di Fabio (University of Bonn), Gertrude Lübbe-Wolff (University of Bielefeld), Peter M. Huber (University of Munich).

B. Constitutional dogmatics as the forum of communication between constitutional scholarship and constitutional jurisprudence

Alongside the close personal connections and the mutual relations, borne of a common subject matter, [130] between the FCC and public law scholarship, constitutional dogmatics serves as the most significant link—by some distance—between them. It serves for both constitutional scholarship and constitutional justice as a common means of communication—a common forum, that is, for mutual exchange, understanding, and influence. It is their common language.

Constitutional dogmatics, however, is nothing more than the branch of legal dogmatics that focuses on the constitution. As such, it does not represent within the circle of domestic jurisprudence any distinctive disciplinary feature of constitutional scholarship. If one looks beyond Germany's borders, however, it quickly becomes apparent that the forum of legal dogmatics is a very German phenomenon—or rather, a disciplinary setting confined to the German-speaking world. It is hardly an exaggeration to say that genuine legal dogmatics is practiced only where, and to the extent that, German jurisprudence exerts an influence. It serves, so to speak, as a kind of brand mark. But because the FCC's methods and manner of reasoning are shaped and guided by dogmatics, it is worth having a look at dogmatics as a particular phenomenon.

1. Dogmatics' aim and function

Dogmatics is defined, on the one hand, by its orientation and *modus operandi*, and, on the other, by its constraining, dual use for legal scholarship and practice. Legal dogmatics is (in the double meaning of the word) oriented toward legal application. In addition to the *scientific community* of legal dogmatics' [131] academic exponents, the ideal or real audience for statements of legal dogmatics are those who participate in the process of producing law, and who, on the basis of and according to the standards of existing law, receive information on the production of new law—e.g. the legislature, administrative organs, courts, or parties to private-law transactions. A working definition of the goal of legal dogmatics is that "it seeks [by the means of legal scholarship] to guide practical decision-making in those positions of the organized world of legal work that are typically held by jurists and whose formal (official) program of decision is oriented toward legal norms" (Morlok 1988, 39 f.). Accordingly, legal dogmatics is "the product of the scholarly treatment of legal materials that aims at mastery of the practical juristic craft" (Morlok 1988, 40) Put differently, by producing a repository of academic knowledge, dogmatics serves as a practical scholarly aid to official legal decision-makers. Put baldly, it is a juristic user's guide focused on currently valid law. Its orientation toward application is thus twofold. On the one hand, it focuses on the law that is to be applied. Its reference point, in this respect, is currently valid law, the *lex lata*. On the other hand, dogmatics is addressed to specific actors—namely, to participants in the practical (i.e. aimed at real social management) production of law. To that end, dogmatics seeks to process and present applicable law in a systematic, standardized way that facilitates understanding and that guides and justifies interpretation and application. [132]

Dogmatics' *modus operandi* can be captured in skeletal form as a three-step process of decontextualization, systematization, and (re)concretization.

The first step involves producing dogmatic figures and concepts. Put simply, this occurs when a legal phenomenon is decontextualized—stripped, that is, both of its connection to a concrete case and set of facts, and (in principle) of its connection to any concrete norm of positive law. The phenomenon, so to speak, is juristically "sterilized." When the legal figure is thus purified of all contingency, there remains a distillation of normative statement—of "pure" law—purged of place, time, and space. Decontextualization helps standardize, rationalize, or stabilize normative expectations.

In a second step, the decontextualized legal principle undergoes a process of systematization that aims at substantive consistency. The "contingency-free" principles are then placed within a hierarchical system that is as comprehensive and as free from contradictions as possible. Taken together, such principles constitute the dogmatic system, which, in its turn, accords those principles rank and influence. This system embodies the (usually unspoken) ideal of legal order and unity. According to this ideal, the dogmatic system incorporates positive law and elevates it to a higher level of abstraction. Thus law becomes a science—a network of systematically connected principles.

In the third and final step, the influence of the system thus developed unfolds during the process of its application through concrete and contingent statements of principle. In a process of (re)concretizing dogmatic insights, the norm of positive law that will determine the case at hand is interpreted by the light of the dogmatic system. [133] The content and status of the legal principle to be applied *in concreto* are essentially determined by means of deductive-systematic reasoning. The dogmatic system furnishes, so to speak, the interpretive matrix for the applicable legal norm. Law thus reemerges from science. The cycle of rationalization thus completed guarantees the scientification of law production—and with it the self-perpetuating indispensability of legal dogmatics.

2. Common medium of legal scholarship and legal practice

Legal dogmatics binds legal scholarship to legal practice and *vice versa*. It spins, as it were, a disciplinary and disciplining thread around them both. Both use and develop it, though they often do so with different intentions and expectations, and by differing means and with different consequences. It is, not least, this ambivalent, hybrid status of legal dogmatics that raises the question whether it is really scholarship. And it is easy to see that this question cannot be answered with a simple Yes or No.

In ideal typical terms that reach the limits of their persuasive power with regard to the FCC, the differing approaches to dogmatics taken by legal scholarship and legal practice can be characterized as follows: while legal scholarship develops dogmatics, legal practice employs it. The former builds the system, the latter uses it (Schmidt-Aßmann 2006, Kap. 1 RN 3). Correspondingly varied are scholars' and practitioners' interest and participation in the individual phases of dogmatic activity. While scholarly attention focuses on decontextualization and harmonization, [134] practitioners attend primarily to (re)concretization—to applying dogmatic concepts and theorems. And while legal scholars routinely occupy themselves with tracing the effect of dogmatic reasoning precisely in the processes of law *production*, legal practitioners cultivate a stronger strategic-tactical relationship with dogmatics, which they use primarily in the *exposition* of law—or, less kindly, in marketing their decisions (Esser 1974, 517 ff.). Both scholars and practitioners make their own uses of dogmatics. Practical decision-makers profit from the scholarly character of legal dogmatics, which allows them to ensure and display the rationality, consistency, and integrity of their own efforts at law production. Conversely, scholarship makes great use of the practical perspective. In addition to testing the fitness of scientific "theory," dogmatics gives scholars an innovative nudge by unleashing reserves of creativity in the serious context of practical interpretation and application. Those who have to decide cases or conduct trials often think differently—and about different things—from those concerned primarily with the purity of their scholarly system.

Of course, the convergence of legal practice and legal scholarship in the communicative realm of legal dogmatics also conceals serious risks. If neither scholarship nor practice observes the limits of its competence, these synergy effects can take the form of collusive cooperation [135] concealed by the cloak of dogmatics. In that case, dogmatics serves as a formula for self-empowerment (Lepsius 2012). By mixing methods and sources of law, legal practice "solves" the competence problem from which it suffers, while legal scholarship employs dogmatics to "eliminate" the problem of validity that dogs its assertions. Propositions of scholarship and provisions of positive law thus come to seem interchangeable, even indistinguishable. The danger grows to the extent that both ambitions—that of system building and that of system using—are pursued by a single actor. Among all domestic courts, this is the case most pronouncedly (and for obvious reasons) with the Federal Constitutional Court.

C. Establishing congenial concepts for standards, interpretation, and exposition

To say that dogmatics' union of theory and practice characterizes the entire German-speaking world—and is not, therefore, a particularity of the relationship between public law scholarship and the Federal Constitutional Court—is not to say that the constitutional dogmatics of the Basic Law is no different from other forms of specialized dogmatics (e.g. private, criminal, or administrative law). The reality is just the opposite. And this circumstance is due, for the most part, to the singular character and influence of the Federal Constitutional Court. The court "profits" not only in a formal sense from the link that dogmatics forges with public law scholarship (which graces its decisions with an aura of scholarly authority), but also, and especially, [136] in a material sense—i.e. in the manner of its engagement with the constitution itself, in which dogmatics' systematic, concretizing, and application-oriented thinking is particularly evident and contributes to the FCC's unique position. What follows is a brief explanation of how this approach, shaped by constitutional dogmatics, affects perceptions and the efficacy of both the Basic Law and the Federal Constitutional Court under the three aforementioned headings: standards, interpretation, exposition. The sketch obviously makes no claim to comprehensiveness in its attention to detail. It does not pretend to do justice to the undeniable commonalities and peculiarities of the Court's judgments. Such an aspiration would be doomed to failure if for no other reason than that the "Federal Constitutional Court" is a unified actor only in an abstract, institutional sense. In reality, one is dealing with two—and, if one counts the chambers, with eight—separate collegial bodies, the composition of which changes constantly over time. In view of this, the best one can hope for here is to identify and extrapolate a few generalizable and representative lines of development. Such an undertaking will show that concepts of standards, interpretation, and exposition were developed by the means—and as an expression—of dogmatics, and that they were conducive to the above-mentioned (III.A.–B.) decisions in favor of (1) a constitutional court that is (2) autonomous and (3) wields powers of review over other courts. Dogmatic concepts incorporated and reinforced those decisions. All these efforts in constitutional dogmatics share the notion of the unity—constantly [137] reproduced, rooted in values, and giving rise to values—that is conceived of as a system and is known as the "constitution."

1. The constitution as the pervasive concept of unity

Conducive to a constitutional court whose potential powers of review make it nearly omnipresent and omnipotent is the concept of a constitution that provides the standard for all constitutional jurisprudence and that permeates the entire (domestic) legal order. The interpretation of the legal order as a pyramidal, multilevel structure—within which the highest level of the hierarchy (the constitution) seeks to exert the broadest possible influence over the subsequent levels of legal concretization and individualization—corresponds to the pyramidal model of adjudication discussed earlier (III.C.1.). This interpretation is more than a logical extension of the constitution's supremacy over all other domestic law. For the concept of supremacy is, in the first place, merely a formal one: in the case of a conflict between norms, constitutional norms take precedence over all other domestic norms.

When norms collide, the constitution trumps. But this means of resolving conflicts says nothing at all about the constitution's concrete scope and the extent to which it guides ordinary law. This is not a question of supremacy (or even of validity); it is a question of the constitution's content—although the argument of supremacy is often adduced to justify a wide-ranging substantive understanding of the constitution.

Two dogmatic concepts enable one to study this understanding of the constitution most vividly and most memorably. [138] One is the model of the system of values, and the other is the so-called constitution-conforming interpretation. We have already discussed the proposition established in the 1958 Lüth judgment (BVerfGE 7, 198 ff.) that the Basic Law's fundamental rights section embodies an "objective system of values," which has a "radiating effect" on all areas of law (above III.C.2.). True, talk of values yielded some time ago to talk of the (infelicitously styled) "objective legal content" of fundamental rights. Factually and substantively, however, this change did nothing to weaken the idea of the multi-functionality and universal relevance of fundamental rights as decisions of constitutional values. Quite the contrary: additional dimensions and functions of fundamental rights were gradually set forth, particularly as rights to benefits and participation (for which the Numerus-Clausus judgment was foundational, BVerfGE 33, 303 ff. (1972)), as the state's duty to protect (for which the first Abortion decision was seminal, BVerfGE 39, 1 ff. (1975)), and as determinative guarantees of protection for organizational and procedural law (see the Higher Education judgment, BVerfGE, 35, 79 ff. (1973)). According to these judgments, fundamental rights exert something like an omnidirectional radiating effect.

The instrument of "constitution-conforming interpretation" (*verfassungskonforme Interpretation*), which the FCC has employed consistently and has placed at the disposition of the specialized courts as well, helps implement the constitution's radiating effect on statutory law. In such cases, the object of interpretation is not the constitution itself, but the statute. [139] The precondition for such a "constitution-conforming interpretation" is that traditional methods of interpretation can derive various meanings from a provision of ordinary law, but at least one of those interpretations is incompatible with constitutional requirements. The principle of constitution-conforming interpretation posits that, when this happens, the applier of law has a constitutional duty to discard the unconstitutional interpretation and embrace a constitution-conforming alternative. The First Senate justified this approach in a paradigmatic case as follows:

> For the Basic Law, as the supreme domestic law, is not only the standard for assessing the validity of legal norms from domestic legal sources; each of these norms must also be interpreted substantively in harmony with the Basic Law. Accordingly, the text of each legal norm receives, as needed, a supplementary sense or, when the other preconditions are met, each must be developed in

harmony with the Basic Law. The Basic Law, too, is part of the comprehensive legal order, which must be understood as a totality of meaning and must underlie every interpretation of domestic law. (BVerfGE 51, 304, 323 (1979)).

With the instrument of constitution-conforming interpretation, the Federal Constitutional Court furnishes for itself—and for all other courts, such as the specialized courts of last resort, that are called upon to construe statutes authoritatively—far-reaching possibilities for correcting the legislature and its handiwork (statutes). Anyone who considers the FCC's relationship with the legislature must look not only to the 632 cases, in which the Federal Constitutional Court over the last sixty years has invalidated federal (452 times) [140] or state (180 times) norms as unconstitutional, but also to those cases—not reported statistically, but likely much more numerous—in which a statute is partially invalidated although its text remains unchanged (which is the practical import of a "constitution-conforming interpretation"). The supremacy of the constitution soothes the constitutional state's conscience for this distortion of the separation of powers, and is supplemented by the rather labored argument that correcting a law through a "constitution-confirming interpretation" spares the legislature the harsher sanction of quashing the law outright. Constitution-conforming interpretations have been subjected to the complaint that they are not really (statutory) interpretations at all, but rather norm quashing in a different guise, justified by confusing—or at least blending—the questions of content and validity. The question to be answered by interpretation—what the statute means—is regularly mingled or muddled with a question usually answered by quashing or confirming the challenged norm—whether the statute as interpreted is valid under the constitution (Lembke 2009). Despite this fundamental—and hard-to-answer—objection, constitution-conforming interpretations have enjoyed lasting popularity and are characteristic of the (postwar) German variant of thinking from the perspective of the constitution (Löwer 2005, section 70 RN 126 f.).

The ideas of both the multi-functionality of fundamental rights and of constitution-conforming interpretation can be readily linked to the idea of optimization, as Robert Alexy's theory of principles has powerfully shown (Alexy 1986): [141] as principles, legal positions guaranteed by the Basic Law strive for the greatest possible realization. In this way, thinking from the perspective of the constitution morphs into the pursuit of constitutionalization.

2. Constitutional interpretation as interpretation sui generis

The special status of both the constitution (among sources of law) and of the Constitutional Court (among judicial bodies) benefits from the proposition, now widely accepted, that constitutional interpretation differs fundamentally in methodological-dogmatic terms from normal statutory interpretation. This requires some explanation, since the Basic Law, in form and origin, is also "only" a statute and owes its influence not least to the fact that, as the supreme law, it can guide other statutes as well as sub-statutory norms. All the same, the idea of the uniqueness of constitutional interpretation has taken hold—even though the FCC has neither explicitly nor extensively defended it, nor even very aggressively invoked it. This lack of justification is hardly surprising, however, given that the Court, which otherwise shows little aversion for verbosity, has often been rather tightlipped when it comes to questioning its own methods. One can hardly hold this against the justices: they are, after all, commissioned to decide cases, not to compose methodological treatises. In the bulk of the Court's decisions—and one can surely say the same of the specialized courts—no syllable is wasted on the interpretive method preferred or employed, [142] nor, in many cases, can that method be reconstructed reliably from the stated reasons of decision. To generalize, one can say that Karlsruhe doctrine does not follow a canon of interpretive rules that is reflected in methodological consistency or uniformly practiced in its judgments. Instead, the FCC embraces a methodological pragmatism not untypical of courts of last resort. The Court does not cling to any interpretive theory with its attendant interpretive methods. Its reflections about *theories* of interpretation do not get in the way of its actual *practice* of interpretation. In general, the applicable interpretive method is determined on a case-by-case basis. And that method is often the product of mixing multiple interpretive theories or methods as needed in the particular case.

All of this would be hardly worth mentioning were it not for the fact that the FCC invokes the classical canons of statutory interpretation—those associated (not quite accurately) with the name of Friedrich Carl von Savigny, namely the grammatical, historical, systematic, and teleological—as a constitutional standard for the work of the specialized courts. For example, in a 2009 decision the Court defined the constitutional "limits of judicial findings of law"—which are derived from Article 20, 2, 2–3 GG and compliance with which is, accordingly, reviewable by the Constitutional Court—as follows:

> The interpretation of ordinary statutory law, including the choice of interpretive method, is a matter for the specialized courts, the correctness of which is not to be reviewed comprehensively by Federal Constitutional Court. The Federal Constitutional Court limits its [143] review to assessing whether the specialized court's findings of law respected the basic decision of the legislature and made acceptable use of recognized methods of statutory interpretation (BVerfGE 122, 248, 257 f. (2009)).

The Court adopted a similar approach in its 2010 Honeywell decision, in which it summarized its powers to engage in so-called ultra vires reviews of decisions of the Court of Justice of the European Union (BVerfGE 126, 286, 302 ff., especially 305 ff. (2010)). But nothing in the Court's jurisprudence suggests that the same rules apply to the FCC's own interpretation of the constitution. Moreover, while the FCC has repeatedly addressed the boundaries of legal development—or, more precisely, of *statutory* development—by ordinary courts (notably in its 1973 Soraya decision (BVerfGE 34, 369 ff.) and in the 2009 just quoted (BVerfGE 122, 248 ff.)), there is still no concept or notion of *constitutional* development by the Constitutional Court. There is thus no standard by which one can distinguish between *interpreting* the constitution and *developing* the constitution (should the latter take place). But that is hardly an uncomfortable circumstance for a Constitutional Court that wields the power of authoritative constitutional interpretation (Roellecke 2010, section 14 RN 31f.).

If one looks closely, the proposition that constitutional interpretation represents an exceptional case for interpretive methodology rests on wobbly ground. This is true in part because the idea that specialized courts engaged in statutory interpretation adhere more or less strictly to the "Savigny Quartet" has little [144] basis in forensic reality. Even among specialized courts, dogmatic jurisprudence—i.e. thinking from the perspective of a (fluid) system—has largely degenerated into mere lip service to the classic methodological guidelines, which are happily trotted out when it suits, but which rarely constitute the true grounds of decision. But this does nothing to alter the fact that the notion of constitutional interpretation's exceptionalism has gained currency, and that the FCC generally enjoys greater freedom when it interprets the Basic Law than the specialized courts enjoy when they interpret statutes.

A brief look at the FCC's treatment of fundamental rights gives at least a small impression of how the Court's dogmatics inflected interpretation works. The Court's treatment of fundamental rights is essentially systematic. But this dogmatic system is not rigid and closed, but fluid and open, and dominated by two central (though not at all parallel) thoughts: (1) the aim of giving fundamental rights the greatest possible effect; and (2) the idea of proportionally ordering all legal interests. While the first thought points beyond the individual case towards an extensive—not to say comprehensive—interpretation and application of fundamental rights, the second idea serves as a means of calibrating effective fundamental rights protection both in the legal order at large and (especially) in the individual case (Jestaedt 1999, 42 ff.). The building blocks of the dogmatic system serve these two basic rules. They mark out the basic reflective framework of constitutional [145] interpretation, and they define the parameters of the available resources of argumentation. A few of the core structural elements of the dogmatic system of fundamental rights developed by the FCC can be painted with broad brushstrokes. Whatever fundamental right is at issue, the Court almost uniformly employs a three-step schema to consider complaints of rights violations: (1) the scope of fundamental rights protection; (2) state infringement of the right; and (3) the justification for the infringement. (That this scope-infringement-justification schema is not contained in the constitutional text no longer merits mention or reflection.) An additional building block of the system is thinking in terms of special protections, on the one hand, and fundamental, comprehensive catchall protections, on the other. This applies equally to liberty rights and to equality rights. The truly startling feature is the generally unbroken quality of fundamental rights protection discussed earlier (III.C.2.) Systematic thinking strives for gapless protection of fundamental rights and has no use for the notion of rights protection limited to certain activities or spheres. In keeping with this rights-expanding approach is the idea that the "typical rights-endangering situation" (BVerfGE 61, 82, 108 (1982)), in which a citizen finds him- or herself vis-à-vis the State, is more important than the elements of the right as formulated by the constitutional legislature. Consequently, there are no insuperable barriers to ferreting out, via interpretation, novel fundamental rights protections for novel situations of risk. The miraculous multiplication of fundamental rights under the Basic Law has found one of its most significant catalysts in the previously discussed multidimensionality of fundamental rights guarantees (above III.C.2. and IV.C.1.). Whether and which dimension of protection is available has been, to [146] all appearances, more a question of the right-bearer's concrete need for protection than of the content of a given right. But the expansion of fundamental rights—or rather, the expansive understanding of the scope of fundamental rights protection—has entailed a broadly parallel (one could even say complementary) development in the limitation of fundamental rights. To the extent that the promise of fundamental rights protection is understood to be universal and comprehensive, there arises a systemic need to expansively understand and implement the possibilities of limitation. Karlsruhe's jurisprudence satisfies this need in practice, albeit tacitly, by leveling the differentiated limitation regime envisioned by the constitutional text and subjecting it to values balancing. The proportionality concept, which was originally developed in the context of liberty rights, has become the centerpiece of all justifications of rights infringements. As such, it reaches even the structure and dogmatics of the general equality clause.

On the one hand, the FCC's open and dynamic system of fundamental rights dogmatics allows it (not least by homogenizing the structures of protection) to designate and treat practically all legal questions as fundamental rights questions. On the other hand, applying the great "emollient" (Ossenbühl 1995, 909), the principle of proportionality—which, for systematic reasons is equally comprehensive—allows the Court to shape the effective protection of fundamental rights in individual cases, as well as the scope of the legal protection the Court provides, in a nuanced, differentiating way. Put differently: the dogmatic figures that guide constitutional interpretation could hardly be better devised for a [147] methodologically pragmatic Court. They give the Court reason to interpret constitutional guarantees in the broadest imaginable way *in abstracto*, as well as reason to calibrate the effective protection of constitutional rights much more narrowly *in concreto*. This approach—which is at once systematic and case-oriented (and thereby open-ended)—is decisively responsible for the fact that, even after sixty years of Constitutional Court review of specialized court decisions, the time has not yet arrived when this prominent form of constitutional review has become superfluous, and when the extraordinary remedy of the judgment complaint can be abolished as unnecessary for the protection of rights.

3. Establishing congenial expository concepts

The way the FCC presents its findings is much less important than the issues, just discussed, of standards and interpretation. But presentation, too, is part of forming a complete picture; it, too, provides a sense of the exceptional position of the Constitutional Court and of constitutional law. As a supremely telling expression of both *the dogmatic approach* and of the *academicization* of the Court's jurisprudence, both Senates use (virtually without exception) the same format of presentation. With rare exceptions, the Senates' discussion of the merits has two parts. In the first part—what Oliver Lepsius has aptly styled the "standards section" (Lepsius 2008a,111 ff.)—the Senate sets forth the constitutional standards (with little regard to the case at hand), analyzes them in their systematic context, and considers their regulative impact. [148] In the second part, the subsumption section, the Court applies the standards to the concrete circumstances of the case. In structure, manner, and style, the standards section is virtually indistinguishable from a scholarly treatise, such as a commentary. It forms the dogmatic heart of the decision, in which both of the primary functions of dogmatics—decontextualization and systematization—unfold in all their purity. The constitutional professoriate devotes its scholarly attention almost exclusively to the standards sections' general, systematic observations, which reach beyond the confines of the concrete, individual case. Apart from rare cases, only a handful of specialists (such as Basic Law commentators) who are interested in the specific outcome of the case pay more attention to the subsumption section.

That the Court itself views the standards section as the most important part of a decision—as the generalized essence, if you will, of its interpretation and application—is reflected in the fact that the Court's self-citations in later decisions refer almost exclusively to the standards sections of earlier judgments. That the Court directs its argumentation primarily to the system, and not to the case, is an expression of how thoroughly its jurisprudence is suffused by dogmatics. [149]

V. An Improbable Success Story

A. Evolutionary improbability

The Federal Constitutional Court is an extraordinarily powerful and influential court, in comparison with both domestic courts (e.g. the so-called specialized courts generally, the federal supreme courts in particular, or the constitutional courts of the individual *Länder*) and international judicial bodies (e.g. foreign constitutional courts or international courts that function like constitutional courts, such as the European Court of Human Rights in Strasbourg). The object of these reflections has not been merely to demonstrate that (and how) the Karlsruhe Court has been so incredibly successful and influential. It has also been to provide a small sense of how unforeseeable, evolutionarily improbable, and unplanned the development of the "Karlsruhe Republic," which the FCC has brought to pass over the past sixty years, has been. The festive atmosphere surrounding the Court's sixtieth anniversary led some observers to speak of a "Karlsruhe miracle." One must remember that this is no less a miracle of the Basic Law, which at its birth was equally unlikely to become Germany's most enduring and effective, successful and felicitous constitution. And yet, both successes are burdened by having transgressed boundaries, and carry with them the risk of exaggeration and overenthusiasm—all the more so because institutionalizing the power of the last word inevitably conjures the guardian's dilemma: *Quis custodiet* [150] *ipsos custodies*? Thus having the last word and exceeding the limits of one's competence (Mayer 2000) can, functionally and institutionally, no longer be unambiguously distinguished.

B. An export-ready success model?

The Federal Constitutional Court is considered a leading export. And that is certainly true if one looks at normative structures—i.e. to the Court's institutional and organizational design, and to its functional and jurisdictional endowment. With respect to the global rivalry between the American model of integrated constitutional justice and the Austrian model of a specialized constitutional court, the FCC has increased, in a substantial way, the significance and attractiveness of the latter.

But, in at least two respects, significant caveats are in order. First, even among those systems that were clearly influenced by the German model in their choice of an institutionally autonomous constitutional court—Spain and Portugal, for example, as well as several Central or Eastern European states after the fall of the Iron Curtain—the introduction of the FCC's most distinctive procedural innovation, the individual constitutional complaint, remains a rare exception. And it has not been for lack of importance or efficacy that the individual complaint has not been embraced elsewhere. Indeed, other jurisdictions may have opted against the individual complaint precisely because they feared the very sort of constitutional court domination that the FCC highlighted all too clearly by means of [151] the judgment complaint against lower-court decisions. Second, the German model cannot simply be copied or transplanted by adopting legal foundations similar to the Basic Law or the BVerfGG. For the Court's nature and operation depend as much on the software of legal culture (defined in the broadest sense) as on the hardware of positive law. For how a constitutional court understands the constitution; which interpretive methods to employ and how to employ them; what levels of prestige and acceptance the court enjoys among the state's governing bodies, the other courts, the general public, and each individual; with what skill its members are chosen and with what professionalism and in what spirit they fulfill their duties—these are questions (and only a few of the questions) that written laws do not answer. Here entirely different factors and effects are at work—personal and institutional, evident and latent, transparent and diffuse—none of which can be fully grasped in their reciprocal influence or intentionally "made" in their entirety.

C. The Federal Constitutional Court—a model for the future?

Many observers insist that the FCC—and with it the Basic Law—has passed its zenith. Just as the German federal constitution has been relativized by Germany's being embedded in international and (especially) supranational structures (Grimm 1990), so [152] European integration with its two rival high courts (the ECtHR and the CJEU) has relegated the FCC from the first rank to the second (Papier 2006). And there is something to be said for the view that the FCC's future role will be determined increasingly within the "European confederation of constitutional courts" (*europäischer Verfassungsgerichtsverbund*) (Voßkuhle 2010b). But, as in the case of nation states and their constitutions, one should greet premature swan songs and narratives of decline with skepticism and calm. In any case, in light of the role that the FCC has played and continues to play in Germany's free democratic order, and of its role as a model for foreign constitutional courts and international tribunals, there is no reason to welcome or hasten such developments. Even if individual FCC decisions occasionally, and deservedly, arouse fierce opposition because of an overstepping and legislature-confining constitutional interpretation, there is still no other court that, given the needs of our legal culture, could take the FCC's place in terms of judicial poise and juridical quality. The Federal Constitutional Court, then, as model for the future? Yes, indeed.

3
The Standard-Setting Power

Oliver Lepsius

I. Constitution and Constitutional Interpretation

Under the Basic Law, the Federal Constitutional Court is part of the judicial authority. Its competences include deciding cases on the basis of extraordinary remedies. Art. 93, 1 GG lists the most important of these proceedings: constitutional complaints by which an individual may challenge violations of Basic Rights, disputes between the Federal Government and the Länder governments, and abstract judicial review of legislation. Art. 100, 1 GG adds the so-called concrete norm control in which the question of the constitutionality of statutes is referred to the Federal Constitutional Court by an inferior court. These are not the only procedural forms in the Basic Law, but the most important ones.[1]

The Federal Constitutional Court cannot act on its own volition. It has jurisdiction when presented with a legal dispute of a particular constitutional quality. Such a dispute must be rooted in constitutional law, either because norms of the Basic Law itself are in question or because the jurisdiction is conferred on the Court through constitutional law. The principle "ubi non accusator, ibi non iudex" (where there is no accuser, there is no judge) applies to the judicial authority of the Constitutional Court as much as to that of every other court. It is, however, limited by the additional principle: "Where there is no constitutional dispute, there is no jurisdiction of the Constitutional Court."

The actual jurisdictional range of the Karlsruhe Court, however, is not fully defined [162] by the Basic Law's limitation of the Federal Constitutional Court's role to resolving constitutional disputes. At least, the general political perception of the Court's role extends beyond its mere attribution of jurisdictional procedures. The last word, in the sense of being the authoritative interpreter of the constitution, is routinely awarded to the Court. In short, the Court is supposed to be the supreme

[1] For example, the Forfeiture of Basic Rights (Art. 18); Party Prohibition Cases (Art. 21, 2); Electoral Supervision (Art. 41, 2); Impeachment of the Federal President (Art. 61); Impeachment of Judges (Art. 98, 2, 5); Deviation Referral (Art. 100, 3); even the federal legislature has conferred on the Court additional jurisdiction via statute, for example, in the Political Party Law (enforcement of a political party prohibition), in the Law on the Parliamentary Investigative Committees (procedural supervision), in the Law on Parliamentary Supervisory Board, or in the Law on Electoral Oversight (on the details, cf. Voßkuhle 2010a, RN 216f.).

The German Federal Constitutional Court: The Court Without Limits. Matthias Jestaedt, Oliver Lepsius, Christoph Möllers, and Christoph Schönberger, published by Oxford University Press under licence (2020).
DOI: 10.1093/oso/9780198793540.001.0001

guardian of the constitution (Lembcke 2007), a characterization the Federal Constitutional Court above all claims for itself (Bundesverfassungsgericht 1957, 144–9; BVerfGE 1, 184 at 196 (1952); BVerfGE, 119, 247 at 258 (2007)). "Like a bolt of lightning it struck into the structure of state functions established by the Basic Law" (Schlaich 1981, 101). "We have the last word," purported the Court's former vice president, Hassemer (Hassemer 2008b, 38). But is that true? Are the other constitutional organs not also called to perform constitutional interpretation (also skeptical Jestaedt 2007a, 12f., 29 f.)? On the contrary, do we not live in an "open society of constitutional interpreters," as Peter Häberle claims (Häberle 1975, 297; see also Sunstein 2009)? Is the Court's authority not restricted to deciding cases and, therefore, should it not leave the underlying constitutional consensus open to discussion?

The true power of "Karlsruhe" emerges at this juncture. Its decisions reach beyond the particular case (cf. Lerche 2004, 522 f.). The interpretation of the Basic Law, which arises from a constitutional dispute, transcends the case to be decided. That is the Federal Constitutional Court's declared aim. It considers itself the "definitive interpreter and guardian of the constitution," the "binding authority in constitutional questions" (BVerfGE 40, 88 at 93 f.—(1975)). Its doctrine is widely accepted as a form of general-abstract constitutional interpretation, which extends beyond the case-related concretization of the constitution [163]. As an institution, the Court profits from the supremacy rule the Basic Law establishes in Art. 20, 3 according to which the legislative, the executive, and the judicial branch are bound by the constitution. The principle of the "supremacy of the constitution" is repeated for the Basic Rights in Art. 1, 3. They bind all authorities as directly applicable law. This supremacy is expressly attributed to the text of the constitution only and does not necessarily extend to the jurisprudence of the Federal Constitutional Court. What is remarkable is that the "supremacy rule" exercises an institutional effect: in practice, the Basic Law is valid in the way that the Federal Constitutional Court interprets it, and the scholars and commentators interpret it in this sense so much that Rudolf Smend could certify at the tenth anniversary of the Court that the constitution was practically binding in the jurisprudential construction (Smend 1968, 582). The irony residing in the phrase "in practice" should, however, not be overlooked. Of course, there is a theoretical difference between the validity of the constitution and its application by the Court in specific cases. Yet despite this distinction between the constitution and its application, despite the distinction between the legal rule and the Court applying this rule, in a socio-juristic conception, the constitution is valid in the interpretation given to it by the Court. This view, of course, runs the risk of conceptually confusing the supremacy of the constitution with the jurisdiction of the Constitutional Court. Substantive constitutional law merges with the law of constitutional procedure: the supremacy rule of constitutional law radiates out to include the exceptional jurisdiction of the Constitutional Court. In practice, the Basic Law is valid in its application by the "Karlsruhe" judges.

One should clearly distinguish, however, [164] between the supremacy of the constitution in substantive terms and the jurisdiction of the Federal Constitutional Court. The Court's mandate for constitutional interpretation is the mere corollary of its authority to decide individual cases. In other words, the supremacy of the constitution is, indeed, always substantively valid, but can only be implemented institutionally when the legal recourse to the Federal Constitutional Court is available. In contrast to the legislature and the government, the Federal Constitutional Court cannot act on its own volition; the exercise of its competence depends on the decision of others to bring a concrete case before the Court. In practical terms, therefore, the constitution cannot be valid only as the Federal Constitutional Court interprets it. Without doubt, it is also binding when there is no Karlsruhe doctrine, as was the case, for example, in the first years of the Federal Republic or as is the case after a constitutional amendment. But this insight threatens to relativize the Court's plenitude of power as the supreme guardian of the constitution.

The Court's competence to make final decisions exists only in casuistic form, that is to say, only in deciding constitutional disputes in concrete cases (cf. Schlaich 1981, 126). Its claim to final decision-making authority, however, clearly extends beyond particular cases, referring specifically to the constitution as an entirety. Still, one may not derive a seamless position of institutional supremacy for the Court from the substantive supremacy of the constitution. Peter Lerche has already put this aptly: In the concrete case, the Federal Constitutional Court has the last word. But one cannot extend the last word beyond the respective case generally. And Lerche (2001, 335 f.) himself adds that it exceeds any understanding of proper adjudication to answer conclusively concrete questions converted into an abstract form. What we encounter as an expression of supreme guardianship of the constitution can be nothing other than the consolidation [165] of casuistic individual decisions, for ultimately the Court can only speak through its decisions. Its constitutional interpretation is procedurally limited, in particular by the necessity to decide a specific legal question.

Nevertheless, the effects of its decisions extend beyond the resolution of the dispute in the individual case. One routinely reads the Karlsruhe judgments from another perspective: as decisions regarding the basic orientation of the political system, as the contouring of the socially permissible, as admonitions about moral necessity. At the same time, constitutional courts are understood as political actors (Häberle 1979, 436 ff.; Landfried 1984; Schneider 1999a; Eberl 2006, 8 ff.). One emphasizes their positive contribution to the acceptance of the constitutional order (Schaal 2000a) or to the quality of the federal German democracy (Kneip 2009, 337–47)—designating them as the "repair shop of parliament" (Schneider 1999b)—or denounces them for intervening in politics and for becoming the "substitute legislature" (Scholz 1999).

In practical terms, therefore, the Federal Constitutional Court does not merely decide cases. On the contrary, it formulates values. And these values do not exhibit a political or relativistic nature. They are, rather, the expression of the highest possible legal bond. Constitutional doctrine and legal politics at this point must merge with one another. Calling to mind famous decisions about abortion, tax law, protection of non-smokers, and rules about long-term unemployment benefits, to name just a few examples, one may rightly ask where the legal bond ends and the shaping of ordinary law begins.[2] Put abstractly [166], in the course of giving effect to the legal bonds of the political process, constitutional adjudication accentuates the legalization of politics (Grimm 2001, 20 ff.; Wahl 2003, 124). The reproach that the Court makes politics, Court Vice President Winfried Hassemer declared laconically, is old, repetitive, and, in essence, apt (Hassemer 2007, 82). Ultimately, only a critical public may limit the judicial politics of Karlsruhe (Hassemer 2008a, 10). On Hassemer's account, the decision-making authority of the Court, apparently considered not subject to any limitation, is derived from a material logic as an inherent feature of judicial pragmatism which cannot be fenced in by legal methodology, but only by legal and judicial sociology (Hassemer 2007, 144–51). Neither civil society nor political actors understand the Court's function solely in doctrinal terms, but rather also in the Court's capacities in the arena of judicial politics. And apparently this is also the case in parts of the Court itself. Put differently, there is obviously a discrepancy between the Court's authority to decide cases and the actual effect of its decisions, which, extending beyond the resolution of legal questions, involve the setting of a political agenda as well as the manifestation of values that are accepted and sanctioned as the ultimately binding interpretation of the constitution. The full extent of the Constitutional Court's power and the Court's political significance are based not on its authority as a court to decide legal disputes, but rather on its task of providing a substantive framework for political action (cf. Habermas 1992, 294 ff.). One may consider this a corollary of constitutional adjudication or its "essence." [167]

II. Exceptional Status through Method

A general, abstract authority for constitutional interpretation as such, for the establishing of substantive frameworks, or for reasoning about values or state objectives (*Staatsaufgaben*) does not result from the authority to decide cases. Constitutional interpretation is solely a means of deciding a concrete legal dispute according to the standard of the Basic Law. Constitutional interpretation serves an ancillary function in the substantive decision; it is not an end in itself. But how can the Federal Constitutional Court fulfill such a broad political and social function

[2] BVerfGE 39, 1—Abortion I (1975); BVerfGE 88, 203—Abortion II (1993); BVerfGE 93, 121—Property Tax (1995); BVerfGE 121, 317—Nonsmoker Protection (2008); BVerfGE 122, 210—Commuter Tax Exemption (2008): BVerfGE 125, 175—Hartz IV Unemployment Benefits (2010).

via the instrument of constitutional interpretation, when its competences are still only those of a court that decides cases? After all, even the Court's current president has made clear that the Court acts as a constitutional accessory defined by statute (Voßkuhle 2010a, RN 18). The actual position of the Federal Constitutional Court, therefore, requires explanation. It is certainly not derived from the order established by the Basic Law. Nor does the principle of constitutional supremacy entail the institutional supremacy of the Constitutional Court. How, then, can one explain the significance of the Karlsruhe Court? My assertion is that the Court itself has created its exceptional status through its distinctive manner of fulfilling its adjudicative duties (cf. more narrowly Ehmke 1963, 67–9; Schlaich 1981, 126–37; also Schenke 2009, 58, 61). To be sure, the Constitutional Court is part of the judiciary, for it ultimately decides legal disputes. Yet from a functional perspective, the Court has become something else; it has conceived itself not merely as a judicial authority, but rather it has reinvented itself as a new power: [168] a power that sets standards. The standard-setting power exceeds judicial authority by far, because the effects of the Karlsruhe decisions, whether constitutional-legal or political, transcend the judgment's binding force. In other words, the decisions claim a broader legal significance than suggested by their narrow holdings. However, the standard-setting power, by its nature, falls behind the lawmaking power of the legislative branch, even if the Federal Constitutional Court interprets the Basic Law with an authority that reaches beyond individual cases and although its interpretations are considered authoritative for the lawmaking process, too (Lepsius 2008a, 114).[3]

A. Division of the reasoning into standards and subsumption

The Federal Constitutional Court makes use of a distinctive technique for reaching and justifying decisions, which it elaborated over the course of many years, and which today it applies habitually. The Court regularly divides the reasoning of a decision into two blocks. The first block identifies the general statements on the interpretation of the constitution. In terms of linguistic style, these statements do not differ from an instructional textbook. Here is an especially good example *pour prendre le ton* (BVerfGE 124, 300, 320 f.—Wunsiedel (2009)):

[3] Cf. Möllers (2005, 136–45) on this point as well as on the legitimation of the quasi-legislative legal production of the case law. Probably the most influential theory on the legitimation of constitutional adjudication in a democracy remains Ely (1980). According to his "representation reinforcement theory," the legislative function of constitutional interpretation is appropriate only as a correction to representation deficits in the political process; therefore, it is primarily to supervise the process, but not to abstractly deduce values. Nino (1996, 199 ff.) has abstracted the theory from the American context and generalized it. Ely's representative theory justification of constitutional adjudication, however, has received a limited hearing in Germany, for example by Habermas (1992) and Riecken (2003). It does not guide the Karlsruhe Court's adjudication.

> Art. 5, 1 GG guarantees everyone the right to freely express and disseminate his opinion. Opinions are shaped by the subjective relationship of the individual to the content of his statement (cf. BVerfGE 7, 198 at 210). Taking positions and advocacy are characteristic of them (cf. BVerfGE 7, 198 at 210; BVerfGE 61, 1 at 8; BVerfGE 90, 241 at 247). In this regard, they cannot be proven as true or untrue. Opinions are accorded protection of the Basic Rights regardless of whether they are considered justified or groundless, emotional or rational, dangerous or harmless (cf. BVerfGE 90, 241 at 247). Citizens enjoying this protection are not legally held to personally share the values underlying the constitution. Though the Basic Law, indeed, builds on the expectation that citizens accept and give effect to the general values of the constitution, it does not compel loyalty to these values (cf. BVerfG, Judgments of the First Chamber of the First Senate of March 24, 2001—1 BvQ 13/01—, NJW 2001, p. 2069, 2070 and of September 15, 2008—BvR 1565/05—NJW 2009, p. 908, 909). Art. 5, 1 also protects opinions directed at fundamentally changing the political order, independent of whether and to what extent these are realizable in the framework of the Basic Law's order. The Basic Law trusts in free debate as the most effective weapon even against the purveying of totalitarian and inhuman ideologies. Accordingly, even the purveying of national socialist thought as a radical rejection of the legitimate order is not per se excluded from the realm of protection found under Art. 5, 1 GG. To counter these genuine dangers, the free order of the Basic Law is directed primarily toward civil engagement in free political discourse as well as state enlightenment and education in the schools according to Art. 7 GG.

In such general terms, the Court establishes the standard that will lie at the foundation of the case. The Court often exerts considerable effort in the cultivation and exposition of the standard. The reader can assume that [170] these statements are carefully formulated and precisely voted on in the judicial panel ("Senate"). Here the Court sets the course for the interpretation of the substantive constitutional law in question, with regard not only to the present case, but also to the understanding and elaboration of the constitution in general. The statements do not in any way refer to the particular case. Instead, they derive their coherence from the general-abstract connection to the pertinent provisions of the Basic Law. This "standards part" is also formally demarcated in the reasoning of the decision. As a rule, it bears the outline number "C.I." It stands at the beginning of the merits, which are usually designated with the outline letter "C" (because typically part "A" addresses the subject-matter and the procedural history, while part "B" considers the admissibility of the constitutional suit).

The application of the standards to the facts of the case then follows, though the Court clearly distinguishes it by designating it as "C.II." The specific case first enters the reasoning in this second part, the "subsumption section." The standards already formed in general-abstract terms are now applied to the specific issue the

Court has to decide. The Court regularly introduces this subsumption section with phrases like, "The challenged provision does not live up to these standards," or "The statute does not satisfy the standards of the constitutional law explicated here."[4] Only now does one appreciate the considerations relevant for the decision. Of course, the Court does not always employ [171] this technique, but it has become the common structure of its reasoning, independent of the type of proceedings and the substantive focus of the case. By now, one can speak of a standardized method of reasoning.

B. Consequences of this division

At first glance, the separation between the substantive constitutional interpretation in the standards section and its application to the facts in the subsumption portion facilitates the clear structuring of the reasoning. Looking more closely, this practice certainly has considerable consequences for the interpretation of the constitution and the jurisdiction of the Federal Constitutional Court. Because of this separation, it is extremely rare for subsumption statements to affect the further development of the standards (cf. Lepsius 2008a, 112). This is because the presentation of the standards proceeds abstractly and is placed before their subsumption. During the establishment and subsequent refinement of the standards, the Federal Constitutional Court need not take heed of the facts or contexts of earlier decisions. In this way, the Court disconnects, without much ado, its constitutional interpretation from the legal disputes, which alone empower the Court to interpret the constitution (where there is no accuser, there is no judge).[5] [172] Thus arises an abstract tier of the constitution termed "standards," which is treated in a purely normative way without any reference to the facts of the case. It should be recalled, however, that it was these very facts that have established the Court's authority in the first place. A reliable statement on the binding effect of the judgment can only be reached if the facts of the case are taken into account in the subsequent processing of the decision. That the constitution had been interpreted in this way and not otherwise is not intelligible without reference to the case which lies at the bottom of it all.

The Federal Constitutional Court consciously suppresses this connection between the factual context and its constitutional interpretation. Highly

[4] The formulation is taken from BVerfGE 115, 118 at 140—Air Safety (2006); BVerfGE 117, 1 at 37—Inheritance Tax I (2006). Of course, one can phrase them quite differently when the legal challenge is unsuccessful: the challenged provision satisfies these standards.

[5] Cf. also Volkmann (2011, section II), who, among other things, describes German constitutional law thusly: from the fact to the norm, from the form to the content, from the limitation to the programming, from the part to the whole. These tendencies are made possible by the formation of standards, more specifically, standards are the methodological consequences of this development.

context-specific statements tend to be abstracted from the facts, taken from their political context, neutralized, and legally objectified. The practical consequence of this approach is that in the standards section, the Federal Constitutional Court incidentally cites numerous previous decisions, but as a rule the passages cited only stem from the standards section of those decisions. The Court gives the impression of constitutional interpretation that is neither limited by time, nor dependent on a particular set of facts. One can then speak of constitutional interpretation that is unhistorical and non-political, ahistorical as well as acontextual. The Court naturally has a vital interest in this. Since it is [173] bound by the constitution and its legal results must be derived from the constitution, the Court benefits in terms of the acceptance of its reasoning if its decisions can be presented as something other than the expression of a contextual or factual constitutional interpretation. Instead, the Court can emphasize the aspects of its decisions perceived to extend beyond the particular case, to be more enduring normatively, and not bound by contemporary outlooks. The removal from context eases justification considerably, and that is an all-the-more-promising strategy when the Court holds the means for this in its own hands: the dissolution of the normative statements from their original context and from political interests.

However, when the development and updating of the standards is presented as a discourse divorced from concrete political conflicts and without a political orientation, which, in other words, is geared toward a heightened scientific posture as well as toward the justification of general-abstract, timeless normative principles, then this begs the question: what became of the political contextualization spirited away out of the process of standard formation? If constitutional adjudication refers to the actual workings of law and politics (Beaud/Pasquino 2007; Jestaedt 2011), there must be a methodological place where the legal and the political process can be coupled. The standards section has the potential to be such a space. But can it in fact fulfil this coupling function, when methodologically it is an expression of a non-political, general-abstract constitutional interpretation? Of course it cannot. Therefore, the coupling can only be successful in the subsumption section. And indeed by methodologically extending standards formation to the subsumption section, the Federal Constitutional Court created a corresponding category in the form of the principle of proportionality, by which it can ensure that the application of standards to the individual case can be rationalized and, at the same time, [174] that decisions regarding political balancing, control, and practicality can be respected, without the supremacy of the constitution giving way to the primacy of the political.

With the principle of proportionality, the Federal Constitutional Court achieves renewed remarkability, for politics must subject its actions to the rationality of the Court. It is the Federal Constitutional Court which, by applying the principle of proportionality, decides on the room for maneuver in politics. This results in an institutionally one-sided coupling of politics and law, specifically, according to the rules set by the Court itself, which are supposed to be an expression of constitutional obligation. In this sense, one can quite rightly speak of a form of superseding politics (cf. Lepsius 2008a, 112).[6]

C. The standards as incontestable intermediary rules and as a vehicle for expansion of competence

The Basic Law itself recognizes the distinction between legislative, executive, and judicial power (Art. 20, 2, 2 GG, Art. 1, 3 GG). However, there is not a one-to-one correspondence when it comes to the Federal Constitutional Court. Neither does the Court merely act as part of the judicial branch nor does it act in the field of legislation. As we saw, its decision-making power rests on the intermediary level of standard-setting. This is where [175] its actual authority resides. The Court understands the constitution as a standard (Lerche 2001, 337–9), which is at its disposal in both an institutional and substantive sense. Let us consider the normative character of standards somewhat more closely.

Constitutional standards distinguish themselves from both the general-abstract provisions of the Basic Law (positive constitutional law) as well as from individual-concrete judgments, which apply such provisions in the light of legal disputes and case references. Standards are intermediate to the concretization. As such they stabilize decision-making expectations, but they do not guarantee them. They form expectations in regard to constitutional adjudication without determining it. In terms of the theory of norms, standards operate on an ambiguous intermediary level, which, on the one hand, is a layer of concretization settled inside the norms of the Basic Law, but which, on the other, lies above the low point of concretization of the doctrinal decision. Standards are not norms ("rules") whose status can be expressed in categories of legitimacy. But neither are standards values, which rest on an aggregation of preferences.[7] The degree of obligation of standards results from their general-abstract derivation from the constitutional text, on the one hand, and from their sanctioning in a concrete case, on the other.

This enables standards to overcome the problem of the dual existence of norms. In one sense, norms are valid in general-abstract terms without [176] needing to be applied to a concrete set of facts. People obey legal norms without having to

[6] Cf. critically Jestaedt 2011, section IV, where he discusses "superseded politics," which finds its compensation in objective theories of interpretation, in the dogmatic quality of the process of legal production with its orientation toward system, or in the proportionality principle.

[7] Cf. also Habermas 1992, 309–16, who discusses this question in terms of the dichotomy of norms and values. Norms and values distinguish themselves from one another through their connections to obligatory or teleological action, through their binary and gradual coding of the legitimacy claims, and through their absolute and relative binding force, respectively. They are also differentiated from each other according to the criteria that the coherence of the respective systems of norms and value must satisfy.

be sanctioned individually. The legitimacy of the legal order rests ultimately on the voluntary recognition of the law, for a compulsory enforcement of the legal order would hardly be possible and, besides, would presuppose a police state. On the basis of their general-abstract validity, norms already display a guiding influence on action. In another sense, though, the normative command manifests itself only during a concrete, individual act of implementation, in other words, in an official or judicial sanctioning of the norm. What the norm demands beyond voluntary obedience first becomes evident in the administrative act or in the court judgment. The same norm is valid and has an effect, therefore, in differing forms, general-abstract and individual-concrete, and these differing forms of appearance are entrusted to different institutional authorities, specifically the legislative and executive branches. Or in the words of Konrad Hesse, who later became a justice on the court (Hesse 1959, 8): a constitutional norm's legitimacy claim is not strictly identifiable with the conditions of its realization. Instead, it contributes to these conditions as a distinct element.

With the technique of standard-setting, the Federal Constitutional Court establishes an intermediate norm in a diffuse, general-individual realm, which traverses the difference between abstract and concrete validity. The standard claims a concretization of the general-abstract constitutional norm and, simultaneously, a generalization of the individual-concrete areas of application. As norms, standards attain an epistemological status that is otherwise denied to legal norms, especially when, in considering questions of competence, we refer legal norms [177] back to the institutions that are responsible for their establishment as well as their application. Standards are norms of an intermediate realm, not of the world of the three powers, legislative, executive, and judicial.

Standards have the more wide-ranging potential to overcome the hierarchical structure of the legal order. The Basic Law establishes a hierarchy of norms and distinguishes between the levels of constitutional law, statutory law, legal decrees, regulations, and individual acts (court judgments, and administrative actions). The binding effect of norms rises in descending order: the legislature is only bound to the constitutional order, while the administrative and the adjudicative authorities are bound to statute and law (Art. 20, 3 GG). Therefore, there is a constitutional connection between the hierarchical structure of the legal order and that of the system of competences. Standards can leverage this connection while they consider the legal order in substantive and unified terms. Later we will encounter standards that counteract the difference between constitution and statute in that they declare structural decisions in statutory form to be constitutionally relevant standards, thereby elevating legislative decisions in rank. The constitutionalization of tax law serves as an example of this procedure. But, conversely, standards also work for the leveling of the hierarchical order. Recall the Court's practice of a constitution-conforming interpretation (*verfassungskonforme Auslegung*) or its use of the eternity clause (Art. 79, 3 GG) directed at "simple" constitutional law as a standard for the judicial review of constitutional amendments. As an example of this approach, we will come back to the "Treaty of Lisbon decision" later. But it also serves as an example of how the Court limited the interpretation of the constitutional amendment in Art. 13, 3, 4 GG to allow for electronic eavesdropping in private residences (BVerfGE 109, 179 at 316–19 (2004)). In any case, [178] standard-formation aiming to produce a general-abstract statement invites the disregard of differentiations in terms of the hierarchy of norms and, consequently, also in terms of jurisdiction.

Standard-setting is, therefore, also a precondition for different methodological practices, themselves questionable, with which the Federal Constitutional Court has extended its decision-making power, such as the constitution-conforming interpretation of ordinary law (for a critical view Lembke 2009), the constitution-conforming interpretation of a constitutional amendment (BVerfGE 109, 279 at 316–19—Electronic Eavesdropping in Private Residences (2004)), the finding of "merely unconstitutional" compared with voiding the statute (on the nuances Schlaich/Korioth 2010, RN 380 ff.), or the debate over the "identity of the Basic Law" (BVerfGE 124, 300 at 321, 329— Wunsiedel (2009); BVerfGE 125, 260 at 324—Data Preservation (2010)), and the finding on an "identity review" (BVerfGE 123, 267 at 353 f.—Lisbon (2009). Such strategies dismantle the hierarchical structure of the legal order in the name of a substantive flattening at the meta-level and can only work when the meta-level standard, in turn, does not refer to a tier of norms, which can be unambiguously localized. Arguing about standards, therefore, is a prerequisite for many other creative judicial findings of the Federal Constitutional Court.

Ultimately, standards conceal the different justificatory connections between norms and values in terms of logical reasoning (cf. Habermas 1992, 313), because they present themselves formally as an expression of norms and substantively as an expression of values. This veiling does not strike one negatively, because with the Court's standards a Janus-faced norm structure enters the hierarchical framework of the legal order at an intermediate level. [179] No one else beside the Constitutional Court itself has access to this level. Since the Court sets the standards, the legislature cannot modify them, not even by a constitutional amendment. Certainly, by amending the constitution the legislature can change the wording of the Basic Law within the parameters of the eternity clause of Art. 79, 3 GG. But once again only the Federal Constitutional Court can decide the question of whether and how a constitutional amendment modifies the standards established by the Court itself.

The "extraction" of standards from the constitution explains the special function of the Federal Constitutional Court which lies between the application and the creation of legal norms. Standards blend the isolated competence to resolve disputes with the substantive authority for constitutional interpretation.[8] They must

[8] More than fifty years ago, Lerche (1961, 700 f.) described the problem as the threefold function of constitutional adjudication: the dispute-resolving, law-declaring, and norm-materializing functions.

be divorced from constitutional interpretation in the individual case and, thereby, make it possible for the Court to furnish its substantive interpretation with a decision whose influence extends beyond the concrete circumstances of the case. On this intermediate level, the Court is both institutionally and substantively unassailable. Its decision-making authority should be understood and described as the power to set standards—as a fourth (or third-and-a-half) power with an authority[180] that lies between adjudication and legislation, between the resolution of cases and the setting of legal frameworks.

By assuming the standard-setting authority, the Federal Constitutional Court also distances itself from its status as a court. In its so-called "Status Report" of 1952, the Court already pursued its promotion from a part of the judiciary to a constitutional organ (on this, see Schönberger earlier, 8–9 as well as Jestaedt earlier, 43–44, a status not provided for in the wording of the Basic Law (Thoma 1953 (1957); more recently, Häußler 1994, 23–8, already skeptical Schlaich 1981, 133). The self-empowerment as a standard-setting power completes its self-installation as a constitutional organ. For only thus can it assume its elevated status as a constitutional organ. Only thus does it exempt itself from any laws enacted by other powers, be they statutes or even constitutional amendments. The supremacy of the constitution is extended institutionally to the Court's jurisdiction. The Court accords itself an institutional status, which only befits the constitution. But the converse is also true. The institutional competence of the Court is extended to the constitution in a substantive sense as well. Taking the expression to its fullest extent, one can say that the success of the Court depends on its self-invention as a standard-setting power, both institutionally and substantively. The guardian of the constitution mutates into the master of the constitution.

The function of standard-setting power did not fall into the Court's lap as a result of, for example, the unswayable peculiarities of the political process in the modern constitutional state. The Court acquired this position itself [181] through an exceptional decision-making technique. One can see in this a strategy of self-empowerment, at least of self-aggrandizement, a strategy that oversteps both the institutional and substantive boundaries of constitutional adjudication, while an intermediate category not foreseen in the constitution is found in the normative framework: the standard.

"Intermediate formulas, measurements and standards," should characterize constitutional court decisions, but they require a disciplining method, which Lerche calls the "opinion procedure." This would be the necessary middle tier between rational principle and a decision in an individual case. But then uneasiness overcomes one, "when in these methodological precincts 'extremely sharp' boundaries are popularly drawn and concepts are 'endlessly clarified' or 'otherwise very precisely defined,' where ideally it is only a matter of nuances and where critical respect must be safeguarded against the secretive and the secret."

Indeed, the Court uses the term "standard" in virtually all of its decisions.[9] Nevertheless, the theoretical and jurisdictional significance of this category of norms has as yet received little attention in the constitutional law literature.[10] Therefore, let us consider the formation of constitutional standards more closely.

III. Standard Formation in Section "C.I."

It is time to provide some examples of these fundamental features. Before we come back to the proportionality principle as the central "C.II." standard in the subsumption section, we should cast a glance at the "C.I." problem. Two famous decisions of the late 1950s, the Elfes and the Lüth decisions, illustrate how the decontextualization of constitutional adjudication and the institutional elevation of the Federal Constitutional Court via substantive standard formation began. Both decisions should be read in conjunction (Grimm 2001, 202-204).

A. Elfes: the subjectivization of the objective law.

In the Elfes decision (BVerfGE 6, 32, 36 ff. (1957)), the Federal Constitutional Court does away with the limitation of its constitutional interpretation to the interests of the complainant. If the Federal Constitutional Court were "merely" a court, and not the general-abstract "guardian of the constitution," a constitutional complaint would only empower it to assess the case as far as the legal interests of the complainant go. The constitutional complaint only serves to protect against violations of Basic Rights conceived as subjective rights. It does not serve as a protection of objective constitutional law. This function is assigned to the judicial review of statutes, which can only be initiated, however, by certain constitutional organs [183] (Art. 93, 1, 2 GG). In the Elfes decision, the Court brought about a transformation of the constitutional complaint from a remedy which protects individual rights to a remedy whose purpose is the safeguarding of objective constitutional law. That is an important prerequisite of being able to serve as the "guardian of the constitution" in general, for otherwise this most broadly conceived competence depends on the "contingency" that a constitutional organ

[9] The Federal Constitutional Court uses the formula of a constitutional or Basic Law standard in each of its by now 150 volumes of decisions. In pure quantitative terms, the use of this formula has increased. While in the volumes from the first half of the Court's existence (therefore, cases from the year 1951 to approximately 1981), numerous decisions get by without a reference to a standard, such references have clearly increased since then. Meanwhile, there is hardly a substantive decision of the Federal Constitutional Court that does not refer to a standard.

[10] Cf., e.g., Schlaich 1981, 111 f., 120, 124; Lerche 2001, 336–40, 356–8; Lepsius 2008a, 111–17; elaborated by Jestaedt 1999, 44–53 in reference to the example of the unlimited interpretation and balancing.

initiates an abstract norm control proceeding or that in a constitutional complaint the subjective right coincides with objective constitutional law. In other words, the procedural form would limit the Federal Constitutional Court's scope of review. Admittedly, it could frequently take stances interpreting the constitution during different proceedings, but the entirety of constitutional law would not be at the Court's disposal at any given time.

The transformation of the constitutional complaint procedure into an objective proceeding (cf. Gusy 2001) is not brought about by procedural means, as one might assume. It stems, rather, from the constructive elaboration of substantive constitutional law. Art. 2, 1, GG guarantees to every person the right to the "free development of their personality." The Federal Constitutional Court, however, derives from Art. 2, 1 the "general freedom of action" with the consequence that every action enjoys Basic Law protection or, put differently, every state action with external effects on an individual becomes an interference with a Basic Right which requires justification. In its justification scrutiny, the Court stretches the text of Art. 2, 1 again by arguing that the state may be allowed to interfere with the Basic Right to general freedom of action via any [184] legal provision that is formally and substantively compatible with the constitution. The wording of the Basic Law defined the limitation clause at this point very precisely, confining it to a "triad of limitations." Consequently, the Federal Constitutional Court expands its extensive area of protection under Art. 2, 1 ("general freedom of action") via an expansive statutory reservation of powers and understands the statutory reservation of the "constitutional order" under Art. 2, 1 as "any statute in accordance with the constitution." What has the Court gained by this?

At first glance, this constitutional interpretation appears to perfect the freedom guarantees of the citizen. From now on, the citizen always moves in a zone protected by Basic Rights. His or her Basic Rights protection does not depend on the threshold requirement of certain modes of behavior ("unfolding of the personality") being worthy of the Basic Rights. Nor is there any quarrel about which institution may determine the value of an action. The Federal Constitutional Court does not want to address this issue, so it opts in favor of freedom and leaves the determination of the scope of freedom in the hands of the citizen. Hence riding in the forest enjoys Basic Rights protection (BVerfGE 80, 137—Riding in Forests (1989); dissenting opinion by Grimm, 164), and even traffic lights become an interference with Basic Rights, which, to be sure, does not ease the annoyance over a red light where the traffic lights were set up in accordance with the law.

Looking more closely, it appears to be a case of easy come, easy go.[11] For what remains of any genuine gain in freedom if the state can eliminate it through any legal provision in accordance with the constitution? The general freedom of action

[11] Cf. on the case and person of Wilhelm Elfes (1884–1969), Schönberger in this volume, 15; also Fiedler in Menzel 2000, 76–83.

enshrined in Art. 2, 1 either turns into the obligation to tolerate proportionate restrictions or the right to a minimum standard of rationality that the legislature has to observe when making laws. (For an early critical view, see Ehmke 1963, 82–6.) In the interpretation of the Basic Law favored by the Federal Constitutional Court, namely one that does not heed the provision's wording, Art. 2, 1 ultimately guarantees a claim to a rational justification of state action.

The effect of the "Elfes construction" first becomes clear on the third look. The whole constitutional order was rendered subjective. The Federal Constitutional Court is the winner in this process. For one, it can at least review any sovereign action (its external effect, therefore presupposing a citizen is affected) whatsoever on a substantive basis via the catch-all Basic Right provided under Art. 2, 1 (supportive Kahl 2000). Additionally, it is certain that a complainant will always be found for a constitutional complaint so that the Court can perforce extend its review to include objective constitutional law. For it must scrutinize both the formal and substantive legality of state action as part of its Basic Rights review. Whether the legislative process or the legislative powers were observed becomes a necessary preliminary question for the review of a violation of subjective Basic Rights.

The preferred interpretation of substantive law (here of Art. 2, 1 GG) has, therefore, a procedural effect. De facto, the constitutional complaint turns into the citizens' claim to judicial review, and the Federal Constitutional Court benefits from it, because one can use Basic Rights to evaluate state action in its entirety (for a critical view, Bethge 2007). En route, the procedural obstacle [186] to the standard-setting power had fallen: objective law was rendered subjective.[12]

B. Lüth: the objectivization of subjective law

Shortly thereafter the substantive hurdles also fell. This resulted from presumably the Federal Constitutional Court's most famous decision: the Lüth decision of January 15, 1958 (BVerfGE 7, 198 (1958); cf. Wesel 2004, 131–8). In conjunction with the Elfes and the Pharmacy (BVerfGE 7, 377 (1958)) decisions, the Lüth case

[12] That is standing doctrine today. Cf. BVerfGE 125, 39—Sunday Store Hours (2009): the Christian churches can challenge Berlin's liberalization of store hours via a constitutional complaint and contest the violation of the constitutional provision protecting Sundays and holidays as days of rest from work and for spiritual renewal, even though the issue is not one of Basic Rights, but rather one of objective constitutional law. A protective duty of the legislature, derived from Art. 4, 1 and 2 of the Basic Rights section (freedom of conscience, freedom of the exercise of religion), serves as a procedural cover here. The petition's opponents (Berlin House of Delegates and Senate) question the churches' right of complaint. The Federal Constitutional Court, however, saw no problems in regard to the permissibility of the constitutional complaint (ibid., 39, 74). The legal problem here is not whether the store hours law disturbs holidays, but rather whether the churches can contest it as holders of Basic Rights under Art. 4, 1 and 2. In an analysis of this judgment, Wißmann (2011) writes that the Federal Constitutional Court opens undue free play in decisions. He criticizes rendering objective law subjective, which effectively privileges certain circles procedurally.

established the Basic Rights theory of the Federal Constitutional Court. In brief, one could say that Elfes stands for the procedural framework: any interference with the general freedom of action can be contested by a constitutional complaint such that in practical terms the constitutional complaint procedure mutates into a judicial review complaint for citizens and obtains [187] a mandate for objective norm control. The Pharmacy decision stands for the review doctrine and the intensity of judicial scrutiny, in particular the case-related preparation of the limitation clause as a precursor of the principle of proportionality that was developed on this basis shortly thereafter.[13] Finally, Lüth stands for the implementation of the supremacy of the constitution, specifically the transition of subjective Basic Rights into an objective order of values, which benefits from the constitutional hierarchy of norms and is regarded as the standard of the entire legal order.[14] With Lüth, the path to the standard-setting power is open in substantive terms, for here subjective rights turned into objective norms (Papier 2009, RN 5).

The Basic Law does not strive to be a value-neutral order, the Federal Constitutional Court declared at the outset of its reasoning, and it established in its Basic Rights section an objective order of values. This expresses a principled enhancement of the binding force of Basic Rights:

> This system of values, which finds its center and its dignity in the free unfolding of the human personality inside the social community, must be considered as the fundamental constitutional decision for all areas of law; legislation, administration, and adjudication receive from it guidance and impulse. So obviously it also influences private law. No private law provision may contradict it. They all must be interpreted in its spirit. The legal content of the Basic Rights as objective norms unfolds in private law through the medium of the provisions, which directly dominate this area of the law. Just as new law must harmonize with this Basic Rights system of values, the content of older law currently in force is guided by this system of values; from this system of values [188] a particular constitutional content enters the older law, which from that point forward determines its interpretation. A dispute among private individuals about rights and duties from the civil law codes of conduct influenced by the Basic Law in this way remain, in both procedural and substantive terms, a private law controversy. The private law is interpreted and applied in such cases, even if its interpretation has to follow the public law, that of the constitution. (BVerfGE 7, 198, 205 f.)

Basic Rights, therefore, are not merely binding the state in relation to its citizens. They also influence the entire legal order. Even the legal relationships among

[13] On this, see in this volume 93 ff., especially 112 ff.

[14] The literature on the change of course in the theory of Basic Rights is, of course, overwhelming. I limit myself to only referring to Goerlich 1973; Jarass 2001; Wahl 2004.

citizens can be evaluated in reference to the Basic Rights. That is a pivotal change of course (cf. Wahl 2004, RN 2–5), for it extends the legal effect of the Basic Rights beyond subjective defensive rights to a dimension that, to be sure, is triggered by an individual injury, but that in terms of content has an effect beyond the individual; specifically, it is substantive in a general-abstract, objective sense. Rainer Wahl speaks of a rebirth of the legal order from the spirit of the Basic Rights (Wahl 2004, RN 1; cf. also Grimm 2001, 307–11). The Federal Constitutional Court thereby founded a universalizable substantive standard, the scope of which extends beyond the concrete case and which empowers the Court to substantively review statutes even apart from their individual relevance to the concrete case. As executed directly by the "Elfes doctrine," the constitutional complaint, which serves to protect the subjective Basic Rights of the complainant (Art. 93, 1, 4a GG), mutates in favor of the Court into a mandate for objective control.[15] [189]

This initially purely substantive legal interpretation of the Basic Rights as an order of values once again has significant institutional consequences. First, the Lüth judgment made the Federal Constitutional Court what it is today (Hennis 1999, 492). The development of its adjudication enhanced the significance of the Federal Constitutional Court as an institution (Schulze-Fielitz 2009, 14). The Court naturally strengthened its own position by reinforcing the supremacy of the constitution, objectivizing the hierarchy of norms and giving it substance in the form of Basic Rights—instead of reverting to the organizational provisions of the constitution. Two strategies are essential for this. On the one hand, the Court again pursued a purely substantive approach, in which the central issue is the content-based interpretation of the constitution. On the other hand, its task of subjective legal protection is rendered objective, thereby lowering a crucial jurisdictional hurdle. This enables the Court to exempt itself to a great extent from limits on its authority. It is free first of all from the substantive bond to the constitution, which begins to live an autonomous normative life as an "objective order of values," whose growth and [190] flourishing alone lies in the hands of the Court (not in any case in those of the constitution-amending legislature). But it is also free from the

[15] Correspondingly, the Federal Constitutional Court has insisted that the constitutional complaint does not exhaust itself in the protection of subjective Basic Rights, but also has the task of "protecting, interpreting, and elaborating" objective constitutional law (so BVerfGE 98, 218, 243—Spelling Reform (1998); BVerfGE 124, 300, 318—Wunsiedel (2009)). Therefore, the Federal Constitutional Court [189] itself decided constitutional complaints, which had in the meantime been withdrawn or whose petitioner had died, so that the subjective interest in legal protection was thereby removed. The procedural desubjectivization of the content-based objectivization makes itself evident here: when the jurisdiction of the Court is established, it does not relinquish its substantive claim to decide, even if the function of the constitutional complaint, which lies in subjective liberty guarantees (one thinks of the procedural hurdles demanded of the complainant for a constitutional complaint to have his or her Basic Rights currently and personally violated), is no longer being fulfilled. The Court does not (only) intend to protect subjective rights with its decisions, but rather it extends to objective law protection its review authority that derives from its duty to protect subjective rights. The Federal Constitutional Court granted itself this competence; it derived neither from the Basic Law nor from the Federal Constitutional Court Law (cf. Wißmann 1999 for a critical view).

procedural requirements, which must be fulfilled in order to establish the Court's jurisdiction. Finally, it is free from the procedural connection of the decision-making authority to the subject-matter of the dispute. In the Lüth judgment, one can observe especially well, how the substantive constitutional interpretation became the vehicle of self-empowerment. What is interesting, ultimately, is how a jurisdictional problem (review authority) leads to a substantive law solution. Today, one rather imagines than actually detects procedural or jurisdictional limits on the Court's review authority. The plethora of opportunities for access provided by procedural law—alongside the constitutional complaint, there are above all judicial review proceedings, disputes among constitutional organs ("Organstreit"), and Federation-Land disputes ("Bund-Länder-Streit")—permits the Court to "impregnate" the entire legal order with its "constitutional interpretations and to extend its own interpretive claims" (Schulze-Fielitz 2009, 14; cf. also Schuppert/Bumke 2000, 48–62).

The elevation of subjective rights to objective standards finds its continuation in the separation of the standards and subsumption sections of decisions. One can already notice this separation in the Lüth judgment. The Court begins with abstract expositions on the meaning of the Basic Rights, conceives them as an objective order of values, and considers the relationship of the Basic Rights to ordinary law. It is only after this that these principles are applied to the case. Since we are standing at the birthplace of modern German theory of Basic Rights, we should examine more closely the case which triggered this judgment. For it is [191] to be expected that, in 1958, the First Senate had chosen to create a universalizable constitutional standard through the objectivization of subjective rights not without cause, but rather in view of the case to be decided. Both the legal question and its symptomatic meaning for the young Federal Republic and, not least, the institutional setting of the still-young Federal Constitutional Court are of decisive significance for the preferred solution.

Erich Lüth (1902–1989) was a delegate for the German Democratic Party (DDP) in the Hamburg Assembly during the Weimar Republic, a pacifist, and an opponent of National Socialism. In 1946, he became the Director of the Hamburg State Press Office. Overcoming the National Socialist past and reconciling with Israel were special wishes of his. Lüth was part of the democratic Germany that was lost in 1933 and upon which the young Federal Republic built in a decidedly anti-National Socialist manner. Lüth observed with anger how the old National Socialist elite again gained a foothold in the new Federal Republic. These included Veit Harlan (1899–1964), director of several anti-Semitic propaganda films, among them the notorious *Jud Süß*. Harlan symbolized the pervasive type of compliant careerists, who readily served National Socialism, but did not see their actions as ideologically infected by it. In the denazification process, Harlan was classified as an "exonerated person." Harlan's first postwar film, a tearjerker with the title *Unsterbliche Geliebte* (Immortal Beloved), was supposed to have its premier in 1950 during the "Week of German Films." Lüth called for the film not to be shown and called on the public to boycott the film. It became a scandal, and the film distributor was concerned about loss of revenue so it obtained an injunction against Lüth from a Hamburg district court, [192] which viewed Lüth's calls as an incitement to boycott contra bonos mores prohibited by Section 826 of the Federal Civil Code (BGB). Lüth's boycott offends against the "democratic conceptions regarding law and morality held by the German people," the district court concluded, and prohibited Lüth's proclamation. Lüth raised a constitutional complaint against the injunction arguing that the judgment violated his Basic Right to freedom of speech.[16] The Federal Constitutional Court affirmed Erich Lüth's claim.

It is a classic legal dispute when freedom of opinion and the protection of morals and personal honor come into conflict. What gave this constellation of facts its spice was the National Socialist background and the symbolic significance for the strengthened social influence of the former National Socialist elite, which used private law to defend itself against the civic courage of those denouncing them. Also at issue was the supposed neutrality of the private law, which is surrounded by the aura of the non-political in the German legal tradition. This case shows how a provision that is per se above suspicion, a provision that only seeks to regulate the legal relations between citizens, can be turned into a weapon in the social-political contest between opinions. The "non-political" provision, therefore, had political effects. What remains of the freedom of speech, if it could be limited in social interactions through private law statutes, merely because these were directed at non-state actions, i.e. non-political legal relations among citizens? The Federal Constitutional Court's justices, composed overwhelmingly of opponents of National Socialism, could hardly permit a supposedly non-political private law to privilege the former National Socialist elite in the conflict of opinions.[17] [193]

Section 826 BGB covers damage caused by intentional actions contra bonos mores ("vorsätzliche sittenwidrige Handlung"). The section applies, for example, to cases such as the relatively recent one involving Rolf Breuer, former CEO of Deutsche Bank, who compromised the creditworthiness of Leo Kirch, a late media tycoon, through public statements, which allegedly drove Kirch into bankruptcy. Clearly, this involves a tangible private law conflict. The problem in Lüth, however, was whether the district court had to take into account the Basic Rights (freedom of speech) when applying a provision of the civil code in a private law dispute. Indeed, according to Art. 1, 3 GG, the lawgiver of the BGB is just as bound to the Basic Rights as the district court, applying the BGB. Nevertheless, Art. 1, 3 plays no

16 The case is vividly worked up and evaluated in Henne/Riedlinger 2005.

17 Cf. also Schönberger 2011, who pays tribute to the Court as midwife of the [193] second German democracy. Early on it distanced itself with great consistency from the poisoned legacy of the National Socialist period (see also Herbert 2006, 96–102).

role at all in the reasoning of the district court's decision, and Section 826 BGB is not in principle an unconstitutional norm. Its application in this case simply fails to recognize the meaning of the freedom of speech. The consequences of the Federal Constitutional Court's solution are on display here. By declaring the Basic Rights an objective standard of value, it makes the application of the private law a question of constitutional law. Thus a civil dispute turns into a constitutional proceeding, which, in turn, renders the Federal Constitutional Court competent to scrutinize whether the application of the BGB provisions complies with the objectivized constitutional standards.

The Federal Constitutional Court used the opportunity to cast a wary eye over the approach of the district court, which applied its own moral standards with the help of the criterion "contra bonos mores" in Section 826 BGB, as it did when it evaluated Lüth's statements as an intrusion against the "democratic legal and moral understanding of the German people." [194] Vague legal provisions that are applicable to countless situations, so-called "general clauses" (*Generalklauseln*), the Federal Constitutional Court instructed the district court, make use of criteria like "contra bonos mores" to function as "breaches" for the "radiating effect" the Basic Rights have on private law.[18]

C. Institutional causes

The strategy of the substantive objectification, therefore, also had an institutional component, specifically, to deny the civil courts its own content-based scrutiny, which makes recourse to general clauses like "contra bonos mores" or "bona fide" using these as a gateway for supra-positive legal agendas. The Federal Constitutional Court had good reason to be wary here. For the general clauses had already been instrumental in the National Socialist reinterpretation of the traditional legal order after 1933, because they were amenable to interpretation in the spirit of the National Socialist Weltanschauung or of the Nazi's notion of Volksgemeinschaft (people's ethnic community) (see Rüthers 2005; on the methodological context Lepsius 1994). After the Second World War, the Federal High Court of Justice (BGH) continued this approach by exchanging the values, but maintaining the method. It simply replaced the discredited National Socialist content with a natural law renaissance (Cf. Weinkauff 1960; for analysis Kühl 1998). By making recourse to natural law, this approach allowed supra-positive ideas to influence the application of the law, threatening the supremacy of the constitution

[18] Cf. BVerfGE 7, 198 at 206. The Court relies here on Günter Dürig, who had denoted the general clauses as entry points for the Basic Rights into the civil law and whose writings had also otherwise influenced the Senate deliberations, as Böckenförde (1989, 26) verifies.

and, by implication, the position of the Federal Constitutional Court. One must not forget that the Federal Constitutional Court in the 1950s was the newcomer [195] and in Karlsruhe was located in the vicinity of the Federal High Court of Justice, which saw itself in the tradition of the Reichsgericht and sought to maintain a corresponding ethos.

The elevation of the Basic Rights to an objective order of values plucked natural law from the hand of the Federal High Court of Justice. The legal order in its entirety, with its general clauses, was to be interpreted in light of the constitution, therefore, in the spirit of the Federal Constitutional Court's doctrine. This not only allowed the supremacy of the constitution to establish itself versus the supra-positive ideas (natural law and substantive justice, substantive values ethic) circulating in the postwar era. It also enabled the Federal Constitutional Court to assert itself institutionally opposite the self-possessed federal courts like the Federal High Court of Justice, the Federal Labor Court, or the Federal Administrative Court, which briskly followed their own paths in the 1950s.[19]

With the "objective order of values" as a substantial meta-standard, the Federal Constitutional Court reacted to several institutional challenges and legal issues. The Lüth judgment proved itself above all to be a time-bound decision to a high degree. In other words, the justification of the Federal Constitutional Court's Basic Rights theory breathed the air of the fifties; it is not the expression of inherent objective necessities, systematization, legal dogmatics, or preconceived and abstractly justifiable theory. [196] Without the National Socialist context of the case, the recourse of the district court to morality, and the institutional competition of the highest (ordinary) federal courts, which in the 1950s had conceived and practiced diverse strategies for the incorporation of higher law, the Lüth case arguably would have been decided differently. Also, the choice of words in the formula of the "objective order of values" betrays the philosophical climate of the 1950s. From which follows that the constitutional interpretation of the Federal Constitutional Court is not explicable entirely on its own merits. Neither can one derive the grounds of the decision from the text of the Basic Law or from a technical bond to the constitution. Obviously intermediate steps and premises lie at the basis of the constitutional interpretation, which is only partly indicated in the Lüth decision. The reasoning of the Court is understandable only by contextualizing the facts of the case: the issue of jurisdiction, the competing federal courts, the intellectual situation of the time, and, of course, the concrete legal circumstances.

[19] Under its President, Hans Carl Nipperdey, the Federal Labor Court had already utilized the direct third party effect of the Basic Rights in labor law, hence quite openly making recourse to the Basic Rights in labor law questions. The Federal Administrative Court under its President Fritz Werner drew on the Basic Rights to render the received administrative law subjective (Werner 1959; for analysis Schönberger 2006). Both approaches challenged the institutional position of the Federal Constitutional Court as guardian of the constitution.

D. Further processing of standards

This may appear to many as something self-evident. The problems of interpretation begin, however, once a standard produced in a distinctive decision-making context becomes normatively autonomous and is transposed into an entirely different set of circumstances. This is precisely what occurs during the further processing of a standard. Although a standard is greatly indebted to a distinctive case constellation, it soon begins to lead an independent existence in normative terms, detached from the historical context in which [197] it can be solely understood. In the Lüth decision, the standard was still developed with a view to the solution of the concrete case. Over the years, however, the factual relativity of the normative solution faded from view, and the Federal Constitutional Court's practical division between the standards and subsumption sections promoted this. The consequence is that during the deciding of a new case, the contexts surrounding the origins of judgments that contributed to the formation of standards are typically blended out. One can see this clearly in the "objective order of values." Neither the Federal Constitutional Court nor constitutional scholars ask whether the formula of the "objective order of values" has a specific anti-National Socialist animus and, therefore, is no longer productively applied to present problems. Today, nobody questions the application of this objective order of values to legislatives acts, although in its original context it was unambiguously directed against the judiciary. It is doubtful that the then novice Federal Constitutional Court would have found fault with a statute of the still rather green Bonn Republic in light of the objective order of values. The Court's addressee was the judiciary, not parliament. Over time, however, one generally forgot about the institutional context of the "objective value" reasoning in the Lüth case and began to extend it thoughtlessly to parliamentary statutes as well.

The objective binding effect of the Basic Rights on all state authority, however, raises a considerable institutional problem. Why should the legislature be bound to the objective legal dimension of the Basic Rights to the same extent as the administrative or adjudicative power? It is important to bear in mind that the invention of the Basic Rights as an objective order of values was not intended to submit the legislature to the Basic Rights. However, since the original context of constitutional interpretation went by the board during the subsequent elaboration of the Basic Rights, normative statements tended to be extended beyond their one-time intended legal [198] effect without this extension being noticed and discussed. For only if one had the contextual limitations of the binding effect in one's sight, could one perceive this extension in the first place. Yet in Germany this is simply not the case. The contextual limitations of constitutional interpretation are not taken into account during its further processing. Decisions incorporate neither history nor context. The facts may interest legal historians, but practitioners do not concern themselves with them, because any contextualization adversely affects the generalization and dogmatization of the decision in question.

In regard to the "objective order of values," a partial all-clear signal can be given. The concept was from the beginning too undifferentiated in order to serve as a standard amenable to subsumption. In the 1970s, its use in adjudication had already decreased, while in the eighties it vanished into oblivion. Meanwhile, the Federal Constitutional Court had differentiated the objective legal content of the Basic Rights in various other ways (as participatory and procedural rights, organizational maxims, duties to protect) and recoupled these dimensions to the primarily defensive, subjective function of the Basic Rights. In any case, the Court accentuates again and again the legitimacy-reinforcing function of the theory of objective rights for subjective law and refrains from drawing upon the objective dimension of rights even in prominent cases that invite solutions by reference to the objective legal content of the Basic Rights (especially, e.g., BVerfGE 115, 118 at 152—Air Safety (2008)). In this sense, one can speak of a re-subjectivization of the objective legal content of the Basic Rights (Kahl 2010, RN 12; cf. also Bethge 2007). This does not necessarily require the creation of new subjective rights, but rather the insight that an objective reinforcement of a right needs an applicable individual claim. [199] Objective legal effects were conceived accessory to subjective legal positions. Thereby, the Court could forestall the structural dangers for the constitutional order, which lie in the objective functions of Basic Rights, without diminishing the wide appeal of the subjective rights in society (Capitant 2001, 175–89). Put differently, since the meta-standard "order of values" was not subsumable, standards applicable in more limited areas had to be developed. Nevertheless, the Lüth case remains the binding clasp between all objective law manifestations of the Basic Rights. And, accordingly, in the course of the differentiation of specific objective Basic Rights dimensions, no regard was shown for a binding effect that is incrementally tiered and tailored for specific powers. This is the essential legacy of the strategy of a substantive objectivization begun in the Lüth case: expansion of both the institutional binding force and the substantive bindingness at the expense of criteria that induce both procedural and jurisdiction limitations.

Let us do a cross check. Is the holding in Lüth already legal history or still good law? A dogmatically trained German jurist cannot answer this question, for he or she does not want to contextualize the decision. If he or she would contextualize it, one could no longer integrate the decision into the standard formation. The present status of the Lüth decision, therefore, must remain unclear. On the one hand, it is the source of the objective theory of the Basic Rights, while, on the other, its current empties out into a delta. May its source dry up? Conversely, if one historicizes and contextualizes the judgment, the justificatory effort naturally increases for the [200] area-specific differentiation of the Basic Rights' objective dimensions. The image would change: the current emptying out into a delta would turn into separate streams with their own distinct sources (read: cases as sources). More than a few constitutional scholars consider this as a danger for the unity and consistency of the legal order and lament the relinquishment of systematization.[20] But this is once again only the reflex of a fundamentally substantive orientation in German legal thinking, which is fixed on the general-abstract norms and neglects their factual contexts (illuminating Ehmke 1963, 77–81).

E. Decontextualization instead of distinguishing

"C.I." sometimes reads like an exposition worthy of a textbook. In the early decades, the standards section often contained content-rich constitutional discussions. The style was not so apodictic as we often find today. In the decisions, the Court discusses assumptions and considers functional issues. Discussions about premises were led, reasons were given that went beyond mere claims to validity and self-quotations, even if in retrospect there is nothing to romanticize.[21] In recent decades, by contrast, the Court is ever more inclined to substitute the justification of standards with a reference to its own case record. In the meantime, such chains of self-citation are routine. The Senates give the impression of unshakable continuity. One is meant to get the impression that the doctrine of the Federal Constitutional Court develops without interruption and displays a high degree of calculability. The use of self-citation signals that we find ourselves in an abstract constitutional discourse, in which the issue is not the solution of concrete legal problems, but rather the textual interpretation of the constitution independent of its concrete application. The Court cultivates its standards and carefully develops them further, all the while attempting to avoid ruptures in its own argumentation. If it wants to counter the impression of decisionistic legal findings, it must maintain the continuity of its material constitutional interpretation. The Court feels bound by a substantive constitutional interpretation that is ultimately its own understanding of the constitution, as it manifests itself in the jurisprudential doctrine. Constitutional interpretation thus shifts from the constitution to constitutional adjudication. The standards themselves become those portions of constitutional law which provide the foundation for the restructuring and new creation of constitutional law. This ensures the institutional and interpretive sovereignty of the Federal Constitutional Court, because no other power can gain access to its "standards."

[20] Cf. the debate in connection with Lepsius (2010a, 194–204), who draws into question the future viability of the idea of the material unity of the legal order and its claim to system in administrative law.

[21] Cf. the then and now pertinent analyses by Ehmke (1963) or Schlaich (1981). Ehmke wanted to understand and discuss the reasoning of decisions from their contexts; he propagated an American approach to some extent. Schlaich wanted to tie the judgments' reasoning more closely to the text of the constitution. Both bemoan the independent disengagement of the decision-making culture, whether it is from contexts or from the normative text.

The Court faces the problem produced by itself, that the normative foundation of validity has shifted from the bindingness of the constitution to the bindingness of standards. Since constitutional interpretation emerges primarily in the form of standard formation, the Court becomes dependent on its own doctrine. It cannot simply deviate from its own standards, for [202] this would mean it would either confess to previous errors or incur the denunciation of judicial politics. Likewise, the Federal Constitutional Court cannot even rely on the technique which high courts routinely employ to ensure the coherence of doctrine and, at the same time, preserve freedom of decision-making for new cases: the technique of "distinguishing," that is, the distinction of facts in regard to their normative treatment. The common law courts have raised this practice to a higher art form (Fikentscher 1975, 62 ff., 95 ff.; Schauer 1987; Postema 2002, 595–499). They are easily able to maintain varying and sometimes even divergent grounds for decisions by differentiating the respective cases on the basis of facts and establishing corresponding classifications of cases. The facts of the pending case create freedom for normative flexibility and dynamic development of law. However, this technique is not at the disposal of the Federal Constitutional Court because of its "C.I." approach. Since the original facts of the cases are simply irrelevant for the formation of standards, standards cannot be further elaborated through the practice of distinguishing prior cases. That is the price paid for the decontextualization of standards and for references to previous standards, specifically, for the fact that the statements referred to in a decision are separated out from their original context, transferred to a new context, and combined into a new whole (as described by Jestaedt 2009a, 532).

IV. Proportionality as the "C.II." Standard

A. The relational function of proportionality

There can be a violation of the constitution even in the application and interpretation of a rule, which in constitutional law terms is per se beyond suspicion. The unconstitutionality in this instance rests not in the legislation, but rather in the application of the statute by officials or by a court. The concrete problem residing in the Lüth decision is whether freedom of opinion can be limited by a general law like Section 826 BGB, in other words, restricted by a rule which pursues a goal that is itself neutral in terms of opinion. According to Art. 5, 2 GG, freedom of opinion finds its limits in such general laws. But the Lüth judgment demonstrates that it might not come down to a general-abstract qualification of the statute as an "abstract provision that is neutral regarding opinions," but rather that under certain circumstances such otherwise neutral statutes can in effect produce limitations on opinions. Therefore, the same statute in one case provides a constitution-conforming legal foundation, while in another case it does not. This makes evident how the effect of legal rules is dependent on the procedural situation of its enforcement. Rules may not be evaluated solely in a general-abstract form that is reducible to its validity. It comes down to the context of its application. And it is precisely that insight—which the Federal Constitutional Court, when constitutional provisions are at issue, can cover up with the help of the standards section, because there is no court above it—that has to decide between the validity and the effectiveness of the constitutional norm. [204]

The question of the differentiated constitutional relevance of a statute, which is not in principle unconstitutional but which turns out to be unconstitutional under certain circumstances, evades treatment in the standards section. The unified image of a situation-dependent casuistic can be lost during the review of the potential impact of constitutional law on the application of ordinary law. The principle of proportionality takes hold at this point, not formulated as a substantive standard (as in "C.I."), but rather as a relational one. It is conceived as a means-end check, which first asks, which goal the legislature intended to pursue, and then if the chosen means matched the goal in a threefold sense: Are the means at all suitable for promoting the goal (suitability)? Are there less restrictive, though equally well-suited means (necessity)? And finally, do the interests which the legislature intends to safeguard outweigh the interests which the means in question impairs (appropriateness)? The elaboration of this relational standard (on the structure Merten 2009, RN 50 ff.) is probably the Federal Constitutional Court's greatest juristic achievement; one, incidentally, it shares with German constitutional scholarship.[22]

B. The processing of normative and factual aspects in proportionality

The formation of a standard of proportionality enables the Court to resolve cases without modifying general-abstract standards and without being subject to pressure to adapt casuistically. Since the proportionality principle is generalizable, it can, in turn, be seen as a (relational) standard. The proportionality standard preserves the impression of a substantive coherence and methodological rationality during adjudication oriented around individual cases. The Federal Constitutional Court can appear as "guardian of the constitution," even if it has to decide thousands of constitutional complaints on a daily basis. The claim to being a constitutional organ remains intact, even if the bench actually performs as a supreme

[22] From the extensive literature on this subject, see, e.g., Lerche 1999 and Schlink 2001. One can speak here of a constitutional invention, which rivals the supremacy of the constitution or hierarchical structure of the legal order. Besides, the proportionality principle numbers among the great world export hits of German legal scholarship (cf., e.g., Grimm 2007; von Arnauld 2008).

appellate court. Or put differently, the proportionality principle facilitates the existence of general-abstract, substantive constitutional standards, because both the factual circumstances of the individual case as well as the situational application of the statute under review can be isolated from these.

The proportionality principle, however, accomplishes even more than this. First, it facilitates the concretization of the standards according to the circumstances of the case, above all at the appropriateness stage of the review process. It also couples law and politics, above all when the purpose of a statute is determined and its suitability and necessity is established. The political process has the right to determine ends. For the purposes of the constitutional review, however, these ends are nevertheless ultimately substantiated by the Court via interpretation of the statute's aim. Politics still determines [206] the choice of means, which the Court nevertheless reviews for their suitability, necessity, and appropriateness.

Both the determination of the goal (1) and the appropriateness stage of the proportionality review (4) are conceived as normative tests. At the suitability (2) and necessity (3) stages, by contrast, the review involves aspects also lying in the realm of facts. Whether the means are suitable or whether there are less restrictive, equally well-suited means can only be assessed in view of concrete circumstances. One cannot go any further here with generalizable normative standards, for the facts first enable legal control.

This presents a problem for the Federal Constitutional Court as standard-setting power: it cannot naturally purport the authority to have the last word in regard to facts. Ultimately, everybody can contribute to factual issues. A general claim to judicial authority (or a claim to authority of lawyers in general) would be far-fetched if other than in evaluating purely normative questions. Conversely, that may explain why in section "C.II." the Federal Constitutional Court also prefers to decide its cases on the basis of appropriateness while the other stages of review (goal determination, suitability, and necessity) are almost never relevant to the decision.[23] In view of its jurisdictional [207] claims, one can understand why the Court prefers to resolve cases with normative implications as legal questions, which is to say, reaching decisions on the basis of appropriateness. That is also understandable for other reasons: the Federal Constitutional Court has trouble fact-finding (cf. Ossenbühl 1976; Bryde 2001). Indeed, it can collect selective evidence (Section 26 BVerfGG), but it is not a court of record that is charged with determining facts.

[23] In the adjudication of modern security legislation, one can clearly observe this development, focusing especially emphatically on the factually relevant stages of review (in more detail Lepsius 2010b), certainly also because the weighing of freedom against security exhibits a structural imbalance. Individual liberty rights and collective security interests are not commensurable. One may also point out, for example, that the unconstitutionality of the launch authority under section 14, 3 of the LuftSiG (Air Security Law of January 11, 2005) had already been established after the review for suitability (BVerfGE 115, 118 at 140 ff. (2006)). The Senate certainly did not stop here, but decided the case in material reliance on Art. 1, 1 GG throughout all four stages of review. [207] The public discussion of the decision, however, focused only on the dignity issues (for further discussion Lepsius 2006).

In a strict practical sense, the Court depends on facts that the "lower courts" or the legislature have provided. Institutionally, it would be hard to fathom how a Senate in Karlsruhe could find facts underlying a statute better, for example, than the federal legislature or those underlying a legal dispute better than a specialized court. Nevertheless, the Federal Constitutional Court cannot simply be satisfied with the fact-finding as it is presented to the Senate. Just think about constitutional complaints based on a violation of freedom of speech. They depend on the circumstances surrounding the particular expression of opinion, as the Lüth case already proved.[24]

Considering the significance that facts have for the proportionality test, the Federal Constitutional Court increasingly demands that the legislature provide empirically verifiable data to support its deliberations about goals and means. Occasionally, for example, the Senate reviews whether [208] parliament collected complete data, whether the result is comprehensible, and whether the data is properly weighed (as examples BVerfGE 106, 62 at 152 ff.—Elder Care (2002); BVerfGE 125, 175 at 227 ff.—Hartz IV Unemployment Benefits (2010)). In such cases, the Federal Constitutional Court treats the Bundestag much as an administrative court treats the district agencies' discretionary authority. Special difficulties arise when the legislature justifies the goal of the provision with prognoses, because the factual basis on which a statute is issued is being extrapolated. Indeed, the Court customarily accords the legislature a certain degree of discretion in estimating, evaluating, and reaching prognoses.[25] However, it limited this straightaway by mandating duties to observe, review, and amend.[26] In some cases, the Court accepts the legislature's treatment of facts, other times it does not. One must not overlook that the choice of one or the other depends on the standard of proportionality. When the Court cannot resolve a dispute as well on the appropriateness issue, for example because the balancing can be reviewed only with great difficulty (conflicts among goals; too many divergent interests, which do not lend themselves to being reformulated unambiguously into two legally protected interests that are balanced with one another; commensurability problems like freedom vs. security or need vs. budget), the Court can divert to the factually oriented stages of review like suitability and necessity and demand the corresponding evidence as prerequisite for its capacity to review.[209]

[24] Additional examples would be BVerfGE 93, 266 at 295 ff.—Soldiers are Murderers (1993), in which the Federal Constitutional Court complained that the lower courts had not properly comprehended the meaning of the insults, or BVerfGE 94, 1 at 10 f.—Flyer at the Conference on Scopenhauer (1996) as well as BVerfGE 107, 275 at 282—Shock Ad Benetton II (2003), in which the Federal Constitutional Court admonished the lower courts to consider the context of the utterance. [208]

[25] More recent examples are BVerfGE 102, 197 at 218—Casinos (2000), BVerfGE 115, 276 at 309—Sports Betting (2006), and BVerfGE 125, 260 at 329—Data Retention (2010).

[26] BVerfGE 49, 89 at 130, 142 f.—Kalkar Nuclear Power Plant (1978); BVerfGE 88, 203 at 310 f.—Abortion II (1993); BVerfGE 95, 267 at 314—East German Farmers Cooperatives Old Debts (1997); BVerfGE 111, 333 at 360—Brandenburg University Law (2004).

C. Linking law and politics?

The Court requires certain information, so that it can apply its relational standards of review. But who guarantees that this data was decisive in the political process or that it can even be provided? Was this data, which the Federal Constitutional Court afterwards deems relevant for the purposes of its test of proportionality, collected and taken into account? Entirely different considerations may have played a role in the legislative process. Parliament should also be permitted to issue statutes from its gut. The political motives for the chosen statutory solution will regularly not coincide with the provisos that the Federal Constitutional Court requires for its legal control. Ultimately, the political process follows other rules than the test of proportionality. It must overcome other obstacles. Above all it must reach compromises to build majorities. But compromises obscure means–ends relationships more readily than they illuminate them. For the prerequisite of compromise is that all participants yield, that packages be put together, and that additional dependencies be created such that where possible the means cannot be unambiguously assigned to multiple ends. Compromises enhance the capacity for political action (cf. Simmel 1923, 248–51; Waldron 1999, 266 ff., 282 ff.). Proportionality facilitates the control of legality. Compromise and proportionality are no natural allies, or put differently: the rationality of politics operates differently than the rationality of review.

What was praised at the outset as the special achievement of the proportionality principle, preparing a place for linking [210] law and politics (on the fundamental problem, see Jestaedt 2011), at second glance proves itself to be a hindrance. For the Court's manner of processing the results of political will formation is guided by its standards. The link becomes one-sided. Ultimately, the principle of proportionality does not evolve from institutional, jurisdictional, or procedural need to produce a mode of coupling of democratic legal politics and the control of democracy under the law-governed state.

The genesis of the proportionality principle displays the traits of the German *Rechtsstaat* tradition, not those of democratic theory. The Federal Constitutional Court regularly gives either the *Rechtsstaat* principle, general legal principles, or even the Basic Rights and their nature in general as the constitutional source of the proportionality principle (cf. Hirschberg 1981; Stern 1993; von Arnauld 2000; Merten 2009, RN 24 f.). Put differently, the constitutional derivation of proportionality is not clarified. One typically makes use of vague references to different, preferably abstract principles. But that does not present a significant problem, for naturally when it comes to standards it is not possible to definitively determine from where it stems and how it is derived. It is common knowledge that the standard's status ensues from an intermediate layer in normative terms, which cannot be integrated unambiguously into the hierarchical structure of the legal order. It is clear, however, that the principle of proportionality does not stem from the principle of democracy and, consequently, respect for democratic legal politics does not number among its core functions.

Proportionality's aim was first to prevent a form of Basic Rights protection according to the standards of the ordinary law, a [211] narrowing that, above all, came out of the Court's expansion of its Basic Rights protection when it interpreted Article 2,1 GG to encompass a general freedom of action (BVerfGE 6, 32—Elfes (1957); BVerfGE 80, 137—Riding in the Forest (1989)). The proportionality test's aim was also to maintain the supremacy of the constitution against the influence of statutes on the Basic Rights (cf. Lerche 2009, RN 13 ff.) while at the same time ensuring the standards' generality and level of abstraction against their necessarily restrictive application in a specific area. Its goal was finally the calculability and rationalization of the subsumption section. These are all goals in the *Rechtsstaat* tradition, and they were optimally reached.

One thing, however, the proportionality principle did not achieve: the peculiarities of the political process play at most a secondary role in the theoretical formulation of the proportionality principle. Whether and to what extent these peculiarities can be taken into consideration in the course of the review is a question of their practical usefulness in the individual case, but cannot be secured already ex ante in the test design. In other words, the Federal Constitutional Court can use the proportionality principle to enforce the rationality of its review, which rests on the functional prerequisites of the *Rechtsstaat* and of the Basic Rights, but it does so at the cost of those underlying the political process. As a result, the political process is forced to proceed on two tracks (on the problem in a typological sense, Stone Sweet 2000; cf. also Scholz 1999, 8). The political process must not only justify a statute politically in the Bundestag, the Federal Council (Bundesrat), and possibly in the committee which mediates between the Bundestag and the Federal Council ("Vermittlungsausschuss"), but rather must also consider legal justifications before the Federal Constitutional Court.[27] Political and constitutional justification, however, follow different courses. Consequently, the Federal Constitutional Court forces its rationality standards on the political process, even if the political process cannot always furnish these institutionally or does so only with great difficulty (cf. Gusy 1985; Heun 1992).

Think of a statute, for example the so-called Hartz IV benefits for long-term unemployed people, which passed through the mediation committee and thus can be nothing else but a compromise between opposing interests of the coalition parties and the Länder. How did the Court react (BVerfGE 125, 175 (2010))? After it created substantive guidelines in the standards section with considerable effort, the

[27] Schlaich already referred to these problems (1981, 114 f.): one cannot send the legislature into battle for an all-encompassing statutory concordance reconciling the opposing interests of the Federal Government and the Länder, minorities and associations, and urge [212] the mediation committee (Art. 77, 2 GG) to seek a last minute compromise and then compare these highly political procedures with the serenity of a courtroom in Karlsruhe.

Court produced an unmediated entitlement to benefits with the pathos of human dignity. Then it whittled down this entitlement in the subsumption section to a claim of citizens to an enforceable decision and a technocratic burden of proof for the legislature (for a criticism, Rixen 2010a). This judicial practice of linking politics and law provided Hartz IV recipients with five additional Euros. But the price for the constitutional order is far higher: the political process is burdened with rationality expectations, which run contrary to its functional conditions and do not strengthen its capacity for action. Even the constitutional standards suffer. An entitlement claim to a minimum standard of living, deriving from the right to human dignity and having an unmediated constitutional status, fizzles out to literally small change. There is a divergence between the pathos of the standards in "C.I." and the pettiness of its legal consequences in "C.II."

That poses problems for the technique of standards formation, [213] in particular its substantive portions. Can the Court still satisfy its own claims to standards formation, when the case is decided ultimately on procedural, not substantive, grounds (claim to an enforceable judgment)? The technique of decision-making through standards, in the end, roots in substantive issues. It conceives of the supremacy of the constitution as that of a substantive order derived from the Basic Rights. It reveals its weaknesses when criteria of the institutional differentiation become necessary or when the factually oriented diversification of legal problems is pending. [214]

V. Problems in Standard-Setting

A. Dynamic over time

The period of great substantive constitutional interpretation appears to be passing. Most of it has already been determined, and when the Federal Constitutional Court decides today, it may not ignore the standards it has already developed. It can hardly establish new grand constitutional standards because of the abundant case law. When the Court dares a new roll of the dice today, it opens itself to the critique of constitutional scholarship. Even the times when constitutional theory followed the Court so complaisantly that one could accuse it of Federal Constitutional Court positivism (Schlink 1981, 161; contrary view Lerche 2002, 649) are drawing to a close. The more recent grand designs of the Court (e.g., the Basic Right of computers, identity checks of the Treaty of Lisbon judgment, Hartz IV Unemployment Benefits) find emphatically more critical scholarly reception (in the example of the Basic Rights theory Höfling 2003; Kahl 2004) than one can detect in previous decades. One reason is that the derivation of standards can be reviewed for consistency with earlier doctrine detailed in the 140 volumes of official decisions. More and more wishes remain unfulfilled. Not without good reason has one held against the Federal Constitutional Court that it may not demand compliance with its decisions, especially from the specialized courts, when it itself does not adhere to them (Schlink 2007). One can put it simply: the Federal Constitutional Court needs argumentative [215] flexibility. Why should it not change its doctrine now and then? Why would one want to be tied down to standards that were suited to the 1970s or the 1980s? Why should new problems not be decided according to new standards?

Does the standard-setting's formula for success take its toll? Indeed, standards do not draw their persuasive power from contextual considerations. Rather, they are based on the constitution. Therefore, they have a normative quality which makes them independent of changing circumstances and the vibrant diversity of cases. Their claim is threatened by a change in doctrine, and the Federal Constitutional Court has practically never discarded its standards.[28] Their normative status, rooted in the supremacy of the constitution, relieves them above all of the classical instruments with which the courts are able to weaken the binding force of older decisions and ensure the flexibility of doctrine. The Federal Constitutional Court cannot relativize its cases by distinguishing prior ones, that is to say distancing itself from statements made before by referring to the altered factual and legal situation. It is precisely this classic instrument of high court adjudication that does not work in standard formation. For the formulation of standards does not take account of changes in underlying criteria, which is precisely what the interpretive device known as *distinguishing* makes possible. Instead, standards are composed with indifference to the underlying factual circumstances. This is a salient property of standards, which accounts for the great success of the Federal Constitutional Court's adjudication [216]. If it intends to remain true to its method, the Court can hardly begin to declare standards with reference to the peculiarities of the case. Then, however, it risks losing its own institutional claim as guardian of the constitution. Otherwise, the Court decides cases just like other courts. Standards can evolve, but they cannot be changed.

The momentum of legal development inevitably outruns the standard-setting power. It is not well-equipped to keep pace with this dynamic movement, because its legitimacy (as determined by the path chosen by the Federal Constitutional Court itself) flows primarily from the binding force of the constitution, and, therefore, is of a substantive nature, rather than from its competence to decide disputes, which is to say its legitimacy is not derived from procedure. It is a self-inflicted institutional tragedy that the dynamic of legal development becomes a problem for a court, an institution which one should assume is accustomed to reacting to

[28] As exceptions one may cite the doctrine of the party state as well as the financing of the parties. Even the change in the doctrine on abortion (BVerfGE 39, 1 (1975), on the one hand, BVerfGE 88, 203 (1993), on the other) at any rate bears witness to a significant extension of the underlying standard for the protection of life.

changing circumstances. When the Bundestag changes statutes, it is doing what it ought to do. But when a court changes standards, it has a problem.

One does not need clairvoyant powers to predict that the period of grand standards is past. For the general-abstract, coherent constitutional interpretation of the "C.I." sections conveys ever less the complete picture. The future belongs to the small standards, that is, the contextual differentiation of the predetermined into classes and sub-classes of cases. The methodological home for this, however, is the subsumption section. But as this section tends to become more important, the doctrine of the Karlsruhe's Court also becomes unmanageable. "C.II.": this is where the action is! And it is, in fact, [217] the section decisions and no longer the Senate judgments where the current doctrine first becomes evident (cf., e.g., Höfling/Rixen 2000). From 2004 until 2010, the Federal Constitutional Court published a selection of its section decisions (BVerfGK) in a newly founded official collection alongside the Senate decisions (BVerfGE). Since then, selected section decisions appear on the Court's official website. That is not accidental, but instead shows how the emphasis of doctrine has shifted.

B. Functional sub-standards in the liberty rights

We have already observed for quite some time how highly differentiated sub-standards have developed. The standards for freedom of assembly migrated into the subsumption section; the decisive factor is found almost exclusively in the section decisions (cf. Hoffmann-Riem 2011, RN 19–85). The constitutional protection of property, to name another example, also depends on which role the property plays in the individual exercise of freedom and which social aspects the object of property displays (cf. in more detail Badura 1994, RN 76; Wieland 2004, RN 27). We encounter graduated standards, which rise and fall with the social and individual reference points of the object of property. This can be formulated as a rule of thumb. In practice, this leads to a highly differentiated property law doctrine, in which real estate, share ownership in the means of production, or the property of legal entities are protected less than the property in moveable goods, for example (cf. BVerfGE 50, 290, 335 ff.—Codetermination (1979); analysis in Lepsius 2010d, RN 54 ff., 74 ff.). One cannot [218] speak of a unified standard in the protection of property. In fact, the law differentiates between the social and individual functions of property in terms of what is demanded by the constitution's "social obligation" of property (Art. 14, 2 GG). The absence of a unified standard in the protection of property could only be lamented if one presupposed a phenotype of property and overlooked that the legal order already set up property relations as a bundle containing highly different combinations of rights and duties. The differentiation ends only with expropriation, which is defined formally as deprivation of private use (normally of the power over disposition) (BVerfGE 58, 300 at 330 ff.—Liquid

Extraction (1981); BVerfGE 100, 226 at 243—Preservation of Historic Monuments (1999)). As a result, a graduated standard provides the foundation for constitutionally protected property, whose level of protection, however, cannot be set without consideration of the social function of property. To put it differently, the decisive legal questions do not concern the general standard of the property guarantee, but rather the differentiation and delimitation of the classes of cases. The doctrine on the freedom of profession yields a similar picture. Here, we also encounter graduated standard formation, which is differentiated according to the choice and exercise of profession, according to earnings for the purpose of individual subsistence, and according to general equality of opportunity for acquisition (competition). Again one can ask whether the Federal Constitutional Court (or even the literature on constitutional law) succeeds in expressing the differentiation of the level of protection which is derived from the application to specific instances of earning activity, in the form of a standard. Basically, the rule of thumb [219] for the protection of property applies here as well: the higher the relevance for individual freedom, the higher the protection of profession and earnings.

The non-juristic reader may not be surprised that the protection depends on the significance of the Basic Right for the guarantee of the freedom of the individual and increases with the rising significance of the individual liberty. This all-around sensible statement, however, does not easily lend itself to be reflected in standards. For it makes the standard dependent on a criterion, which cannot be determined in general-abstract terms: the role of the law for the liberty of the individual. The criterion decisive for the case may be formulated normatively only in a manner that is highly generalized, but, therefore, not easily cast in concrete terms. The real challenge is to differentiate among generalizable criteria for enhanced and reduced Basic Rights protection. But even the differentiation of such classes of cases must remain open to the circumstances of the individual case. So, for example, the freedom of profession must be guarded more firmly, because the individual's existential implications are more obvious than those of the earning activity of legal persons. In corporations, for example, there is only indirect control of the individual (if at all in associations or foundations). Since standard formation is primarily oriented toward normative characteristics, only with difficulty can it incorporate such functional and social differentiations.

C. Standards in the law of state organization

Thus far we have examined standards derived from the Basic Rights. But how does it stand with [220] standards in the part of the Basic Law concerning the law of state organization, the legislative process, and separation of powers? Here we see quite a contrary picture. Standards do not play much of a role there, and that says something about the quality and the deficiencies of standards. One thinks about the attempt of the Second Senate to find a standard in Art. 68 GG for the issue of whether the Federal Chancellor's motion of confidence is permissible if it is only posed for the purposes of bringing about new elections, even though the government is supported by a parliamentary majority. In 1983, the Court made a stab at a standard by deciding that a motion of confidence that is directed only at the dissolution of parliament presupposes as an "unwritten operative fact" of Art. 68 GG that the Federal Chancellor cannot rely on the ongoing support of a majority in the Bundestag (hence BVerfGE 62, 1 at 42—Dissolution of the Bundestag (1983)). In particular, the Federal Constitutional Court had in mind the statements of the FDP fraction in the Bundestag, which in the Court's view justified Chancellor Helmut Kohl's assessment that he could not be certain of the votes of the FDP, even though this party had just left the old, joined the new coalition and elected Helmut Kohl Chancellor. The Court evaluated in detail results of mid-term elections to Länder parliaments and resolutions at party conventions (BVerfGE 62, 1 at 50–62) in order to affirm the fulfillment of its own prerequisites and to declare constitutional the dissolution of the German Bundestag just weeks before its reelection. The 1983 standard involving unwritten factual indicators of ongoing support of a parliamentary majority no longer played a role in the 2005 decision on the dissolution of the Bundestag in response to the no-confidence vote of Chancellor Gerhard Schröder directed at mere dissolution (critical, therefore, the dissenting vote of [221] Jentsch, BVerfGE 114, 121 at 174–7—Dissolution of the Bundestag (2005)). In the 2005 decision, the Senate accepts as sufficient "the justified assessment of the Chancellor that the Federal Government's capacity to act is compromised by the majority relations in parliament" (BVerfGE 114, 121 at 162). The Court abandoned the substantive contours of the 1983 standard. With the fact-finding means at the Court's disposal, the Senate's principal argument ran, it could not reach conclusive findings regarding the Chancellor's alleged loss of his parliamentary majority (BVerfGE 114, 121 at 155). In 2005, the Senate was no longer confident it could do what it did in 1983. Certainly, Schröder's approach that came out of the blue was not as transparent as the situation in 1983, when the coalition breach by the FDP was thoroughly documented. Instead, the Senate forfeited the standard of review and substituted it with respect for the matching statements of the Chancellor, Bundestag, and the Federal President.[29]

However one may judge these decisions on their merits, they nevertheless demonstrate the boundaries of standard formation in the law of state organization. The legal problems in this area do not lend themselves to substantive review, for they

[29] Moreover, the decision is internally contradictory, because it demands that the decision of the Federal Chancellor must be supported by facts (BVerfGE 114, 121 at 160), but leaves these facts to the Chancellor's prognosticating assessment. The significance of the factual circumstances for the no-confidence vote directed at dissolution is duplicated and, in this case, answered differently. The decision is often criticized (cf., e.g., Schenke 2006; Schoch 2006; Ipsen 2007; in principle correct, also the dissenting opinion of Jentsch, BVerfGE 114, 121 at 170–81).

involve conflicts of competence, jurisdictions of constitutional organs, and procedural questions. Moreover, they cannot be dissolved from their respective political interests, as the [222] non-analogous decision of 1983 concerned with the coalition breach by the FDP shows. A standard derived from that situation cannot be carried over to the entirely different political context of 2005 and the different political motives of the Federal Chancellor as initiator of the procedure. As a result, the formation of the standard fails due to the unsuitability of the legal dispute for substantive resolution as well as due to the contexts, which simply cannot be explained away.

This observation repeats itself when we think about other legal questions in the law of state organization, which actually lend themselves in principle to resolution by standards. Consider the *Wesentlichkeitslehre* ("fundamentality test"), a doctrine that assigns specific areas to legislative action and forecloses executive rulemaking in those areas. This doctrine allocates the rulemaking power between the legislative and executive branches; it was one of the most discussed problems of German constitutional law from the seventies to the nineties (cf. Staupe 1986; Lerche 2009, RN 54 ff.). There is, indeed, ample case law, yet the Federal Constitutional Court did not produce a generalizable standard. It identified the relevant areas reserved for legislation with a view to their relevance for the Basic Rights. Therefore, the Court requires regulation by parliamentary statute, not executive ordinances, in all areas with relevance for individual rights. The Court, however, did not manage to answer which subjects are supposed to be addressed by parliamentary statute and which policy issues may be regulated by executive rulemaking and ordinance. It decided on a case-by-case basis: sometimes a statute was required, sometimes an ordinance sufficed. Obviously, it did not reach the twofold question concerning, first, which rules to produce, to guarantee accordingly in an organizational sense, to legitimize democratically, and to clarify in a theoretically satisfying framework and, second, by which authority (legislative, executive, but also judicial lawmaking) to do so. The issue is governed by a test which keeps in mind the Basic Rights of those who are affected by the rules in questions tending to contextual answers. For example, the Court affirmed the fundamentality of sex education in schools so that a statute was required for its regulation, while it denied the fundamentality of the spelling reform, which thus could be implemented by circular decrees. A further negative example of failed standard formation would be the definition of the delegation [223] requirements of Art. 80, 1, 2 GG. In this instance, the Court had only limited success interpreting the relevant features of the provision, requiring the legislature to outline the "content, purpose, and extent" of executive rulemaking in the delegating statute (see Nierhaus 1997). Naturally, other issues of the law of state organization, such as, for example, the division of powers between the federal and Länder levels, the legislative process, or the need for consent to federal statutes, elude materialization with the aid of standards. The boundaries of standard formation become evident just when the jurisdictional and institutional aspects become relevant, and that is typically the case in the law of state organization. Standard formation then conceives the legal problem in substantial terms, but not in its entirety.

The surprising thing about this ultimately obvious insight—that standards do not work well in the law of state organization—is quite another matter. In the Federal Constitutional Court's case law record, the entire area of the law of state organization is astonishingly free of theory; one could also say that it remains amorphous (cf. Lepsius 2004, 376–81). As radiant as the doctrine is in the realm of Basic Rights theory, it is just as pale in the law of state organization. Opportunities to develop such a theory, making clear which actions by which powers with which forms of action,[30] whether this results from the rule of law, federalism considerations, or democratic theory, are rarely found,[31] with one important exception, [224] specifically, the theory of the chain of legitimation ("Legitimationskette") referring to the question of the democratic legitimation of state action.[32] As oriented toward standards as the Federal Constitutional Court is when the Basic Rights are involved, when a materialization is possible, it therefore proceeds just as well without standards when such an approach is not relevant. In this circumstance, we encounter a casuistry largely without orientation points, which instead orients itself mostly around individual cases and constitutional practice. Consider, for example, a decision from the year 2005, where the Court conceded to the Bundestag the right to issue ordinances in certain cases, which, in turn, equipped the Bundestag with a form of action that constitutionally belongs to the executive branch [225] (BVerfGE 114, 196—Amendment Decree (2005); for critique, see Möllers 2007), and adapted it as a central argument in state practice. Meanwhile, it is used in precisely this way. Understood as a negative, contrasting

[30] Ehmke (1963, 89) had already called for this, though he turned against a substantial interpretation of the constitution that ends in a closed system, and urged instead the incorporation of state law considerations, especially those stemming from the principle of democracy, into the interpretive technique (functional-legal constitutional principles) (on this last point, also Heun 1992). Schulze-Fielitz (1997, 9) termed the Federal Constitutional Court a "functional-legal border-crossing commuter."

[31] A dictum from the year 1984 achieved passing popularity. [224] In it, the Federal Constitutional Court paternalistically lectured the Green party, which had just joined the Bundestag, about why its desire for the Bundestag to institute a statutory regulation for the rearmament with Pershing missiles was doomed to failure. The constitutional law literature later gave this highly context-dependent statement a life of its own and stylized it to an oft-cited organizational theory of the Federal Constitutional Court. In the rearmament decision, BVerfGE 68, 1 at 86 (1984), the Court declared that the organizational and functional distinction and separation of authorities normatively set by Art. 20, 2 GG facilitates in particular the distribution of political power and responsibility as well as the control of the bearer of power; the principle aims at state decisions being as proper as possible, that is, made by the organs that are best positioned for this according to their organization, composition, function, and procedure, and it intends to exercise a moderating influence on state authority in general. In practice, however, this dictum of the Federal Constitutional Court, cast in general-abstract terms, led to a privileging of the executive at the expense of the Bundestag and was already, therefore, unpersuasive constitutionally.

[32] Hardly any theme has occupied the law of state organization in the last twenty years as this one has. It was initiated by doctrine traceable to Böckenförde (1987) in BVerfGE 83, 37—Right to Vote by Foreigners in Schleswig-Holstein (1990) and in BVerfGE 83, 60—District Assemblies Hamburg (1990). In the meantime, the once clear principles have become more flexible and lost their normative edge (cf., e.g., BVerfGE 107, 59—Water Association (2002)). On the stringency of the theory of the chain of legitimacy, see Jestaedt 1993.

template for the formation of standards, this decision is still ironically consistent in that it stems from a constitutional court: one can expect little understanding for the hierarchical structure in an ordinary legal order and the need to assign statutes and ordinances to different powers (as expressions of the different forms of action by the parliament and the administration) from a constitutional court whose approach to the formation of standards works to a considerable degree by lowering the hierarchy of norms (standards as intermediate norm, constitution-conforming interpretation of ordinary law, legal control even of constitutional amendments through meta-standards).

At any rate, in the realm of the law of state organization, the Federal Constitutional Court displays a remarkable reserve viz-à-viz the inherent logic of the political process. It trusts here in the self-control of the other constitutional organs and understands itself as one actor among several. Institutional and jurisdictional aspects express themselves as restraint in the control intensity, however, without these resting on a theory of institutions or an understanding of competence with underpinnings in democratic theory. Rather, practical considerations permit the Federal Constitutional Court to exercise restraint in the law of state organization. One could also say that it is the inability to treat certain legal problems with standards that then leads it to respect the political process.

In regard to the political process, the doctrine shows a Janus-faced countenance. If the actions of the political process have implications for the Basic Rights, the Federal Constitutional Court makes recourse to an extremely standard-bound form of legal control, in [226] which the inherent logic of politics can hardly be taken into account in a constitutional theory sense. That may appear plausible from the perspective of a form of Basic Rights review that is favorable to liberty, but it leaves questions unanswered in regard to an institutional understanding that has concerns beyond any implications for Basic Rights. For usually, the Court will review the actions of state organs differently, when they do not infringe on Basic Rights. Then, there tends to be a lack of standards for issues in the law of state organization, so that respect among organs and powers takes on greater significance. That also means that among state organs, the lawmaking parliament is subjected to a more stringent standard of review than other powers, because the typical form of action by parliament is the statue, and, according to the Elfes decision, thus a limitation of Basic Rights. Ultimately, the capacity for developing standards decides the issue of the intensity of judicial scrutiny, that is, the extent to which legal questions lend themselves to substantialization and decontextualization. On the contrary, the Court did not explicitly develop a theory of institutions grounded in a theoretical distribution of powers, with which the extensiveness of review could be related not only to Basic Rights and constitutional reference points generally, but rather also to the democratic aspects of an issue and to those having to do with the fitness of specific institutions to decide specific issues (cf. Möllers 2005, 398 ff.; cf. for the European Union Roland 2008; Möllers 2008b, 172 ff.).

Such an approach would offer the opportunity, for example, to differentiate the review standard according to the different procedures before the Court. One could apply the review standard more strictly to constitutional complaints than in abstract norm control cases, because the former serves subjective legal protection, because the facts had been processed in detail by the lower courts, and because the individual involvement assured a proportionality review of the Basic Right in question. In the abstract norm control procedure reviewing statutes, by contrast, the concrete effect of the provision [227] can only be conceived hypothetically, so that proportionality review by necessity must be grounded on nonspecific assumptions. In any case, the necessary factual basis (suitability, necessity) for the proportionality test is mostly absent, and the reviewable Basic Right infringements lack the necessary concretization of the affected legal interests (appropriateness). The consequence must be that in constitutional complaints the extensiveness of review is more thoroughgoing than in the abstract norm control procedure, and that in the concrete norm control procedure it occupies an intermediary level. Such a distinction would generate opportunities for procedural law, as the standard of review for Basic Rights permits bonding with the respect of a constitutional organ for parliament that is rooted in the separation of powers and the democratic principle. However, the Federal Constitutional Court blocked such an approach when, in the Elfes decision, it adapted the constitutional complaint to the review of statutes and adhered to the objective quality of legal protection for the constitutional complaint. With the received approach oriented toward standards, such a differentiation between judicial review procedures and constitutional complaints would be hardly possible, whether dictated by the law of state organization or concerns for the constitutional process. Specifically, what has grown together through the use of standards must be separated procedurally by reference to the substantive legal effects: subjective and objective constitutional law.

D. Development of new standards

Let us turn to fields where the technique of standard formation bears riper fruit. Since the Court [228] has already established standards for most constitutional questions, there is rarely the opportunity to create new ones. With the ongoing extension and reinforcement of standards, the flexibility and dynamism of doctrine necessarily diminishes. Seldom does the Court come upon an unplanted field, on which it can blithely sow standards. Sometimes, it can harvest anyway. Two more recent examples may illuminate the problem and practice of the creation of new standards.

Let us consider first of all the Treaty of Lisbon case, in which the Second Senate derived a new standard for the limits of transference of sovereignty to the European Union from a Basic Law-based elaboration of the democratic principle (BVerfGE

123, 267 at 340 ff (2009)); see also Möllers in this volume 191–2. Here the Court established a new standard and distanced itself from the argumentation of the Maastricht decision (BVerfGE 89, 155 at 182 ff. (1993)), which was based more firmly on the sovereignty of the member states. In the Treaty of Lisbon decision, it carried over the then reigning sovereignty concept to the democratic principle and declared both as the boundary of permissible delegation.[33] In the course of the text, the judgment's reasoning took on ever more emphatically the style of a state theory for the twenty-first century developed out of the democratic principle. Georg Jellinek would have been delighted. Such rather broad creations of principle must be conceived as an independent constitutional amendment of the Karlsruhe Court, when it is not possible to disguise it as the updating of received standards. Ergo the Treaty of Lisbon decision was especially fiercely criticized for its strategy (cf., e.g., Grimm 2009a; [229] Halberstam/Möllers 2009; Schönberger 2009). Matthias Jestaedt (2009b, 503) even speaks of a "wondrous proliferation of standards."

In the Treaty of Lisbon decision, the Court took the additional step of claiming the authority for protecting the constituent power of the people. The violation of a constitutional identity established in the eternity clause of Art. 79, 3 GG is a trespass on the constituent power of the people, because the alteration of fundamental constitutional principles is not included in the power of the legislature. When we read the self-confident statement in the Treaty of Lisbon decision, "the Federal Constitutional Court watches over it" (BVerfGE 123, 267 344 (2009)), then this statement can also be understood in this way in regard to the conflict of powers between the constitution-amending legislature and the people creating a new constitution: the Court protects the power of a people that exists only in constitutional theory, namely that of the *pouvoir constituant*. However, this is not conceivable in constitutional law terms. Constitutional law cannot regulate the constituent power of the people, for the constitution is the product of a previous *pouvoir constituant*. The legitimacy of the constitution always stands normatively under the Damocles sword of a revolutionary act of new constitution-making. However, the Karlsruhe Court only has the existing, currently valid constitutional order to thank for its existence and competence. In terms of constitutional law, the concept of the people is limited to the *pouvoir constitué*. There the people is always a group of individuals with specific rights. As *pouvoir constituant* the concept of the people belongs to constitutional theory, but it is not part of the constitution itself. Here the concept of the people remains an abstract category of an imaginary collective. The mental construct of the Court's notion becomes coherent with one unspoken premise: the Constitutional Court became what is a trustee of the *pouvoir constituant*.[34] That would certainly be as if the child arranged the birth of his or her grandparents. [230]

[33] On the revised sovereignty argument, see Grimm 2008, 108–23.

[34] Cf. the relatively early dictum of the former President of the Federal Constitutional Court (Benda 1979, 114): "The Federal Constitutional Court is legitimated to share the *pouvoir constituant* under the auspices of constitutional interpretation."

The *pouvoir constituant*, however, needs no protection from the Constitutional Court, because its power derives from a revolutionary act. The Court, therefore, cannot bind the democratic principle in the sense of the eternity clause with the constituent power of the people, for Art. 79, 3 GG can only mean the people in its function as *pouvoir constitué*, but not a people in its function as *pouvoir constituant*, because this precedes the constitution, and with it the normative claims of Art. 79, 3 GG. What the Court presents here as interpretation of the democratic principle in the sense of the eternity clause, in fact turns out to be a strategy of self-empowerment. One awards oneself the power of the last word at the expense of other constitutional organs, claiming a concept of the people for support, which the Basic Law cannot regulate at all. Otherwise, the Basic Law must be able to pull itself out of the swamp by its own hair like Baron Münchhausen; failing that it must achieve what is impossible in norm theoretic terms, specifically, to set the legitimacy of the constitution in the constitution itself. Here, the incriminating position from the Lisbon Decision illuminates one thing, namely, that an externally directed duty to control, which is rooted in the vague, if not nebulous, formulation of "identity of the constitution," is a new creation of the Constitutional Court, which not only surpassed the already very principled formulation of Art. 79, 3 GG ("the principles laid down in Articles 1 and 20") in terms of openness, but rather also substituted constitutional psychology cloudiness for it.

In another case that is substantively not less controversial, the Senate conceals the overturning of its decision behind a supposedly well-established [231] standard, which, however, only at first sight resulted from the proffered self-quotations. I am speaking here of the Hartz IV Unemployment Benefits decision of 2010 (see also Möllers in this volume, 182–3). There the Court justified for the first time an unmediated constitutional entitlement to the guarantee of a minimum standard of living. The First Senate derived this monetary entitlement from the human dignity of Art. 1, 1 GG conceived as a Basic Right in connection with the social state principle of Art. 20, 1 GG, which ranks among the purely objective provisions of the Basic Law. The human dignity principle operates as a foil for the social state mandate by establishing an actionable subjective claim. This (new) Basic Right has an autonomous significance as an entitlement in the form of a claim to concrete (monetary and nonmonetary) benefits (BVerfGE 125, 175 at 222 (2010)).

The justificatory technique is illuminating. First, the Court repeats its allegedly established standards. Previous decisions cited for this purpose, however, formulated the state's obligation to guarantee a minimum standard of living only as an objective command, not as a Basic Rights claim.[35] The central innovation

[35] The Court even quoted (BVerfGE 125, 175 at 222): BVerfGE 40, 121 at 133 (1975); BVerfGE 45, 187 at 228 (1977); BVerfGE 82, 60 at 85 (1990); BVerfGE 113, 88 at 108 f. (2005); BVerfGE 123, 267 at 362 f (2009). Yet none of these earlier decisions acknowledges a Basic Rights claim. The last of these cited decisions, the Treaty of Lisbon decision, formulates the duty of the state to provide living conditions for its citizens that meet the standards of human dignity. All of the cited decisions stress the principle of legislative discretion.

of the Hartz IV decision is the conversion of the state's objective into a subjective legal claim of the bearer of Basic Rights. This outcome, however, cannot be derived from previous decisions. It does not become clear how a frequent shifting back and forth between the [232] objective aspects of Art. 1, 1 GG and Art. 20, 1 GG as well as the subjective law interpretation of the human dignity provision can produce a Basic Rights claim to social benefits. But it is precisely this that has to be meticulously justified. Instead, the Federal Constitutional Court lists the asserted principles one after another, but ultimately does not prove the newly created legal results (cf. BVerfGE 125, 175 at 222–4—Hartz IV (2010); for criticism see Rixen 2010b). The central assertion that the claim to benefits is provided by the constitution, even if there is no legislation in place, is justified with a decision that just does not support the outcome.[36] The decontextualization of the prior decisions used in the Court's reasoning facilitates their utilization in a new problem set and conceals what remains in dire need of justification. It makes possible the alleged transfer of standards to new case constellations. These standards, however, stem from an entirely different institutional context (binding the legislature instead of the judiciary) and different Basic Rights features (the positive dimension of the Basic Rights instead of their defensive one). All the sins of standard formation appear to climax here: subjectification of objective law, objectification of subjective law, unclear substantive basis in the text, nontransparency of the case constellations in the elaboration of earlier standards, negation of the institutional contexts, and substantivization of the legal questions exhibiting the necessary prerequisites in terms of jurisdiction and the law of state organization. Certainly, [233] the Court's shifting interpretation of Art. 1, 1 GG, where in one sentence it highlights subjective suability and in another the objective state services dimension of the provision, facilitates this sloppy practice. Here, a standard is not elaborated contextually by way of precedents, but rather by appeals to fundamental constitutional principles (human dignity, social state), which lowers the reasoning. How can one assess such a legal finding of the Federal Constitutional Court in terms of its constitutional binding force? Does the principle of human dignity become a judicial joker card? What degree of contextual binding force may one expect from the doctrine of the Federal Constitutional Court? Neither the constitutional text nor constitutional doctrine provides further assistance. And that is completely symptomatic of the establishment of new standards.

[36] BVerfGE 125, 175 at 224 refers to BVerfGE 107, 275 at 284—Benetton Shock Ad II (2003). There, the "claim to benefits" is directed toward an advertising ban according to the general clause of section 1 of UWG (*Gesetz gegen den unlauteren Wettbewerb*), a provision concerning unfair competition. The cited case is not comparable because it (1) requires action of the administrative or judicial branches, but not, as in the Hartz IV case, the legislative branch, and (2) requires the protection of the classical, liberal, and defensive dimension of the Basic Rights, not the financial support of the state.

E. Problems with proportionality

We saw that the advantage of the proportionality principle is its ability to present substantively divergent decisions methodologically as the expression of overlapping structural constitutional principles. In other words, to reconcile casuistry and doctrine, results and standards with one another, to take account of individual circumstances of the case and permit exceptions without adversely affecting the unity of the legal order. Admittedly, the proportionality principle does not always work. There are limits to the standard technique on level "C.II." Numerous types of cases preclude the application of the proportionality principle. Entire areas of the law do not lend themselves to a means–end review, because [234] there is typically only one means for the achievement of the goal.

Tax law comes to mind. There is only one means of meeting the state's financial needs: taxes. The suitability and appropriateness of the means do not lend themselves to review, and the appropriateness test would presuppose verification of the use of the taxes, which contradicts its own nature and interferes in the budgetary sovereignty of parliament.[37] One encounters limits even in criminal law: The justification of punishments has been a controversial topic for centuries. The Siblings Incest decision of the Federal Constitutional Court illustrates the problems arising from the interrelationship of punishment and its purpose. If one applied the proportionality principle strictly in the case of the siblings' incest, there would have been no justification for the imprisonment of the incestuous brother, because there would have been no purpose that sufficiently outweighed the infringement of personal freedom. This calculable outcome and the subsequently predictable general excitement that would have resulted if the Court declared imprisonment in incest cases unconstitutional moved the Senate to settle the case with a sense of decency solidly in place since the time of Hammurabi. Obviously, recourse to the standards of the Basic Law does not take one any further here.[38] The application of proportionality encounters further problems associated with the general clauses (Wißmann 2008, 231 f.), because the facts do not allow the unambiguous determination of either the purpose or the means. We have already referred to the dependence of facts and empirical expositions in the review of suitability and necessity. This particularly produces problems if statutory requirements take into account anticipated developments. Finally, the review of appropriateness confronts great difficulties when too many [235] conflicting legal interests are involved and when no diametrically opposed rights are at issue. Legislation on security matters falls just as readily in this category as does economic regulation. Especially in the

[37] Cf. on a tax law case Lepsius 2015, see further in this volume 120–1.

[38] BVerfGE 120, 224—Incest (2008). The alternative becomes clear in the dissenting opinion of the Senate's President Hassemer, Professor of Criminal Law (at 255 ff.), who investigated the case logically for its proportionality and came to the conclusion that the incest provision was unconstitutional.

area of economic regulation, the legislature pursues several goals simultaneously (high level of service provision, universal provision of service, lower cost, effective competition) and employs a number of different means at the same time (access to a network, business and administrative duties, tariff control, supervisory, organizational, and procedural duties). Such bundles of means–ends complicate considerably the review of appropriateness (Lepsius 2010d, RN 74 ff.). The Federal Constitutional Court can at most become involved in a comprehensive assessment, but then it must make decisions on social values and would find itself in a genuine political field, namely that of compromise.

Conversely, one can maintain that this field is especially favorable for the proportionality review of legal questions amenable to that form of judicial scrutiny. Typically, these are conflicts involving opposing legal positions without precedential or empirical ambiguities, therefore, generalizable conflicts of interests between legal subjects. Numbered among these are private law questions as well as classical fields of the interventionist state and the citizen, but not conflicts of interests among several parties, distributional issues under social law, or the regulations in economic law as well as general precedential decisions. But that is where the relevant political themes are: distributional conflicts. This presents problems for the Federal Constitutional Court: It cannot maintain as easily the logical consistency and strictness with which the proportionality principle was applied before. Either the Court develops new approaches to the [236] subsumption problem, or it withdraws certain types of issues from intensive judicial scrutiny, opting instead for a form of review focusing on abuse or arbitrariness. In each case, the previous judicial orientation need be scrutinized according to one-sided substantive legal standards with the consequence that the Court has to answer the question of the legitimation of its actions all over again. These issues can no longer be addressed simply with reference to a substantive constitutional obligation. Supplementary considerations of an institutional and jurisdictional nature and derived from democratic theory are unavoidable, if one does not want to end up politicizing the institution and the selection of judges and answer the question of who watches the watchers with a response beyond the psychology of judges.

But even in regard to "classic" issues (normatively generalizable conflicts with only two opposing interests), the question arises whether unanimity of results expected by the proportionality principle can still be guaranteed. Voices in the literature complain in any case that the inordinate use of the proportionality principle has already led to an exaggerated casuistry (Merten 2009, RN 2). That is illustrated by the growing significance of the section decisions, in which legal development is taking place in many areas of the law, from freedom of association to the protection of intellectual property, because the underlying standards can no longer be elaborated normatively and any necessary adaptation is achieved casuistically.

VI. Standards or Precedents?

One could claim that this demonstrates a structural feature of high courts. The connection to a norm, which is loosened in practice, can be supplemented by an orientation toward the distinct decisions and sometimes substituted by it. Instead of allegiance to the constitution, there is allegiance to constitutional interpretation. Precedents then guarantee the predictability and rationality of the decision. Can adjudication oriented toward standards be understood as a form of the law of precedent? Does not the Federal Constitutional Court face the same problem as other high courts, and does it not react to this problem with similar means?

If this throws into question the distinctiveness and originality of the Federal Constitutional Court, one is inclined to answer yes. In fact, there is a considerable difference between the setting of standards, on the one hand, and reasoning with precedents, on the other, as the approach of other courts demonstrates, above all those in the common law world. One thinks here especially of the U.S. Supreme Court). Why can standards not be understood and utilized as precedents?

A. Meaning of facts in legal reasoning

The Federal Constitutional Court reduces the binding force of its previous decisions by editing out the application factual circumstances on the normative level. The obligation does not depend on a comparison of facts, but rather on a normative consensus. It is defined first of all [238] in a substantive legal and general-abstract sense, while in the United States it is cast primarily in terms of jurisdiction and procedural law, therefore, in an individual and concrete sense (cf. Lepsius 2007, 320–6). In the United States, legal norms are not treated in a general-abstract way, but rather in an institutional perspective. Rules are to be understood in reference to their origin and application; they do not exist apart from the contexts of their political and institutional origin. Only with great difficulty can one identify timeless, comprehensive, or transpersonal purposes of norms. In these instances, Americans speak of principles, which first take effect when they are broken down into concrete case norms. When the U.S. Supreme Court invokes its precedents, their (self-)binding force depends not only on the normative assertions presented there, as tends to be the case with the Federal Constitutional Court, but rather the decisive issue is whether the previous set of facts is comparable to the facts of the present case.[39] Only with a factual analogy may the comparable application be subsumed under the normative statement, for the norm had, indeed, been formed for

[39] For an early comparison of the functional legal interpretive principles of the Federal Constitutional Court and the U.S. Supreme Court, see Ehmke 1963, 72–7; Großfeld/Roth 1995; Kau 2007, 408–22. For a comparison of the European Court of Justice and the U.S. Supreme Court, see Höreth 2008.

the resolution of a certain factual issue. Therefore, one questions whether the conflict of interests is identical. Have the parameters changed? Empirical investigations play an important role here (cf. Rosen 1972; Monahan/Walker 2010; see also Lepsius 1997, 143–63, 239–51; more generally Mertz 2008). But in the framework of the factual analogy, normative questions, *policy issues*, are also considered. What effects does the [239] precedent have, and how are these effects to be evaluated in reference to the case to be decided? Normative aspects (effectiveness, purposefulness, distribution of power, need for change), therefore, are integrated in the retrospectively directed analysis of the case materials. That has the advantage of not degenerating into abstract discussions of norms and values. Instead, it is possible to consider normative issues in a social, economic, and political setting, in other words, in an identifiable framework. This framework is provided by the facts of the precedent. The context is historically given and, therefore, can be handled on an empirical basis.

This interest in the origins of precedents and the contextual conditions for their effectiveness also has consequences for the internal politics of the legal profession. If a considerable portion of the discussion of the binding force of precedents involves factual issues, jurists lose their exclusive right of access. For in contrast to legal norms, everyone can contribute to a discussion of facts. That also explains the high status that interdisciplinary approaches enjoy in American legal scholarship (cf. Lepsius 2007, 335–40). Historical analyses, sociological considerations, psychological evaluations, economic valuations, all can be relevant for the treatment of the factual context, which decide the normative relevance of the precedent in the result.

As a consequence, pure forms of normative interpretation have not taken hold in the United States. If a court limits itself to purely normative considerations, its decisions will find a limited reception. It would be received as suspect, because the conflicts of interests remain concealed behind the interpretation of norms. Hence, Americans feel a healthy mistrust of abstract normative presentations. In their eyes, [240] what in Germany is understood and valued as the expression of depoliticization, rationality, and allegiance to the constitution seems to be disguised politics.

Another difference is evident. American decisions are composed individually with a personal style. The opinion names the author, and the judges address one another by name. Affirming and diverging viewpoints (concurring and dissenting opinions) are typical. One debates openly, engaging the positions of colleagues on the Court and seeking opposing arguments. Especially on the Supreme Court, the judgment's reasoning fragments occasionally, because a consensus is only achievable by compromising on particular sections of the opinion. Not infrequently, justices will vote with different majorities. They participate in a legal interpretation of the majority in one section, and then join the minority in another. The predictability of decision-making suffers under such an approach. But that is not an insurmountable problem for a case law-based legal culture, because normative discourse is not conducted in a general-abstract manner, but rather ever more novel factual situations are decided on the basis of existing precedents.[40]

B. Attaining majorities and compromises among justices

A different decision-making style is cultivated in Karlsruhe: judgments are not authored. Occasionally, not always, the alignment of majorities is made public, though not broken down individually by name. Justices decide in secret deliberation according to the content of the arguments and evidence (Section 30, 1 BVerfGG). The Senate always decides, not an individual. This lends the decision a depersonalized character. "The Basic Law speaks, not the judge," is a valid characterization of this attitude. The fact that dissenting opinions, the publication of which has been permissible since 1970,[41] figure as only carefully calculated exceptions contributes to the objectification of decisions (cf. Lamprecht 1992; Kau 2007, 472–83). One finds the pros and cons of the Senate deliberations built into the reasoning of the judgment. If one calls out justices of the Federal Constitutional Court for inconsistencies, meanderings, or something simply obsolete (*obiter dicta*) in their judgments, one receives an answer in confidence that one should be forgiving, because it is due to the requirements of majority formation in the Senate. The case reporter (*rapporteur*) prepares the vote on the decision, makes the rounds to achieve a majority for his or her vote, and seeks a compromise for this purpose. That is understandable in view of the decision-making in the Senate. The division of the decision into the standards and subsumption sections also eases the production of majorities, because fundamental consensus can be cultivated in the standards section [242], while in the United States the case itself is sometimes decided by detailed considerations, which are carefully sculpted for this purpose.[42] In other words, the Court in its decision-making ultimately stands under the same need to

[40] The negative effects of this approach should not be underestimated. It becomes ever more difficult for American legal scholarship to order the great number of precedents into a functioning typology ("systematize" would certainly be the false verb here). This is rarely achieved in American constitutional law in any case. The last work to achieve something like this (Tribe 2000) was no longer reworked by the author after the third edition, because such a portrayal of the valid American constitutional law no longer seemed possible to him.

[41] Allowed under the amendment of Section 30, 2 BVerfGG; put into practice for the first time by the justices Geller, von Schlabrendorff, and Rupp in BVerfGE 30, 1 at 33 ff.—Constitutional Amendment Affecting Art. 10 GG (1971). There had been prior deviations from Court decisions (BVerfGE 20, 162—Spiegel Affair (1966)), which then led to the amending of the BVerfGG.

[42] The judgment on the protection of nonsmokers offers an example (BVerfGE 121, 317 (2008), especially the dissenting opinions of justices Bryde and Masing, at 378 ff., 381 ff.). Justice Masing, e.g., complains about the conceptually attained, shifting, contradictory reasoning of his Senate. The Senate knocked a balanced concept out of the hand of the legislature and pointed the way toward an extreme solution, which was disproportionate, however, due to the absence of a balancing of interests and which conceals the risks of paternalism (on earlier paternalistic tendencies, see also Schulze-Fielitz 1997, 8 f.).

compromise as the legislature, and it operates as if it detaches itself from a general-abstract verdict on norms, whose justification, of course, may not refer to either the facts or the acting justices.

C. No precedents from Karlsruhe

This brief comparison to the legal reasoning and to the decision-making practice in the United States cannot [243] be pursued further here (on this issue, see Levi 1949; Atiyah/Summers 1987; Sunstein 1996; 1999). However, it may clarify the distinctive manner in which the Federal Constitutional Court elaborates its own doctrine, not as precedents, but rather as normative emanations of general-abstract standards. Consequently, in Germany one does not speak of precedents or leading cases of the Federal Constitutional Court. One is not interested in previous cases for the purposes of deciding a case, but rather for its contribution to the interpretation of the constitution. The model of statutory interpretation is utilized while at the same time held at arm's length, because statutes are not at issue when standards are in play. Instead, the object of interpretation is a condensation of particular doctrine put together by constitutional court justices. That is clear, for example, in the fact that there is hardly any literature in Germany on the interpretation of court decisions (cf., e.g., however, Kähler 2011). Theories of method revolve instead around the normative type of statute at issue. The Federal Constitutional Court is also implicitly indebted to this tradition. It interprets its own decisions as if they were general-abstract normative texts, in other words, as if they were statutes in a structural sense. And it can only do this because it has already formulated its decisions in the "C.I." part in the style of general-abstract norms, namely as standards.

One may refer to another idiosyncrasy. In contrast to what is practiced in this essay, the Federal Constitutional Court cites its own decisions only by the volume number of the official collection, the first page number of the decision, and finally—mostly in parentheses—the specific page references. It provides neither the year of the decision nor any information about the parties to the decision or the issues addressed. The case becomes simply a number. That is a widespread, long-standing practice in Germany [244]. The Federal High Court of Justice and the Federal Administrative Court proceed in exactly the same way, and already the *Reichsgericht* cited in this manner. Yet two important pieces of information are lost in the citation. The year of the decision is not made clear, nor is the name of the proceedings or an abbreviation of the case given. Of course, experts know what blockbuster is concealed behind codes like "6, 32," (Elfes) "7, 198," (Lüth) "39, 1," (Abortion I) or "89, 155" (Maastricht). With most other code combinations, it is not clear to them which case is behind the reference. What does "BVerfGE 81, 242" stand for, and in which year was this case decided?[43] Conversely, one may certainly ask which German jurist wants to know? The information deficit is obviously not perceived as a problem. And that is understandable. The date and facts do not convey significant information for the German jurist. In a general-abstract norm discussion it is simply not significant from which year the decision stems or which issue underlies it. Consequently, one can understand the idiosyncratic citation practice, on the one hand, as an expression of the distinctive German elaboration of doctrine and its transformation into a normative discourse analogous to statutes. On the other hand, one can evaluate it as the prerequisite of the desired dehistorization and decontextualization of the judiciary. The factual dimension is already effaced from whatever is cited and through it the dogmatic elaboration of the normative statement is ensured. General standards or formation of a system [245] naturally presuppose abstraction from the context of origin.

It also becomes evident here that in the German practice legal interpretation distinguishes itself from that of the underlying facts. It holds tightly to the norm, not to its application (Lepsius 2008b, 43–7). Interpretation is not treated institutionally and procedurally, but rather it is detached from any connection to application of the respective rule. That is also questionable, because legal norms are indeed valid abstractly, but are effective only in their concrete application. Whoever does not incorporate the effect of the norm into its concrete application reduces the legal character of norms to abstractly valid declamations. On this level, which precedes any legal effects, one can naturally concoct without risk, because no decision-making impact results from abstract statements on norms (these remain reserved for the subsumption sections).

D. Dogmatization instead of contextualization

This strategy of decontextualization and dehistorization, of which the citation practice is only the most striking example, allows the Federal Constitutional Court to render its own doctrine dogmatic (Jestaedt 2009a, 533). When, with the help of these decision-making techniques, normative statements are separated from the factual issues they once were meant to resolve, then constitutional interpretation begins to take on a life of its own in the jurisdictional authority of the Federal Constitutional Court. The Court can freely make use of the newly arising intermediary category "constitutional standard," because it is not limited in the formulation or in the [246] further development of standards by any reference to facts or type of proceeding. When this formerly competence-dissolving element

[43] BVerfGE 81, 242—Trade Representative (1990): an important decision on the third party effect of the Basic Rights in contract law, precursor of the still more famous decision BVerfGE 89, 214—Bail (1993).

is no longer at issue, because the Federal Constitutional Court declines to integrate facts into the formulation of a standards component, it is able to free itself from formal and material limitations on its competence. The citation practice of the chain of references to previous standards sections functions as a substitute for justification (cf. Jestaedt 2009a, 520–33). Indeed, the bond to the constitution remains as the central substantial limitation on competence, but in reality this bond to the constitution represents allegiance to its own standards, into which a concrete constitutional adjudication has congealed. Everything is nevertheless constitutional adjudication bound to the constitution, so that institutional conflicts over competence are superseded by the materialization of the constitutional order. Consequently, judge-made constitutional law is not an issue in Germany and has not become an idea with any currency (as deftly analyzed by Jestaedt 2005, 50–2). We also do not speak of legal development driven by constitutional justices, though it occurs often in fact.

VII. On the Future of the Standard-Setting Power

Let's look at two cases from recent doctrine with a view to what possible future the standard-setting power has today. Is everything working optimally? Or are there signs of erosion that demand auxiliary strategies? The examples are less about grand formulas, such as identity scrutiny or human dignity than the perpetuation of a comparably more differentiated doctrine. For the everyday practice of the Federal Constitutional Court, they may provide more meaningful examples than spectacular decisions like Treaty of Lisbon or Hartz IV Unemployment Benefits. At the same time, they give us an impression of the justificatory difficulties often confronting the justices in Karlsruhe. Both cases also show what obstacles the perpetuation of existing standards encounter—and which strategies the Federal Constitutional Court itself has designed, in order to preserve the standards it has developed, on the one hand, and to attain solutions to cases that are nevertheless flexible and still compatible with standards, on the other.

A. First rescue attempt: consistency and other methodological experiments

For the first example, I will make recourse to the judgment on the tax exemption for commuting costs—a decision that was received with public delight, because it reintroduced the tax deduction for travel to the workplace (BVerfGE 122, [218] 210—Commuting Allowance (2008)). The Bundestag had decided that travel should first qualify for a tax deduction after twenty-one kilometers, and offered essentially fiscal considerations as support, but also noted that it was the result of a compromise between the Federation and the Länder. The Bundestag simply needed more revenue, and sought to achieve this through a gradual elimination of tax deductions. The Federal Constitutional Court, however, did not consider purely fiscal considerations a substantive basis for making the cutoff point after twenty kilometers. When the legislature introduces the commuting allowance, it has to develop it consistently, according to the Court. The new regulation did not follow a permissible tax law principle (e.g., as discussed in German tax law doctrine, the principle of responsibility, the factory gate principle). Consequently, it was struck down as a violation of the general principle of equality under Art. 3, 1 GG. One may read the judgment as a perfectly standards-bound permeation of tax law. However, the seemingly so technical decision was not, in fact, factually convincing (for a detailed critique, see Lepsius 2009 and 2015).

The problems begin with the fact that tax laws are not reviewable in terms of their conformity with liberty rights under the Basic Law, because, first of all, taxes cannot be portrayed as restricting actions and legal positions protected under the Basic Rights and, secondly, the means–ends review under the proportionality principle is not applicable, because no less restrictive, though equally well-suited means, is available for the general financing of the state.[44] Consequently, the only available standard of review [249] is the equality principle. Insofar as it is a question of differentiations relevant to the concept of personality, the Federal Constitutional Court has not erected any higher justificatory hurdles, but rather demands merely a substantive basis of legal justification for the unequal treatment. The conflict revolves ultimately around this: which concretization requirement may the Federal Constitutional Court demand from the legislature?

Greater challenges to the equality principle are raised in factually defined areas of tax law, in order to prevent a loss of control. Since the 1990s a reservoir of tax law principles has developed, and the principles are applicable as tax-based constitutional standards for the review of equality issues (e.g., financial performance of the tax payer, objective net income principle, among others). These standards, however, are hard to derive from constitutional law, because the Basic Law treats taxes solely as an issue of legislative and administrative powers, but does not establish substantive stipulations. On the contrary, the Court extrapolates the principles from ordinary law (e.g., Income Tax Law) and then raises them to the status of constitutional law during the review of unequal treatment. Their status in the norm hierarchy is highly unclear. Why does the Federal Constitutional Court apply principles that it derived from the Income Tax Law, a parliamentary statute, to the equality principle as a constitutional discrimination standard? From where does

[44] Admittedly, all this would be disputed by the Federal Constitutional Court and parts of the literature. The Federal Constitutional Court, for example, gladly reviews the appropriateness of taxes, although the inapplicability of the proportionality principle leaves no maneuvering room for it (cf. on this legal question more narrowly, Waldhoff 2008b; Kirchhof 2000; Kirchhof 2003, 12 ff; from the perspective of legislation, Schenke 2007).

the Court derive the power to adopt the decisions of the legislature over tax burdens as constitutional standards? The consistency requirement, derived in highly general terms from the equality, rule of law, and federal state principles, serves as the central supportive argument (Kirchhof 2003, 45). This provision is a variant [250] that is more comparable to the principles maintained recently in judge-made law, with which the Court has considerably narrowed the room for the maneuvering of parliamentary legislation (consistency, duty of conceptual compliance).[45]

The Federal Constitutional Court fuses ordinary law with constitutional law here and translates decisions on political structure into constitutional standards. It develops a network of structuring provisions. The constitutional derivation (subjective or objective law), content (state organization or Basic Rights core), and status (constitutional law or statute) of these provisions remains unclear. In the review of tax laws, the Federal Constitutional Court sinks ever deeper into self-generated standards of competing and even opposing constitutional principles, and even ordinary law principles. The standards have taken on a life of their own as an alternative constitutional law, which circumvent the fundamental decisions of constitutional law (Basic Rights/law of state organization, subjective/objective law, constitution/statute).

There is hardly an area of politics where the legislature is so tightly leashed as tax law, even though one can find no substantial provisions in the Basic Law regarding taxes and the constitution has turned over the tax legislation, an area of law that is especially deeply influenced by political and economic change, to the political process. Ultimately, there is hardly any other [251] area of politics, where checks in the political process work better than in tax law, whether it is through the demands of compromise or directly through elections. Not only are electoral campaigns conducted around tax reform, but also historically the idea of representation began with tax legislation ("no taxation without representation"). The Federal Constitutional Court could, therefore, return its control in no other area of law as assuredly as tax law, especially since the application of the Basic Rights to tax law is possible only to a limited degree (only general review of equal treatment without a proportionality test).

The Court-driven constitutionalization of tax law, therefore, is not welcome in constitutional law terms, and it could only occur at the price of considerable constitutional legal denunciations in the political process. This is because it put statutes requiring compromise and subject to long-term political and economic changes under extreme pressure to display coherence, and measured them against expectations of system-wide equity, which collide with the political idiosyncrasies of tax

[45] Consistency: BVerfGE 98, 83 at 97—Hessen Garbage Law (1998); BVerfGE 98, 265 at 301—Bavarian Law for the Extension of Pregnancy Assistance (1998); duty of conceptual compliance: BVerfGE 121, 317 at 357–60—Non-Smoker Protection (2008). This doctrine is the object of intensive criticism; Masing speaks of the "risk of paternalism" (dissenting vote on BVerfGE 121, 317 at 381 ff.; from the literature Hanebeck 2002; Dann 2010, among others).

legislation. The Court sought an exit out of this tight squeeze by declaring the legislature's own principles of tax burdens to be the applicable constitutional standard. Still, this strategy was an impermissible mingling of norms from different hierarchical levels (ordinary law and constitutional law) that cannot be justified with methodological demands like consistency, non-contradiction, and conceptual compliance as expressions of substantive standards. The supremacy of the constitution is no longer being implemented here, but rather a form of systemic justice of ordinary statutory law, which finds no basis in the text of the Basic Law [252].

B. Second rescue attempt: area-specific exceptional standard

In the Wunsiedel decision of 2009, the Court ruled on the constitutionality of Section 130, 4 of the Criminal Code (Strafgesetzbuch), which the Bundestag intended to use to prohibit the annual neo-Nazi march in celebration of Rudolf Heß's birthday in the Upper Franconian town of Wunsiedel. The criminal sanction restricted the right of free expression (Art. 5, 1 GG). Such a restriction is only justifiable when the prohibition qualifies as a "general law" within the meaning of Art. 5, 2 GG. A "general law" in this sense is a provision which is not directed at the expression of opinion as such, but instead has an impact on expression that is completely independent of the content of the opinion.[46] Section 130, 4 of the Criminal Code, however, cannot be defined as a general law,[47] since the Bundestag intended it to prohibit just the march. At issue, [253] therefore, was a so-called "special law," that is, the contrary of a "general law," such that the Lex Wunsiedel would be held unconstitutional if one applied the constitutional standards properly.

Nevertheless, the case came out differently. The Federal Constitutional Court permitted a limitation on the freedom of opinion in the form of a "special law" on an exceptional basis. It sought to honor the "historically formed identity of

[46] To simplify, the issue was the refusal to make the necessary differentiations in the definition of "general law" in the sense of Art. 5, 2 GG (cf. in more detail BVerfGE 124, 300 at 322—Wunsiedel (2009)).

[47] This was disputed in the lower courts, since previously a broad interpretation of the concept of the "general law" prevailed, so that even Sections 185 and 186 of the Criminal Code (criminal liability for defamation, libel) as well as previous formulations of Section 130 of the Criminal Code (incitement to hatred, defamation of ethnic groups) had been considered general laws, because they protected a general legal interest and affected freedom of opinion only indirectly. That was long-standing doctrine (cf., e.g., BVerfGE 28, 282 at 292—Political Activity of Soldiers (1970); BVerfGE 39, 334 at 367—Political Allegiance of Civil Servants (1975); BVerfGE 47, 198 at, 232—Electoral Broadcast of the KPD/ML (German Communist Party) (1978); BVerfGE 69, 257 at 269—Electoral Broadcast of the German Center Party against abortion laws (1985); BVerfGE 90, 241 at 251—Auschwitz Lie (1994); BVerfGE 93, 266 at 291—Soldiers are Murderers (1995); BVerfGE 102, 347 at 360—Shock Ad Benetton I (2000); BVerfGE 111, 147 at 155—German National Party Assembly (2004)). As the previous court, the Federal Administrative Court had qualified section 130, 4 of the Criminal Code as a general law, since it served the "public peace" as a neutral legal interest (BVerwGE 131, 216 (2008)). The Federal Constitutional Court rejected this interpretation and narrowed its previously more broadly worded interpretation of the "general law" (cf. in more detail on this question Lepsius 2010c, 529–31; Enders 2008, 1095).

the Federal Republic of Germany" through a "distinctive constellation of circumstances that is not applicable to other conflicts" (BVerfGE 124, 300 at 329 (2009)):

> In view of the fact that the injustice and horror of the National Socialist tyranny over Europe and other parts of the world do not fit into general categories, and because the emergence of the Federal Republic of Germany was understood as an alternative to it, an exception from the prohibition of special rights for statutes directed at opinion is immanent to Art. 5, 1 of the Basic Law for provisions which set limits to the propagandistic affirmation of the National Socialist regime between 1933 and 1945 (BVerfGE 124, 300 at 327 (2009)).

The Wunsiedel decision has noteworthy consequences for the practice of standard application. The First Senate first reaffirmed the standards for freedom of opinion—even for National Socialist opinions. It upheld and narrowed the extensive concept of the "general law," which previously guaranteed flexible limitations. The "C.I." standard for freedom of opinion was made extremely strong in a general-abstract form. The Senate attempted to preemptively close all possible entryways leading to the softening of doctrine favorable to the expression of opinion and to foreclose a perforation of the protection under Art. 5, 1 GG. The Senate then waived [254] the strict standard during the subsumption phase of the case. Via a one-time exception, the Federal Constitutional Court closes an eye to Section 130, 4 of the Criminal Code. At first glance, there are neither doctrinal nor methodological grounds for the exception. It is aided only by the idea of a distinctive constitutional reservation, which is grounded in the identity of the Basic Law. The Court kisses it awake from its sixty-year slumber. The construction's historical validity is suspect, because the constitution's framers reacted explicitly to the National Socialist's arbitrary, violent rule with the provisions on militant democracy, the forfeiture of Basic Rights, or even the eternity clause, such that there is no room for a subcutaneously conceived general constitutional reservation. Above all, however, this decision verifies that the Federal Constitutional Court encounters limits in its practice of standard formation. One could maintain the standard favoring the freedom of opinion under Art. 5, 1 over the years only through an extensive interpretation of the reservation of the "general laws" clause. In time, it became ever more implausible, why abstractly formulated statutes, however factually relevant to the expression of opinion (e.g., the culpability for defamation, incitement, legal limitation of political activity of civil servants or soldiers), still qualify as "general laws." The criminal sanctions for the Heß procession rendered obvious that the incorporation of ever more limitations on expression into the category of "general laws" had become a problem. The Court reacted to this by rejecting its own standards—and humbled the Federal Administrative Court, which had applied this standard unfailingly (BVerwGE 131, 216 (2008)). One may also express this differently. The Federal Constitutional Court ensures the standard [255] when it defines the scope of the right, while it permits situation-specific exceptions under the limitation clauses. However, this is not justified by the special circumstances of the case, therefore not via a distinguishing of the facts, but rather the Court grounds it in the special circumstances of the enactment of the norm, while at the same time it asserts a constitutional reservation, otherwise slumbering since the Basic Law came into force. Such arguments can naturally first be brought into consideration once all the framers of the constitution are deceased.

C. Crossroads

Both of the more recent strategies for maintaining general standards and for finding a way out of the thicket of existing standards encounter serious objections. A considerable future problem for the Federal Constitutional Court becomes apparent here. (For an early diagnosis, see Schulze-Fielitz 1997, 25.) If one generalizes such cases, then the Court stands at a crossroads. Either it adapts its standards for specific situations, thus working with classes of cases rather than standards, or it must suspend its standards casuistically by permitting explicit exceptions. But the strategy of the Wunsiedel decision, to create new constitutional reservations from the identity of the Basic Law, works only once. By the second time at the latest, the Court runs the risk of being charged with judge-made constitutional law, in other words, being denounced for usurpation of authority and arrogance of power. This argumentative technique will not continue seamlessly and allow application to any new constellations of facts. The Federal Constitutional Court risks [256] maneuvering itself into a crisis, because its prestige, its institutional position, and the respect for its decisions were attributable to the technique of standard formation and because the bond to the (self-produced) constitutional standards represented the foundation of the Court's legitimacy.

It is necessary to develop new techniques of reasoning. Ultimately, this can only be remedied by an enhanced consideration of the factual circumstances of the case. In other words, it lies in a decision-making style which is more oriented toward precedents like that cultivated by the U.S. Supreme Court and many other high courts. However, this no longer allows the maintenance of the "C.I." and "C.II." distinction. The act of subsumption must have a direct influence on the interpretation of the constitution as the normative foundation of the decision and no longer can it be separated from it stylistically and systematically. The consequence would be an argumentative stratification of constitutional interpretations according to factual situations and their connections to issues (formation of case categories according to sets of facts). And this would presuppose that empirical, contextual, and, finally, historical facts would elucidate an important doctrinal question, for only with the precise investigation of the object of decision can one determine the future binding effect of the interpretation. Only those who actually master previous cases can predict which constitutional interpretation is suited to which set of facts. An additional consequence of this is that constitutional interpretation will not remain a purely normative pursuit, which exclusively empowers jurists (and in particular constitutional justices). Instead, it is transformed into an interdisciplinary process with a division of labor, in which social scientists must help [257] elucidate important factors. In the future, one will no longer be able to get by with constitutional *Dogmatik* or a purely normative validity discourse. For this risks leaving behind hard-won goals like the unity of the constitution, a unified theory of rights, or a substantial orientation toward the system (early critique by Ehmke 1963, 89). Constitutional interpretation will be differentiated contextually and temporally. In terms of standards, the freedom of expression of citizens will differ from that of soldiers, civil servants, or neo-Nazis (as it already is today in practical terms). The property guarantee of the freeholder or partial owner will standards-wise differ from owners of moveable property or intellectual property (as it already is practically today anyway). The solutions of the year 2020 will be quite different from those of the 1950s. These can hardly be consolidated into one standard, which can be updated over sixty, eighty, one hundred years. A temporal and contextual differentiation of constitutional interpretation should not be understood as a history of decline. That is already unavoidable on the basis of the passing of time and the dynamic quality of legal life.

Otherwise, a turning away from standards toward precedents would also ensure that German adjudication could take up international and especially European usages. Other high courts and constitutional courts are prevented from following the Federal Constitutional Court's strategy of forming standards by the historical and institutional circumstances surrounding their respective origins. Typically, courts reach decisions on the basis of a more intense casuistic approach. In other words, they rely more on precedents and formulate judgments in less abstract and general terms than the Federal Constitutional Court does. The American Supreme Court falls in this category just as does the Court [258] of Justice of the European Union in Luxemburg and, above all, the European Court of Human Rights in Strasbourg. Precedents are the more flexible form of decision, which is well adapted to dynamic legal development, because they are content with contextual limitations. If the Federal Constitutional Court orients itself more decidedly toward precedents, this would lessen the rivalry between Karlsruhe, Luxemburg, and Strasbourg. At the moment, the Federal Constitutional Court intends to mediate this conflict by cooperation with standards (cf. Kirchhof 1998; Steiner 2009; Voßkuhle 2010b, 238 f.). It will lose this battle, because its rivals do not answer with standards, but rather with precedents.[48] If the European Court of Human Rights

[48] BVerfGE 128, 326—Preventive Detention II (2011) offers a good example. In order to explain why the issue was decided entirely differently than in 2004 (BVerfGE 109, 133—Retroactive Preventative Detention I), the Senate made reference to a decision of the European Court of Human Rights, whose result the Senate claimed to be enforcing. The Federal Constitutional Court cannot admit openly

evaluates the general right of personality and freedom of the press in the case of Caroline of Hannover differently than the Federal Constitutional Court,[49] then this cannot involve disagreement about the standards. Rather, it is nothing more than a different assessment of a factually specific issue within a broader consensus in principle on the meaning of a common European Basic Rights standard. Such divergences are not resolved by drawing them into the standards, are not repaired with an interpretation that aims at producing conformity with the Convention or with common European meta-standards. Rather, [259] they should be resolved by allowing a case-related form of reasoning, which in particular assesses the right of personality differently according to the textual bases (e.g., the ratio decidendi either pertains to the tabloid press or to the freedom of the press in general; the ratio decidendi pertains either to the general right of personality in public or specifically to public persons, with the benchmark changing once children are present etc.).

D. First strategy: contextual differentiation

Therefore, what would one advise the Federal Constitutional Court to do? First, it should rethink the technique of standard formation in such a way that the context of the decision and the factual references are introduced more fully into the composition of standards. That would lead to a manner of forming standards of review that are oriented more intensely on the particular case categories and, therefore, to a differentiation at the sub-standard level, as is already apparent, today, in the adjudication of the sections. Ultimately, the Court faces the problem how to prevent the ossification of its doctrine in standards. Also, it cannot escape the historicization of its own doctrine. A sixty-year-old will not be measured by his or her youth, whether by their youthful sins or heroic deeds. The Court needs a strategy for opening more flexibility in decision-making without disrupting earlier judgments or having to smash and strangle standards. Such room for maneuvering in decision-making is best achieved through distinguishing, that is, through a stratification of normative statements in particular areas. Clearly, the problem with this is that the previous doctrine is not prepared methodologically [260] for the act of distinguishing, because it does not impart the necessary criteria for differentiation from the facts. Instead, the doctrine presents itself in terms of standards that are general and abstract. To a degree, the previous judicature must be reworked

to overturning a decision of its own. In this case, the correction of its own doctrine is justified with foreign doctrine, although the European Convention on Human Rights stands within reach of an ordinary law under the Basic Law. Now the guardian of the constitution in effect tolerates another shepherd at its side.

[49] BVerfGE 101, 361—Caroline of Hannover II (1999), on the one hand, The European Court of Human Rights, EuGRZ 2004, 404, on the other. On the problem, Merli 2007; Oeter 2007.

contextually, in order to reveal the corresponding argumentation reservoir. But the Federal Constitutional Court cannot complete this task, for it only has the competence to reach new decisions, and is simply not in a position to correct its own earlier decisions.[50] An important assignment for constitutional scholarship is to stand at the side of the Federal Constitutional Court.[51] However, that also means that the commentary on the Court must change its character fundamentally, for until now it has negated the context of the decision and understood its task as the system-oriented perfection of the material standards. The literature would be better off not setting goals for itself that run parallel to doctrine, but rather work on what the judicature itself is not in a position to do.

If one achieves new flexibility for decision-making by contextualizing and historicizing the decisions of the Federal Constitutional Court, then not only would the Court itself profit, but also even the political process would. The sheer scope of the standard-setting constitutional doctrine steadily narrows the opportunities [261] to form policy. In a five-, six-, or even seven-party parliament and with further diffusion of the combinations for political majorities, it is already becoming increasingly difficult to produce workable, sustainable compromises. Considering the present partisan circumstances and the reshaping of politics produced by European and international law, the Federal Constitutional Court must also take into account the state organs' practical and substantive capacity to act. In any case, political actors suffer from a progressive narrowing of their options for action. This has a paralyzing effect in a democracy, which draws meaning from the malleability of life circumstances and the alterability of decisions. Consequently, there is an overarching constitutional interest in achieving more decision-making for all powers, not just for constitutional adjudication. Hence, the Federal Constitutional Court should reflect the institutional decision-making context of the other powers in the intensity of its control efforts. It should not take an institutionally egoistic posture by asking only whether other organs meet the requirements of its legal control. Also, contextual *distinguishing* of constitutional doctrine helps in this regard, because the political process does not need to censor its potential actions preemptively on the basis of Constitutional Court-generated standards that are hard to render concrete. It can instead focus on the political expediency and persuasiveness of its actions. One can achieve the politically desirable relativizing of old constitutional court decisions by a contextual differentiation. Such an approach even elegantly ensures the consideration of those democratic and institutional aspects

[50] A truly rare case of the correction of its own doctrine occurred in the 2011 judgment on preventative detention. Cf. n. 48. Procedurally, this was only possible through a decision of the European Court of Human Rights that was handed down in the interim. In material terms, the Federal Constitutional Court could only correct its own standard through the adoption of that of a foreign court. The reception of the foreign standard is supported by the Court's own doctrine as an interpretation of the Basic Law that is compatible with international law.

[51] On this relationship, cf. especially Lerche 2002.

of decision-making that have hitherto been neglected. The democratic deficit of previous decision-making techniques [262] can be partially remedied without requiring a demanding democratic theory.

E. Second strategy: differentiation of competences

In addition to a contextual form of distinguishing, there is also one involving competences. The binding effect of standards should differ according to the type of legal proceeding from which the decision stems (cf. Schlaich 1981, 115). The judicial review of statutes pursues an objective goal of legal protection, whereas constitutional complaints serve the protection of subjective Basic Rights. The Federal Constitutional Court focuses the review in a correspondingly differentiated way. In constitutional complaint proceedings, the issue is the review of the injury of subjective rights, while in judicial review procedures subjective legal control is largely excluded and objective control is dominant. It is to be expected that the Court's scrutiny becomes broader in constitutional complaints, because they involve the countering of individual intrusions of Basic Rights. At the same time, the general-abstract effect of the decision in constitutional complaints decreases, because a concrete case is being decided and not the legal situation overall. It is typically different in judicial review procedures. There the Court's scrutiny will be narrower, for the abstract validity of the statute is being reviewed, not the concrete effect, and one cannot appraise the individually differentiated consequences for the most diverse dimensions of the Basic Rights without a reference to a case. On the contrary, the general-abstract binding effect of the Federal Constitutional Court decision increases, because it involves primarily the validity and not the effect of the statute. [263]

One such differentiation of the scope of review, according to the criteria of subjective/objective, general-abstract validity/individual-concrete effect that is tied to types of proceedings, is also institutionally plausible in view of the graduated obligation, which Art. 20, 3 GG imposes on the production of the law by different powers. According to the provision, administrative and adjudicative authority are both more strictly bound, for they are legally obligated by statute and law, respectively, while the legislative obligation is weaker bound under Art. 20, 3 because only the constitutional order limits the legislature. This graduated degree of obligation is transferable to the constitutional law of procedure as a tiered form of judicial review. In a norm control procedure, which is typically directed against statutes and, therefore, the legislature, there is a lower level of obligation than in constitutional complaints that are usually concerned with judgments of the inferior courts. Put differently, the constitution awards parliamentary action a larger degree of discretion than it allows judges. The Court's scrutiny should reflect the different powers' varying levels of constitutional obligation.

The Federal Constitutional Court, however, has nullified this central constitutional distinction through its standard-setting technique, while it developed the constitutional complaint into a procedure for objective legal protections, thereby smoothing out the differences from the judicial review procedure. For the scope of review, it is ultimately a matter of indifference which type of procedure provides jurisdiction. The Federal Constitutional Court operates as guardian of the constitution, not as a judicial body. It ignores the supremacy of the constitution under Art. 20, 3 GG, differentiated institutionally and in terms of a norm hierarchy, in favor of the general limitation of state action under the Basic Rights provided by Art. 1, 3. Put differently, it slights, once again, the law of state organization in favor of the Basic Rights, or the structural law in favor of the substantive law.

The irrelevance of the procedural form makes itself especially evident in [264] the formation of the standard. The procedural context simply has no effect on it. The Court ignores it even in the further elaboration of the standards. It cavalierly cites its own decisions without taking into consideration the procedural context, such that in constitutional complaints recourse is made to standards from norm control procedures and vice versa. Of course, this is not per se objectionable. But for the binding effect and range of the standards, the procedural context of the decision is important information. The central constitutional differentiations like subjective Basic Rights and objective constitutional law or the ferrying of the order of competences into the hierarchy of norms first becomes clear. Therefore, one must pay careful attention to the type of procedure and the participants in the procedure when elaborating standards. One may not, as is unfortunately the practice, search through the 140 volumes of decisions with an exclusively substantive perspective for those places that fit one's purpose precisely. Such an approach threatens to degenerate into arbitrariness in view of the overflowing reservoir of statements from the decisions in the last sixty years that could be used to formulate standards.

The differentiation of competences could even enable the Federal Constitutional Court to face a debate about its legitimation that is looming on the horizon. For it is becoming ever clearer that the standard-setting technique used till now, as well as the self-empowerment of the Court as guardian of the constitution associated with it, raises theoretical questions about legitimation. The legitimation of the Federal Constitutional Court results institutionally from the order of competences under the Basic Law (Arts. 93–94 and Art. 100), in other words, from exceptional jurisdictions, and the legitimation follows from the supremacy of the constitution, which is to say, [265] the obligation to the constitution. Standard-setting thins out both strands of legitimation, because both depend on assets of the Court, in particular on the ability of the Court's procedural leveling of types of proceedings that establish jurisdiction, on the one hand, and the redirecting of the obligation to the constitution toward the setting of standards, on the other. The Court should make use of differentiations of competences just for reasons of institutional self-protection.

In any case, with both these strategies, the contextual and jurisdictional differentiation specifically, the Federal Constitutional Court can live on as a standard-setting power, even if in modified and redirected form. This path allows it to survive the emerging legitimation claims and inquiries about its methodology. With this path the Court may find shelter in stormy times. In its present form, however, standard-setting has no future. That clarifies recent doctrine, in which more and more problems emerge in the method: differentiation of standards according to area-specific section decisions, refuge in stratospheric grand formulas like human dignity or constitutional identity, competition from European courts. But also in positive terms, the recent Karlsruhe adjudication shows how a differentiated form of standard formation can look. Just see the doctrine on modern security and anti-terror statutes after September 11, 2001. At this point, the Federal Constitutional Court arrived at a standards oriented strategy to counter effectively the generalization, dissociation, and jurisdictional non-differentiation, all driven by legislation (cf. Gusy 2010; Poscher 2011). The approaches pursued by the Federal Constitutional Court move in the direction of a contextual [266] and jurisdictional differentiation: enhancing of the simple (police-)law with its individual attribution as opposed to objective security ascription; demand for facts in the risk assessment by the executive; avoidance of state theoretical meta-discourses about security as state duty; justification of special areas of freedom resistant to balancing; hesitation about objective theories of the Basic Rights; repositioning of the review of proportionality onto a factual dimension; just to name a few (for further analysis Lepsius 2010b, 39ff). It can, therefore, succeed.

Ultimately, there are many constitutional courts, but the Federal Constitutional Court is simply unique in its functioning as a standard-setting power. If one wishes to preserve this distinctive German contribution to the world heritage of constitutional theory, one must refine it. Only those who adapt remain true to themselves. That goes above all on one's sixtieth birthday. For sure, it is too early for retirement.

4

Legality, Legitimacy, and Legitimation of the Federal Constitutional Court

Christoph Möllers[*]

"... the Basic Law is more likely to suffer from being challenged too little than from being challenged too much." *Rudolf Smend (1962)*

I. Introduction

In the rich literature on constitutional law in Germany, the question of how to justify the Federal Constitutional Court is posed rather rarely.[1] If so, it is usually answered by simple reference to the constitution: the Court monitors the observance of the Basic Law, just as the Basic Law provides for it. This answer seems remarkably unsatisfying not only in terms of comparative law. Indeed, the legitimation of constitutional and high courts remains among the central questions of constitutional scholarship in most democratic orders, while the limited interest among German legal scholarship represents an irritating exception.[2] The simple answer is above all not especially persuasive in substantive terms. The reference to law must, indeed, serve as the decisive argument inside a legal order (Raz 1975). It is the only possible response from a [284] *court*, for otherwise it would give up its role as a court. But this reference is not sufficient for the theoretical question at

* In remembrance of Klaus Schlaich, the brightest academic observer of the Federal Constitutional Court. Thanks for research assistance and criticism to Alexander Tischbirek, Johannes Bethge, Andrej Lang, Jelena von Achenbach, and Tim Wihl.

[1] Cf. Abromeit 1995 on the fundamentally different sovereignty concepts in Great Britain, Switzerland, and the Federal Republic.

[2] This statement must be read before the background of the vast literature on individual decisions. Cf. as corrective so far as it goes, Grimm 1976; Gusy 1985, 132 ff.; Roellecke 1987; Simon 1994, RN 42–60; Böckenförde 1999a. A reason for this appears to be that the Court gets by with concepts of social and constitutional transformation instead of making use of normative political theories, as is pervasive in Western constitutional traditions (Ebsen 1985; Walter 2000; for a critique of the category of constitutional transformation, Voßkuhle 2004), so then a development is justified, because it occurred. Jellinek's assertion about the "normative power of the factual," however, is only an expression of the category impoverishment of the constitutional scholarship of the Imperial period (Möllers 2011, 18 ff.), not a serviceable point of departure for an analysis of legitimation.

The German Federal Constitutional Court: The Court Without Limits. Matthias Jestaedt, Oliver Lepsius, Christoph Möllers, and Christoph Schönberger, published by Oxford University Press under licence (2020).
DOI: 10.1093/oso/9780198793540.001.0001

stake. Legal scholarship limiting itself to positive law neglects its intellectual duties. It suffers from a false self-identification with the work of judges, confusing law, and legal scholarship. This is especially true for constitutional law that is dependent on political and other social contexts.

In the following, those courts designated "constitutional courts" are courts which have the authority to review and reject parliamentary statutes in reference to the constitution. Such an authority can rest in a *specialized* court. That is the case with the Court, which is the only court in German law that can reject statutes and which is exclusively focused on the application of constitutional law. Different from a supreme or high court, all its pronouncements produce constitutional law and can directly bind the democratic legislature, whereas in the American case, all federal courts can decide constitutional questions alongside mere statutory problems.

The institution of constitutional review may result from different considerations: the final control of lower courts by a high court, the adjudication of conflicts between federal levels in order to ensure the legal unity of a federal space, the need to settle conflicts among political organs, and the judicial application of fundamental rights even against the legislature. In its "uniquely ample" competencies [285] (Helms 2006, 65), the Court draws from all of these considerations. It rules on claims of one political organ against another, on federal disputes involving different levels of government, on constitutional complaints of individual citizens, and on lower court references for a review of particular statutory provisions.

Constitutional review by a court does not necessarily follow from the supremacy of the constitution, even less so do specialized constitutional courts (Nino 1996, 189 ff.). Contrary to a common myth in Germany, there is no inevitable development from constitutionalism to constitutional review by a court (Gusy 1985, 30f.). At this point in time, the model of a specialized, powerful constitutional jurisdiction is advancing globally (Ginsburg 2008; Hirschl 2004); but it is not the only possible institutional solution to the protection of constitutional supremacy. Many European countries do not have a specialized court devoted to constitutional questions. Some do not recognize any control of constitutionality through courts (Brünneck 1992; Brunner 2002). The worldwide spread of this kind of institution began after 1945, and then, once again, after 1989. Indeed, it is a typical institutional reaction to totalitarian experiences.

The following essay will examine the question of constitutional review in the case of the German Basic Law and the Court. Its core assumption is that there is no one-size-fits-all model for the justification of constitutional review, but that such theories are dependent on different layers of political and social context. The argument presented here for the most part refers to the Court as an institution. [286] Taking into account its procedural and organizational structures, therefore, it will only occasionally deal with the Court's specific case law. This piece makes a three-part distinction. I begin with the legality of the Court. The question is: to what extent does the concept that the Court is bound to law and merely applies the law support its actual practice (II.). After that I take a look at the legitimacy of the Court in terms of the factual social acceptance of its decision-making practice (III.). Finally, and most extensively, I turn to the normative justification of the Court, by asking about good reasons for the present institutional configuration of the Court (IV.). This section will be distinctly more detailed than the others for two reasons: first, because a thorough theoretical preparation is necessary; and second, because a relevant answer requires delving into the specific decision-making structures of the Court. In a concluding reflection, I will then examine the interrelation of all three above-mentioned elements (V.).

I will try to connect the undertheorized German debate on constitutional review, which is also a bit introverted, both comparatively and in terms of disciplinary boundaries, with discussions in other disciplines and legal orders. Is this a "critique" of the Court? If by critique one means an examination which is interested in arguments (Jaeggi 2009), certainly so. Under this condition, it is also clear that in a scholarly context, in which arguments matter, the justification of an institution is not conceivable without critique [287]. Only an engagement with the Court, which does not limit itself to institutional positivism rooted in constitutional law, can explain and justify the institution. [288]

II. Legality: On the Legal Obligations of the Federal Constitutional Court

A. The legal court

Does it make sense to question the legality of the Court? Can a constitutional court act illegally? On an initial level, the question must be answered in reference to the provisions in which the Basic Law and the Federal Constitutional Court Law establish this particular court. The Court is so expressly and extensively regulated that it becomes difficult to doubt the legality of its activity. The Parliamentary Council, the German constitutional assembly of 1948/49, ultimately intended a strong form of constitutional review, even if the discussions about it were multifaceted. The still unambiguous decision for a specialized form of constitutional control determined the debate of postwar German legal scholarship, whose much-derided "constitutional court positivism" (Schlink 1989; previously on this subject Schlaich 1981, 139) consisted less in the acceptance of the Court's judgments than in accepting the Court as an institution without developing any reasons which extended past the reference to its mere "legality."

Therefore, scholarly discourses from other countries like the United States (Kahn 2002) or Israel (Hirschl 2004, 172 ff.), in which a supreme court transformed itself into a constitutional court, are not suited for the German case with the Court's legally flawless founding history. [289] The vast literature on the so-called "counter-majoritarian difficulty" (Bickel 1962; Kramer 2004; furthermore, see Kielmannsegg 1988, 401 f.) originating in the United States, and, more specifically, the phenomenon of a court that is not democratically accountable yet capable of rescinding majority decisions, has sparked a global discussion that is not helpful in describing the Court and many other post-totalitarian constitutional courts worldwide.

At the first level, it is plausible that the firm and unambiguous legality of the Court's establishment could supplant the question about its legitimation. At the second level, however, this reference to legality has much more to it: it involves an obligation to standards, over which the Court itself does not have control and which can only be changed through democratic decisions. Hence, it is thoroughly controversial whether such an idea of legality is suitable to constitutional law in the first place (for critique, Dworkin 1977). Should constitutional courts perhaps orient themselves toward self-developed standards of justice on a case-by-case basis rather than exclusively toward positive law (**IV.3.**)? Anyhow, as long as we understand a court as an organ, whose actions are legally bound, and so long as courts make reference to legal obligations in their decisions, the relevance of legality cannot be denied. But what does that exactly mean in the German case?

B. The Court's statutory obligation

The Court is bound by the Basic Law and by parliamentary statute (Schlaich/Korioth 2010, RN 32 ff.; Voßkuhle 2010c, RN 29). Indeed, the obligation to the parliamentary statute is significant. Even if the Court has the power to nullify statutes, it still remains bound by all those statutes it has not rejected. Thus, one could theoretically think of other courts judging the actions of the Court, for example, if its justices were accused of intentionally misinterpreting legal provisions and thereby making themselves criminally or civilly liable. That such a conflict does not occur in Germany is due to the collegial culture of the German judiciary, not to the formal structure of the legal order. The Spanish and Italian cases demonstrate that such conflicts between the constitutional court and criminal and civil courts may indeed arise (Hansen 2008).

Even if the Court can be understood as the highest institution defining legality under German law, the question of how to construe the legality of its actions in ordinary law terms is not irrelevant. It illustrates a remarkable structural dilemma. On the one hand, the Court can only draw its authority from complying with constitutional and statutory law. For, as a court, it has to justify its own decisions by reference to specifically legal reasons (Möllers 2005, 95 ff.). On the other hand, compliance with law is factually weakened through various factors in the case of the Court. First, most statutory rules that obligate the Court [291] are applicable to the Court only. This is especially true for the provisions of the Federal Constitutional Court Law which regulate the selection and appointment of the Court's justices, and its legal procedures. Such targeted regulations, however, lack a certain legal routine that can only be established through a multitude of cases as well as instances of application. A lack of legal routine then hinders secure structures of legality (Weber 1922, 477 f.).

Secondly, the observance of these specific regulations, as we have seen, cannot be controlled, because the Court serves as the highest court. In terms of procedural law, it is a "judge in its own affairs." This further weakens its claim to legality, which relies on independent review mechanisms as a central element to its persuasiveness.

Finally, a constitutional court has the opportunity to interpret norms of ordinary statutory law in the light of constitutional norms or principles. It can thereby resort to arguments that are simultaneously more fundamental and vaguer than the comparably unambiguous procedural rules.[3] The interpretation of the latter in the light of constitutional principles does not correspond to any ideal of legality, however. The Court has shown a very pliable handling of its procedural law not only in individual cases, but also in a remarkably more fundamental [292] manner by appointing itself the "master of its procedure" and by claiming "procedural autonomy" for itself (Schlaich/Korioth 2010, RN54 ff.; Klein 2001, 510 ff.). "Master of the procedure" under the Basic Law, however, is the legislature, which defines the procedural rules, not the Court, which should apply them. Then again, there may be good reasons for the Court's free dealings with its procedural rules, but such reasons must be distinguished from a strict obligation to the law. The statutory obligation appears to be less potent for the Court than for other courts, partly for structural reasons and partly for those resting in the peculiarity of its jurisdiction.

C. The Court's obligation to the constitution

This weakening of statutory obligations could be justified with the reference to the Court's duty to the constitution. Legally, though, this is not correct, as we have seen, because the Court is bound by all statutes it has not formally found to be unconstitutional. While the Court's bond to statutory law seems precarious for this reason, one might consider its obligation to constitutional law quite unproblematic. With a closer look, however, further questions arise. [293]

The first question results from the Court's self-understanding. To what extent does the Court consider itself an element of the constitutional order rather

[3] One example is the principle of subsidiarity of the constitutional complaint.

than an authority that guards over the observance of the constitution from the outside of this very order? Evidently, a dilemma arises for every high court at this point. High courts can only justify themselves in reference to a legal order, which they interpret without further controls. The problem is accentuated in the case of the Federal Constitutional Court. For it claims to determine its own position within the legal order in two different ways. First of all, the aforementioned self-designation as "master of the procedure" illustrates the Court's claim to control the very rules that are meant to restrain it. Because its procedural law is regulated in statutes and in the constitution, the Court's claim dissolves not only its statutory obligation, but also its constitutional boundaries. The same applies for its quasi-official self-designation as a "constitutional organ"—a claim the Court has successfully made ever since its first conflict with the Federal Government in the 1950s (Collings 2015). Although the legislator has come to accept this status, it is so far not derivable from the text or structure of the Basic Law, which simply treats the Court as part of the judiciary (for reasoning, see below IV.C).

A second, more general limitation of the constitutional obligation results from the open wording of the constitution itself. Provisions like Art. 1, 1 GG, which protects human dignity, provide, on the one hand, a very strong normative claim, and yet, on the other hand, they remain vague and contested. Is Art. 1 GG really a legal provision [294] or is it rather a programmatic principle? Does it constitute a subjective right or an objective value? What does dignity mean? Even if the semantic problem is particularly manifest here, a higher degree of uncertainty is typical of all constitutional law. It would be mistaken to understand the openness of constitutional provisions as a mere deficit. Constitutions must be open to continued development in order to provide the political process with a certain leeway. A court, however, that is supposed to give a purely legal reasoning which does not allow for political compromises (Taylor 1995, 130) is faced with a serious problem; for the openness of the constitutional text inevitably dilutes that court's claim to legality.

There is still another question that has drawn great attention in German legal scholarship: how can the Court's specifically constitutional standard be demarcated from the statutory standard, which is to be heeded by the lower courts? As a pure constitutional court, the Court may only apply constitutional, not statutory, law in its review of court judgments. How may this be possible if the obligation to statutory law itself is entrenched in constitutional law, as is the case in Germany (Hermes 2002; Jestaedt 2001)? The Court itself developed pragmatic formulas to solve the problem by looking for "specific" constitutional problems. And to be sure, there is no clear systematic solution to this, as Kelsen (1929b, 40) has already noticed. The dazzling array of constitutional law literature on this question is a further indicator of an unfruitful [295] fixation on the decision-making perspective of the Court.

D. Circular legality

All in all, even in the German case with its strong formalist tradition, the claim that courts are bound by law is far from self-evident. While courts interpret their own jurisdictions, high courts find themselves in the unusual situation of only having to apply individual rules tailored to their own institution, which are not reviewable by any other court. Moreover, the authority of rejecting statutes invariably leads to more freehanded interpretations of statutory law. Hence the legality of constitutional court practice is structurally deficient. The tautological notion—anything is legal that courts designate as legal—does not help either. For the point of an obligation through legality is precisely that this bond determines the practice of the courts in advance, not that this obligation first arises in the very moment a court decides.[4] [296]

In other words: when the Court itself, by and large, develops constitutional standards, then the paradigm of legality does not suffice for justifying its practice. If legality refers to an external obligation, legality can establish legitimation. For compliance with legal obligation is able to justify the Court's practice. When legal obligation, however, turns out to be merely situational and self-referential, a legality loop with uncertain justificatory content arises. Whether or not the Emperor is wearing clothes cannot be determined with the reference to legality then. [297]

III. Legitimacy: On the Recognition of the Federal Constitutional Court

In what follows, the notion of legitimacy denotes the acceptance, the factual recognition of the Court, by those affected by its decisions (Weber 1922, 775). For our purposes, one should distinguish between two sub-types of legitimacy: acceptance of the Court itself (A.) and acceptance of the entire constitutional order to the extent that it is protected by the Court.

A. The popular court

In regard to the first form of legitimacy, the very high popularity the Court enjoys among the general public in Germany is uncontested (Lembcke 2006; Vorländer/Brodocz 2006). It has enjoyed this level of support almost throughout its entire history. This degree of acceptance has, indeed, drawn

[4] Fundamentally skeptical about the background problem of whether we can conceive the normativity of law as binding in the future, Müller-Mall 2012.

criticism, even by representatives of the Court itself. For in this attachment to a judicial institution, one can discern a yearning for a conflict-free form of political decision-making, which absolves from the efforts of self-determination in a representative democracy. The aura of a wise, substitute emperor, who reigns beyond the imperfections of everyday politics, [298] may live on in the general admiration for the Court, conjuring up associations with a discredited authoritarian tradition (Höffe 1999, 176). Of course, this reading is not necessarily correct, for it assumes that the difference between a court and an authoritarian leader is widely ignored. Whoever welcomes the powerful position of the Court in the institutional order of the Federal Republic, whoever esteems the Court more than, for example, parliament, still need not support the substitution of the latter by the former.

More interesting than this general observation is a glance at the specific organizational prerequisites for the Court's wide popularity. Most likely, the public success of the Court results in large part from the constitutional complaint procedure. For it opens a direct channel to the Court for everybody who can claim a basic right. With this opportunity, which cannot be taken for granted even in constitutional democracies, the Court comes into direct contact with the concerns of citizens. And the Court's considerable discretion in procedural affairs provides it with the opportunity to accept and decide cases even at a relatively early procedural phase. Therefore, the Court does not only serve as the court of final review, which is summoned directly by the people, but often also as the only court [299] making decisions at all (IV. C.). The Court's self-understanding as "procedurally autonomous" has a concrete impact here.

Clearly, the Court does not lack acceptance. Whenever the Court itself became the object of political attacks or public protests in recent history, this could not permanently diminish its popularity (Collings 2015): at the beginning, it had to prevail against a governmental majority and against ordinary courts which were dominated by former National Socialist judges (Häussler 1994, 22 ff.); in a later phase, it appeared to have too slight regard for the progressive agenda of the social-liberal coalition; and, finally, in the middle of the 1990s, it met resistance from the opposite direction with decisions perceived as left-leaning (Lamprecht 2009, Isensee 1996, 1088 f.). Each of these phases diminished the Court's popularity temporarily, but in none of these cases did it sustainably change its positive public perception. The Court's technique of decision-making that is simultaneously non-political and directed toward the public good, especially in the constitutional complaint procedure, is the main reason for the staying power of its popularity. To what degree these causes can also be understood as normative reasons for the Court's justification will be reviewed below (IV.B.).

B. The Federal Constitutional Court as a "factor of social integration?"

A second type of legitimacy that we have to look at relates to the Court's contribution to the legitimacy of the constitutional order in its entirety [300]. It is clear that a popular state organ casts its light on the order of which it is a part. Furthermore, influential contributions to German constitutional theory ascribe to the Court the task of facilitating and improving social cohesiveness. "Integrating society" has been a leitmotif in German constitutional scholarship since Rudolf Smend's works in the early Federal Republic (Smend 1968), which, however, carry on some of his thoroughly anti-republican ideas (Möllers 2011, ch. 4) from the Weimar era (Smend 1994). One may doubt (Schlaich 1981, 136) whether the later Smend intended to entrust the Court with said task of integrating the federal German society, as is often written and even claimed by the Court itself in its "status report" (for a critical view: van Ooyen 2005, 140 ff.). As always, Smend's texts remain ambiguous on this question. The simple identification of integration and constitutional adjudication is probably an attribution from his disciples. For the early Weimar Smend, "integration" was a formula for the emergence of a strong political community, which showed little appreciation for either the plurality of modern society or the formalization achieved by law. If there is something that separates Smend's theory from the anti-pluralist tradition of German statism, it is his sense for the dynamic and procedural aspects of a constitutional order and his rejection of a clear distinction between the state and private spheres. With these important insights, Smend was uncommonly successful in the Federal Republic (overview in Möllers 2008b, 32 ff., 38 ff.). [301]

Nevertheless, it remains unclear what Smend exactly means by "integration" and how that concept could be applied to the Court (Haltern 1997, 41ff.). Precisely because the formulation seems to rest on a vague intuition, it is rarely contested. On a literal reading, integration means a process of "de-differentiation." But whether social cohesiveness is built on any form of homogeneity seems dubious. It runs counter to a general tendency of modern social theories, which explain the functioning of society essentially via the possibility of internal differentiations (among many Nassehi 2006, 396 ff.). Likewise, it contradicts all theories of democracy that stress the need for plurality and disagreement. This objection is even weightier, because there is no theory behind the concept of integration that deserved that name. Smend's primary contribution remains a hardly understandable outline (Smend 1994; benevolent analysis in Badura 1977).

Finally, a distinctive problem of the integration concept in constitutional adjudication is that constitutionalism may only be conceived on the basis of the *differentiation* of politics and law. Whether the integration concept can undo this differentiation [302], however, appears more than doubtful. As we have seen, constitutional courts may organize an institutional linkage between law and politics, but this linkage is not properly described as "integration," precisely because it shall guarantee the distinctions between law and politics (van Ooyen 2005, 142). By way of example, a legal order in which law and politics were "integrated" would probably not recognize independent courts, whereas a concept that reduces constitutions to sheer moral catechism (Schaal 2000b, 174 ff.) neglects not only the peculiarities of modern societies, but also the very point of modern constitutions.

Despite these objections, integration theory has experienced an empirically grounded renaissance in German political sciences (Schaal 2000b; Vorländer 2002, 18 ff.). Here it is mostly tied to empirical evidence about the popularity of the Court. Nevertheless, it appears difficult to derive a higher level of acceptance of the entire order from the popularity of the Court. In fact, one would have to conduct a controlled counter experiment that investigated the popularity of a fictitious constitutional order without the constitutional court. The Court's contribution to public debate is, indeed, emphasized by many studies. But even if one could attribute to it an empirically measurable power to create general acceptance for the constitutional system, this effect would appear, on the one hand, very selective, and, on the other, not typical of court decision-making. For constitutional court decisions normally form the endpoint of a discourse over constitutional politics, not its beginning [303].

C. Acceptance problems of constitutional adjudication

Popular acceptance is of particular significance for courts. Indeed, no form of political rule can ensure its own claim to decision-making authority solely with commands and compulsory enforcement. And courts in particular do not have such formal means of execution at their disposal anyway. They are dependent on other authorities. They require enforcement of their decisions by the executive. For the systematic implementation of decisions with great substantive scope, they also need the support of the legislature (exemplarily Rosenberg 1991; Landfried 1984, 125 ff., 147 ff.; von Beyme 1997, 300–12). Courts lacking this structural support remain helpless, as a President of the United States is alleged to have put it once in reference to the U.S. Supreme Court Chief Justice: "John Marshall has made his decision, now let him enforce it!"[5]

Among ordinary courts, the need for acceptance can be satisfied through procedure. A court decision that is unacceptable to the parties or the general public can be understood as an anomaly inside of an otherwise acceptably functioning legal system: higher courts can reverse that decision, while other courts can decide

[5] The quote, however, is apocryphal. The decision in question is "Worcester v. Georgia," 31 US 515 (1832).

differently. The individual court is embedded in the entire system. All the same, the most important procedural mechanism for the production of [304] factual acceptance is the individualization of decisions (Luhmann 1975, 121 ff.; cf. also Shapiro 1981, 1 ff.). Courts decide as independent organizations and they will only hear the very specific concerns of the parties to the very particular case. Therefore, it is difficult for the losing party in such a case to mobilize opposition to the result. The decision is withdrawn from political generalization by this procedure. It appears acceptable and, therefore, legitimate.

Both conditions of legitimacy, the embedding in the entire legal system and the individualizing effect of the court procedure, are hardly available for constitutional courts. In a concentrated system like the German one (see I.), the constitutional court decides as if it were in a system with a single actor. The decision, therefore, is ascribed to the institution, not the legal order. And even in the American system, which is neither specialized nor concentrated, the challenging of a statute before a lower court creates the expectation of a subsequent conclusive decision by the Supreme Court. Moreover, constitutional courts cannot individualize decisions in the same way as other courts can. In the cases of a review of a statute or of the validity of an election, the decision's scope extends well beyond the parties to the proceedings as it even may include the entire democratic community. There are judicial techniques to limit this effect. Nevertheless, [305] a structural problem of constitutional adjudication still remains. When courts in general are especially dependent on acceptance, and constitutional courts lack procedural mechanisms of creating such acceptance at their disposal, they must develop alternative strategies to compensate for that deficiency.

D. Strategies of self-legitimation—and its institutional limits

Indeed, the Court does use strategies of self-legitimation to enhance the acceptance of its own decisions. Among these measures is a strategy of informal communication with the public. Further efforts include questions like which cases are decided sooner and which later, which ones get an oral argument and which a press release. Neither of these questions is determined by law or by internal rules. Strategies even involve commentaries on the Court's own decisions in interviews or scholarly publications by individual justices themselves. Obviously, the Court considers the political consequences of a decision (Vanberg 2004; Sieberer 2006). This "political" stock-taking is certainly nothing out of the ordinary (Wittig 1969). Even lower courts take account of the consequences of their decisions. This may even be part of proper legal methodology, so long as the consideration of consequences is normatively guided (Lübbe-Wolff 1981). However, [306] in the case of constitutional adjudication, the consideration of consequences is omnipresent, paramount, and, thereby, politicized.

This is not the place to pursue such strategies in detail, since we do not know enough about the inner life of the Court (Vanberg 2004; Kranenpohl 2009). But what we do know is that there are weighty structural limitations to such mechanisms of self-legitimatization.

The first and most important limit stems from the simple fact that constitutional courts normally owe their acceptance to the legal character of their practice: they guarantee rights in the form of the law.[6] Nonpartisanship, independence, and legal reasoning are typical properties, which provide for the acceptance of an entirely untypical court like the Federal Constitutional Court. All strategies of self-legitimation, which are not based on law, are consequently highly precarious, once they become discernable. If the Court becomes visible as a strategically acting agent, it will lose acceptance. This is a decisive difference from political organs. Legitimacy is cross-referenced with legality.

Internally, all such strategies of self-legitimation, moreover, are practically limited through the fact that the Court does not function as a hierarchical organization. The normative equality of the judges as well as their independence provide few formal opportunities to restrict their behavior outside the court [307]. Indeed, the president represents the Court externally and operates as a formal supervisor of the justices.[7] Nevertheless, he or she can neither influence the behavior of the justices nor control their external representation. The president does not even have any informal instruments at his or her disposal, as he or she can neither assign cases to specific justices, nor issue evaluations for future promotions, to guide the constitutional justices (Geiger 1979, 26ff).[8]

Perhaps rightly so, the Court's "public relations" should be limited to oral arguments as well as the pronouncement and publishing of its judgments. If the popularity of the Court is due to the supposedly non-political techniques of reaching decisions, the most secure long-term strategy is withdrawal from the public. If the bottom line of this section is that the popularity of the Court is empirically robust, but structurally threatened, the Court may be well-advised to avoid the political public outside the confines of the Court's specific procedural forms. [308]

IV. Legitimation: On the Justification of the Federal Constitutional Court

The question of the Court's justification, understood neither in reference to positive law nor to factual acceptance, will now occupy us in this central section of the

[6] See below IV.B.

[7] S. 5, 1, 1 and s. 9 of the Bylaws of the Federal Constitutional Court.

[8] Clearly, this was still the case before the coming into force of the bylaws in the discussion surrounding the "status report," in which the president of the Court sent a negative commentary and the vice president an affirmative one to the Federal Justice Ministry.

study. The question is difficult, because the criteria for such a justification are uncertain and potentially multifaceted. One of this section's key propositions is that there is a middle road between a purely legalistic approach to this question and an over-generalized attempt that applies American or other constitutional theories to one specific case. An adequate response has to work its way from the general and normative to the specific and contextualized. Initially, I will try to determine the particular function of constitutional courts (**IV.A.**) before different models of legitimation of constitutional adjudication can be developed (**IV.B.**), in order to finally take up a more specific institutional analysis of the Court (**IV.C.**). The bottom line will not be any general claim in favor of or against constitutional review as it can be read so often, particularly in the American debate, nor will my own approach to legitimation in constitutional law be applied to our case (Möllers 2008b, 136ff.). I will rather aim to identify the very specific justificatory problems of a quite unique court like the Federal Constitutional Court. [309]

A. The court between law and politics

1. The constitution as coupling and separation of law and politics

Constitutions as supreme norms are not simply the hierarchical apex of a legal system. While constitutions found and organize a political system, they are also part of this system. Put differently, in constitutional orders the political system stands behind the supreme norm, just as conversely the legal order stands behind the political institutions. Constitutions structure the relationship of law and politics. They politicize the production of law, by connecting the legal system to a political process, and they legalize this political process through its obligation to superior legal rules (Luhmann 1973; Luhmann 1990; Grimm 2010, 9 ff.; Preuß 1994, 11 ff.). All other "functions" of constitutions (Peters 2001, 76 ff.) are derivative of this foremost task: the limitation and legalization of political power, the installation of a political organization, and the enabling of political action.

In democratic constitutional states, to which alone the following considerations apply, this mechanism legitimates both, law and politics, by cross reference to each other. The legal order can found its claim to obedience only by reference to the democratic conditions of lawmaking. Otherwise, this claim remains authoritarian.[9] [310] The political process, by contrast, can only prove itself democratic because it is bound to certain rules, which ensure that standards of democratic equality, generality, and openness are met.

"Legalization" hereafter refers to decisions that exclusively, or at least extensively, invoke legal or juristic reasoning. Court decisions display the most intense degree

[9] Hershovitz's critique of Raz's model of authority (2003) is representative of the theoretical problem.

of legalization. For they are reached by independent decision-makers subordinated only to the law, who direct themselves only to certain limited cases and reach judgments normally only after the fact. Conversely, we can designate practices as "politicized" for our purposes when they are justified with political, therefore programmatic, preferences, to which there are legitimate alternatives, and which are issued with the intention of achieving an extensive, future-oriented design. The politicization of a certain issue can also consist of opening the decision-making structure to alternatives and introducing it into a public debate. Evidently, the fact that constitutional court decision-making tends to blur this distinction to a certain degree does not speak against its descriptive value. As "constitution" finally, we hereafter describe the coupling of both decision-making forms, which should generate the above-suggested reciprocal justificatory effect. [311]

An important function of constitutions is the preservation of the institutional *differences* between law and politics, in order to guarantee their reciprocal means of justification (Grimm 1995a, 97 ff.; Roellecke 1987, RN 33–9). Both the politicization of the judiciary and the legalization of politics are problematic. The functioning of the constitution, in other words, proves itself precisely by making room for differing decision-making structures. A constitution, therefore, should not integrate law and politics, but rather connect them in a form that distances both from one another.

2. Political and legal constitutions

This important function does not necessarily require the establishment of a constitutional court. Constitutional orders without constitutional adjudication, such as in Scandinavia, Australia, New Zealand, or the classic case of England, demonstrate this. In these orders, one can rely on the fact that parliament and the ordinary courts guard the legitimating cycle between law and politics in other ways. Such alternative mechanisms may include, for example, a high degree of voluntary compliance with the law (or social homogeneity) in the works of parliament, as in Westminster, the establishment of constitutional committees in parliament or a decentralized judicial control of statutory application rather than of statutes themselves. [312] Traditionally, the English parliament was not just a legislative organ, but the central location of the coupling of politics and law. The English legislative process is rule-bound. Mere compliance with these rules is mostly left to the political system. Indeed, the English system has no written constitution, but it has a constitution nonetheless, because action in the political system is guided by norms (emphatically Gardner 2009).

It is thoroughly controversial in constitutional theory whether there are universal reasons for or against the establishment of constitutional adjudication. But in view of the multiplicity of functioning constitutional orders, little speaks in favor of arguments that apply regardless of the considerable differences between legal orders and political cultures. In terms of comparative law, much depends on the significance that a political community accords its constitutional text, if it even has one. Is it understood as a legal text, which is entrusted to the courts, as was mostly the case in the German postwar era? Or is the constitutional text understood as a political founding document, a program, the realization of which is the responsibility of the legislature above all, as in the states of the Atlantic revolutions? In the words of Franklin D. Roosevelt, the constitution is "a layman's document, not a lawyer's contract" (Roosevelt 1938). The answers to these questions are not self-evident, even if the legalistic tradition of the Federal Republic (Lepsius 1982) mostly ignored the possibility of a political constitutionalism. It is probably not accidental that mostly post-totalitarian states propagate a legalistic understanding of constitutionalism. Bad experiences with the political process encourage its intensive legalization. [313] Against this backdrop, the Court globally became an influential model for constitutional orders in middle and Eastern Europe, southern Africa, and Latin America.

As a result, the constitutional connection between politics and law has a more political design in one system or a more legal one in another. These differing designs can be placed on a scale. Between a purely political coupling in the parliament and a decentralized system of judicial control, in which all courts also directly apply constitutional provisions, ranges the establishment of special organs like a parliamentary constitutional committee (for a typology Bryde 1982, 97–105)—or even a specialized constitutional court. These organs modify received institutional forms from the legal system or from politics for their specific task.

3. In particular: constitutional courts between law and politics

But what are the consequences when a specialized constitutional court is entrusted with the linkage of law and politics? Does it function as a political or as a legal actor? On the one hand, constitutional courts are organized in the traditional form of a court and act accordingly. Notably, they decide cases only when petitioned in a specific proceeding. [314] Before this background, the finding that constitutional courts are "in effect" political organs is often proclaimed to be a surprising discovery, not least of all from political scientists. Thus, political scientists first recognized the "political" character of constitutional courts in the U.S. (Dahl 1957) after the Second World War, later also in other countries (Stone Sweet 2000), and held it against a formalistic legal approach, though the political character of constitutional review had long been a topic, for example, in the German discussion of the Weimar Republic (for an overview of the history, see Laufer 1968, 4 ff.).[10]

[10] The oft-cited and influential book of Stone Sweet (2000) is an example of a typical form of argument, in which the novelty of his own politicization thesis is continually emphasized against the background of "traditional" understandings of the separation of powers and concepts of legal obligation, without giving any evidence at all for the latter claim. Actually, in Europe, one must reach back to the period before 1800 to discover corresponding concepts of juristic method. Even the distinction between a "European" and an "American" conception of a separation of powers is unpersuasive in its simplicity (on this Möllers 2008b, ch. 1).

But why is it plausible to understand constitutional courts as political organs, and what exactly is described with this epithet? First off, virtually every legal system with a constitutional court treats it as a political organ when it comes to the appointment of judges, who are often selected through a parliamentary or some other political procedure (Bobek 2013). In addition to that, the political character of a constitutional court is evident in its position at the pinnacle of the hierarchical court system, which corresponds with a substantive competence to guard the unity of the entire legal order. This is already [315] atypical for a court, which normally reaches decisions within very firm substantive limitations.

This understanding is admittedly based on a relatively weak concept of politicization, since it even pertains to supreme courts which do not have the power to nullify statutes. A stronger concept of politicization points at continuing influences of the appointment procedure in the court's decision-making behavior. In this regard, one may first have to examine how, if at all, the composition of the court in terms of the judges' political convictions differs from that of the political organs that selected them. Does the court have a distinct composition, which refers to criteria that are specifically oriented toward the legal system, or does the court merely act as a sort of parliament in miniature, which only replicates the political majority/minority relationships (this thesis for the U.S. Supreme Court in Dahl 1957)? Such an analysis is attempted by attitudinal approaches, which try to explain court decisions through the political preferences of individual justices (Segal/Spaeth 2002, 86 ff.; for an overview Hönnige 2007, 34; critically Robertson 2010, 13 ff.). These approaches seem persuasive for legal systems where the judges communicate little with one another internally (as in the U.S. and in Brazil), where individual judges write the decisions, and where there is a certain skepticism toward the capacities of formal legal rules (Daxbury 1997 showing that this, too, applies to the U.S.). After all, there are remarkably successful attempts to predict U.S. Supreme Court decisions with the help of such models (Ruger et al. 2004).

For other legal systems, it is more difficult to assess [316] how the law itself and the deliberative process within the court can change the judges' preferences, especially when the opinions of the court are the communal product of a whole judicial body. To the extent that it is possible to quantify the political convictions of judges and the political tendencies of court decisions, this may cast new light on the significance of court procedure. Certainly, such research is always in danger of succumbing to a self-fulfilling prophecy, because it can hardly prove the existence of determined political convictions before a judge's entry onto the court. Even so, researchers would be hard-pressed to provide a methodologically consistent clarification of the continuing effect of such attitudes in the decision-making practice of a court. And even if such stable convictions endured, which is a problematical assumption (Sunstein 1986), it would not be clear whether these convictions could be easily conferred into the specific deliberative and justificatory methods of a court decision. Although this seems to be the case in the U.S. Supreme Court, this does not seem representative for every other constitutional court.

A second factor that would have to be incorporated into such research is still more difficult to grasp for empirical and quantitative approaches, namely the influence of genuinely legal arguments in a given case. If it was completely contested, the law could be neglected altogether. But despite a century of realist and critical debunking this still seems to be an implausible assumption. Rather, the politicization of an issue in public debate and the degree of its determination by constitutional reasoning do not appear to be directly related to each other (Möllers 2011, 183 f.). Highly politicized questions may be perfectly clear as a matter of constitutional law, whereas questions that receive no or little attention in the political process can be highly controversial in legal discourse, and vice versa. So far, constitutional law has differentiated itself from politics in most [317] constitutional states such that unequivocal correlations between political and constitutional controversies cannot be established. The U.S. is again a special case in this regard, and, therefore, not a good model for theoretical efforts.

As a result, in order to assess the degree of a court's politicization, one has to understand the legal problems in question. Correspondingly, parts of neo-institutional research recognize that courts not only make law, but rather that the law also binds and limits their decisions (Smith 1988, 91 ff.; Lhotta 2003, 147 ff.). This relativizes the thesis of the constitutional court as a political actor. Empirical research must grapple with constitutional law as an "independent institutional variable" (Lhotta 2003, 147). Vice versa, legal scholarship must consider the political contexts of constitutional decisions. [318]

As a result, defining constitutional courts as political actors may be accurate with regard to certain specific elements of the institution, but not in view of constitutional courts at large. Such courts are created and staffed in political procedures, their rank in the constitutional structure and the scope of their decisions makes their action genuinely political. But, on the other hand, it would be fruitless to reduce their specific procedures as well as their way of reasoning to mere superstructures or epiphenomena of politics. To be sure, this may happen and may have happened in countries like Russia or the United States, but even these developments can only be described in a conceptual framework that accepts the law as a relevant factor. When characterizing constitutional courts, the differences from the purely political organs are at least just as important as the parallels. Otherwise, the point of constitutional adjudication would be mistaken.

4. The fundamental legitimacy problem of constitutional adjudication

Constitutional courts claim a comprehensive decision-making power. In some cases, the judgments of the Federal Constitutional Court are even expressly accorded the force of statutory law (s. 31, 2 of the Federal Constitutional Court Law). But in contrast to a parliamentary procedure, a court procedure is designed exclusively, not inclusively. The parties to a constitutional case may bring a legal question before the court, which potentially concerns "everyone." But "everyone" will not participate in the case, while participation appears especially important when the decisive constitutional criteria are controversial or uncertain. Thus, the decision-making procedure does not fit the scope of the decision; and as a matter of self-determination this poses a problem. The urgency of this problem depends on the type of procedure and its respective participants. Where [319] constitutional organs, specifically government and parliamentary opposition or the federal level and a Land, dispute with one another, the participants in the case represent the whole democratic community. This is less clear, however, in the case of a constitutional complaint by an individual against a statute, in which democratic organs are heard, if necessary, but, in the German case, without being full-fledged parties to the case. Here, the Court's ruling on an individual complainant's claim potentially concerns the entire democratic legal community with direct effect. Already the representation of the "legislature," which, under the Basic Law, is not a single separate organ but rather a combination of different organs, seems hardly possible in this type of proceeding (Schlaich 1981, 108f.). Here, one might see an *overrepresentation of the parties* and of their concerns. The constitutional complaint procedure promotes, as we have seen, the popularity of the Court particularly well. Ironically, however, constitutional complaints advanced by an individual holder of fundamental rights appear especially contestable from the perspective of institutional justification. Other properties of the constitutional court procedure intensify this excluding effect. Only very rarely does an oral argument take place before the Court, thus providing the sort of public debate one generally demands of decisions with democratic implications. In contrast to a parliamentary procedure, the constitutional arguments presuppose legal knowledge. All of these properties tend to render the process exclusive in a sense typical of normal court cases,[320] yet not necessarily appropriate for a legitimate general decision-making procedure.

In addition to its exclusivity, constitutional court decision-making procedures are characterized by other properties which are typical for adjudication. Such decision-making takes place under the conditions of judicial independence, which, however, also means political independence. Judges shall simply *not* be held politically accountable for the consequences of their decisions. In addition, court decisions are issued in response to the initiative of the petitioner (Bryde 1982, 105). The petitioner's concern thus is the actual motive of the procedure. Even decisions, which have proven themselves false in the perspective of the court, can only be corrected when a subsequent case opens up the possibility of a second decision. That way, constitutional court decisions may not be simply corrected like political ones. The Court does not have a coherent position on self-correction, but it generally tends to not undertake such corrections openly (Seyfarth 1998, 94 ff.). This is partly due to the fact that legal reasoning, in contrast to political arguments, treat the court's opinions as the only one possible solution to a case according to the law. Unlike in the parliamentary process, a changed majority cannot simply assert the opposite result without calling into question its own decision-making logic. Open self-corrections rather provide reasons for doubts about the court's claims to a purely rational reasoning.

5. Hybridization of decision-making techniques

When faced with the alternatives of establishing either a supreme federal court or a genuine constitutional court, the Parliamentary [321] Council decided in favor of the latter (Schiffers 1984, VIII ff.; v. Doemming/Füsslein/Matz 1951, 669 ff.). At first glance, the creation of such a specialized body for constitutional adjudication could be understood as the ultimate form of constitutionalism, as the strongest possible institutional guarantee of the constitution. That is wrong for two reasons. First, if one takes the political element in constitutionalism seriously, then there is no such thing as an ultimate form of constitutionalization, and constitutionalism has to remain conceptually distinguished form judicialization. Secondly, the decision in favor of a specialized constitutional court is by no means a decision in favor of a complete judicialization of constitutional review, but rather a politicized transitional form of adjudication. The establishment of a constitutional court meant that constitutional review would not simply be turned over to ordinary courts and that constitutional questions would not be worked out in detail in the usual judicial process. Instead, a *specialized* constitutional court that is *contiguous with the political system* would rule on the supreme law of the land.

Only specialized constitutional courts have specific procedural rules at their disposal, which expressly acknowledge the scope of their decision-making claim, as is the case with the Court. The altered procedures of constitutional courts recognize, but also bring about a distinctive form of, internal [322] politicization: for instance, the oral argument changes its character and its function when an exchange of legal arguments, in which exclusively specific legal questions should be considered, turns into a type of hearing where the affected parties can express their concerns. As we will see, this is, indeed, typical of procedures before the Court. Furthermore, the internal decision-making process receives a different character through the publication of dissenting opinions. Also, the language of the decisions is less technical than in the case of ordinary courts, the reasoning is less "juristic." Finally, constitutional court arguments are often closer to political theory than to legal doctrine (Robertson 2010; Lasser 2004). One can read all these phenomena as an internal politicization of court procedure. In this sense, politicization is not, however, synonymous with a loss of the court's independence from political organs, parties, or majorities. It rather means a convergence of types of arguments, which seem familiar from the political system, but are now being heard in court.

This coupling of politics and law can lead to a hybridization of political and judicial forms, even though judicial forms clearly dominate in the case of the Constitutional Court. Other institutional arrangements of constitutional review also show such hybridizations. Here parliamentary bodies draw closer—from the opposite direction—to courts in terms of their procedural forms. Institutions that might initially be conceived as either legal or political prove astonishingly to resemble one another when they exercise the task of constitutional review. [323]

This final insight is significant to avoid provoking a dilemma of legitimacy of constitutional review. The fact that it is not crucial to establish constitutional courts in every democratic order does not mean that such courts must necessarily suffer from legitimation deficits. More precisely, democratic lawmaking and control of legality are combined with one another in all democratic systems. But every form of the coupling leads to inconsistencies, the diagnosis of which does not represent a sweeping objection against the selected institutional arrangement. Before we consider more closely the possibilities for the legitimation of constitutional courts, we shall first examine the consequences of constitutional court decisions with regard to the relationship between politics and law.

6. Consequences: legalization of politics—politicization of politics—politicization of law

Even when looking at the consequences of their decisions, constitutional courts require special arrangements precisely because, on the surface, they first and foremost resemble *courts.* On the one hand, we have seen that a [324] decision rejecting a statute can have a general scope of application. On the other hand, however, constitutional court decisions still do not have the same consequences as parliamentary decisions. Kelsen's quip of constitutional control as "negative legislation" (Kelsen 1929a, 54 f.; concurring Stone Sweet 2000, 135 ff.) is misleading (Schlaich 1981, 132 ff.; Hönnige 2007, 244). The provision providing for the statutory effect of a Court judgment cannot guarantee the same degree of general applicability as with parliamentary statutes. In practical terms, the Court often needs the statutory elaboration of a judgment by parliament, before its judgments can attain general effect. For instance, if a court declares racial segregation in schools or the discrimination of women in family law unconstitutional, discernible consequences of such decisions for the sum of all affected only become effective if the legislator translates the decision into a general rule, which is suitable for general application. So, whether or not this effectively happens is a question that is not for the courts alone to decide. In comparison with other courts, the Court has attempted to resolve this problem very proactively. It regularly sets time limits for the legislature to implement certain judgments. Occasionally, it has even drafted its own transitional rules (Schlaich/Korioth 2010, RN 378 ff.). Here the Court acts even more like the legislature, and thereby further aggravates its legitimation problem.

Ultimately more important for the effectiveness of judgments than the mere attempts of the Court [325] at implementation by means of procedural law may be another question, though. For the role which a constitutional court's definition of legality plays in a particular political culture may differ. Then the question arises of if and how a political community is prepared to recognize the decision of a constitutional court as at least a provisionally authoritative conclusion of a disputed issue. Indeed, extensive constitutional court decisions are particularly dependent on the cooperation of the political system. Therefore, Kelsen`s identification of the political significance of constitutional court decision-making with the concept of legislation seems erroneous.

If one analyses the effect of constitutional court decisions in reference to the distinction between politics and law, the findings become more and more complex: traditionally, we think of the *legalization of politics* by constitutional courts. Constitutional courts supervise the political process by use of a judicial proceeding; constitutional court decisions subject the political process to additional legal precepts. As we have seen, this statement, however, is immediately relativized by the fact that this form of "legalization" follows special rules. For with regard to specialized constitutional courts we are dealing with a modified form of judicial decision-making.

Moreover, the effect of constitutional adjudication is not reducible to the phenomenon of the legalization of politics. If a constitutional court repeals the prohibition of a political party, when it finds that a governmental decision requires a legal basis provided by parliament, or when it enhances the information rights of [326] the parliamentary opposition, then these stipulations lead to a *politicization of politics*. In the first case, the political process is allowed to keep a political alternative. In the second, a politically relevant decision must be made in a public process with the participation of the opposition; it cannot be treated as an exclusively internal matter of the executive. In the third case, the opposition is provided with additional instruments to instigate political debate in the general public as well as in parliament. Politicization of politics, then, means that the political process, which is based on public openness and the development of alternatives, is supplied with even greater openness and even further alternatives.

Ultimately, constitutional court decisions can even lead to a *politicization of the legal system*. What exactly does that mean? We have already seen that constitutional court decision-making displays properties that can be explained by the court's proximity to the political system. These properties have a retroactive effect on entire legal system. Indeed, in the German system of a specialized constitutional adjudication, to which there is direct access, the Court usually does not supervise the legislature directly, but rather the ordinary courts in their handling of the constitution when interpreting statutory law. In this constellation, the constitutional court supplies constitutional standards to be applied by the ordinary courts. During this process, in any case, a distinctive form of politicization [327] is discernible, because constitutional norms simply provide a more fundamental form of legal reasoning than is the case with arguments drawn from civil, criminal, or administrative law. Freedom of religion, much discussed in all democratic constitutional states, may serve as an example. Whether a teacher may wear a veil while teaching in public schools can be addressed on an individual case basis according to civil service regulations—or it can be treated as a wide-ranging question of religious freedom, which must be answered on a more fundamental level. In fact, there are good arguments for referring to religious freedom here. Our point is another one, however. The incorporation of constitutional arguments into legal reasoning with statutory law involves a doctrinal shift toward more fundamental considerations. Instead of answering the unspectacular question about functionally appropriate work attire for teachers, even lower courts find themselves confronted with the question of what place religion should have in the public sphere.

Under certain circumstances, constitutional court decisions even contain express references to the political system. When the Court obliges civil courts to take into account freedom of opinion when applying contract law or the law on compensatory damages because of its constitutive significance for democracy, a politicization of the legal system is at play, which commits the latter to look out for the functional conditions of the political order.

With this background, an important function of constitutional courts may consist in limiting this politicization of the law to their own institution, and thereby shielding the ordinary courts. [328] For in their decisions the ordinary courts can refer less to these fundamental principles themselves than to the constitutional court's understanding of the constitution. That way, constitutional courts can legitimate the legal system by subjecting a certain issue to a specific review, which functions differently from both the political system and the "normal" legal system. For this reason, the idea of a federal supreme court, which is not restricted to constitutional review, has long been discussed in the German constitutional debate (Schiffers 1984, XIV) but ultimately rejected. For with such a solution, ordinary courts would have directly adopted constitutional standards. The legal system would have been less intensively politicized, but one could also say for the case of the early Federal Republic: less radically democratized in view of its conservative and politically tainted corps of regular judges.

So, a complex picture results, in which constitutional courts bind the political process through judicially reviewable rules, which we designate as legalization, as much as they contribute to the opening of the political process for alternative opinions and actions. At the same time, they stimulate the legal system through "constitutional standards," which distinctively politicize the law. This takes us back to the question of justification.

B. Models of justification and their critique

The properties of constitutional court decision-making defy easy answers to the legitimation problems outlined above [329]. These issues have long been debated above all in the American literature. In German constitutional law, however, this discussion only plays a modest role. For the course of our argument, we have seen that the reference to legality is not sufficient to reconstruct the justification of the court. A more precise concept of its justification is needed. Such justification models must rest upon the function of constitutional review to simultaneously couple and differentiate law and politics. In the following, I intend to critically review six models of justification of constitutional adjudication. Subsequently, I will discuss the extent to which such models can be used to justify concrete institutions like the Court.

1. Justification through democratic legality

Legality may have a justificatory effect as far as the production of law itself satisfies criteria of legitimacy. In a democracy, constitutional adjudication may find its justification in the democratic process. This [330] argument, as we have seen, holds special significance for the order of the Basic Law, because the Court was expressly instituted by the constitutional convention. Its legitimation results from the democratic will of the constitutional assembly and of the legislature. The constitutional text demands a coupling of law and politics through legal forms and judicial control.

Of course, we have already seen objections to this model of justification through democratic legitimacy. For the obligatory effect of democratic statutes proves to be uncertain, if not weak, precisely in the case of constitutional adjudication. The members of the Parliamentary Council, as they supplied the Court with its range of competencies, were well aware of the fact that the court would begin its own normative existence by developing and elaborating constitutional standards. The relative vagueness of constitutional law provisions in comparison with those of statutory law was not unexpected to them, either. Hence, the reference to an—at least procedurally—precisely defined, democratic, legitimated mandate is not to be denied. Nevertheless, it does not remain fully satisfactory in terms of the theory of legitimacy. It is not sufficient for resolving the highlighted problem of legitimacy for several reasons.

First of all, in the vast majority of cases, constitution-making acts are not democratic, even if they [331] institute a democratic order (Elster 1991, von Beyme 1968). This objection has also been raised for the Basic Law. Indeed, the legitimizing effects of the mere democratic act of constitution-making tend to fade over time. Instead, the constitution retains its legitimation, above all, through the possibility of making changes therein, for only this openness to change allows for its application to those who did not have the opportunity to participate in the original decision on the document.

For the Court, this is not an overly dramatic problem. First, the Basic Law is still not very old. The democratic process that brought it into being did not take place that long ago and it still has a certain legitimating effect for the present. The founding generation's claim to binding authority still appears persuasive and understandable today. Moreover, the institutional side of the Basic Law has been actualized through procedural legislation. Second, the Basic Law is comparably easy to amend. And it was indeed very often amended over the last sixty years (for a comparative analysis see Lorenz 2008, 84ff.). This also means that a democratic process, capable of constitutional amendment, is able to react—and has in fact reacted—to decisions of the Court. This capacity for amendment incorporates the Court's doctrine into the process of democratic legitimation and, therefore, into actualized legality. The question about legitimation loses its urgency because of such opportunities for democratic reaction, even if the Court's doctrine does not [332] appear to show great respect for the intentions of the constitution-amending legislature (for critique Jestaedt 2002, 204 ff.). Different from an old constitution, which is almost impossible to amend, as is the case with the U.S., the reference to positive constitutional law in Germany effectively denotes an actualized relation to the democratic process.

By contrast, the reconstruction of a democratic mandate becomes more difficult through the so-called eternity guarantee of Art. 79, sec. 3 in which the constitution precludes amendments to certain provisions. This clause protects principles like democracy, the social state, and human dignity. When the Court interprets this clause, it creates constitutional law which can no longer be changed by a political procedure. A legitimacy problem arises for all those born into the system without having a chance to participate in its elaboration. We will return to this issue when we look at doctrine below (IV. C.).

Further doubts about the model of democratic legality result from the different requirements for ordinary legislation as opposed to constitutional amendments. Because the Court, being a specialized constitutional court, does not review ordinary statutory law, but creates fresh constitutional standards through each of its decisions, the reference to the constitution-maker's democratic legitimacy and the constitution-amending legislature's opportunity for revisions becomes problematic. The democratic capacity for action is very strongly constrained by the requirements for qualified majorities. The requirement that decisions be made by enhanced majorities in no way corresponds to the democratic ideal. Qualified majority requirements [333], such as those necessary for a constitutional change, favor the status quo. From the perspective of democratic equality, these requirements diminish the opportunity of all participants of the democratic community to take part in a majority decision. Moreover, they reduce the opportunities for those who would rather see a change in policy. If a constitutional court rejects a democratic decision, then this decision is certainly directed against at least a simple majority. An opportunity to correct such a rejection through constitution-amending legislature often appears to be precluded in this set of circumstances. For in many cases, the political possibility of composing anew even an ordinary statutory decision by simple majority will not occur.

2. Legitimation through safeguarding the democratic process

Another model of the justification of constitutional adjudication draws on the necessity to secure the democratic character of the political process with legal means. The law constitutes the rules, which legitimate politics.

Such an understanding of legitimacy is reflected in certain types of proceedings in the German law of constitutional procedure [334]. In American constitutional theory, this kind of justification of constitutional review became the point of departure of one of the most influential theories of constitutional adjudication: the model of representation reinforcement (Ely 1980, 73 ff.; on this Haltern 1998). A court must intensify its scrutiny whenever the affairs of minorities, which are not represented in the political process, are concerned. This very distinctive argument, tailored to the social structure as well as the electoral law of the U.S., certainly requires modification in other constitutional orders. Nevertheless, the idea of democracy protection can be reconstructed more generally (for example, Möllers 2005, 136ff.; Troper 2003; Nino 1996, 199 ff.). In democratic constitutional states, democracy is not understood as the brute expression of a political will, but as decision-making according to a formalized procedure. Above all, one must ensure that all members of a political community receive the same opportunity to participate in the political process. This requirement has many implications for the legal order, extending from electoral law to freedom of opinion. Insofar as these requirements are contested on a fundamental level, it is for the constitutional courts to oversee the observance of such rules.

In this model, therefore, constitutional review does not represent the demands of the historical constitution-maker, but it safeguards the present-day legislature's claim to legitimation through the possibility of concurrent control. For this reason, constitutional courts do play a very special role in a democratic order (very extensive Barak 2006, 20 ff.), just as the subsequent claim for justification of a constitutional court cannot be clarified without a precise view of the functional conditions of a particular democratic order. [335] It is no accident that the intensity of constitutional court interventions into the inner workings of the political process—for example, into parliamentary decision-making—varies widely in different constitutional systems. For they correspond with different understandings of democracy. Originally, the French Conseil constitutionnel was supposed to see about the legislative process only—particularly so, however, in order to confine the parliament's claim to decision-making power with respect to the government (Schnapper 2010, 62ff.). This was mainly a reaction to the negative experiences with parliamentary systems of government in the Third and Fourth Republics. In contrast, even though the American Supreme Court intensively reviews the electoral law, it very rarely occupies itself with the inner workings of the legislative process. Its doctrine hardly aims at the protection of parliamentary minorities (for an overview see Pildes 2004). This illustrates a strongly adversarial and majoritarian understanding of democracy. The German Court, on the other hand, has protected rights of the parliamentary opposition in quite a few decisions (cf. recently BVerfGE 124, 161—Minor Interpellation (2009), Meinel 2016). This underlines an understanding of democracy that values rule-governed behavior and consensus. The democracy-ensuring function of constitutional courts is certainly an important element of its justification. But the validity of this point does not only depend on the concrete organization of a democratic order, there are further objections to it.

First, the democracy-ensuring function may only explain a small part of the decision-making practice of a constitutional court. It would only suffice [336] for the justification of constitutional adjudication as a whole, if one intended to limit the decision-making competencies of the court to the democratic principle. Still, not every constitutional rule simply serves the guarantee of democratic representation. Some obviously also facilitate protection against decisions whose democratic legitimacy is not in question.[11]

An additional objection is more fundamental. It is at least an open question, to what extent can a democratic process be safeguarded through the observance and review of certain rules, or whether it is rather more a constant challenge for each democratic order to continuously elaborate and modify its decision-making mechanisms. Is it plausible in terms of democratic theory to have a pre-defined conception of national citizenship that does not permit further elaboration within a democratic process? Should parliamentary procedure meet a constitutional ideal of democratic deliberation, which can be reviewed and enforced by a court? Or else are not democracies more like the ship that one repairs while underway (Neurath 1932, 206)? And, consequently, can there even be an Archimedean point of democratic theory, from which an unambiguous criterion of democracy was applicable (Bryde 2000, 67 ff.)?

A static fixation of certain concepts of democracy can also be problematic in terms of democratic theory. This becomes evident when the U.S. Supreme Court can nullify the statutory limitation of private party spending [337] in the name of the openness of the democratic process.[12] Here two concepts of democracy collide. On the one hand, there is the idea of democracy as a marketplace, in which all opinions shall be able to circulate freely. On the other hand, there is an emphasis on political equality in the democratic process, which should not be overcome by differences in personal wealth.[13] We will have a closer look at this problem with regard to the Court's doctrine below (**IV. D.**).

[11] The exaggerated content of democratic theory arguments becomes especially clear in contributions which classify any Basic Rights protection as democracy promoting (Kneip 2006, 268 f.) or indeed declare the distinction between ordinary statutory law and constitutional law as unremarkable (Kneip 2006, 275 f. reaches the same conclusion for different reasons.)

[12] Citizens United v. FEC, 130 S. Ct. 876 (2010).

[13] For a comparable problem in German law, see BVerfGE 118, 277—Duties of Transparency and Accountability (2007). On the methodological problem that the decision is less about the application of norms than about the exchange of different guiding principles, see Volkmann 2010, 79 ff.

If meaningful democratic theory must always reflect its own relationship to democratic decision-making, too, then an orientation toward democratic statutes appears more convincing than any highly theoretical and juristically inclined thoughts that try to reach beyond specific political decisions. When different conceptions of democracy clash, both with arguments in favor of them, it appears persuasive to provide the democratic process itself with the power of definition on the appropriateness of certain democratic rules. The meaning of constitutional standards like the one contained in Art. 20, 2, 1 GG that "All state authority stems from the people" appears uncertain. The model of justification through a safeguarding of democracy, therefore, has its own value, which is, however, limited, and threatens to be reversed into a paternalistic model, in which the dynamism [338] and openness of the system's design may be lost. Concerning the coupling of law and politics, the question remains how it is possible to preserve the democratic character of political will formation without depriving democracies of the opportunity to regularly redefine their own procedures.

3. In particular: justification through the safeguarding of federal autonomy

The safeguarding of federal structures is among the most traditional tasks of modern constitutional court adjudication. Oliver Holmes declared on behalf of the U.S. Supreme Court: "I do not think the United States would come to an end if we lost our power to declare an Act of Congress void. I do think the Union would be imperiled if we could not make that declaration as to the laws of the several States" (Holmes 1913, 295 f.). In fact, one of the few commonalities of the American and German systems of constitutional court control is that both originate from federalism. And this interrelation is far from incidental. For two autonomous political levels need an independent review authority, which supervises their respective competences. For this reason, constitutional courts are to be found more typically in federal than in unitary systems (Beaud 2005). The protection of federal competencies is a special case of legitimation through the safeguarding of democracy. The integrity of two political unities, which are bound to one another institutionally but which must also be marked off from one another in order to guarantee their respective democratic processes, is assigned to a court. The review of competencies [339] in a democratic federation shall ultimately guarantee that the appropriate democratic subject is to decide on a certain question. Indeed, the German law of constitutional procedure provides a multitude of specific procedures for disputes between the Federation and the Länder.

It is not surprising that similar objections apply both to the role of a constitutional court as a guard of federalism and with respect to its more general functions of democratic safeguarding. Even the distribution of federal competencies requires adaptation to changing needs. New ideas arise in the political process about which substantive problems should be regulated centrally in a uniform way and which in a decentralized manner that allows diverse approaches. At the same time, the question whether to regulate a certain problem at the upper or lower federal levels is often not separable from the political question about how it should be regulated. American constitutional law offers many examples of this observation. Gun control, for instance, is debated in a context that includes fierce disputes about the federal level being permitted even to issue such legislation (documentation in Möllers 2005, 387 ff.). Therefore, the nullification of a federal statute for reasons of competence is also perceived as political advocacy on the federal level. This correlation is also reflected in the American party system, where from the very inception of the republic one of the two parties has been inclined to understand itself as the advocate of the member states, while the other [340] has put greater trust in the regulatory competence of the federation.

There is no corresponding politicization in German constitutional law. Moreover, in the case of conflicts of federal competencies, the constitution is often quickly amended by political consensus. Most changes to the Basic Law, indeed, concern the federal distribution of competencies. Here too, when the constitutional legislature is effectively capable of acting, this justifies a stricter scrutiny in the court's review. But when the constitutional legislature cannot adapt the federal system of competencies, constitutional court control provides the political practice with greater room for maneuver. This correlation is evident both in the doctrine of the U.S. Supreme Court and the European Court of Justice. In both cases, the courts react to the very harsh constitutional requirements of formal amendments to the system of competencies with a less strict standard of review of said competencies.[14]

Ultimately, a possible legitimating effect of such a review of competences by constitutional courts depends on various factors. Precisely when the constitutional rulebook is not easy to change, an intensive form of control creates new legitimation problems. Furthermore, the implicit presupposition to such a legitimating effect, that constitutional courts can act as neutral arbitrators between the federal levels, is in any case precarious. Although constitutional courts are politically independent, they formally stand on the side of the higher federal level. More important still is the fact that cognitively constitutional courts constantly take a holistic perspective on the legal order, instead of merely focusing on the partial orders of the states. They are devoted to the entire legal order, even if they shall only protect portions of it in a given case. Consequently, according to all comparative law experience, it is typical that constitutional courts in federal systems ultimately prove to be agents of centralization. They empower the central level, for example, through favorably construing discrimination prohibitions. This has occurred in the United States and in the process of European integration alike (Cappelletti/Seccombe/Weiler 1986). This challenges the notion of the courts' impartiality.

[14] For this reason, the Federal Constitutional Court's requirement that European treaties may constitutionally only be amended by consensus (BVerfGE 89, 155—Maastricht (1993); BVerfGE 123, 267—Lisbon (2009)) inevitably leads to a freer interpretation of EU powers by the European Court of Justice.

4. Legitimation through protection of minorities

Under the Basic Law, the Court's justification is construed less from the perspective of the democratic majority but rather from that of the minority. Historically, the Parliamentary Council established the Court to protect minorities, specifically, the opposition and individuals (see, Stüwe 2001 and Hönnige 2007), not least because of the lessons from the National Socialist era. The Court should serve as an institution that could set limits on the political majority, under certain circumstances even on the constitution-amending majority. This interpretation is not a German idiosyncrasy but rather common throughout countries that have decided to adopt constitutional adjudication in response to a totalitarian past. How persuasive is the model of a constitutional court that derives its legitimacy from the protection of minorities? [342]

First of all, the model of minority protection, as already indicated above, is not inconsistent with the model of safeguarding democracy. If democracy is the system in which a minority can become the political majority, and conversely (clearly in Kelsen 1929a), then the rights of political minorities serve as a guarantee of the democratic order. Many constitutional courts make that explicit with regard to the right to freedom of opinion. A constitutional court simultaneously protects the political minority and the democratic order when it enforces freedom of opinion against the legislature. This also appears to be conceptually consistent with the distinguished right of the Court to review the actions of the democratic legislature as the guardian of minorities. Democratic majorities have no need to call upon the Court. Nevertheless, the thesis that constitutional courts draw their legitimacy from the protection of minorities exhibits both ambiguities and systematic deficiencies.

At first, it is important not to equate minorities with the bearers of basic rights. The bearers of property rights or of the right to religious freedom can both be part of the political or social majority as well as representatives of privileged parts of society. It is difficult to identify majority and minority when the right to property of a multinational concern wins out over the land-use plan of a municipality. For a very long time, the Court's doctrine on religious freedom has protected the actions of the Christian majority milieu in a comparatively broad manner. As Muslims began more and more to call on religious freedom, [343] this protection was limited.[15] One cannot speak of minority protection in this instance.

Fundamental rights and minority protection refer to different, incommensurable categories. Not accidentally, empirical social science research on American constitutional adjudication started out with the thesis that the Supreme Court was an organ which represented political majorities in terms of its composition and decision making practice (Dahl 1957; for Germany, critical of the Federal Constitutional Court, Massing 1970 and 2005, 129). Finally, from a political

[15] Cf. the determination of the realm of protection in BVerfGE 24, 236—Rag Collector (1968) and in BVerfGE 104, 337—Religiously Sanctioned Slaughter (2002) [344].

perspective, one can perceive the fact that constitutional courts in most cases attest to the constitutionality of legislation as another legitimation-enhancing argument for the legislature. For now, the majority also has the constitution at its side. Hence, it appears only possible to consider constitutional courts to be agents of minority protection in very specific circumstances, if at all.

The distinction between fundamental rights protection and minority protection raises the question of the latter's legitimating impact beyond merely securing the parliamentary opposition. While one can attribute an independent value to the protection of rights, this is not equally the case with the category of the minority. In most cases, the invocation of minority status may be translated as the invocation of rights that shall apply equally to anybody. The conceptual flaw of the idea [344] of minority protection is that it is generally only applicable when there is a common reference point for determining the appropriate object of protection. For otherwise one could not identify majority and minority save for such a standard of equality that first of all implies the priority of the majority before the minority (Sadurski 2008, 85 ff.).[16] From the fact that minorities are especially in need of protection, it follows that we protect them *because* they are minorities. We protect them because and to the extent that they have rights, which could be especially endangered due to their status as minorities. Ultimately, the reference to the role of constitutional courts in minority protection is at best an imprecise formulation of the task of protecting fundamental rights.

5. Justification through fundamental rights protection

It appears more convincing, after all, to derive the legitimacy of a constitutional court from fundamental rights protection. Although today it is treated as self-evident, fundamental rights protection represents a much more recent function of constitutional courts than the preservation of federal structures. At the outset of the nineteenth century, the U.S. Supreme Court asserted its interpretation of the constitution against the political organs of the Federal Government and the states. Nevertheless, it was not until the second half of the nineteenth century that the [345] Court began to review federal statutes for their compatibility with fundamental rights (Friedman 2005, 279 ff.). The first case in which a federal law was struck down to protect a fundamental right led to the Civil War ("Dred Scott v. Sanford," 60 U.S. 393 [1856]). Like many post-totalitarian courts, however, the Court was expressly established for the protection of fundamental rights. Certainly, a model of justification made in reference to the protection of fundamental rights presupposes an idea of what fundamental rights are and who is to have jurisdiction

[16] For the same reason, the fear of what Tocqueville designated as the "tyranny of the majority" has at least unfortunate connotations as formulated. When tyranny makes pains to distinguish majority and minority, it already applies a standard of normative equality. Correspondingly, one empirically only finds true human rights protection in functioning democracies.

over them. A coupling of law and politics must allocate fundamental rights somewhere within this distinction. Such an allocation is not at all obvious.

Whenever the protection of fundamental rights shall justify the establishment of a constitutional court, they are mostly understood as defined individual legal spheres, in which the political process may not intervene at all or, if so, only under certain conditions. Here the court is protecting an affected person's individual volition within a particular sphere, for example that of religious activity. From its origins to the present, the American understanding of fundamental rights is oriented around a conception of interpreting these rights as a clearly defined pre-political space for action, on which the legislature may under no circumstances intrude. Under the Continental European tradition, by contrast, in France (Gauchet 1995) as in Germany (Wahl 1979), a different understanding of fundamental rights has long dominated, which obliges the legislature to frame and substantiate fundamental rights. Parliament conferred and rescinded fundamental rights for German citizens to protect themselves from administrative seizure. Court protection of fundamental rights consisted [346] of the search for a statutory foundation for a limitation of "freedom and property." Administrative intrusions triggered the competence of the legislature, which undertook the protection of rights through political elaboration.[17] The legitimacy of the courts consisted in protecting citizens from the executive, which, at the same time, facilitated the legislature's actions. Not accidentally, the demand for a court review of the legislature in the Imperial period and in the Weimar Republic stemmed from those parts of academia and the judiciary that were hostile to parliament (Caldwell 1997, 145 ff.; Kübler 1963).

The dispute over an appropriate theory of fundamental rights, the question whether rights are to be understood as legally defined spheres, as programmatic political duties for the legislature, or, indeed, as moral claims has raged since the early nineteenth century critique of law by Bentham and Marx. In the twentieth century, said dispute was invoked in making a case for or against the institution of constitutional adjudication (on one side Waldron 2006, 1364 ff.; the other side Dworkin 1977). One may distinguish between two levels of this confrontation. On the one hand, it is about the reason of the validity of fundamental rights. On the other hand, it concerns their protective function and their scope. The answering of both questions is difficult to pursue separately. Nevertheless, one must keep them both distinct from one another. Are fundamental rights the result of a political decision, or do they have a moral foundation? Do they only offer protection against the actions of the public authority or do they protect against other forms of action as well?

If one intends to classify possible answers to both questions rather crudely, then a liberal understanding of the constitution, which understands rights as pre-political

[17] Strictly understood, a pre-political concept of the law is presupposed here, too, which initiates the need for concrete political elaboration.

spheres that establish negative rights requiring the state to forgo action (Allan 2001), encounters a political understanding of the constitution, which interprets rights as objects of political elaboration and even allows for a notion of rights as claims against the state or even against other citizens (Bellamy 2007; Nino 1996). Fundamental rights can be limited to the determination of state-free spheres. But they can also contain a claim to a proportional elaboration of such spheres by the legislature—or even claims to government assistance. Finally, fundamental rights can even be "objectified" and understood as norms, which operate without a subject, as "values," which must be taken into consideration for the understanding of the entire legal order.

Now, it seems hardly possible to determine the justificatory value of fundamental rights protection for constitutional adjudication separately from the respective court's concrete understanding of these rights. As guardian of a politics-free sphere of individual freedom, the court carries out a genuinely liberal task: it protects the individual from politics. The further away the fundamental rights conception is from the concrete concerns of the individual, the more uncertain this achievement becomes and the more decisions will draw on colliding various different spheres of freedom.

According to the liberal understanding of fundamental rights, for example, the question whether a dangerous criminal should be set free or held in preventive detention only affects the fundamental rights of the criminal. The security concerns of the general public can be [348] articulated politically. There is, however, no fundamental right for protection against criminal acts. On the other hand, a more far-reaching, objectifying understanding of freedom can under certain circumstances even grant constitutional rights to potential victims.[18]

What are the implications for constitutional adjudication? A narrow, liberal understanding of fundamental rights has the advantage that constitutional complaint procedures can only involve the rights of the complainant herself. There is a very close connection between the person of the complainant who initiated the procedure and the application of fundamental rights. *It is the actual freedom of the complainant which justifies the review authority of the court, not the potential freedom of all others.* The more extensive the notion of fundamental rights becomes, the more the concerns of those actually and potentially affected are judicially taken into consideration, although they are not actually represented in the proceedings. This problem becomes clearer if one considers the Kantian insight that the definition of an individual's legal sphere will always affect all the other rights holders as well. The definition of a subjective right requires democratic legitimation, for bound up with

[18] It is important to see that these differing constructions need not contain predeterminations about the ultimate results of the protection. Perhaps a perpetrator will *ultimately* have more rights in a legal order which objectivizes Basic Rights, as in Germany, than in a legal order which does not, like the American one.

it is a decision on the distribution of freedom for everyone. The more extensively constitutional courts deal with fundamental rights, the more pressing the question of their legitimation becomes.

Finally, with a more wide-ranging notion of fundamental rights, they are no longer just a matter of protecting individual opportunities for action, but rather of limiting them, too. For example, the Court [349] not only confines the right to life to a citizen's individual right to not have his life burdened by the state. But, moreover, it derives from said fundamental right to life even a duty to place a criminal penalty on life-threatening actions like abortion. Here, court doctrine diminishes individual freedom as well as the leeway of the democratic legislature.[19] This reflection is not a substantive critique. It only demonstrates that the Court's need for legitimation increases along with expanded notions of fundamental rights. Put differently, an outward-reaching interpretation of fundamental rights involves a politicization of adjudication, because it widens the perspective on the specific case. For, on the one hand, the concerns of a larger number of affected parties must be included in the proceedings, while, on the other hand, fundamental rights also serve to limit individual freedom. Looking back at the example of preventive detention: the multitude of all persons potentially affected by a criminal is not distinguishable from the entire democratic community. So, with the taking on of duties to protect fundamental rights, which oblige the legislature to take action, the Court assumes a new role in the institutional game of powers. For it initiates political action, to which—as a court—it should only react.

A notion of fundamental rights as "objective values" [350] converges constitutional law with an independent moral discourse (Alexy 1986; for critical view see Burchardt 2004, 204ff). In many respects, fundamental rights are here understood as universal super arguments (Dworkin 1984). The principle of proportionality is interpreted as a type of generally valid grammar of justice for solving cases (Kumm 2010). Under this reading, the institutional legitimation of constitutional adjudication lies in the independent deliberation of moral reasons, not the application of law. The "objectification" of fundamental rights further distances the matter in dispute from the participants in the procedure.

The lesson is clear. Because fundamental rights can be understood either as legal claims or as political programs in need of fulfillment, entirely different possibilities for the coupling of politics and law conceal themselves behind the task of fundamental rights protection by constitutional courts. To the extent that independent

[19] The example stems from the Court's doctrine on abortion (BVerfGE 39, 1—Abortion I (1975); BVerfGE 88, 203—Abortion II (1993)). It is characteristic of the problem discussed above that these decisions were not occasioned by a constitutional complaint, but rather by a procedure to resolve disputes between two constitutional organs. Consequently, there is not even a specific holder of fundamental rights involved in the case. In Sweden, one found this doctrine so dauntingly politicized that this was even used as an argument against the introduction of constitutional adjudication (Lamprecht/Malanowski 1979, 15).

constitutional courts protect a sphere of individual opportunities for action under the constitution from limitation through the political process, they have very good arguments on their side. However, as one argues for a notion of fundamental rights that is more far-reaching and de-subjectified, the more politicized and in need of legitimation is the Court's claim to decision-making, for it moves further and further away from the structure of the constitutional complaint procedure. [351]

6. Legitimation through deliberation and expertise

A constitutional court's actual level of legitimacy may be due after all to the opportunity for a politically independent exchange of reasons both between the justices and between the court and the parties. The idea of establishing legitimacy through the open exchange of arguments and counterarguments has gained in importance with reference to the idea of "deliberative democracy" (Elster 1998, 8 ff.; Manin 1987). Scholarly literature has meanwhile applied this conception to constitutional courts (recently Ferejohn/Pasquino 2010).

In concrete terms, this begs the question whether courts should fulfill the high rationality and morality expectations which are addressed by such decision-making techniques, and, if so, why courts are better fitted for this than other actors like parliaments, governments, or independent administrative agents. Institutional arguments point to the issue of judicial independence here. For the latter may facilitate an exchange of reasoning among justices that satisfies other standards of rationality than is the case among politically dependent actors. This model, therefore, is of interest for the Federal Constitutional Court in particular, because it allows for the creation of legitimacy through the institution itself without having to refer to the observance of norms. It is an attractive theory for a court that keeps developing its own standards. Such a model is suitable precisely because the Court has a high degree of expertise, since the vast majority of the justices consists of former federal judges and law professors. [352]

At this point, of course, at least four objections come to the fore. First, the idea of legitimation through the give and take of reasons also requires the inclusion of *all* affected parties in the discussion (Habermas 1992, 151 ff.). The idea that a circle of experts or judges could simply simulate this incorporation is, indeed, current in the recent international law literature (Slaughter 2004, 203 ff.), but it is not justified by the theory. The model is poorly suited for court procedures for two reasons, the first of which is its exclusive character. The other is that judgments authoritatively put an end to the discourse, for which, in this theory, there may be a pragmatic, but certainly not a normative, justification. The second objection is that the model, as interpreted, calls for wide-ranging institutional independence. When every decision argumentatively has to be justified anew over and over, then this discourse operates neither by commitment to rules nor to norms. To put it pointedly: a deliberative institution can no longer be bound to any form of law. It is simply independent. This leads to a third objection: is it even possible to perceive such an institution as part of a political order conforming to legal norms, namely to a constitution? If the idea of the constitution consists in the interrelated distinguishability of law and politics, then the concept of deliberation abolishes this distinction. If reasons are exchanged in parliament as well as in court, one of these institutions may be better suited for that than the other. Nevertheless, they both no longer follow different logics. But does not such a court rather resemble a court of morality or reason than a court of constitutional law? Fourth, [353] the assessment of a constitutional court's capacity to truly engage in deliberation differs significantly in comparative terms (Ferejohn/Pasquino 2010). Some courts do not appear to interact especially intensively either internally or with the parties.

7. Intermezzo: models in context

All of the aforementioned models grasp certain elements of a justification of constitutional courts. At the same time, they appear neither self-sufficient nor consistent. A legitimate institutional setup or even a legitimate doctrine of constitutional review cannot be derived from one of these models alone or a combination of all of them. Nevertheless, many theories of constitutional adjudication claim to be universal at a level extending beyond a particular legal system.[20] However, these theories at least implicitly ignore not only the political and social contexts, but also the entire level of positive law, which forms part of these contexts. It appears more convincing, by contrast, to refer to the legitimation models as mere elements of a reconstruction of justificatory problems. These problems, however, require further elaboration.

In a democratic constitutional system, it is for the constitution-maker and the legislature to carry out such elaborations. [354] For their decisions are democratically legitimated and can, therefore, be raised as an objection to the abstract arguments of legitimation theories. The analytical starting point must be the priority of the concrete democratic decision over the theoretical argument for legitimacy (following Rorty 1991). Put differently, one should be skeptical about legitimation theories that do not purport to govern simply as natural law, but which still always know better than a democratically legitimated legislative organ that has opted in favor of a strong form of constitutional court review. That does not mean that such a theory's arguments are simply to be excluded. However, they need to be embedded in the context of democratic lawmaking, they need to argue *within* this context.

But how is such argumentation conceivable? Here again, we recognize a discursive feedback effect, because the inclusion of positive law, as already seen, links legality and legitimacy, though the content of legality often remains uncertain. Therefore, it is important to see that a theoretical observation of positive law from

20 Paradigmatic for the German discussion is the pioneering, idiosyncratic, though also incomplete, form of argument in Habermas (1993, 324 ff.).

within the legal order is still different from a legal argument. The former does not entail a claim of legality, but it is rather about the development of the law's own theoretical presuppositions and about the disclosure of internal contradictions. This shall now be demonstrated with the example of Germany's Court.

A reconstruction of the Court's legitimation will not adhere to a simple formula, in which one applies institutional factors, in order to calculate an unambiguous result. The point is rather to develop a set of arguments for a critical [355] or affirmative reconstruction of the Court's achievements. A comprehensive result of the sort, "The court is/is not legitimated," cannot be expected from this. Instead, institutional peculiarities, models of legitimation, and objections against precisely this model must be correlated in order to unfold a consistent description of the legitimating contributions and problems of the Court.

C. Legitimation structures in the Federal Constitutional Court's procedure

1. Status: the Federal Constitutional Court as a constitutional organ

The "status" of a constitutional court in between the political system and the legal system is, as we have seen, not easy to determine. It oscillates between both of them, it reveals a hybrid character, but it nevertheless retains the institutional form of a court. The decision of the Parliamentary Council for a constitutional court and against a federal supreme court speaks in favor of this mixed form. Despite this, the Court, unlike other state organs, is not accorded its own chapter in the Basic Law. Though the Herrenchiemsee Conference had intended this, it was no accident that the corresponding provisions were absent in later drafts (Schiffers 1984, XIV). The Basic Law incorporated the Court as a special court among others in the chapter on the adjudicative authority, but not as a constitutional organ.

The early Court was faced with double animosity between politics and law, which [356] is not surprising, given the fact that the Court—as a new institution—still had to find its role. On the political side, above all the Federal Government was not willing to allow its political room for maneuver to be limited by a court (Häussler 1994, 22 ff.). On the other side, the Court was confronted with an assertive system of ordinary courts. Notably the Federal High Court of Justice, as part of the politically conservative elite of specialized jurists, was not ready to bow before a new, politicized form of constitutional adjudication with judges whose expertise in the technical aspects of specialized law was in doubt (Faller 1990, 187 et subs.). Animosities from both sides also implied a dispute about recent history. Like a large proportion of the political representatives, the Federal High Court of Justice was politically discredited. The early Court, by contrast, was the only institution in which members of the resistance and of the exile community constituted a critical mass. Many of its decisions, particularly the doctrine on civil servant status, also did not spare National Socialist collaborators (Frei 1996, 69 et subs.).

Against this background, the Court finally redefined itself as a constitutional body in its famous "status report." This entailed the proclamation of the Court's emancipation in terms of budget and protocol. Composed by Gerhard Leibholz (Leibholz 1957a), a teacher of constitutional law and victim of National Socialist persecution, the report was controversial, even internally, and encountered strong criticism in the Federal Ministry of Justice, among a minority of the Court itself, and within the scholarly community (Thoma 1953, 165 ff.).[21] Ultimately, the Court prevailed, and at last parliament recognized the Court's status as a "constitutional organ" in the revised Section 1 of the Federal Constitutional Court Law of 1970. [357]

The status report is the Court's small version of "Marbury v. Madison," therefore, a form of self-empowerment that is familiar to us from the history of many other constitutional courts. What is noteworthy about it, first off, is the memoir form—a genuine ode to professors of constitutional law. While German constitutional law scholarship adopted the perspective of the Court at the expense of its own scientific issues, the Court reversed things in this case by camouflaging its own institutional claim to power as a piece of scholarship. It did not incorporate this aspiration into the reasoning of a judgment, as other courts have done, but instead operated at the point of intersection between law, politics, and scholarship. In the memoir, neither politics nor law define the status of the Court. Much rather, it is the "essence" of the relationship between politics and law, as it has scholarly been determined. Leibholz defined the status of the court as a "representative constitutional organ" (Leibholz 1957a, 128 f.), which also exercised "functions of government and legislature." Some judgments would inevitably have the character of "highly political governmental actions." This resulted from the force of law of the Court's judgements. Consequently, the Constitutional Court had to be placed at the same level as the government and parliament and had to be recognized as a constitutional body.

The memoir is well understood as a reaction to the precarious double animosity facing the court then. It even appears convincing that the coupling of law and politics functions cannot operate at just any random hierarchical level. Nevertheless, one will have to disapprove of the status report. For it unveils for the first time a self-conception that enables the Court to define its place in the constitutional order all by itself. [358] That the political system followed the Court in this matter by ratifying its new status as constitutional body into law may have subsequently legitimated this approach. Quite a bit of ignorance regarding the legality, which had facilitated the Court in the first place, is evident in this line of argument, nonetheless. This is especially noteworthy because the Court's ultimate argument for the justification

[21] On the discussion, see the portrayal in Lembcke 2007, 91 ff.

of its own decisions does not play any role in this central question. The rhetorically sophisticated memoir makes no effort to justify its claim by use of the text of the Basic Law. Scholarly, theoretical, and comparative arguments predominate. The contemporary scholarly criticism quickly recognized (Thoma 1953, 165 ff.) that a justification of the memoir based on the Basic Law was hardly possible. But it may be just as questionable to draw budget law and protocol consequences from the mere status of a constitutional body (Voßkuhle 2010c, RN 29).

It is highly remarkable how clearly and openly the Court's members and even the constitutional framers and legislators in the early Federal Republic have emphasized the political significance of the Court. And it is just as astounding how much this insight gave way, little by little, to a purely legalistic view of constitutional law and doctrine. The memoir, however, did not manage to distinguish between the constitutional adjudication's political significance and the Court's classification as a court. As we have seen, the Court in fact takes on a special role in the political system, when it rejects parliamentary statutes and decides upon disputes between political bodies. At the same time, the fact still remains that it does so [359] in the form of court decisions. In words other than those of the memoir (Leibholz 1957a, 128): the Court is neither legislature nor government. It does not participate in "state leadership" (Schlaich 1981, 116 in footnote 56), either. All of these functions require the power of self-initiative. The Court does not define an agenda, and it does not develop its own policies in the political game, even if the consequences of its judgments can have such effects (Heun 2008). As soon as the Court claimed such competencies it would be unclear why its members had to be independent and why the Court had to provide reasons for its decisions. The Basic Law selected the form of a court for the aforementioned coupling of law and politics. Much in the argumentation of the memoir appears to depend on the false identification of mere political significance with policy-making. The same is true for parts of the political theory of constitutional adjudication (IV.B.).

2. The election of judges

The constitutional courts' specific task of a coupling of politics and law becomes evident not least in the fact that the election of judges is an expressly political act. Two political bodies, the Bundestag and the Federal Council, elect the justices of the Court by a two-thirds majority (on different models, Billing 1969, 238 ff.). This manner of political legitimation is not unusual in comparative law terms. We have seen that this provides a starting point for the thesis of the constitutional adjudication's political character. It would be a misunderstanding to consider this as an illegitimate arrangement of powers. Quite the contrary, [360] the idea that powers do not amend themselves is a basic concept of most constitutional systems. Instead, the people or other authorities must create and expand these powers. The self-empowerment of the judiciary—which is independent in its decisions anyway—threatens to withdraw from any control mechanisms. For a body that is granted the authority to reverse democratically enacted statutes also demands, at least at its inception, democratic legitimation. The requirement of a two-thirds majority and the informal distribution of seats on the Court between political parties link a need for political consensus with the facilitation of the Court's internal political pluralization. That is a favorable solution, even if one must not overlook that small parties might be excluded. Like all decision-making rules among coalitions, the process leads to the election of politically moderate justices. This may facilitate the coherence of the Court's case law. To this degree, a legitimation problem is not raised. Since constitutional justices in Germany cannot be re-elected after the end of their term, the Court's independence is strengthened, as is the legitimating effect of the judges' appointments, for no long passage of time may ossify the institution.

The opacity of the election procedure has drawn criticism, however, because, unlike the U.S. system, it lacks public presentation as well as public debate on the candidates (for a thorough account see Epstein/Segal 2005, 87 ff.). The American case is certainly instructive. The U.S. has had public criticism of candidates for a very long time, at least since the nomination of Louis Brandeis in 1916. The sensational character of the American [361] Senate hearings, by contrast, is a comparatively recent phenomenon. The rejection of Robert Bork as justice of the Supreme Court in 1987 provided the high public profile to the process, as it is known today. Whether such a public discussion ensues, however, is not a mere question of statutory law, but rather an expression of public concern, which cannot simply be imposed by law. Institutionally, the public hearing in the American election process is an expression of the conflict of legitimation between Congress and the President, as is typical of presidential systems. This cannot be said about parliamentary systems, in which the government is supported by parliament. Considering that there has never even been a similar hearing procedure for members of the Federal Government, who, in contrast to justices, must perform their work directly in the public eye, a formalized hearing procedure appears inappropriate. All political participants—from the general public to the factions of the Bundestag—are free to publicly discuss public appointments. The Basic Law expressly precludes a parliamentary debate about the persons standing for election as Federal President and Federal Chancellor (Art. 54, sec. 1 and Art. 63, sec. 1). Therefore, this appears even less appropriate for the position of a constitutional justice, which is not conducted publicly. The current mode of election is fully suited to the duty of the Court to reach decisions—with potential political effect, though in the form of court procedure.

3. In particular: expertise through professors as justices

German legal scholarship puts a comparatively strong focus on the analysis of lawmaking by the state. By requiring its junior staff to pass highly respected and competitive state (instead of university) examinations, legal academia and law applicants mutually influence one another in an unusually strong way. [362] The legal system might actually benefit more than scholarship (Möllers/Voßkuhle 2003) from this close connection of theory and practice.

The fact that law professors regularly sit on the Court reveals a similar proximity of theory and practice. From the beginning, the Court has consisted and still consists of renowned teachers of constitutional law like Gerhard Leibholz, Martin Drath, Ernst Friesenhahn, Konrad Hesse, Ernst-Wolfgang Böckenförde, Paul Kirchhof, Hans Hugo Klein, Dieter Grimm, and Wolfgang Hoffmann-Riem. In 2011, nine of the sixteen justices were law professors. Although other constitutional systems also prefer professors as justices, they do not carry this preference to an extreme.

By looking at this court composition, we can identify once again a distinctive variant of the deliberative model of justification. Legal academics may prove to be especially qualified to argue about constitutional law. Whether this justification strategy has the desired effect, however, also depends on one's basic understanding of the constitution. A political understanding of the constitution may be skeptical about the high number of professors on the bench. For from this perspective, everybody is equally entitled to interpret a political document. In the "open society of constitutional interpreters" (Häberle 1975) no special expertise is necessary. It is no coincidence that American constitutional lawyers are surprised at the aspirations of their European colleagues to define the constitutional system with expert knowledge (emphatically Post 2009, 419–21). The constitutional understanding currently prevailing in Germany, which is more firmly based on legalization and systematization of law (for criticism Jestaedt 2006, 81 ff.), may ascribe its own value to the inclusion of professors. [363] It can ensure the quality of decisions and at the same time promote the special character of constitutional court decisions, which, as we have seen, contain argumentation that more closely approximates political or legal theory than do the decisions of ordinary courts.

Since political and legal understandings of the constitution can never be mutually exclusive, it is necessary to strive for mediating positions. Academic legal scholars, who frequently argue for a systematic legalization of the political process, could serve as a counterbalance to court members with a political background. There have been examples of such combinations ever since the Court's inception. Gebhard Müller, Ernst Benda, Jutta Limbach, or Christine Hohmann-Dennhardt are worth mentioning here. If one takes into account that, according to the Basic Law, three justices of each Senate have to be selected from the supreme federal courts, the number of political members regularly lags far behind those from the scholarly community. If the justification problem of constitutional courts lies in the relation between the reach of its decisions and its procedure (see **II.A.**), academic legal reasoning that tends to imply an excessive scope of decisions (Lepsius 2008a, 104 f.) is likely to accentuate this problem. Precisely if the broadening of the scope of decisions is doubtful in terms of legitimacy, and if an important justification strategy consists in limiting the content of the decision, increasing the ratio of professors on the Court can conversely produce legitimation deficits. A more balanced proportion of academics, judges, and "political" members on the Court may seem advisable.

Against this backdrop, the practice of the Court shows a mixed picture. To begin with, the Court owes [364] the internationally noteworthy reputation of its reasoning to the participation of academic legal scholars. It is not always simple to follow the genealogy of Court reasons in detail. One can document connections between the grounds of decisions and academic work, though.[22] Academia does not always have a direct effect on the Court's decision-making, but justices with professorial backgrounds regularly frame their arguments in an academic way. Consequently, the remarkable length of the Court's judgments as well as the broadening of the reach of court decisions is probably not a matter of pure coincidence. The doctrine of the Court often seems to aim at an abstract solution of legal problems rather than deciding on a concrete case. The way in which scholars of constitutional law interpret judgments constitutes a further problem. They are inclined to neglect the factual circumstances of a decision and tend to read and interpret decisions as if they were legal texts (Lepsius 2008a, 111 ff.). Hermann von Mangoldt, one of the founders of the Basic Law, once prophetically remarked: "There is a great risk that an abstract principle will be deduced from a decision of the Court, which will then be applied to other cases without a careful examination of whether the principle should rather not be applied because of the distinctiveness of the case" (cited in Laufer 1968, 91).

In view of the Continental European influences on German legal scholarship, German discourse lacks interpretive techniques which can systematically incorporate historical and political contexts [365] into the analysis of the decision.[23] Another special aspect is the justices' self-interpretation of their judgments in scholarly essays. While justices have done theoretical preliminary work since the beginning of the Court, which they then adopt as justices, it is a more recent development that sitting justices interpret their own decisions.[24] This comes across as a strategy of self-legitimization, which is thoroughly double-edged. Do those interpretations constitute scholarly or quasi-official statements? Are we confronted with an involuntary confession of the court members' failure to provide an adequate justification for a decision that therefore requires further explanation? Or

[22] Examples are the fundamental rights theory of Rudolf Smend, Gerhard Leibholz's theory of the party state, or Böckenförde's conception of democracy.

[23] Oliver Lepsius points out that, until today, authors still refer to decisions of the Court without indicating the decision's date, probably a technique that is unique around the world, which unnecessarily expands the reach of the decision. In the present volume, all cited opinions appear with their dates.

[24] This happens quite frequently in articles that seem to discuss more general topics, but which clearly address concrete cases; sometimes it happens quite openly and it applies to many articles by active justices during publication (Stein 1967; Henschel 1990; Kirchhof 1994 on BVerfGE 89, 155—Maastricht (1993); Grimm 1995b; Hoffmann-Riem 2008 on BVerfGE 120, 274—Right to confidentiality and integrity of IT systems (2008)).

do individual justices want to nail down results, which they could not successfully make prevail in the Senate? Finally, is this not an attempt to extend the reach of a decision, without a legal mandate?

To sum it up: while the inclusion of professors in the composition of the Court constitutes a peculiarity of German constitutional adjudication that gives rise to particular problems, but at the same time brings about unique qualities that suits the strongly legalistic German approach of constitutional thinking, the phenomenon of self-interpretation [366] expresses unease about the Court's limited opportunities to communicate decisions. The dissolution of boundaries between official decisions and, in the end, private scholarly opinions cannot have legitimizing effects for the Court. Finally, the high proportion of scholars on the Court would appear even more legitimate if more justices with political experience were appointed in order to provide a counterbalance.

4. Access—dependence on petition—work load

The procedural access to the Court represents a decisive institutional peculiarity of its decision-making. Courts draw their legitimacy essentially from the fact that they do not decide on their own initiative. This alone justifies their independent decision-making. At the same time, they have leeway to decide whether to reject a legal question on substantive or procedural grounds. One of the most important, and, at the same time, unusual features of the Federal Constitutional Court is the direct access for "everyone" (Art. 93, par. 1, no. 4a) in the constitutional complaint procedure. This generous access rule has led to the Court's reputation as a citizens' court (III.A.).[25] Finally, it sets the protection of fundamental rights as the central justificatory element of the Court.

Two essential procedural requirements limit the access to constitutional complaints.[26] [367] First, the petitioner must allege that one of his or her fundamental rights has been infringed upon by public authority. Secondly, all legal measures must be exhausted beforehand.

The Court has modified the aforementioned prerequisites in two directions. On the one hand, in an early revolutionary decision, it extended fundamental rights protection to all conceivable actions (BVerfGE 6, 32—Elfes (1957)). Not only selected actions like an expression of opinion or religious practice are protected under this reading of fundamental rights and, consequently, accorded access under the complaint procedure. Rather, every free human activity is protected from government limitations by the understanding of general freedom of action created by the Court.[27]

[25] "Citizen" can mean bourgeois as well as citoyen here; the Lüth case can be properly designated as a "political constitutional complaint" (Häberle 1980, 61f.).

[26] A comprehensive representation of the access requirements is not required here (for this Schorkopf 2005; Schlaich/Korioth 2010, RN 194 ff.).

[27] The most well-known critique of this doctrine was formulated by the Court itself in a dissenting opinion by Dieter Grimm (BVerfGE 80, 137, 164 ff.—Riding in Forests (1989)).

Consequently, any public legal restriction can potentially become the object of a constitutional complaint. Secondly, the Court and, in its turn, also the legislature has "objectified" the constitutional complaint.[28] That is to say that the constitutional complaint procedure serves not only the protection of the rights of the petitioner, but also the objective elaboration of constitutional law. Thus, on several occasions, the importance of a case for the evolution of constitutional law [368] has been established as a criterion for access to the Court.[29]

This dual modification has important consequences. On the one hand, it *opens* access through the generalization of fundamental rights protection. On the other hand, it *prioritizes* this access and ultimately limits it by distinguishing important from less important concerns. One could argue that the Court has compensated the obvious "substantive" opening of access with a veiled procedural closure. The Court has not only expressly limited the requests for legal protection in the name of objective criteria when it was overwhelmed with constitutional complaints;[30] instead, in view of the extreme scarcity of resources (Wahl/Wieland 1996), the criterion of objective importance of a case also involves an important distributional decision for the complainants. The Court does not schedule constitutional complaints on a first-come-first-served basis but even significant decisions require a long time. A terminally ill person had to wait almost eight years (1 BvR 347/98 of December 6, 2005). A complainant, seeking to indirectly challenge a highly controversial decision of the European Court of Justice before the Court, raised the complaint after the failure of the EU constitutional treaty in 2006, but received a decision only after the judgment on the Lisbon (EU) treaty in 2010 (2 BvR 2661/06 of July 6, 2010). The state of European integration had evolved significantly in the meantime. Conversely, the Court also uses the criterion of [369] significance to decide cases without requiring the complainant to exhaust all legal remedies. There is—this is decisive—a procedural distributional conflict between subjective and objective understandings of the complaint procedure. The Court gives preference to some cases while putting others on the back burner. The Court's objective understanding of the procedure is taken to the extreme, so that the Court has ignored the withdrawal of a complaint as well as the complainant's death, thereby having reached important decisions even without any complainant.[31]

In terms of legitimation theory, the two steps of opening and objectifying the complaint procedure is not unproblematic, in particular if it is true that fundamental rights protection is the central legitimatory basis for the Court. If the Court

[28] Compare the original draft of s. 90 ff. in Schiffers 1984, 445 f. The Court has spoken of an objective meaning of the constitutional complaint since BVerfGE 33, 247—Klagestop (1972).

[29] Cf. s. 90, 2, 2 of the Federal Constitutional Court Law ("general significance"); s. 93a, 2a of the Federal Constitutional Court Law ("fundamental general constitutional significance").

[30] BVerfGE 94, 166, 213 ff.—Airport Procedures (1996). The case involved a constitutional complaint by foreigners threatened with deportation.

[31] BVerfGE 98, 218, 242—Spelling Reform (1998); BVerfGE 124, 300, 318—Wunsiedel (2009).

as a legal institution draws its justification first and foremost from taking care of the complainant's individual request, and if the Court derives its popularity, and even its self-understanding, primarily from the protection of bearers of fundamental rights seeking legal protection, then the criteria of "objectivity" limiting the subjective side of legal protection become questionable. What is at issue here are criteria which, on the one hand, lie beyond the concern for legal protection itself, and yet, on the other hand, also lie beyond the mere political relevance of the case. It is indeed possible to name such criteria. Thus, certain cases may concern open legal questions, for which other courts and parties are awaiting a constitutional answer. Nevertheless, the application of these criteria decisively changes the justification logic of the Court (see part **IV.D.** for more details). The Court transforms itself [370] from an entity in service of the complainant to a body that is supposed to ensure the coherence of the entire legal system. Both concerns are appropriate, but they must be distinguished from one another. A court deciding objective legal questions cannot derive its justification exclusively from the demands of the bearers of fundamental rights. The more strongly the Court objectifies the access to the Court, the less it can legitimate itself as a court of civil rights. In this regard, even the question of equal treatment of complainants is not resolved.[32] While understandable in practical terms, it is still not at all justifiable when the Court decides cases without any actual petitions. For here, the Court no longer merely addresses concerns of a bearer of fundamental rights in the light of objective criteria. Such concerns are simply nonexistent. Institutionally, the Court is acting as judge without a petitioner, hence no longer as a court at all.

Another institutional problem lies behind the questions of access and of case selection: the overburdening of the Court as a result of the constitutional complaint procedure.[33] The objectification of the constitutional complaint procedure enabled the Court to breathe rigor into its own doctrine, which threatens to unravel because of an excessive amount of complaints. The Court has always rejected the establishment of a voluntary acceptance procedure, in which the Court itself is free to [371] choose its cases. In this constellation, the Court would become unequivocally responsible for the selection of constitutional complaints to be decided. The legislature's preferred solution of a preliminary acceptance procedure is, as was rightly pointed out, an expression of a "dualistic legal morality."[34] On the one hand, the Court can still address all fundamental rights violations, while, on the other, both criteria of acceptance refer to objective conditions: the one refers to the

[32] Contrary to common use, in this context, the subjective component must be defined much more precisely than the objective component. "Subjective" refers to individual concerns of certain legal subjects; "objective" refers to uncertain criteria of greater significance.

[33] The treatment of the problem also documents cycles of political and academic attention. At the end of the 1990s, it was extensively discussed in terms of legal policy (cf. Wahl/Wieland 1996, 1137ff. with further evidence; Benda 1998). Afterwards, the problem disappeared as a theme without being resolved.

[34] Lechner/Zuck 2011, before s. 93a, para. 45 at the end.

"fundamental constitutional significance," and the other to the "enforcement" of the indicated rights.[35]

A pattern emerges, in which the Court primarily decides constitutional complaints involving either the threat of a dramatic, unrecoverable legal loss or an objectively significant question. As such, this might sound like a reasonable solution, but the outcome is something entirely different from a general citizen's complaint. The sheer amount of constitutional complaints obliges the Court to make a selection of cases it will decide on. The legal situation conceals rather than reveals this need for selection. In terms of legitimation theory, the reference to a general protection of fundamental rights for "everyone" clearly loses its plausibility.[36] The relationship between the substantive broadening of fundamental rights protection and the [372] procedural objectification of the access criteria is problematic. The opaque dealing with the flood of petitions finally raises the question to what extent the Court is in a position to define its own agenda and to relieve itself de facto from the individual complaint of a petitioner, which is important for its justification.

5. Internal differentiation of the Court

The internal structure of the Court is directly related to its great workload. Like other constitutional bodies, the Court needs an internal division of labor in order to manage its workload. From the perspective of its justices, the Court's internal organization is one of the central conditions of the Court's work. However, it is certainly a condition very few outsiders understand in depth (Cf. interviews in Kranenpohl 2009). Of course, neither scholars nor judges can be blamed for not knowing each other's perspective. For even if a purely external perspective is ill-suited for describing the Court appropriately, the familiarity with the internal view unavoidably leads to cognitive deficits as well. One knows one's own milieu better, but one does not necessarily understand it better. The normative insight that a view into the internal organization of the Court can have an *explanatory*, but *not a justificatory*, content appears more important than this cognitive problem. Just as in the case of other organizations [373], in particular in the case of parliament and the administration, the internal view helps in understanding successes and failures, but does not have a legitimating effect for the addressees of the decision. From an

[35] Even this second condition is understood objectively. It does not involve an individual case, but rather structural questions of Basic Rights protection, i.e., those affecting several cases (on this Lechner/Zuck 2011, s. 93a, para. 24 ("general negligence"); Schlaich/Korioth 2010, RN 264).

[36] The fact that in other circumstances the Court even asks the legislature to create new types of proceedings to provide a more intensive control of European law reflects a certain institutional indecisiveness in regard to this problem (BVerfGE 124, 267, 355—Lisbon (2009); there the Court states: "Also conceivable, however, is the creation by the legislature of an additional type of proceedings before the Federal Constitutional Court that is especially tailored to *ultra vires* review and identity review to safeguard the obligation of German bodies not to apply in individual cases in Germany legal instruments of the European Union that transgress competences or that violate constitutional identity.")

external perspective—in normative terms—it is always the attributive subject that acts, in our case the Court.

In its present form, the Court consists of two Senates containing eight justices each, which, in turn, are subdivided into three chambers with three justices each (Hermes 2001). The chambers reach a consensus on the distribution of cases and the changing filling of the ninth place. The division into chambers facilitates the management of the mass of constitutional complaints. All justices have three full-time staff members, often lower court judges, who support them in their work. This division of labor entails an easing of the workload. Not least of all it enables internal specialization. At the same time, this differentiation obviously poses a threat to the coherence of the Court's doctrine as a whole. When there is a divergence in the jurisdiction between Senates, the Court can and must formally summon the plenum. Decisions within a chamber can only be taken unanimously. In case of disagreement, the Senate is to decide. In practice, the convocation of the plenum occurs very rarely, probably not only because the Court does not want to reveal internal conflicts. Rather, genuine disagreements between Senates on concrete legal questions are seldom. However, Senates quite frequently set different accents in dealing with fundamental questions.[37] [374] The field of police investigations comes to mind, in which the First Senate is responsible for threats to public safety and the Second Senate for criminal prosecution. Both are ruling on identical provisions, but they do so with thoroughly different tendencies, albeit without contradicting themselves in the process.[38]

The significance of such differences must not be underestimated because other courts and the legislature observe the Court, both of which attempt to anticipate constitutional objections to their decision-making practice and find it difficult to receive orientation from the Court. The publication of selected chamber decisions since 2003 only seems to increase the problem. If the legitimate aim of an official collection of decisions is to provide orientation by canonization, the overabundance of included decisions prevents canonization. It is even more striking that both Senates do not always take notice of each other in their citation practice—another sign of internal pluralization.

As a result, it is not exaggerated to speak of a tendency toward the fraying of doctrine through the large number of decisions and the differentiation of the Court. In terms of legitimation theory, such a pluralization has a similar effect to that of the publication of dissenting opinions, even if this is unintended in this case: it

[37] There are differences between the Senates with regard to the principle of democracy. See Bryde 2000, 63ff.

[38] Cf. on the core area of private ways of life, for example, on the one hand, from the First Senate, BVerfGE 109, 279, 318 ff.—Big Eavesdropping Operation (2004) and BVerfGE 120, 274, 334 ff.—Right to confidentiality and integrity of IT systems (2008); on the other hand, the reluctant remarks of the Third Chamber of the Second Senate in BVerfG, Decision of May 11, 2007, 2 BvR 543/06, Paragraph Number 39 ff.

documents the contingency of the Constitutional Court's modes and patterns of argument—contingency not in the sense [375] of randomness or politicization, but in the sense of a strongly relativized determinacy of constitutional court decisions through its own reasoning—and shows how limited justification qua legality actually is. A genuine resolution of this problem merely through organization seems hardly possible. More justices or more support staff would only accentuate the problem. Solely a restriction of access could provide a remedy.

6. Oral proceedings

Oral proceedings fulfill distinct tasks in different legal orders and different parts of legal systems. Inter alia, they enable the *public* to observe court proceedings. Public oral proceedings are not unusual for the legal system, but rather constitute a basic requirement of the rule of law. However, the question of how oral proceedings in the Court are conducted remains unanswered. Are oral proceedings merely a legal exchange between participants in a trial with the aim of clarifying an individualized set of facts, or does the different function of constitutional adjudication have an effect on the form of oral proceedings?

The law considers oral proceedings as the rule, which may be waived by the parties. In practice, the Court mostly recommends the parties to opt for this waiver, and the parties regularly follow this suggestion. Because of the high number of cases, oral proceedings thus become the exception. The Court itself decides on this exception without rendering the reasons for the decision public. This allows the Court to influence the degree of public attention for a particular case. Of course, the Court can also recommend parties not to opt for the waiver in cases [376] which have received special public attention and therefore require oral proceedings. Two observations apply to both variants. The Court has room for maneuver. It acts with or reacts to the political public.

The design of oral proceedings before the Court confirms this impression. These turn out very differently from those before other German or comparable foreign courts, for example, the U.S. Supreme Court.[39] Indeed, the Court pre-structures the proceedings in written form. Nevertheless, the procedure often resembles a public hearing. Compared to the U.S. Supreme Court, where every hearing has a very limited time frame, frequently a total of sixty minutes, the Court is less strict in limiting the spoken contributions of the participants in terms of content and time. Oral proceedings before the Court often take one whole day—the "Lisbon Trial" even extended over two days. The participants are comparatively free to intervene. Moreover, the interested parties, who have submitted written briefs, are also frequently invited to present an oral argument. Hence, the trial provides the parties as well as further interested participants with the opportunity to publicly

[39] Documentation volumes with the protocols of oral arguments proceedings (Isensee/Schmidt-Jortzig 1999; Schorkopf 2006) offer a vivid insight into the procedure.

formulate a position. For the Court, the oral proceedings help in obtaining a more exact impression of the *factual* side of the case. [377]

Oral proceedings before the Court resemble parliamentary hearings. Under some circumstances, they attract even more public attention than parliamentary proceedings. This was the case, for example, in the Lisbon Trial, in which the oral proceeding produced publicity for a political opposition critical of the European Union, for which parliamentary debate did not provide much space.[40] The Court has room for maneuver in dealing with oral proceedings. It uses them in order to broaden the object of discussion and for a generous inclusion of affected parties. The opposite strategy of restriction would also be conceivable. Internal rules that are not at all oriented toward public attention could determine whether oral proceedings take place or not. Another strategy of restriction could consist of a strict juridification of the trial.

It is important for the acceptance of the Court that it acts as an institution that listens to the participants and that must even incorporate their objections into the decision.[41] With regard to the Court's legitimation, however, the problem of the overrepresentation of case participants in opposition to the democratic majority is particularly acute at this point (**IV.A.**). Oral proceedings put the individual concerns of participants in the public eye and may outshine other legitimate concerns. If the Court reacts to public interest [378], the problem of unequal attention becomes even more acute. The possibility of a live transmission of the decision's announcement, which is reserved to the Court, accentuates this adverse effect.

7. Legal reasoning and the reach of decisions

Legal reasoning is at the very center of every court activity. Through their reasoning, the courts also justify themselves, for what is being explained is not self-evident. This contribution cannot do justice to the Court's technique of legal reasoning, especially since it displays great differences between the Senates and in the course of time. Even the Court's methods of constitutional interpretation cannot be examined in more detail here. Instead, our theoretical reflections on legitimation will be linked with specific aspects of the Court's technique of legal reasoning.

In particular in the beginning of their existence, it is important that constitutional courts set out their modes and patterns of argumentation that serve as the basis of justification for the Court's decision. Constitutional provisions concerning this matter are regularly too indeterminate. The more doctrine there is, the more the Court can have recourse to its own reasoning and develop it further.

[40] This appears to be the case in particular with regard to foreign and European political policy questions issues, in which the Bundestag frequently decides in concord with a substantial portion of the opposition. The policy of the Court to allow petitioner complainants to express themselves extensively compensates, whether intentionally or not unintentionally, for the long-standing absence of a pertinent critique of the European Union in German politics.

[41] S. 30, 1, 1 of the Federal Constitutional Court Law.

The central mode of the Court's self-justification, as we have seen, lies in the reference to the law, which is, in turn, essentially a reference to its own doctrine (for a justice's perspective: Kranenpohl 2009, 394; quantitatively: Schäller 2006, 217 ff.). The increasing self-referentiality in the grounds of the decisions is especially effective in a specialized constitutional court like the Federal Constitutional Court [379], because it stands alone at the hierarchical peak of the legal system and because its reasoning, in contrast to a supreme court, is inevitably of constitutional rank.[42] The reference to law is a reference to the Court itself, a thoroughly precarious construction, which, as such, hardly provides sufficient justification. The fact that, unlike actors in the democratic process, the Court cannot simply change its reasoning accentuates the resulting feeling of unease. The Court is supposed to ensure the continuity of its reasoning. It cannot simply modify its doctrine. The Court is not entitled to change its doctrine merely because of changing majorities or changed understandings. At this point, the attractiveness of a deliberative justification model becomes evident. If the Court could claim from the beginning that its reasoning had a special quality, then both the self-referencing character as well as the continuity of its reasoning would become a solution to the problem. The worldwide success of the argumentative structures and topoi of the Federal Constitutional Court demonstrate that this is not an arbitrary assumption, even though, unfortunately, a scientific and systematic account of this success is still lacking. In fundamental rights doctrine alone, many other courts have taken notice of the Court's reasoning regarding the objective effect of fundamental rights (on this problem, see IV.D. below) or regarding the principle of proportionality. It is these modes of argumentation that make the Court globally one of the most influential constitutional courts in the view of comparative law literature (Robertson 2010, 29). In terms of legitimation theory, this success is also double-edged as the high [380] quality of the Court's reasoning could at the same time serve as a demanding blueprint for other constitutional courts to extend their own competencies.

At this point, of the many complex forms and arguments on which the Court draws in its reasoning, four elements should be mentioned in particular. First, in the composition of its grounds, the Court distinguishes, on the one hand, between general legal findings, formulated in the headnote as well as in a specific section setting out the benchmarks for the legal assessment of the case, "Maßstäbeteil" (Lepsius 2008a, 111), and, on the other hand, the application of these standards to the concrete case. In this way, the reasoning reaches beyond the singular case from the outset. But is not the part on the general legal findings, in contrast to the above (see IV.A.) formulated critique, actually an act of "legislation"? This qualification does not seem persuasive, because the explanation of the Court does not create,

[42] For this reason, the influence of international or other courts which provide the Federal Constitutional Court with new arguments can also be understood as contributing to its legitimation.

but rather limits, political action, and because for the most part it consists of derivations, not orders.

Secondly, in the constitutional complaint procedure, the Court even provides detailed reasons to bearers of fundamental rights whose complaints are unsuccessful. This practice has an evident calming effect on the defeated complainant. On the other hand, it leads to an immense multiplication of constitutional guidelines, for even these grounds often contain important commitments, that other complainants may invoke in future procedures. Those commitments multiply constitutional standards, while at the same time encouraging additional procedures, which produce new obligations. This does not even depend on whether the complaint procedures are successful or not.

Thirdly, in certain cases, the Court is used to acting as "emergency legislature" (Lerche 1995), establishing astoundingly detailed transitional rules before [381] the legislature is able to decide on a new rule.[43] Here, the designation of the Court as a "lawgiver" is, in fact, justified. Still, the legitimation problem is manifest. The reference to substantive constitutional law, which, of course, the Court defines itself, serves the Court as self-justification. The Court argues that the decree of transitional rules creates a situation more in tune with constitutional law. Hereby, it certainly ignores its own institutional role. It does not understand itself as being part of a constitutional order with an internal division of labor, but rather as a body that defines this order from the outside. Let me carry this point to an extreme for illustrative purposes: The benevolent dictator, who, after a coup d'état, orders the protection of human dignity, secures a high-ranking norm in breach of other constitutional law. But nevertheless, speaking from a constitutional point of view, this is hardly a desirable state of affairs.

Fourth, very early on, the Court decoupled different types of proceedings from standards of review: in a subjective procedure like the constitutional complaint, the Court also reviews objective constitutional law, which has nothing to do with the legal interests of the claimant. Thereby arises a kind of fundamental right to an objectively correct state action (rare critique, Franßen 1991, 83 ff.). On the other hand, the Court also reviews fundamental rights in objective procedures, like in proceedings that concern the abstract review of a statute (*abstrakte Normenkontrolle*), in which personal legal infringements are not at issue. In this type of proceeding, a constitutional body can invoke fundamental rights even if a claimant who asserts his or her individual fundamental right is lacking. Standard of review and procedure diverge.

Ultimately, these tendencies of the Court to extend its reasoning [382] are not unproblematic in terms of the Court's justification (above IV.A.). They detach the

[43] Cf., for example, BVerfGE 33, 303, 305—Numerus Clausus (1972); BVerfGE 72, 330, 333—Financial Balancing Equalization I (1986); BVerfGE 100, 104, 106—Retirement Benefits Reconciliation Alignment of Pensions III (1999).

content of the decision from the structure of the court procedure. Therefore, the pervasive self-referential reasoning of the Court requires a critical examination by scholars and the political public. Although this observation might appear trivial at first glance, it is not. Many perceive political critique of the Court as a crisis phenomenon. This analysis is flawed. In order to justify itself, the Court is reliant on political and academic critiques, for otherwise its reasoning becomes lost in self-referentiality. Moreover, the academic critique of the Court is, indeed, impressively precise and detailed even in terms of comparative law. Still, it lacks sustainability. While for decades civil and criminal legal scholarship take shape through the formulation of their own more consistent alternative viewpoints to those of the Federal High Court of Justice, scholars of constitutional law, in spite of initial criticism, often quickly take the Court's decisions as given.

The engagement of the legislature with court decisions is still of greater importance. The formally binding character of court decisions was the object of a thorough but largely inconclusive jurisprudential discussion (precise reconstruction by Ipsen 1980). Formally, certain decisions of the Court have legal force. Whether the reasoning of the opinion also attains force of law is controversial. In terms of legitimation theory, there is a strong argument against such a binding force. It would limit the scope of democratic opinion-forming and thereby discourage change (Hoffmann-Riem 1974; Sunstein 1999, 24 ff.). Here again the representational deficiencies become apparent and have an effect. Still, the discussion [383] on whether the reasoning attains legal force is largely of academic nature. The reverse perspective seems to be much more important. There is no doubt that the political process in the Bundestag takes decisions of the Court very seriously. Although this is appropriate in principle, it is also clear that the responsibility for dealing with constitutional court decisions rests in parliament itself. If the political process uses constitutional law as a pretext for not having to decide political questions politically, it is also responsible for falling into a trap of constitutionalization that is ultimately detrimental to both institutions (assessment in Schuppert/Bumke 2000). Political actors prematurely accusing the opposite side of acting unconstitutionally contribute to a further (self-)limitation of the political process. This self-limitation inhibits the development of political alternatives in the aftermath of elections. However, it also places undue responsibility on the Court. So in addition to expansive legal reasoning by the court, there is a strategic handling of said reasoning in the political process. Bottom line: procedural law facilitates an overly expansive reasoning, the Court uses this opportunity, and scholarship and politics accentuate this tendency. This is rather detrimental to the justification of the Court.

8. Standard-setting: an example

A recent decision on human dignity in social welfare law shows how complex the relation between standard establishment, standard extension, and the political process actually is. Drawing on an idea of the Federal Administrative Court, the Court has long recognized a right to [384] a decent minimum standard of living that it derived from the guarantee of human dignity (BVerfGE 40, 121, 133—Orphan's Allowance (1975)). At the same time, it was always clear that no specific minimum amount for social assistance could be derived from Art. 1, 1 GG.[44] When the Court had to decide on the constitutionality of the amount of the Hartz-IV standard rates, it was in a dilemma. On the one hand, it could not simply determine a specific minimum amount of money, which would derive from the human dignity principle, and yet, on the other hand, it was difficult for the Court to establish that the constitution is silent on the question. In the end, it developed a procedural rather than a substantial standard, which triggered a new, difficult legislative process. Regarding the nature of the claim founded on the principle of human dignity, the Court found:

> In order to ascertain the extent of the claim, the legislature has to realistically and comprehensively assess all expenditure that is necessary for one's existence in a transparent, expedient procedure on the basis of reliable figures and plausible methods of calculation. (cf. BVerfGE 66, 214, 223 (1984); BVerfGE 68, 143, 153 (1984); BVerfGE 99, 246, 260 (1998); BVerfGE 112, 268, 280 (2005); BVerfGE 120, 125, 155 (2008); BVerfGE 125, 175, 225 (2010)).

From where does the Court draw this conclusion? Here again, references to the Court's own doctrine are characteristic. Still, none of the cited decisions concern human dignity nor the social state principle.[45] The standard applied by the Court is new. On which grounds does [385] this standard lead to the repeal of individual provisions? The Court declares:

> The standard benefit of Euro 345 according to s. 20, 2, 1st clause of the Second Book of the Code of Social Law, old version, has not been calculated constitutionally because the structural principles of the statistical model, which the legislature itself selected and made the basis of its assessment of the necessary subsistence minimum, has been deviated from without a factual justification. (BVerfGE 125, 175, 238 (2010)).

That is an astonishing application of the guarantee of human dignity. It appears problematic in terms of democratic theory because it treats the legislature as a government agency, which is bound by specific rules (on this below **IV.D.4.**). Above

[44] That is the direct consequence of the vagueness of provisions, which leads to the so-called Sorites Paradox. If 345 Euros a month does not violate human dignity, and 344 also does not etc., then why does 1 Euro? In order to make this problem invisible, it is necessary to abstain from the determination of an exact amount (for attempts at a solution, Bung 2008).

[45] All of these decisions establish the principle of a "realistic assessment" of taxation, i.e. an assessment on the basis of reliable figures.

all, it is difficult to make a connection with the guarantee of human dignity. The recognized right to a social minimum standard of living is transformed to a right to a rational legislative process (in more detail below **IV.D.4.**).

Therefore, it appears as if the Court had seen itself compelled by its own doctrine to develop a novel constitutional standard. Ultimately, however, it remains unclear whether the decision reached by the Court actually helped the parties of the initial proceedings, who did not demand a more rational decision of the legislature, but rather claimed that the state guarantees a higher standard of living to individuals. The political process once again had no other choice than to engage with the decision in a new legislative process.

Ultimately, this example shows several characteristics and dilemmas of the Court's justificatory technique. The Court's own doctrine is the decisive standard of its reasoning. This type of self-binding is necessary for two reasons. First, [386] in most cases the constitutional text alone does not provide a sufficient basis for deciding on cases. Yet the Court also has to decide on cases where the text of the constitution does not supply detailed guidance. Second, doctrinal self-binding is required to make the Court's jurisprudence more comprehensible. Nevertheless, the Court can still opt for not finding fault with the legislature for the lack of constitutional standards. Would the simple finding of the Court that the social law provision at issue did not adversely affect the standard of living in a manner that is detrimental to human dignity be any less plausible? Hence, a logic of self-reliant standard-setting emerges, which preserves doctrinal consistency without aiding the parties or the political process. There is a risk that the Court's reasoning only serves to resolve the Court's own reasoning problems.

9. In particular: dissenting opinions

Since the change in the Federal Constitutional Court Law in 1970, dissenting opinions may be published. Once again, however, the Court has co-defined its own procedure. Before the change in the law, the Court had already published a, then still anonymous, dissenting opinion in its decision on the *Spiegel Affair* in 1962 (BVerfGE 20, 162, 178 ff. (1966); on this Ipsen 2009, 274f.). How can we assess dissenting opinions in terms of legitimation theory?

For such an assessment, it is important to distinguish between the German practice and the practice of the globally influential U.S. Supreme Court (Millgram 1985; Roellecke 2010). In American law, individual justices compose judgments and other justices may choose to join [387] or not. This is the case on all levels of federal jurisdiction. In this respect, dissenting opinions are nothing unusual, but rather the norm. In the German legal system, by contrast, deliberations are secret.[46] Deliberation and voting by courts must be held in secret. Consequently,

[46] S. 43 of the German Judiciary Act (DRiG). Hence, the Court initially violated the law, which the legislature only subsequently legitimated.

the possibility to issue a dissenting opinion is an exception that is reserved to the Court. Dissenting opinions attest to the exceptional position of the Court, the relative openness to interpretation of constitutional standards, and the possibility of alternative interpretations of constitutional law. This can be seen as a rapprochement of the Court with the political discourse. The judgment's reasoning itself provides for alternative points of view. As the Court discloses voting ratios, the judgment is practically no longer supported by the Court as a whole, but rather by a number of justices, in certain constellations even by only half of the Senate. This is significant in terms of legitimation theory because it suggests that all of the arguments put forward against democratic majoritarianism are equally applicable to a collegiate court in absolutely the same way (pointedly Waldron 2006, 1363 f.). Dissenting opinions reveal the Court's decision-making while, at the same time, calling into question the Court's legitimation to "do justice" in the individual case. What is at issue here is a phenomenon of hybridization (above **III.B.**).

In its practice, the Court seems to be fully aware of this. Dissenting opinions are relatively rare. The Court seeks to avoid them. Such avoidance strategies have their price: In [388] case of differences of opinion, all the divergent views must be introduced in the reasoning. Obviously, this leads to a lack of consistency.[47] The fact that the Court is composed of eight justices often implies that in difficult cases there is only a choice between a divided decision and a decision full of tensions or even contradictions.

Is it questionable, in terms of legitimation theory, to publish voting ratios and dissenting opinions? This does not seem to be the case for two reasons. First, the absence of dissenting opinions would not eliminate the openness of interpretation or the controversial nature of constitutional standards. Instead, they would manifest themselves in other ways. The openness of interpretation created by dissenting opinions expresses the unavoidable ambiguity of every constitutional text. The disclosure of the Court's formation of opinion corresponds more closely to a deliberative legitimation ideal than the concealment of internal conflicts under the veil of an unclear reasoning.

Secondly, the ambiguity of a reasoning that comprises dissenting opinions is at any rate clearly distinguishable from a party politicization of the Court's jurisprudence, at least in its practice of legal reasoning. An obvious formation of political camps within the Court, as is observable in the U.S., in Spain, and to an astonishing degree even in Switzerland, would hardly be acceptable. In this case, it should rather be for parliament to decide. However, the Court's practice of reasoning is different. Dissenting opinions cannot definitely be assigned to a specific political [389] camp. Ultimately, the doctrine of the Court is currently rather too reluctant

[47] More recent examples are BVerfGE 107, 59—Water Association Lippe (2002) and BVerfGE 112, 118—Conciliation Committee (2004) (in which the majority did not seem to have reached an agreement, although there was a dissenting opinion).

to resort to the instrument of dissenting opinions. It is necessary to distinguish between the fact that, in the eyes of the participants and the political system, diverging justifications can have an adverse effect on the legitimacy of a judgment and the comparatively higher level of legitimation that can be achieved through a conflict over the right justification of a case, that is carried out openly.

D. Structural problems of jurisprudence: four samples

Up till now, the present discussion has not been concerned with the actual doctrine of the Court. This is partly due to the fact that there are already plenty of such analyses, whereas the Court's institutional side still remains significantly underexposed. In four samples, we will attempt to place the insights gained with respect to the institutional side of the Court into relationship with the content of doctrine. The analysis will not address specific legal questions in depth. Nor will it aim to do justice to the Court's achievements. Instead, the following structural problems, whose selection is based on the developed legitimation models, will be considered: the definition of unalterable constitutional boundaries, the doctrinal approach to democratic decision-making, the objectification of fundamental rights protection, and the control of European integration. The analyses will trace potential connecting lines between the legitimatory/institutional arguments developed here and the Court's jurisprudence. [390]

1. Unalterable law and constitutional change: human dignity

The Basic Law recognizes unalterable provisions, which according to the so-called "eternity clause" are not subject to constitutional amendment (Art. 79, 3 GG). The Court has referred to these unalterable provisions in order to define realms of normativity under the Basic Law, which are forever withdrawn from any interference by the political process. If law is exclusively conceived as a relationship between legal subjects, then it certainly appears difficult, if not impossible, to consider individual norms as unalterable and absolute. A glance at the Court's doctrine on human dignity confirms this objection that might sound theoretical and abstract at first sight. The expansive interpretation of human dignity represents an international peculiarity (McCrudden 2008, 665).

According to a still dominant, though increasingly controversial, viewpoint, which is also shared by the Court itself, human dignity protects an absolute, closed realm, which is not subject to balancing at all (overview in Goos 2011, 21-74). Human dignity is of central significance to the justification of the Court. It defines the Court as a guardian of a last refuge of humanity. At the same time, the use of human dignity is particularly risky, because the meaning of the formula remains uncertain, while the institutional consequences of its application are especially serious. The democratic process is thus extensively limited on shaky argumentative ground. More recent judgments of the Court reveal problems resulting from this constellation: the [391] problem of consistent derivation, the problem of implicit relativization, and the problem noted above concerning the autonomization of the guarantee's standards. In its decision on the Aviation Security Act, the Court struck down a statutory provision authorizing the state to shoot down a passenger plane, captured by terrorists, even when carrying innocent people. The decision is clearly grounded on the human dignity guarantee. As the Court put it:

> Taking as a starting point the idea of the constitution-creating legislature that it is part of the nature of human beings to exercise self-determination in freedom and to freely develop themselves, and that the individual can claim, in principle, to be recognized in society as a member with equal rights and with a value of his or her own, the obligation to respect and protect human dignity generally precludes making a human being a mere object of the state. What is thus absolutely prohibited is any treatment of a human being by public authority which fundamentally calls into question his or her quality of a subject, his or her status as a legal entity by its lack of the respect of the value which is due to every human being for his or her own sake, by virtue of his or her being a person. When it is that such a treatment occurs must be stated in concrete terms in the individual case in view of the specific situation in which a conflict can arise (…). (BVerfGE 115, 118, 153—Aviation security (2006))

This formulation equates the declaration that the state may not treat a person instrumentally, merely as an object, with his or her status as legal subject. Nevertheless, the state can obviously make anyone "an object" in the form of law, in other words treat an individual instrumentally, without calling into question his or her status as an addressee of law. The passage inaptly mixes up legal technique with legal ethic. With a view to the provision under examination, the Court explains further:

> Also the state which in such a situation resorts to the measure provided by s. 14, 3 of the Aviation Security Act treats them as mere objects of its rescue operation for the protection of others. The desperateness and inescapability which characterize the situation of the people on board the aircraft who are affected as victims also exist vis-à-vis those who order and execute the shooting down of the aircraft. Due to the circumstances, which cannot be controlled by them in any way, the crew and the passengers of the plane cannot escape this state action but are helpless and defenseless in the face of it with the consequence that they are shot down in a targeted manner together with the aircraft and as result of this will be killed with near certainty. Such a treatment ignores the status of the persons affected as subjects endowed with dignity and inalienable rights. By their killing being used as a means to save others, they are treated as objects and at the same time deprived of their rights; with their lives being disposed of unilaterally by the state, the persons

> on board the aircraft, who, as victims, are themselves in need of protection, are denied the value which is due to a human being for his or her own sake. (BVerfGE 115, 118, 154 (2006)).

In other words, the killing of persons on the basis of mere suspicion, who have contributed nothing to the present danger, in order to save others, is unconstitutional. The result is convincing. Under current doctrine, the shooting down of a plane can be considered as a disproportionate intrusion into the right to life.

Nevertheless, the Court wants more. It strives for a reasoning that draws on the inalterability of the human dignity guarantee. However, if one reads the passage just cited, it becomes clear that it owes its force of persuasion to the fact that in the present case human *life* is being sacrificed in a certain situation. To simply "use" someone in this way does not appear contrary to human dignity per se (Dreier 2004, RN 53 with further evidence). Even tax obligations treat taxable persons as objects. Taxpayers are instrumentalized for the production of revenue of which they may get no share. This is precisely why the Court links the prohibition of instrumentalization with the right to life. Only the connection between the [393] "objectification formula" used here and the right to life enables the reader of the judgment to understand where the normative problem of the case actually lies. However, the Basic Law defines the right to life as an ordinary fundamental right that is limitable (Art. 2, 2 GG), while the scope of human dignity remains excessive. The reasoning is excessive because it suffers from conceptual self-overstraining.

The opposite problem becomes evident in another context, in which human dignity becomes virulent, namely the protection of the "core area of a person's private life," which should prevent police officials from interfering with an individual's absolute sphere of intimacy. The complicated construction forbidding the police to proceed to a systematic, continuous surveillance of one's living room should also draw on the inalterability of the human dignity guarantee. Only such a reasoning allowed the Court to measure a constitutional amendment, the introduction of a so-called big eavesdropping operation, against the requirements of the human dignity guarantee. In the words of the Court, this protected core area includes for instance:

> (t)he possibility to express inner processes like sentiments and feelings as well as reflections, opinions, and experiences of a highly personal nature, without having to fear being surveilled by state officials. This protection also covers expressions of emotions, of unconscious experiences as well as expressions of sexuality (BVerfGE 109, 279, 313—Big Eavesdropping Operation (2004)).

Communication about serious crimes, however, does not fall in this core area (BVerfGE 109, 279, 319 ff. (2004)): an individual who notes his or her murders in a diary or who tells his or her lover about them in bed does not enjoy absolute protection. This implies that the state must potentially have knowledge even of a person's intimacy sphere, in order to know whether communications are absolutely [394] protected or not. The requirement to take into account the content of communication transforms the supposedly absolute form of protection of the intimacy sphere into a relative procedural form of protection. Ultimately, there is no absolutely protected realm (criticisms in the dissenting opinions of Jaeger and Hohmann-Dennhardt in BVerfGE 109, 279, 383 (2004); see also Lepsius 2005, 437), but only "instrumental rational relativity" (Peterson 2004, 316) of the protection of human dignity. This dilemma permeates the Court's jurisprudence on human dignity from its beginnings. It appears that the Court *always* cites Art. 1, 1 GG "in conjunction with" another fundamental right or constitutional provision. The actual interplay between illimitable and limitable fundamental rights protection remains unclear (For an attempt of a reconstruction see von Bernstorff 2008, 32f; for criticism see Goos 2011, 191ff.).

It does not follow from these remarks that an absolute protection of human dignity, which limits itself to the most severe state transgressions such as torture, would be inconceivable.[48] However, the broadening of the scope of the guarantee of human dignity and its linkage with other fundamental rights unavoidably results in a relativization of the concept. The Court seems to feel compelled to steer a middle course, which no longer provides absolute protection, by the very need to draw absolute constitutional boundaries and the fear of a conclusive definition of the core of human dignity. Behind all this lurks the dilemma that however controversial a conclusive definition of human dignity by the Court may be [395], the Court cannot renounce its duty to protect human dignity. Only a much more reluctant usage of the human dignity clause can contribute to remedy this dilemma.

2. Democratic rules and democratic openness

In contrast to many older democratic constitutions, the Basic Law has ensured the emergence of a democratic order not only through the establishment of institutions, but also by anchoring a particular principle of democracy in the constitutional text (Art. 20, 2, 1 GG). The constitutional protection of the democratic order from itself belongs to the classic catalogue of constitutional models of legitimation (IV.B.). At the same time, we have seen that it can be questionable in terms of legitimation theory when jurisprudence consolidates a specific democratic ideal. For it is an essential task of the democratic process itself to attempt different forms of democratic legitimation.

[48] However, a clear technique of regulation is required here. As a model, the Basic Law prescribes exemplarily that those in custody may not be subjected to mental or physical mistreatment (Art. 104, 1, 2 GG). This provides the normative basis for an absolute prohibition of torture. This interpretation only starts to become questionable when one stylizes the rule into a "principle,", which can be balanced against other, likewise objective Basic Rights, for example, the right to life (logical implications consequently in Teifke 2011).

For a long time, the Court was very reluctant to refer to the principle of democracy. Apart from a few earlier decisions, only in the 1980s did the jurisprudence of the Court begin to address the principle more intensively. This jurisprudence has always been very controversial. From that period on, the Court has drawn on the principle of democracy and systematically related provisions in order to establish standards for administrative organization, for the concept of the "people," for electoral law, and for the rights of the parliamentary opposition (for an overview see Dreier 2006, RN 113 et. subs.). The constitutional framework set out by the Court includes a broad spectrum of standards ranging from conditions for the act of election to requirements for law enforcement [396]. In view of comparative law, the constitutional requirements are of unparalleled rigor.

In an additional line of jurisdiction, the Court establishes further criteria for the legislative process, which enable the Court to proceed to a review that is partly procedural and partly substantive in nature. It postulates standards of legislative rationality (critical discussion in Schlaich/Korioth 2010, 323 ff.; Dann 2010; on special cases Möllers 2010; Lepsius 2009). This rationality review consists of two elements. The *first* involves the processing of facts by the legislature. In the 1970s, the Court granted the legislature considerable latitude for prognosis in the assessment of the consequences of statutory regulations in a ground-breaking decision (BVerfGE 50, 290, 331 ff. —Codetermination (1979); on the inconsequentiality of the distinctions developed there, Schlaich/Korioth 2010, 319 ff.). Of course, this formulation already contained the nucleus for an unusually strict standard of review, because the Court did not justify its supposed judicial self-restraint with the democratic legitimation of the legislature, but rather with its own limited capacity for the establishment of facts. The argument is more reminiscent of a Court addressing an administrative body rather than the democratic legislature (prophetic critique in Schlaich 1981, 110 f; Bryde 1982, 326 ff.). The administration must account for its treatment of a specific state of affairs. The legislature, however, carries out a political assessment of social developments, which cannot be equated with the treatment of circumstances of "fact" and cannot be retraced in the same manner (Lepsius 1999).

In the meantime, the duties of the legislature to systematically monitor the factual situation in society have grown considerably (overview in Huster 2003). From now on, if the legislature presumes a situation, it must monitor this situation and make corrections in the event of factual changes. Such a duty, as we have seen (IV.C.), may even be derived from the guarantee of human dignity. At the same time, an intensified control of the parliamentary legislative process also illuminates the inner workings of the political process. Thus, the Court objected to the introduction of documents into the legislative process because the affected parliamentary committee did not have the opportunity to take sufficient account of them (BVerfGE 101, 297, 307—Home Office (1999); BVerfGE 120, 56, 75—Conference

Committee (2008)). Even in the innermost realm of politics, the Court imposes cognitive duties.

A *second line* of jurisprudence requires the legislature to take consistent decisions (critical overview in Dann 2010; affirming reconstruction in Bumke 2010). This standard seems to derive from administrative law, too. The legally bound administration should not contradict itself for reasons of equality. For the legislature, by contrast, inconsistencies virtually constitute a necessity in the case of new majorities in parliament and government initiating a political reorientation, or in a situation in which political parties reach compromises in order to achieve a majority. The Court mostly combines the duty to ensure consistency with the principles of equal treatment and proportionality, which considerably broadens and intensifies the review program (see already Bryde 1982, 328). However, it is precisely the application of the principle of equal treatment toward the legislature that runs the risk of producing circular reasoning (Sadurski 2008, 98 ff.). In this line of jurisprudence, decisions [398] of the legislature are struck down because their *justification* did not meet the rationality standards that the Court derived from the principle of equality (BVerfGE 122, 210, 230 ff.—Commuting Allowance (2008); on this Lepsius 2009, 261). Consequently, the Court struck down a statutory provision which the Court deemed to distinguish inconsistently between different types of restaurants in its "no smoking decision"; on the other hand, the Court allowed the legislature to prohibit smoking in public places in general (BVerfGE 121, 317, 374—Smoking Prohibition (2008)). It is difficult to understand how standards for the consistent determination of different types of restaurants can be derived from Basic Rights guarantees. By contrast, it is not evident why the Court should have a mandate to explicitly permit the legislature a greater degree of interference than was provided for in the challenged statute. In this instance, the fundamental right protects neither the freedom of the affected party nor the democratic legislature's scope for decision-making.

This line of jurisprudence is based on an understanding of democracy that becomes problematic against the background of the aforementioned existing legal obligations. For other than the administration, which is bound by statute and which must rationalize its decisions through justification, respect for the democratic parliamentary election also requires the recognition of an element of voluntarism, which necessarily involves inconsistencies. The Court, however, frequently treats the legislature as a mere issuer of decrees, which must act in a way that is rationally comprehensible. But if the legislature must act in a rationally comprehensible manner, the question arises whether political programs and preferences still make sense, as long as the electorate [399] should not be obligated to justify its vote "rationally," too. The ascertainment of facts always has a political dimension and political opinion formation requires compromises, which, as compromises, are intrinsically inconsistent, and so the Court ultimately sets a rationalist ideal of democracy against democratic (or political) practice. Thereby, it consolidates the status quo to the detriment of new regulations. In some fields of law such as tax law, the Court even undertakes a redistribution from bottom to top.[49] While the guarantee of democratic rules, for example in electoral law, offers a strong justification for the doctrine of the Court, this certainly does not apply to the application of rationality standards.

3. Subjective rights and objective law

In the foregoing discussion, we have already encountered the relationship between the subjective and objective dimension of fundamental rights on several occasions: when discussing the legitimation model of fundamental rights, when examining access to the Court, and when looking at the relationship between types of proceedings and standards of review. Few constitutional courts objectify fundamental rights as emphatically as the Federal Constitutional Court (Wahl 2004). In this reading, fundamental rights are norms which have an effect on the entire legal order, even in constellations [400] where there is no intrusion into the individual sphere of liberty (critical analysis in Poscher 2003). Fundamental rights can even condense into duties requiring action by the legislature, which must become active on the factual initiative of the Court. Objectification means de-subjectification.[50] The fundamental right produces effects to which no subject can appeal. Strictly speaking, it stops being a right to the extent that rights are supposed to protect a concrete power of the will. Through this modification—this is decisive here—an objectifying interpretation of fundamental rights detaches the construction of fundamental rights from the concrete procedural requests of a bearer of these rights. The meaning of fundamental rights protection changes, and with it also its legitimating function. Legitimation through fundamental rights protection means first and foremost legitimation by reference to the concrete requests of an individual. If the fundamental right is objectified, this individual claim disappears. In this way, the connection between the procedural initiative, which permits the Court to become active, and the fundamental right disappears. The Court no longer protects rights. It becomes a guardian of objective law on the occasion of a procedural initiative. This is, for instance, the case when the Court imposes a prohibition on sale on Sundays on the basis of a constitutional complaint, although no individual or religious society is actually prevented from exercising its rights to religious freedom

[49] In this context the Court demands, for example, that the regulation of exemptions such as the commuting allowance (BVerfGE 122, 210 (2008)) and the taxable base be "consistent" (BVerfGE 93, 121, 136—Assessed Value II (1995)); on the excessive content of the decision, see the dissenting opinion of Böckenförde (Ibid., 149 ff.). New regulations, however, were no longer enforceable, so that the commuting allowance remains in force and no further wealth tax was introduced.

[50] Therefore, many of the phenomena that the literature wrongly identifies as objective effects of the Basic Rights are simply not that. When a state civil court penalise an expression of opinion (BVerfGE 7, 198, 1958—Lüth (1958)), its decision interferes with the individual-subjective practice of freedom of opinion. The fact that this intervention takes the form of private law is insignificant (precise reconstruction in Canaris 1988).

by other persons buying and selling on Sunday (BVerfGE 125, 39, 73 ff.— Sundays in Advent [401](2009); for criticism Wißmann 2011). The Court protects objective "values" without having a mandate to do so.

The aforementioned case points out the problem. Of course, considering the vote count, it remained very controversial even in the Court. The normal case in terms of fundamental rights dogmatics, however, does not differ categorically, but merely gradually, from this more controversial case: in the usual case, a fundamental right is weighed against other fundamental rights or other constitutional values in order to justify an intrusion into that right. This seems unproblematic in cases in which the Court has to decide on the distribution of freedom between two bearers of fundamental rights participating in the court procedure. For example, either the freedom of the press of a newspaper or the right of personality of a celebrity prevails (e.g. BVerfGE 101, 361—Caroline II (1999)). Either the right to property of a house owner or the artistic freedom of a graffiti artist wins out (BVerfG NJW 1984, 1293—Graffiti). But as soon as fundamental rights also serve as the subject matter of a weighing up in cases in which a concrete limitation of freedom is absent, they are used, as has long been recognized by the doctrine, to justify infringements of freedom without this being justified by a concrete claim of a party to the proceeding. The point here is not to criticize the prevailing fundamental rights doctrine (Poscher 2003; Lenz 2006), nor to criticize the objectification of the bearer of fundamental rights as such. The aim is rather to explain the connection with the legitimation of the Court. An objective fundamental rights understanding may still legitimate the Court as guardian of the constitution in the sense of the—as we have seen, notoriously weak—legality model, [402] but certainly no longer as guarantor of individual freedom. A stricter reference to individual complaints would better serve the legitimation of the Court.

4. On the legitimation of a Europeanized Court

The relation between the Basic Law and European Law is one of the most discussed questions in the Court's recent jurisprudence. Thereby, it is obvious that national constitutional courts in all legal systems have greater difficulty with the internationalization and Europeanization of law than do ordinary courts (Alter 2001). While ordinary courts become part of the common European system of legal protection and gain increasing influence through the possibility of referring cases to the European Court of Justice, European integration means a loss of definition competence for constitutional courts because they can only decide on national constitutional law. Lower courts apply the specific law at their disposal, while constitutional courts, also as institutions, are identified with a certain political order and a specific law which is the national constitution. Consequently, national constitutional courts have developed sovereignty reservations to Europeanization (comparing Mayer 2009). The Court has vigorously pursued this strategy and, in doing so, utilized the peculiarity of the Basic Law providing absolute limits to constitutional amendments (BVerfGE 123, 267, 343 ff.—Lisbon (2009).

The point here is not to discuss the difficult questions of Europeanization in depth, but rather to analyze the question of Europeanization exclusively with a view to the question of the Court's legitimation and break it down once again to a fundamental distinction. Assuming that a national constitutional court [403] is usually competent for a review of national acts on the basis of national standards, then two of our models of legitimation seem to provide greater scope to the Court: the federal integrity of the democratic process, and the protection of fundamental rights. The Court has pursued both paths. On the one hand, it has protected fundamental rights against acts of the European public power. On the other hand, it has attempted to set limits to the political process on the level of the European Union. However, so far, the Court has never struck down an act of the European Union.

How should those strategies be assessed in terms of legitimation theory? Three observations help in the search for an answer. First, the Court linked both forms of review by making it possible to lodge constitutional complaints against the German participation in European treaty amendment procedures. "Everyone" can invoke his or her democratic rights of participation and initiate a full review of the German act approving the European treaty. At this point we encounter the subject–object linkage which is already familiar to us: a complainant is now not only entitled to invoke his or her own subjective rights, but can also refer to any objective constitutional provision in order to oppose the integration process. Secondly, the standard of review is higher than ordinary constitutional law because legislative bodies approve European treaty amendments with majorities sufficient for constitutional amendments. The Court has to apply the core of the Basic Law that is not subject to amendment. All statements of the Court that relate to this immutable core are elevated to the same rank of immutability. Thirdly, the Court has made the review of fundamental rights violations by the European Union subject to structural reservations. The Court does not review each individual violation of fundamental rights or competence rules by the EU. It merely reviews structural problems. If, on the one hand, it has subjectified the review of the principle of democracy, then, on the other, it has objectified the protection of fundamental rights.

As a court of the German political order, the Federal Constitutional Court faces a dilemma. On the one hand, it has to respect the democratic decision in favor of European integration, which is also required by the Basic Law itself. On the other hand, it must protect individual complainants against violations of their fundamental rights and their right of democratic participation. The problem is intensified by the fact that the decision in favor of Europeanization is not reversible or correctible in the same way as other democratic decisions. There is not a clean solution to this dilemma. Instead, it appears unavoidable that existing judicial institutions always also assume the control of other sovereign levels, over which they actually do not have jurisdiction. Supranational courts like the European Court of Human Rights or the European Court of Justice have also reserved supervision of this kind for themselves.

In the current state of Europeanization, the Court should not generally give up such control competencies. The Court is still needed as a guardian of fundamental rights. However, the role of a protector of European democracy seems to overburden the Court institutionally. The Lisbon judgment showed all the signs of the blurring of boundaries between judicial activity and the political process, from oral proceedings with very fundamental discussions to long, textbook-like [405] passages of the judgment, which do not tend to legally asses a settled manner but rather attempt to shape future developments. The fact that the judgement was so long, because the Court had to delve into all the claims of the complainants, illustrates the problem. The Court itself has offered the possibility to lodge a constitutional complaint against European integration and has expanded the standards of review so that all pleas become legally relevant. A cross check indicates why the Court reached an institutional limit in its decision: what would have happened if the Court had invalidated the treaty? Not only European integration, but also the legitimation of the Court—which, in the name of democracy, would have struck down a decision provided with overwhelming democratic legitimation—would have entered into a deep crisis. [406]

V. The Boundless Court: Legality—Legitimacy—Legitimation

The remarkable position of the Federal Constitutional Court in the constitutional order of the Basic Law is neither accidental nor unintentional. The intensive constitutionalization of the Federal Republic's legal order is the expression of a distinctive culture of trust in law, which serves as a model for systems with a totalitarian past throughout the world. The strength of the law, of course, also depends on the visibility of its boundaries. The Court has clearly pushed these boundaries over the last six decades. The fact that the Court is bound by law, its legality, provides its democratic legitimation. At the same time, it contributes to its own legitimacy, for the Court owes its popularity to the trust in the disinterested legality of its actions. The Court's obligation to adhere to law is certainly precarious for different reasons. A general reason is that constitutional courts can do none other than develop constitutional obligations themselves. In the case of the Court itself, however, another reason is that the Court, as a "procedurally autonomous" constitutional body, is able to deal with legal obligations in a very independent manner. When the obligation to adhere to law becomes to a great extent a commitment to self-developed standards, this requires additional justification in any event. First and foremost, courts derive their mandate for the further development of the law from their concrete mission to protect law, from the narrow reading of a normative claim provided by the complainant. In particular in the field of fundamental rights, new case constellations allow a further development of the law through an altered understanding of freedom and threats to freedom. [407] However, whilst on the one hand attracting a multitude of constitutional complaints through the opening of admissibility requirements, the Federal Constitutional Court, on the other hand, closes these requirements through an objectification of legal protection, through a selection of cases that is both difficult to grasp and hardly governed by rules, and through a pervasive use of forms of balancing. The constitutional complaint procedure which relates to the protection of individual fundamental rights does not properly fit with the Court's practice of objectifying the law through procedural techniques and extensive fundamental rights doctrine. While the responsiveness of the constitutional legislator gives the Court a robust mandate in disputes over federal competence, and though disputes among constitutional bodies must unavoidably be decided in favor of one or to the disadvantage of the other party, the procedure to which the Court owes most of its popularity appears to be the procedure whose practice is also most strongly contestable in terms of legitimation: the constitutional complaint directed, either directly or indirectly, against a statute.

The objectification of fundamental rights protection is offset by a subjectification of objective legal protection. The Court also reviews fundamental rights to which no bearer of fundamental rights has ever appealed, and, in the context of European integration, it has completely given up the distinction between questions related to the organization of the state and individual constitutional complaints. At the same time, the self-referential quality of the standards has led to the development of very high rationality demands on the democratic legislature, which the Court treats more and more like an administrative body rather than a legitimate democratic body. Moreover, the proliferation of a multitude of standards sometimes conveys the impression that the Court resolves its own justification problems [408] and thereby puts obligations on the legislature without actually being able to help the bearer of fundamental rights.

This critique is formulated before the backdrop of a robust democratic mandate of the Court defined by positive law and its extremely high national and international esteem, which has unavoidably led to a quantitative and qualitative expansion of its decision-making practice. Nevertheless, in the long term, a reduction of the density of the standards as well as a more exact linkage between the specific type of procedure and the Court's review program could be advisable. As a permanent court of last resort which always knows better than the legislature even if there has been no request to the court, the Federal Constitutional Court will do no favors to the constitutional order of the Basic Law, even though the number of invalidated statutes may remain statistically small. For the binding effects of the decisions depend only to a limited degree on the result. Finally, as guardian of inalterable normative statements, the Court quickly reaches its own limits of knowledge. Democratic communities often do not feel at ease with the characteristic openness and relativity of the standards. They hope for places of ultimate normative certainty. Still, whatever form those places take, they always belong to the political community and inevitably share its unavoidable uncertainties. “There is no court of appeal outside the democratic discourse—neither philosophers nor supreme courts—that could make indisputable decisions removed from the possibility of critique. So it is only *in the medium* of democratic discourse that its own foundations can be secured and preserved” (Wellmer 1993, p. 63). [409]

References

Abromeit, Heidrun, "Volkssouveränität, Parlamentssouveränität, Verfassungssouveränität: Drei Realmodelle der Legitimation staatlichen Handelns," *Politische Vierteljahresschrift*, 36 (1995), 49–66.

Ackerman, Bruce, "The Rise of World Constitutionalism," *Virginia Law Review*, 83 (1997), 771–7.

Aders, Thomas, *Die Utopie vom Staat über den Parteien. Biographische Annäherungen an Hermann Höpker-Aschoff (1883–1954)* (Frankfurt, 1994).

Alexy, Robert, *Theorie der Grundrechte* (Frankfurt, 1986); trans. Julian Rivers as *A Theory of Constitutional Rights* (Oxford, 2010).

Allan, Trevor R. S., *Constitutional Justice. A Liberal Theory of the Rule of Law* (Oxford, 2001).

Almond, Gabriel A. and Sidney Verba, *The Civic Culture. Political Attitudes and Democracy in Five Nations* (Princeton, 1963).

Alter, Karen, *Establishing the Supremacy of European Law. The Making of an International Rule of Law in Europe* (Oxford, 2001).

Arnauld, Andreas von, "Die normtheoretische Begründung des Verhältnismäßigkeitsgrundsatzes," *Juristenzeitung*, 55 (2000), 276–80.

Arnauld, Andreas von, "Theorie und Methode des Grundrechtsschutzes in Europa am Beispiel des Grundsatzes der Verhältnismäßigkeit," in A. Hatje and M. Nettesheim, eds., *Grundrechtsschutz im Dreieck von nationalem, europäischem und internationalem Recht* (Baden-Baden, 2008), 41–64.

Arndt, Adolf, "Das Bundesverfassungsgericht," *Deutsches Verwaltungsblatt*, 66 (1951), 297–300.

Atiyah, Patrick S. and Robert S. Summers, *Form and Substance in Anglo-American Law. A Comparative Study of Legal Reasoning, Legal Theory, and Legal Institutions* (Oxford, 1987).

Bachof, Otto, "Bundesverfassungsgericht und obere Bundesgerichte. Zum Streit über die Auslegung des § 80 des Bundesverfassungsgerichtsgesetzes," *Juristenzeitung*, 11 (1956), 272–4.

Badura, Peter, "Staat, Recht und Verfassung in der Integrationslehre Rudolf Smends," *Der Staat*, 16 (1977), 305–25.

Badura, Peter, "Eigentum," in E. Benda, W. Maihofer, and H.-J. Vogel, eds., *Handbuch des Verfassungsrechts* (2nd edn., Berlin, 1994), 10.

Baldus, Manfred, "Frühe Machtkämpfe. Ein Versuch über die historischen Gründe der Autorität des Bundesverfassungsgerichts," in T. Henne and A. Riedlinger, eds., *Das Lüth-Urteil aus (rechts-)historischer Sicht. Die Konflikte um Veit Harlan und die Grundrechtsjudikatur des Bundesverfassungsgerichts* (Berlin, 2005), 237–48.

Barak, Aharon, *The Judge in a Democracy* (Princeton, 2006).

Barenbolm, Peter D., James E. Hickey, Jr., and James R. Silenat, eds., *The Legal Doctrines of the Rule of Law and the Legal State (Rechtsstaat)* (Springer, 2014).

Baring, Arnulf, *Im Anfang war Adenauer. Die Entstehung der Kanzlerdemokratie* (3rd edn., Munich, 1984).

Baumert, Renaud, *La découverte du juge constitutionnel, entre science et politique* (Paris, 2009).

Beaud, Olivier, "De quelque particularités de la justice constitutionnelle dans un système federal," in C. Grewe, O. Jouanjan, E. Maulin, and P. Wachsmann, eds., *La notion de la "justice constitutionnelle"* (Paris, 2005), 49–72.

Beaud, Olivier and Pasquale Pasquino, eds., *La controverse sur "le gardien de la Constitution" et la justice constitutionnelle. Kelsen contre Schmitt. Der Weimarer Streit um den Hüter der Verfassung und die Verfassungsgerichtsbarkeit. Kelsen gegen Schmitt* (Paris, 2007).

Bellamy, Richard, *Political Constitutionalism. A Republican Defence of the Constitutionality of Democracy* (Cambridge, 2007).

Benda, Ernst, "Verfassungskontrolle durch Verfassungsgerichtsbarkeit," in D. Merten and R. Morsey, eds., *30 Jahre Grundgesetz. Vorträge und Diskussionsbeiträge der 47. Staatswissenschaftlichen Fortbildungstagung 1979 der Hochschule für Verwaltungswissenschaften, Speyerer Vorträge 89* (Berlin, 1979), 103–17.

Benda, Ernst, *Entlastung des Bundesverfassungsgerichts—Vorschläge der Entlastungskommission* (Baden-Baden, 1998).

Bernstorff, Jochen von, "Pflichtenkollision und Menschenwürdegarantie," *Der Staat*, 47 (2008), 21–40.

Bethge, Herbert, "Die Grenzen grundrechtlicher Subjektivierung objektiven Verfassungsrechts. Zum aktuellen Stellenwert der Elfes-Konstruktion," in O. Depenheuer, M. Heintzen, and M. Jestaedt, eds., *Staat im Wort. Festschrift für Josef Isensee* (Heidelberg, 2007), 613–31.

Bettermann, Karl August, "Opposition und Verfassungsrichterwahl," in H. Bernstein, U. Drobnig, and H. Kötz, eds., *Festschrift für Konrad Zweigert* (Tübingen, 1981), 723–46.

Beyme, Klaus von, *Die verfassunggebende Gewalt des Volkes. Demokratische Doktrin und politische Wirklichkeit* (Tübingen, 1968).

Beyme, Klaus von, *Der Gesetzgeber. Der Bundestag als Entscheidungszentrum* (Opladen, 1997).

Beyme, Klaus von, "Modell für neue Demokratien? Die Vorbildrolle des Bundesverfassungsgerichts," in R. C. van Ooyen and M. H. W. Möllers, eds., *Das Bundesverfassungsgericht im politischen System* (Wiesbaden, 2006), 519–31.

Bickel, Alexander, *The Least Dangerous Branch. The Supreme Court at the Bar of Politics* (Indianapolis, 1962).

Billing, Werner, *Das Problem der Richterwahl zum Bundesverfassungsgericht* (Berlin, 1969).

Bobek, Michael, *Comparative Reasoning in European Supreme Courts* (Oxford, 2013).

Böckenförde, Ernst-Wolfgang, "Nachwort. Gesetzesbegriff und Gesetzesvorbehalt. Bemerkungen zur Entwicklung und zum heutigen Stand der Diskussion," in E.-W. Böckenförde, ed., *Gesetz und gesetzgebende Gewalt. Von den Anfängen der deutschen Staatsrechtslehre bis zur Höhe des staatsrechtlichen Positivismus* (2nd edn., Berlin, 1981).

Böckenförde, Ernst-Wolfgang, "Demokratie als Verfassungsprinzip," in P. Kirchhof and J. Isensee, eds., *Handbuch des Staatsrechts der Bundesrepublik Deutschland* (Heidelberg, 1987), 1st vol., s 22.

Böckenförde, Ernst-Wolfgang, *Zur Lage der Grundrechtsdogmatik nach 40 Jahren Grundgesetz* (Munich, 1989).

Böckenförde, Ernst-Wolfgang, "The Origin and Development of the Rechtsstaat Concept," in *State, Society, Liberty*, trans. J. A. Underwood (Berg, 1991).

Böckenförde, Ernst-Wolfgang, "Verfassungsgerichtsbarkeit. Strukturfragen, Organisation, Legitimation," in E.-W. Böckenförde, ed., *Staat, Nation, Europa. Studien zur Staatslehre, Verfassungstheorie und Rechtsphilosophie* (Frankfurt, 1999a), 157–82.

Böckenförde, Ernst-Wolfgang, "Verfassungsgerichtsbarkeit: Strukturfragen, Organisation, Legitimation," *Neue Juristische Wochenschrift*, 52 (1999b), 9–17.

Bösch, Frank, *Die Adenauer-CDU. Gründung, Aufstieg und Krise einer Erfolgspartei 1945–1969* (Stuttgart, 2001).

Brodocz, André, "Lüth und die Deutungsmacht des Bundesverfassungsgerichts," in T. Henne and A. Riedlinger, eds., *Das Lüth-Urteil in (rechts-)historischer Sicht. Die Konflikte um Veit Harlan und die Grundrechtsjudikatur des Bundesverfassungsgerichts* (Berlin, 2005), 271–89.

Brodocz, André, "Die souveränen Deuter. Symbolische Voraussetzungen—instrumentelle Rahmenbedingungen—praktische Auswirkungen," in H. Vorländer, ed., *Die Deutungsmacht der Verfassungsgerichtsbarkeit* (Wiesbaden, 2006), 95–119.

Brodocz, André, *Die Deutungsmacht des Bundesverfassungsgerichts* (Wiesbaden, 2009).

Brünneck, Alexander von, *Verfassungsgerichtsbarkeit in den westlichen Demokratien. Ein systematischer Verfassungsvergleich* (Baden-Baden, 1992).

Brunner, Georg, "Der Zugang des Einzelnen zur Verfassungsgerichtsbarkeit im europäischen Raum," *Jahrbuch des öffentlichen Rechts der Gegenwart*, 50 (2002), 191–256.

Bryde, Brun-Otto, *Verfassungsentwicklung. Stabilität und Dynamik im Verfassungsrecht der Bundesrepublik Deutschland* (Baden-Baden, 1982).

Bryde, Brun-Otto, "Die Rolle der Verfassungsgerichtsbarkeit in Umbruchsituationen," in J. J. Hesse, G. F. Schuppert, and K. Harms, eds., *Verfassungsrecht und Verfassungspolitik in Umbruchsituationen* (Baden-Baden, 1999), 197–210.

Bryde, Brun-Otto, "Das Demokratieprinzip des Grundgesetzes als Optimierungsaufgabe," in Redaktion Kritische Justiz, ed., *Demokratie und Grundgesetz* (Baden-Baden, 2000), 59–70.

Bryde, Brun-Otto, "Tatsachenfeststellungen und soziale Wirklichkeit in der Rechtsprechung des Bundesverfassungsgerichts," in P. Badura and H. Dreier, eds., *Festschrift 50 Jahre Bundesverfassungsgericht* (Tübingen, 2001), 1st vol., 533–62.

Bryde, Brun-Otto, "Der Beitrag des Bundesverfassungsgerichts zur Demokratisierung der Bundesrepublik," in R. C. van Ooyen and M. H. W. Möllers, eds., *Das Bundesverfassungsgericht im politischen System* (Wiesbaden, 2006), 321–31.

Bumke, Christian, *Der Grundrechtsvorbehalt. Untersuchungen über die Begrenzung und Ausgestaltung der Grundrechte* (Baden-Baden, 1998).

Bumke, Christian, "Die Pflicht zur konsistenten Gesetzgebung. Am Beispiel des Ausschlusses der privaten Vermittlung staatlicher Lotterien und ihrer bundesverfassungsgerichtlichen Kontrolle," *Der Staat*, 49 (2010), 77–105.

Bundesverfassungsgericht, "Denkschrift des Bundesverfassungsgerichts vom 27. Juni 1952: Die Stellung des Bundesverfassungsgerichts," *Jahrbuch des öffentlichen Rechts der Gegenwart*, 6 (1957), 144–8.

Bung, Jochen, "Das Bett des Karneades—Zur Metakritik der Paradoxologie," in W. Brugger, U. Neumann, and S. Kirste, eds., *Rechtsphilosophie im 21. Jahrhundert* (Frankfurt, 2008), 72–89.

Burchardt, Daniel O., *Grenzen verfassungsgerichtlicher Erkenntnis. Zur Prozeduralität der Verfassungsnormativität* (Berlin, 2004).

Bürklin, Thorsten, "Bauen als (demokratische) Sinnstiftung—Das Gebäude des Bundesverfassungsgerichts als "Staatsbau," in R. C. van Ooyen and M. H. W. Möllers, eds., *Das Bundesverfassungsgericht im politischen System* (Wiesbaden, 2006), 17–32.

Caldwell, Peter C., *Popular Sovereignty and the Crisis of German Constitutional Law* (Durham, 1997).

Canaris, Claus-Wilhelm, *Grundrechte und Privatrecht* (Berlin, 1988).

Capitant, David, *Les effets juridiques des droits fondamentaux en Allemagne* (Paris, 2001).

Cappelletti, Mauro and Theodor Ritterspach, "Die gerichtliche Kontrolle der Verfassungsmäßigkeit der Gesetze in rechtsvergleichender Betrachtung," *Jahrbuch des öffentlichen Rechts der Gegenwart*, 20 (1971), 65–109.

Cappelletti, Mauro, Monica Seccombe, and Joseph Weiler, *Integration through Law* (Berlin, 1986).

Collings, Justin, *Democracy's Guardians: A History of the German Federal Constitutional Court, 1951–2001* (Oxford, 2015).

Dahl, Robert, "Decision-Making in a Democracy. The Supreme Court as a National Policy-Maker," *The Journal of Public Law*, 6 (1957), 279–95.

Dann, Philip, "Verfassungsgerichtliche Kontrolle gesetzgeberischer Rationalität," *Der Staat*, 49 (2010), 630–46.

Doemming, Klaus-Berto von, Rudolf Werner Füßlein, and Werner Matz, "Entstehungsgeschichte der Artikel des Grundgesetzes," *Jahrbuch des öffentlichen Rechts der Gegenwart*, 1 (1951), 1–926.

Dreher, Eduard, "Glanz und Elend der Staatsgerichtsbarkeit. Zum Gesetz über das Bundesverfassungsgericht vom 12. März 1951," *Neue Juristische Wochenschrift*, 4 (1951), 377–81.

Dreier, Horst, "Art. 1 I (Menschenwürde)," in H. Dreier, ed., *Grundgesetz—Kommentar*, 1st vol. (2nd edn., Tübingen, 2004).

Dreier, Horst, "Art. 20 (Demokratie)," in H. Dreier, ed., *Grundgesetz—Kommentar*, 2nd vol. (2nd edn., Tübingen, 2006).

Durner, Wolfgang, "Urteilsanmerkung zu BVerfGE 125, 260—Vorratsdatenspeicherung," *Juristische Arbeitsblätter*, 42 (2010), 391–4.

Duxbury, Neil, *Patterns of American Jurisprudence* (Oxford, 1997).

Dworkin, Ronald, *Taking Rights Seriously* (Cambridge, 1977).

Dworkin, Ronald, "Rights as Trumps," in J. Waldron, ed., *Theories of Rights* (Oxford, 1984), 153–7.

Eberl, Matthias (2006), *Verfassung und Richterspruch. Rechtsphilosophische Grundlegungen zur Souveränität, Justiziabilität und Legitimität der Verfassungsgerichtsbarkeit* (Berlin, 2006).

Ebsen, Ingwer, *Das Bundesverfassungsgericht als Element gesellschaftlicher Selbstregulierung. Eine pluralistische Theorie der Verfassungsgerichtsbarkeit im demokratischen Verfassungsstaat* (Berlin, 1985).

Ehmke, Horst, "Prinzipien der Verfassungsinterpretation," *Veröffentlichungen der Vereinigung der Deutschen Staatsrechtslehrer*, 20 (1963), 53–102.

Ellwein, Thomas, *Das Erbe der Monarchie in der deutschen Staatskrise. Zur Geschichte des Verfassungsstaates in Deutschland* (Munich, 1954).

Elster, Jon, "Arguing and Bargaining in the Federal Convention and the Assemblée Constituante"; *Center for the Study of Constitutionalism in Eastern Europe, Working Paper Number 4* (Chicago, 1991).

Elster, Jon, ed., *Deliberative Democracy* (Cambridge, 1998).

Ely, John Hart, *Democracy and Distrust. A Theory of Judicial Review* (Cambridge, 1980).

Enders, Christoph, "Die Freiheit der Andersdenkenden vor den Schranken des Bundesverwaltungsgerichts," *Juristenzeitung*, 63 (2008), 1092–99.

Enzensberger, Hans Magnus, "Die Helden des Rückzugs. Brouillon zu einer politischen Moral der Macht," *Frankfurter Allgemeine Zeitung*, December 9, 1989.

Epstein, Lee and Jeffrey Segal, *Advice and Consent. The Politics of Judicial Appointments* (Oxford, 2005).

Esser, Josef, "Dogmatik zwischen Theorie und Praxis," in F. Baur, J. Esser, F. Kübler, and E. Steindorff, eds., *Funktionswandel der Privatrechtsinstitutionen. Festschrift für Ludwig Raiser zum 70. Geburtstag* (Tübingen, 1974), 517–39.

Faller, Hans Joachim, "Bundesverfassungsgericht und Bundesgerichtshof. Zum Verhältnis beider Gerichtshöfe in fast 40jähriger Jurisdiktion," *Archiv des öffentlichen Rechts*, 115 (1990), 185–211.

Federer, Julius, "Die Rechtsprechung des Bundesverfassungsgerichts zum Grundgesetz für die Bundesrepublik Deutschland," *Jahrbuch des öffentlichen Rechts der Gegenwart*, 3 (1954), 15–66.

Felz, Sebastian, "Duchesse-Schwerrot. Wie die Richter des Bundesverfassungsgerichts zu ihren Roben kamen und warum diese ein Symbol für die Autorität des Gerichts sind," *Ad Legendum. Die Ausbildungszeitschrift aus Münsters Juridicum*, 5 (2008), 246–9.

Ferejohn, John and Pasquale Pasquino, "Constitutional Adjudication: Lessons from Europe," *Texas Law Review*, 82 (2004), 1671–704.

Ferejohn, John and Pasquale Pasquino, "The Countermajoritarian Opportunity," *University of Pennsylvania Journal of Constitutional Law*, 13 (2010), 353–95.

Fiedler, Christoph, "BVerfGE 6, 32—Elfes," in J. Menzel, ed., *Verfassungsrechtsprechung. Hundert Entscheidungen des Bundesverfassungsgerichts in Retrospektive* (Tübingen, 2000), 76–83.

Fikentscher, Wolfgang, *Methoden des Rechts in vergleichender Darstellung*, 2nd vol., *Der anglo-amerikanische Rechtskreis* (Tübingen, 1975).

Forsthoff, Ernst, "Das Bundesverfassungsgericht und das Berufsbeamtentum," *Deutsches Verwaltungsblatt*, 69 (1954), 69–72.

Franßen, Everhardt, "Verfassungsbeschwerde—eine verkappte Normenkontrolle?," in E. Franßen, et al., eds., *Bürger—Richter—Staat. Festschrift für Horst Sendler zum Abschied aus seinem Amt* (Munich, 1991), 81–91.

Frei, Norbert, *Vergangenheitspolitik. Die Anfänge der Bundesrepublik und die NS-Vergangenheit* (Munich, 1996).

Friedman, Lawrence M., *A History of American Law* (3rd edn., New York, 2005).

Fronz, Michael, "Das Bundesverfassungsgericht im politischen System der BRD. Eine Analyse der Beratungen im Parlamentarischen Rat," *Sozialwissenschaftliches Jahrbuch für Politik*, 2 (1971), 629–81.

Gardner, John, "Can There be a Written Constitution?," *Oxford Legal Studies Research Paper No. 17/2009* (Oxford, 2009).

Gauchet, Marcel, *La Révolution des pouvoirs* (Paris, 1995).

Gehle, Burkhard, "Vorbemerkungen zu ss 93a ff.," in: D. C. Umbach, T. Clemens, and F.-W. Dollinger, eds., *Bundesverfassungsgerichtsgesetz. Mitarbeiterkommentar und Handbuch*, (2nd edn., Heidelberg, 2005), 1241–55.

Geiger, Willi, *Gesetz über das Bundesverfassungsgericht vom 12. März 1951. Kommentar* (Berlin, 1952).

Geiger, Willi, *Vom Selbstverständnis des Bundesverfassungsgerichts* (Hannover, 1979).

Ginsburg, Tom, "The Global Spread of Constitutional Review," in G. A. Caldeira, K. E. Whittington, and R. D. Keleman, eds., *Oxford Handbook of Law and Politics* (Oxford, 2008), 81–99.

Godau-Schüttke, Klaus-Detlev, "Entnazifizierung und Wiederaufbau der Justiz am Beispiel des Bundesgerichtshofs," in E. Schumann, ed., *Kontinuitäten und Zäsuren. Rechtswissenschaft und Justiz im "Dritten Reich" und in der Nachkriegszeit* (Göttingen, 2008), 189–212.

Goerlich, Helmut, *Wertordnung und Grundgesetz. Kritik einer Argumentationsfigur des Bundesverfassungsgerichts* (Baden-Baden, 1973).

Goethe, Johann Wolfgang von, *Poetische Werke, Berliner Ausgabe*, 2nd vol. (Berlin, 1966).
Goos, Christoph, *Innere Freiheit. Eine Rekonstruktion des grundgesetzlichen Würdebegriffs* (Göttingen, 2011).
Gosewinkel, Dieter, *Adolf Arndt. Die Wiederbegründung des Rechtsstaats aus dem Geist der Sozialdemokratie (1945–1961)* (Bonn, 1991).
Grigoleit, Klaus Joachim, *Bundesverfassungsgericht und deutsche Frage. Eine dogmatische und historische Untersuchung zum judikativen Anteil an der Staatsleitung* (Tübingen, 2004).
Grimm, Dieter, "Verfassungsgerichtsbarkeit im demokratischen System," *Juristenzeitung*, 31 (1976), 697–703.
Grimm, Dieter, "Die Zukunft der Verfassung," *Staatswissenschaften und Staatspraxis*, 1 (1990), 5–33.
Grimm, Dieter, *Die Zukunft der Verfassung* (Frankfurt, 1991).
Grimm, Dieter, "Die Meinungsfreiheit in der Rechtsprechung des Bundesverfassungsgerichts," *Neue Juristische Wochenschrift*, 27 (1995a), 1697–705.
Grimm, Dieter, "Politik und Recht," in E. Klein, ed., *Grundrechte, soziale Ordnung und Verfassungsgerichtsbarkeit. Festschrift für Ernst Benda* (Heidelberg, 1995b).
Grimm, Dieter, *Die Verfassung und die Politik. Einsprüche in Störfällen* (Munich, 2001).
Grimm, Dieter, "Proportionality in Canadian and German Constitutional Jurisprudence," *University of Toronto Law Journal*, 57 (2007), 383–97.
Grimm, Dieter, *Souveränität. Herkunft und Zukunft eines Schlüsselbegriffs* (Berlin, 2008); trans. Belinda Cooper as *Sovereignty: The Origin and Future of a Political Concept* (New York, 2015).
Grimm, Dieter, "Das Grundgesetz als Riegel vor einer Verstaatlichung der Europäischen Union. Zum Lissabon-Urteil des Bundesverfassungsgerichts," *Der Staat*, 48 (2009a), 475–96.
Grimm, Dieter, "Identität und Wandel—das Grundgesetz 1949 und heute," *Leviathan*, 37 (2009b), 603–16.
Grimm, Dieter, "The Achievement of Constitutionalism and its Prospects in a Changed World," in P. Dobner and M. Loughlin, eds., *The Twilight of Constitutionalism?* (Oxford, 2010), 3–22.
Gross, Johannes, *Die Deutschen* (Frankfurt/Main, 1967).
Gross, Johannes, *Begründung der Berliner Republik. Deutschland am Ende des 20. Jahrhunderts* (2nd edn., Berlin, 1997).
Großfeld, Bernhard and Herbert Roth, eds., *Verfassungsrichter. Rechtsfindung am U.S. Supreme Court und am Bundesverfassungsgericht* (Münster, 1995).
Guggenberger, Bernd and Claus Offe, *An den Grenzen der Mehrheitsdemokratie. Politik und Soziologie der Mehrheitsregel* (Opladen, 1984).
Günther, Frieder, *Denken vom Staat her. Die bundesdeutsche Staatsrechtslehre zwischen Dezision und Integration 1949–1970* (Munich, 2004).
Günther, Frieder, "Wer beeinflusst hier wen? Die westdeutsche Staatsrechtslehre und das Bundesverfassungsgericht während der 1950er und 1960er Jahre," in R. C. van Ooyen and M. H. W. Möllers, eds., *Das Bundesverfassungsgericht im politischen System* (Wiesbaden, 2006), 129–39.
Gusy, Christoph, *Parlamentarischer Gesetzgeber und Bundesverfassungsgericht* (Berlin, 1985).
Gusy, Christoph, "Die Verfassungsbeschwerde," in P. Badura and H. Dreier, eds., *Festschrift 50 Jahre Bundesverfassungsgericht*, 1st vol. (Tübingen, 2001), 641–71.

Gusy, Christoph, "Vom neuen Sicherheitsbegriff zur neuen Sicherheitsarchitektur," *Verwaltungsarchiv*, 101 (2010), 309–33.

Häberle, Peter, "Die offene Gesellschaft der Verfassungsinterpreten. Ein Beitrag zu einer pluralistischen und "prozessualen" Verfassungsinterpretation," *Juristenzeitung*, 30, (1975), 297–305.

Häberle, Peter, "Verfassungsgerichtsbarkeit als politische Kraft," in P. Häberle, ed., *Kommentierte Verfassungsrechtsprechung* (Königstein/Taunus, 1979), 425–449.

Häberle, Peter, "Verfassungsgerichtsbarkeit als politische Kraft," in: P. Häberle, ed., *Verfassungsgerichtsbarkeit zwischen Politik und Rechtswissenschaft* (Königstein, 1980), 55–79.

Habermas, Jürgen, *Faktizität und Geltung. Beiträge zur Diskurstheorie des Rechts und des demokratischen Rechtsstaats* (Frankfurt/Main, 1992).

Haffner, Sebastian, "Konrad Adenauer: der rechte Mann zur rechten Zeit," in S. Haffner, ed., *Im Schatten der Geschichte* (Stuttgart, 1985), 287–98.

Halberstam, Daniel and Christoph Möllers, "The German Constitutional Court Says "Ja zu Deutschland," *German Law Journal*, 10 (2009), 1241–57.

Haller, Herbert, *Die Prüfung von Gesetzen. Ein Beitrag zur verfassungsgerichtlichen Normenkontrolle* (Wien, 1979).

Haltern,UlrichR.,"IntegrationalsMythos.ZurÜberforderungdesBundesverfassungsgerichts," *Jahrbuch des öffentlichen Rechts der Gegenwart*, 45 (1997), 31–88.

Haltern, Ulrich R., *Verfassungsgerichtsbarkeit, Demokratie und Mißtrauen. Das Bundesverfassungsgericht in einer Verfassungstheorie zwischen Populismus und Progressivismus* (Berlin, 1998).

Hanebeck, Andreas, "Die Einheit der Rechtsordnung als Anforderung an den Gesetzgeber? Zu verfassungsrechtlichen Anforderungen wie 'Systemgerechtigkeit' und 'Widerspruchsfreiheit' der Rechtsetzung," *Der Staat*, 41 (2002), 429–51.

Hansen, Cornelia, *"Guerra de Cortes"—Der Konflikt zwischen dem Spanischen Verfassungsgericht und dem Spanischen Obersten Gericht* (Hamburg, 2008).

Harlan, Thomas, *Veit* (Reinbek/Hamburg, 2011).

Hassemer, Winfried, *Erscheinungsformen des modernen Rechts* (Frankfurt/Main, 2007).

Hassemer, Winfried, "Politik aus Karlsruhe?," *Juristenzeitung*, 63 (2008a), 1–10.

Hassemer, Winfried, "Wir haben das letzte Wort," Interview, *Der Spiegel*, 12th issue (2008b), 38–40.

Häußler, Richard, *Der Konflikt zwischen Bundesverfassungsgericht und politischer Führung. Ein Beitrag zu Geschichte und Rechtsstellung des Bundesverfassungsgerichts* (Berlin, 1994).

Heideking, Jürgen, "Der symbolische Stellenwert der Verfassung in der politischen Tradition der USA," in H. Vorländer, ed., *Integration durch Verfassung* (Opladen, 2002), 123–35.

Helms, Ludger, "Ursprünge und Wandlungen der Verfassungsgerichtsbarkeit in westlichen Demokratien," *Zeitschrift für Politik*, 53 (2006), 50–73.

Henne, Thomas, "Die neue Wertordnung im Zivilrecht—speziell im Familien- und Arbeitsrecht," in M. Stolleis, ed., *Das Bonner Grundgesetz. Altes Recht und neue Verfassung in den ersten Jahrzehnten der Bundesrepublik Deutschland (1949–1969)* (Berlin, 2006), 13–37.

Henne, Thomas and Arne Riedlinger, eds., *Das Lüth-Urteil aus (rechts-)historischer Sicht. Die Konflikte um Veit Harlan und die Grundrechtsjudikatur des Bundesverfassungsgerichts* (Berlin, 2005).

Hennis, Wilhelm, "Integration durch Verfassung," *Juristenzeitung*, 54 (1999), 485–92.

Henschel, Johann Friedrich, "Die Kunstfreiheit in der Rechtsprechung des BVerfG," *Neue Juristische Wochenschrift*, 32 (1990), 1937–44.

Herbert, Ulrich, "Integration der jungen Republik durch Verfassungsrecht?," in M. Stolleis, ed., *Das Bonner Grundgesetz. Altes Recht und neue Verfassung in den ersten Jahrzehnten der Bundesrepublik Deutschland (1949–1969)* (Berlin, 2006), 85–102.

Hermes, Georg, "Senate und Kammern," in P. Badura and H. Dreier, eds., *Festschrift 50 Jahre Bundesverfassungsgericht*, 1st vol. (Tübingen, 2001), 725–49.

Hermes, Georg, "Verfassungsrecht und einfaches Recht—Verfassungsgerichtsbarkeit und Fachgerichtsbarkeit," *Veröffentlichungen der Vereinigung der Deutschen Staatsrechtslehrer*, 62 (2002), 119–50.

Herrmann, Dietrich, "Akte der Selbstautorisierung als Grundstock institutioneller Macht von Verfassungsgerichten," in H. Vorländer, ed., *Die Deutungsmacht der Verfassungsgerichtsbarkeit* (Wiesbaden, 2006), 141–73.

Hershovitz, Scott, "Legitimacy, Democracy, and Razian Authority," *Legal Theory*, 9 (2003), 201–20.

Hesse, Konrad, *Die normative Kraft der Verfassung* (Tübingen, 1959).

Hesse, Konrad, "Der Rechtsstaat im Verfassungssystem des Grundgesetzes," in Konrad Hesse, Siegfried Reicke, and Ulrich Scheuner, eds., *Staatsverfassung und Kirchenordung: Festgabe für Rudolf Smend zum 80 Geburtstag am 15 Januar 1962* (Tübingen, 1962).

Heun, Werner, *Funktionellrechtliche Schranken der Verfassungsgerichtsbarkeit. Reichweite und Grenzen einer dogmatischen Argumentationsfigur* (Baden-Baden, 1992).

Heun, Werner, "Die politischen Wirkungen verfassungsgerichtlicher Entscheidungen," in W. Heun and C. Starck, eds., *Verfassungsgerichtsbarkeit im Rechtsvergleich. Drittes deutsch-taiwanesische Kolloquium vom 2.-3. Oktober 2006 an der Georg-August-Universität Göttingen* (Baden-Baden, 2008), 225–41.

Hirschl, Ran, *Towards Juristocracy. The Origins and Consequences of the New Constitutionalism* (Cambridge/Mass., 2004).

Höffe, Otfried, "Wieviel Politik ist dem Bundesverfassungsgericht erlaubt?," *Der Staat*, 38 (1999), 174–93.

Hoffmann-Riem, Wolfgang, "Beharrung oder Innovation—Zur Bindungswirkung verfassungsgerichtlicher Entscheidungen," *Der Staat*, 13 (1974), 335–64.

Hoffmann-Riem, Wolfgang, "Der grundrechtliche Schutz der Vertraulichkeit und Integrität eigengenutzter informationstechnischer Systeme," *Juristenzeitung*, 21 (2008), 1009–22.

Hoffman-Riem, Wolfgang, "Versammlungsfreiheit" in D. Merten and H.-J. Papier, eds., *Handbuch der Grundrechte in Deutschland und Europa*, vol. IV/I (Heidelberg, 2011), 106.

Höfling, Wolfram, "Kopernikanische Wende rückwärts?," in S. Muckel, ed., *Kirche und Religion im sozialen Rechtsstaat. Festschrift für Wolfgang Rüfner zum 70. Geburtstag* (Berlin, 2003), 329–40.

Höfling, Wolfram and Stephan Rixen, "Stattgebende Kammerentscheidungen des BVerfG, 1986–1998," *Archiv des öffentlichen Rechts*, 125 (2000), 428–76.

Holmes, Oliver Wendell, "Law and the Court," in Oliver W. Holmes, ed., *The Collected Legal Papers* (Mineola, 2007 [1913]), 291–7.

Hönnige, Christoph, *Verfassungsgericht, Regierung und Opposition. Die vergleichende Analyse eines Spannungsdreiecks* (Wiesbaden, 2007).

Höpker-Aschoff, Hermann, "Ansprache," in *Ansprachen zur Eröffnung des Bundesverfassungsgerichts. Ansprachen von Theodor Heuss, Konrad Adenauer, Reinhold Maier, Hermann Höpker-Aschoff, Friedrich Töpper* (Karlsruhe, 1951).

Höreth, Marcus, *Die Selbstautorisierung des Agenten. Der Europäische Gerichtshof im Vergleich zum U.S. Supreme Court* (Baden-Baden, 2008).

Huster, Stefan, "Die Beobachtungspflicht des Gesetzgebers," *Zeitschrift für Rechtssoziologie*, 24 (2003), 1-26.

Ipsen, Jörn, *Rechtsfolgen der Verfassungswidrigkeit von Norm und Einzelakt* (Baden-Baden, 1980).

Ipsen, Jörn, "Verfassungsgerichtsbarkeit und politischer Prozess. Anmerkungen zum "Auflösungs-Urteil" des Bundesverfassungsgericht," in R. Grote, et al., eds., *Die Ordnung der Freiheit. Festschrift für Christian Starck zum 70. Geburtstag* (Tübingen, 2007), 263–74.

Ipsen, Jörn, *Der Staat der Mitte. Verfassungsgeschichte der Bundesrepublik Deutschland* (Munich, 2009).

Isensee, Josef, "Die Verfassung als Vaterland: Zur Staatsverdrängung der Deutschen," in A. Mohler, ed., *Wirklichkeit als Tabu. Anmerkungen zur Lage, Schriften der Carl Friedrich von Siemens Stiftung*, 11th vol. (Munich, 1986), 11–35.

Isensee, Josef, "Verfassungsrecht als 'politisches Recht'," in J. Isensee and P. Kirchhof, eds., *Handbuch des Staatsrechts der Bundesrepublik Deutschland*, 6th vol. (Heidelberg, 1992), 103–88.

Isensee, Josef, "Braucht die Republik einen Präsidenten?," *Neue Juristische Wochenschrift*, 47 (1994), 1329–30.

Isensee, Josef, "Bundesverfassungsgericht - quo vadis?," *Juristenzeitung*, 51 (1996), 1085–93.

Isensee, Josef and Edzard Schmidt-Jortzig, eds., *Das Ausländerwahlrecht vor dem Bundesverfassungsgericht. Dokumentation und Verfahren* (Heidelberg, 1999).

Jaeggi, Rahel, *Was ist Kritik?* (Frankfurt/Main, 2009).

Jarass, Hans D., "Die Grundrechte: Abwehrrechte und objektive Grundsatznormen. Objektive Grundrechtsgehalte, insbes. Schutzpflichten und privatrechtsgestaltende Wirkung," in: P. Badura and H. Dreier, eds., *Festschrift 50 Jahre Bundesverfassungsgericht*, 2nd vol. (Tübingen, 2001), 35–54.

Jestaedt, Matthias, *Demokratieprinzip und Kondominialverwaltung. Entscheidungsteilhabe Privater an der öffentlichen Verwaltung auf dem Prüfstand des Verfassungsprinzips der Demokratie* (Berlin, 1993).

Jestaedt, Matthias, *Grundrechtsentfaltung im Gesetz. Studien zur Interdependenz von Grundrechtsdogmatik und Rechtsgewinnungstheorie* (Tübingen, 1999).

Jestaedt, Matthias, "Verfassungsrecht und einfaches Recht—Verfassungsgerichtsbarkeit und Fachgerichtsbarkeit," *Deutsches Verwaltungsblatt*, 116 (2001), 1309–22.

Jestaedt, Matthias, "Verfassungsgerichtspositivismus. Die Ohnmacht des Verfassungsgesetzgebers im verfassungsgerichtlichen Jurisdiktionsstaat," in O. Depenheuer, M. Heintzen, P. Axer, and M. Jestaedt, eds., *Nomos und Ethos. Hommage anläßlich des 65. Geburtstages von Josef Isensee* (Berlin, 2002), 183–228.

Jestaedt, Matthias, "Rechtsprechung und Rechtsetzung—eine deutsche Perspektive," in W. Erbguth and J. Masing, eds., *Die Bedeutung der Rechtsprechung im System der Rechtsquellen. Europarecht und nationales Recht* (Stuttgart, 2005), 25–79.

Jestaedt, Matthias, *Das mag in der Theorie richtig sein* (Tübingen, 2006).

Jestaedt, Matthias, "Wirken und Wirkungen höchstrichterlicher Judikatur—Rechtsprechung von Grenzorganen aus Sicht der Reinen Rechtslehre," in C. Jabloner, ed., *Wirken und Wirkungen höchstrichterlicher Judikatur. Symposium zum 60. Geburtstag von Heinz Mayer* (Wien, 2007a), 9–33.

Jestaedt, Matthias, "Die Abwägungslehre—ihre Stärken und ihre Schwächen," in O. Depenheuer, et al., eds., *Staat im Wort. Festschrift für Josef Isensee* (Heidelberg, 2007b), 253–75.

Jestaedt, Matthias, "Autorität und Zitat. Anmerkungen zur Zitierpraxis des Bundesverfassungsgerichts," in S. Detterbeck, et al., eds., *Recht als Medium der Staatlichkeit. Festschrift für Herbert Bethge zum 70. Geburtstag* (Berlin, 2009a), 513–33.

Jestaedt, Matthias, "Warum in die Ferne schweifen, wenn der Maßstab liegt so nah? Verfassungshandwerkliche Anfragen an das Lissabon-Urteil des BVerfG," *Der Staat*, 48 (2009b), 497–516.

Jestaedt, Matthias, "Zur Koppelung von Politik und Recht in der Verfassungsgerichtsbarkeit," in S. Korioth and T. Vesting, eds., *Der Eigenwert des Verfassungsrechts. Was bleibt von der Verfassung nach der Globalisierung?* (Tübingen, 2011), 317–32.

Kahl, Wolfgang, *Die Schutzergänzungsfunktion von Art. 2 Abs. 1 Grundgesetz* (Tübingen, 2000).

Kahl, Wolfgang, "Vom weiten Schutzbereich zum engen Gewährleistungsgehalt. Kritik einer neuen Richtung der deutschen Grundrechtsdogmatik," *Der Staat*, 43 (2004), 167–202.

Kahl, Wolfgang, "Grundrechte," in O. Depenheuer and C. Grabenwarter, eds., *Verfassungstheorie* (Tübingen, 2010), 24.

Kähler, Lorenz, *Strukturen und Methoden der Rechtsprechungsänderung* (2nd edn., Baden-Baden, 2011).

Kahn, Paul W., *The Reign of Law. Marbury v. Madison and the Construction of America* (New Haven, 2002).

Kau, Marcel, *United States Supreme Court und Bundesverfassungsgericht. Die Bedeutung des United States Supreme Court für die Errichtung und Fortentwicklung des Bundesverfassungsgerichts* (Berlin, 2007).

Kau, Marcel, "Politische Parteien im Prozess der Konstitutionalisierung—Einfluss und spätere Wirkung dargestellt am Beispiel der Verfassungsgerichtsbarkeit," *Zeitschrift für Rechtsphilosophie*, 6 (2008), 90–105.

Kelsen, Hans, "Wesen und Entwicklung der Staatsgerichtsbarkeit," *Veröffentlichungen der Vereinigung der Deutschen Staatsrechtslehrer*, 5 (1929a), 30–88.

Kelsen, Hans, *Vom Wesen und Wert der Demokratie* (2nd edn., Tübingen, 1929b).

Kelsen, Hans, "Wer soll der Hüter der Verfassung sein?," *Die Justiz. Monatsschrift für Erneuerung des deutschen Rechtswesens. Zugleich Organ des Republikanischen Richterbundes*, 6 (1931), 576–628.

Kielmansegg, Peter Graf, "Das Verfassungsparadox. Bemerkungen zum Spannungsverhältnis zwischen Demokratieprinzip und Verfassungsprinzip," in H. Meier, et al., eds., *Politik, Philosophie, Praxis. Festschrift für Wilhelm Hennis* (Stuttgart, 1988), 397–411.

Kinkela, Claudia, *Die Rehabilitierung des Bürgerlichen im Werk Dolf Sternbergers* (Würzburg, 2001).

Kirchhof, Paul, "Das Maastricht-Urteil des Bundesverfassungsgerichts," in P. Hommelhoff and P. Kirchhof, eds., *Der Staatenverbund der Europäischen Union* (Heidelberg, 1994), 11–24.

Kirchhof, Paul, "Das Kooperationsverhältnis zwischen Bundesverfassungsgericht und Europäischem Gerichtshof," in P.-C. Müller-Graff, ed., *Perspektiven des Rechts in der Europäischen Union* (Heidelberg, 1998), 163–82.

Kirchhof, Paul, *Besteuerung im Verfassungsstaat* (Tübingen, 2001).

Kirchhof, Paul, "Der Grundrechtsschutz des Steuerpflichtigen," *Archiv des öffentlichen Rechts*, 128 (2003), 1–51.

Kirn, Michael, *Verfassungsumsturz oder Rechtskontinuität? Die Stellung der Jurisprudenz nach 1945 zum Dritten Reich, insbesondere die Konflikte um die Kontinuität der Beamtenrechte und Art. 131 Grundgesetz* (Berlin, 1972).

Klein, Eckart, "Verfahrensgestaltung durch Gesetz und Richterspruch: Das "Prozeßrecht" des Bundesverfassungsgerichts," in P. Badura and H. Dreier, eds., *Festschrift 50 Jahre Bundesverfassungsgericht*, 2nd vol. (Tübingen, 2001), 507–32.

Kneip, Sascha, "Demokratieimmanente Grenzen der Verfassungsgerichtsbarkeit," *Politische Vierteljahresschrift, Politik und Recht*, special edition, 36 (2006), 259–81.

Kneip, Sascha, *Verfassungsgerichte als demokratische Akteure. Der Beitrag des Bundesverfassungsgerichts zur Qualität der bundesdeutschen Demokratie* (Baden-Baden, 2009).

Kommers, Donald P., *Judicial Politics in West Germany. A Study of the Federal Constitutional Court* (Beverly Hills, 1976).

Kralewski, Wolfgang and Karlheinz Neunreither, *Oppositionelles Verhalten im ersten Deutschen Bundestag (1949–1953)* (Cologne, 1963).

Kramer, Larry, *The People Themselves. Popular Constitutionalism and Judicial Review* (New York, 2004).

Kranenpohl, Uwe, "Die Bedeutung von Interpretationsmethoden und Dogmatik in der Entscheidungspraxis des Bundesverfassungsgerichts," *Der Staat*, 48 (2009), 387–409.

Kranenpohl, Uwe, *Hinter dem Schleier des Beratungsgeheimnisses. Der Willensbildungs- und Entscheidungsprozess des Bundesverfassungsgerichts* (Wiesbaden, 2010).

Kübler, Friedrich, "Der deutsche Richter und das demokratische Gesetz," *Archiv für die civilistische Praxis*, 162 (1963), 104–28.

Kühl, Kristian, "Kontinuitäten und Diskontinuitäten im Naturrechtsdenken des 20. Jahrhunderts," in K. Acham, K. W. Nörr, and B. Schefold, eds., *Erkenntnisgewinne, Erkenntnisverluste. Kontinuitäten und Diskontinuitäten in den Wirtschafts-, Rechts- und Sozialwissenschaften zwischen den 20er und 50er Jahren* (Stuttgart, 1998), 605–58.

Kumm, Mattias, "The Idea of Socratic Contestation and the Right to Justification. The Point of Rights-Based Justification," *Law & Ethics of Human Rights*, 4 (2010), 141–75.

Lamprecht, Rolf, *Richter contra Richter. Abweichende Meinungen und ihre Bedeutung für die Rechtskultur* (Baden-Baden, 1992).

Lamprecht, Rolf, "Feindbild Karlsruhe. Wie Politiker Urteils- und Richterschelte betreiben—und betrieben," *Deutsche Richterzeitung*, 87 (2009), 145–7.

Lamprecht, Rolf and Wolfgang Malanowski, *Richter machen Politik. Auftrag und Anspruch des Bundesverfassungsgerichts* (Frankfurt/Main, 1979).

Landfried, Christine, *Bundesverfassungsgericht und Gesetzgeber. Wirkungen der Verfassungsrechtsprechung auf parlamentarische Willensbildung und soziale Realität* (Baden-Baden, 1984).

Lasser, Mitchel De S.-O.-I'E., *Judicial Deliberations. A Comparative Analysis of Transparency Legitimacy* (Oxford, 2004).

Laufer, Heinz, *Verfassungsgerichtsbarkeit und politischer Prozeß. Studien zum Bundesverfassungsgericht für die Bundesrepublik Deutschland* (Tübingen, 1968).

Lechner, Hans and Rüdiger Zuck, *Kommentar zum Bundesverfassungsgerichtsgesetz* (6th edn., Munich, 2011).

Lehmbruch, Gerhard, "Die korporative Verhandlungsdemokratie in Westmitteleuropa," *Schweizerische Zeitschrift für politische Wissenschaft*, 2 (1996), 19–41.

Lehmbruch, Gerhard, *Parteienwettbewerb im Bundesstaat. Regelsysteme und Spannungslagen im Institutionengefüge der Bundesrepublik Deutschland* (2nd edn., Opladen, 1998).

Leibholz, Gerhard, "Bericht des Berichterstatters des Bundesverfassungsgerichts vom 21. März 1952," *Jahrbuch des öffentliches Rechts der Gegenwart*, 6 (1957a), 120–37.

Leibholz, Gerhard, "Der Status des Bundesverfassungsgerichts: Eine Materialsammlung mit einer Einleitung," *Jahrbuch des öffentlichen Rechts der Gegenwart*, 6 (1957b), 109–221.

Lembcke, Oliver W., *Über das Ansehen des Bundesverfassungsgerichts. Ansichten und Meinungen in der Öffentlichkeit 1951–2001* (Berlin, 2006).

Lembcke, Oliver W., *Hüter der Verfassung. Eine institutionentheoretische Studie zur Autorität des Bundesverfassungsgerichts* (Tübingen, 2007).

Lembke, Ulrike, *Einheit aus Erkenntnis? Zur Unzulässigkeit der verfassungskonformen Gesetzesauslegung als Methode der Normkompatibilisierung durch Interpretation* (Berlin, 2009).

Lenz, Sebastian, *Vorbehaltslose Freiheitsrechte* (Tübingen, 2006).

Lepsius, M. Rainer, "Institutional Structures and Political Culture," in H. Döring and G. Smith, eds., *Party Government and Political Culture in Western Germany* (London, 1982), 116–29.

Lepsius, Oliver, *Die gegensatzaufhebende Begriffsbildung. Methodenentwicklungen in der Weimarer Republik und ihr Verhältnis zur Ideologisierung der Rechtswissenschaft im Nationalsozialismus* (Munich, 1994).

Lepsius, Oliver, *Verwaltungsrecht unter dem Common Law. Amerikanische Entwicklungen bis zum New Deal* (Tübingen, 1997).

Lepsius, Oliver, "Die erkenntnistheoretische Notwendigkeit des Parlamentarismus," in M. Bertschi, et al., eds., *Demokratie und Freiheit* (Stuttgart, 1999), 123–80.

Lepsius, Oliver, "Braucht das Verfassungsrecht eine Theorie des Staates? Eine deutsche Perspektive: Von der Staatstheorie zur Theorie der Herrschaftsformen," *Europäische Grundrechte Zeitschrift*, 31 (2004), 370–82.

Lepsius, Oliver, "Der Große Lauschangriff vor dem Bundesverfassungsgericht (Teil I)," *Juristische Ausbildung*, 27 (2005), 433–40.

Lepsius, Oliver, "Das Luftsicherheitsgesetz und das Grundgesetz," in F. Roggan, ed., *Mit Recht für Menschenwürde und Verfassungsstaat. Festgabe für Dr. Burkhard Hirsch* (Berlin, 2006), 47–74.

Lepsius, Oliver, "Was kann die deutsche Staatsrechtslehre von der amerikanischen Rechtswissenschaft lernen?," in H. Schulze-Fielitz, ed., *Staatsrechtslehre als Wissenschaft, Die Verwaltung*, supplement, 7 (Berlin, 2007), 319–66.

Lepsius, Oliver, "Zur Bindungswirkung von Bundesverfassungsgerichtsentscheidungen," in R. Scholz, et al., *Realitätsprägung durch Verfassungsrecht. Kolloquium aus Anlass des 80. Geburtstags von Peter Lerche* (Berlin, 2008a), 103–17.

Lepsius, Oliver, "Themen einer Rechtswissenschaftstheorie," in M. Jestaedt and O. Lepsius, eds., *Rechtswissenschaftstheorie* (Tübingen, 2008b), 1–49.

Lepsius, Oliver, "Erwerbsaufwendungen im Einkommensteuerrecht. Anmerkung," *Juristenzeitung*, 64 (2009), 260–3.

Lepsius, Oliver, "Hat die Europäisierung des Verwaltungsrechts Methode? Oder: Die zwei Phasen der Europäisierung des Verwaltungsrechts," in P. Axer, B. Grzeszick, W. Kahl, et al., eds., *Das Europäische Verwaltungsrecht in der Konsolidierungsphase. Systembildung—Disziplinierung—Internationalisierung, Die Verwaltung*, supplement, 10 (Berlin, 2010a), 179–204.

Lepsius, Oliver, "Sicherheit und Freiheit—ein zunehmend asymmetrisches Verhältnis," in W. Merkel, G. Nolte, G. F. Schuppert, et al., eds., *Der Rechtsstaat unter Bewährungsdruck* (Baden-Baden, 2010b), 23–54.

Lepsius, Oliver, "Einschränkung der Meinungsfreiheit durch Sonderrecht," *Juristische Ausbildung*, 32 (2010c), 527–35.

Lepsius, Oliver, "Verfassungsrechtlicher Rahmen der Regulierung," in M. Fehling and M. Ruffert, eds., *Regulierungsrecht* (Tübingen, 2010d), 4.

Lepsius, Oliver, "Kritik der Dogmatik," in G. Kirchhof, S. Magen, and C. Schneider, eds., *Was weiß Dogmatik?* (Tübingen, 2012), 39–62.

Lepsius, Oliver, "Constitutional Review of Tax Laws and the Unconstitutionality of the German Inheritance Tax Law," *German Law Journal* 16 (2015), 1191–215.

Lerche, Peter, "Stil, Methode, Ansicht," *Deutsches Verwaltungsblatt*, 76 (1961), 690–701.

Lerche, Peter, "Zur Funktion des Bundesverfassungsgerichts als Notgesetzgeber, insbesondere im Hinblick auf das Recht des Schwangerschaftsabbruchs," in M. Heinze and J. Schmitt, eds., *Festschrift für Wolfgang Gitter zum 65. Geburtstag*, (Wiesbaden, 1995), 509–17.

Lerche, Peter, *Übermaß und Verfassungsrecht* (2nd edn., Goldbach, 1999).

Lerche, Peter, "Stil und Methode der verfassungsgerichtlichen Entscheidungspraxis," in P. Badura and H. Dreier, eds., *Festschrift 50 Jahre Bundesverfassungsgericht*, 1st vol. (Tübingen, 2001), 333–61.

Lerche, Peter, "Rechtswissenschaft und Verfassungsgerichtsbarkeit," *Bayerische Verwaltungsblätter*, 48 (2002), 649–52.

Lerche, Peter, "Die Verfassung in der Hand der Verfassungsgerichtsbarkeit," in R. Scholz, D. Lorenz, C. Pestalozza, et al., eds., *Ausgewählte Abhandlungen* (Berlin, 2004), 522–8.

Lerche, Peter, "Vorbehalt des Gesetzes und Wesentlichkeitstheorie," in D. Merten and H.-J. Papier, eds., *Handbuch der Grundrechte in Deutschland und Europa*, 3rd vol. (Heidelberg, 2009), 62.

Levi, Edward H., *An Introduction to Legal Reasoning* (Chicago, 1949).

Ley, Richard, "Die Erstbesetzung des Bundesverfassungsgerichts," *Zeitschrift für Parlamentsfragen*, 13 (1982), 521–40.

Lhotta, Roland, "Das Bundesverfassungsgericht als politischer Akteur: Plädoyer für eine neo-institutionalistische Ergänzung in der Forschung," *Swiss Political Science Review*, 9 (2003), 113–53.

Limbach, Jutta, "Globalization of Constitutional Law through Interaction of Judges," *Verfassung und Recht in Übersee*, 41 (2008), 51–5.

Lorenz, Astrid, *Verfassungsänderungen in etablierten Demokratien. Motivlagen und Aushandlungsmuster* (Wiesbaden, 2008).

Lortz, Alexander, "Die Gefahr der Stimmengleichheit—Ein wenig beachteter Sprengsatz in der Konstruktion des BVerfG," *Zeitschrift für Rechtspolitik*, 36 (2003), 36–9.

Löwer, Wolfgang, "Zuständigkeiten und Verfahren des Bundesverfassungsgerichts," in J. Isensee and P. Kirchhof, eds., *Handbuch des Staatsrechts der Bundesrepublik Deutschland*, 3rd vol. (3rd edn., Heidelberg, 2005), 1285–526.

Lübbe-Wolff, Gertrude, *Rechtsfolgen und Realfolgen. Welche Rolle können Folgenerwägungen in der juristischen Regel- und Begriffsbildung spielen?* (Freiburg, 1981).

Luhmann, Niklas, "Politische Verfassungen im Kontext des Gesellschaftssystems," *Der Staat*, 12 (1973), 1–22, 165–82.

Luhmann, Niklas, *Legitimation durch Verfahren* (2nd edn., Neuwied, 1975).

Luhmann, Niklas, "Verfassung als evolutionäre Errungenschaft," *Rechtshistorisches Journal*, 9 (1990), 176–220.

Luhmann, Niklas, "Quod omnes tangit … Anmerkungen zur Rechtstheorie von Jürgen Habermas," *Rechtshistorisches Journal*, 12 (1993), 36–56.

Manin, Bernard, "On Legitimacy and Political Deliberation," *Political Theory*, 15 (1987), 338–68.

Massing, Otwin, "Das Bundesverfassungsgericht als Instrument sozialer Kontrolle. Propädeutische Skizzen zu einer funktionskritischen Formanalyse der Verfassungsgerichtsbarkeit,"

Politische Vierteljahresschrift, Probleme der Demokratie heute, special edition, 2 (1970), 180–225.

Massing, Otwin, *Politik als Recht—Recht als Politik. Studien zu einer Theorie der Verfassungsgerichtsbarkeit* (Baden-Baden, 2005).

Maus, Ingeborg, "Entwicklung und Funktionswandel des Bürgrlichen Rechtsstaats," in *Rechtstheorie und politische Theorie im Industriekapitalismus* (Munich, 1986).

Mayer, Franz C., *Kompetenzüberschreitung und Letztentscheidung. Das Maastricht-Urteil des Bundesverfassungsgerichts und die Letztentscheidung über Ultra vires-Akte in Mehrebenensystemen. Eine rechtsvergleichende Betrachtung von Konflikten zwischen Gerichten am Beispiel der EU und der USA* (Munich, 2000).

Mayer, Franz C., "Verfassungsgerichtsbarkeit," in A. v. Bogdandy and J. Bast, eds., *Europäisches Verfassungsrecht* (2nd edn., Berlin, 2009), 559–606.

McCrudden, Christopher, "Human Dignity and Judicial Interpretation of Human Rights," *European Journal of International Law*, 19 (2008), 655–724.

Meinel, Florian, "The Constitutional Miracle on the Rhine: Towards a History of West German Constitutionalism and the Federal Constitutional Court," *I.CON. Int. J of Constitutional Law*, 14 (2016), 277–93.

Menzel, Jörg, "Vergangenheitsbewältigung in der frühen Judikatur des Bundesverfas sungsgerichts: Beamten- und Gestapo-Urteil," in T. Henne and A. Riedlinger, eds., *Das Lüth-Urteil aus (rechts-)historischer Sicht. Die Konflikte um Veit Harlan und die Grundrechtsjudikatur des Bundesverfassungsgerichts* (Berlin, 2005), 225–35.

Menzel, Jörg, ed., *Verfassungsrechtsprechung. Hundert Entscheidungen des Bundesverfassungsgerichts in Retrospektive* (Tübingen, 2000).

Merli, Franz, "Rechtsprechungskonkurrenz zwischen nationalen Verfassungsgerichten, Europäischem Gerichtshof und Europäischem Gerichtshof für Menschenrechte," *Veröffentlichungen der Vereinigung der Deutschen Staatsrechtslehrer*, 66 (2007), 392–422.

Merten, Detlef, "Verhältnismäßigkeitsgrundsatz," in D. Merten and H.-J. Papier, eds., *Handbuch der Grundrechte in Deutschland und Europa*, 3rd vol. (Heidelberg, 2009), 68.

Mertz, Elisabeth, *The Role of Social Science in Law* (Aldershot, 2008).

Millgramm, Karl-Heinz, *Separate Opinions und Sondervotum in der Rechtsprechung des Supreme Court of the United States und des Bundesverfassungsgerichts* (Berlin, 1985).

Möllers, Christoph, *Gewaltengliederung. Legitimation und Dogmatik im nationalen und internationalen Rechtsvergleich* (Tübingen, 2005).

Möllers, Christoph, "Formloser Sozialstaat gegen rechtsstaatliche Form—Zustimmungsrechte des Bundesrates und Rechtsverordnungsermächtigungen durch den Bundestag—BVerfG 2 BvF 2/03 v. 13.9.2005," *Juristische Ausbildung*, 29 (2007), 932–7.

Möllers, Christoph, *Der vermisste Leviathan. Staatstheorie in der Bundesrepublik* (Frankfurt/Main, 2008a).

Möllers, Christoph, *Die drei Gewalten. Legitimation der Gewaltengliederung in Verfassungsstaat, Europäischer Integration und Internationalisierung* (Weilerswist, 2008b).

Möllers, Christoph, "Vermittlungsausschuss und Vermittlungsverfahren," *Juristische Ausbildung*, 32 (2010), 401–7.

Möllers, Christoph, *Staat als Argument* (2nd edn., Tübingen, 2011).

Möllers, Christoph and Andreas Voßkuhle, "Die deutsche Staatsrechtswissenschaft im Zusammenhang der internationalisierten Wissenschaften—Beobachtungen, Vermutungen, Thesen," *Die Verwaltung*, 36 (2003), 321–32.

Monahan, John and Walker Laurens, *Social Science in Law. Cases and Materials* (7th edn., New York, 2010).

Morlok, Martin, *Was heißt und zu welchem Ende studiert man Verfassungstheorie?* (Berlin, 1988).

Müller, Jan-Werner, *Verfassungspatriotismus* (Berlin, 2010).

Müller-Mall, Sabine, *Performative Rechtserzeugung* (Weilerswist, 2012).

Nassehi, Armin, *Der soziologische Diskurs der Moderne* (Frankfurt/Main, 2006).

Naumann, Richard and Hans Spanner, "Die Berufsbeamten und die Staatskrisen," *Veröffentlichungen der Vereinigung der Deutschen Staatsrechtslehrer*, 13 (1955), 88–194.

Neurath, Otto, "Protokollsätze," *Erkenntnis*, 3 (1932), 204–14.

Niclauß, Karlheinz, "Der Parlamentarische Rat und das Bundesverfassungsgericht," in R. C. van Ooyen and M. H. W. Möllers, eds., *Das Bundesverfassungsgericht im politischen System* (Wiesbaden, 2006), 117–28.

Nierhaus, Michael, "Bestimmtheitsgebot und Delegationsverbot des Art. 80 Abs. 1 Satz 2 GG und der Gesetzesvorbehalt der Wesentlichkeitstheorie," in J. Burmeister, ed., *Verfassungsstaatlichkeit. Festschrift für Klaus Stern zum 65. Geburtstag* (Munich, 1997), 717–32.

Nino, Carlos Santiago, *The Constitution of Deliberative Democracy* (New Haven, 1996).

Oeter, Stefan, "Rechtsprechungskonkurrenz zwischen nationalen Verfassungsgerichten, Europäischem Gerichtshof und Europäischem Gerichtshof für Menschenrechte," *Veröffentlichungen der Vereinigung der Deutschen Staatsrechtslehrer*, 66 (2007), 362–91.

Ossenbühl, Fritz, "Die Kontrolle von Tatsachenfeststellungen und Prognoseentscheidungen durch das Bundesverfassungsgericht," in C. Starck, ed., *Bundesverfassungsgericht und Grundgesetz. Festgabe aus Anlaß des 25jährigen Bestehens des Bundesverfassungsgerichts*, 1st vol.: Verfassungsgerichtsbarkeit (Tübingen, 1976), 458–518.

Ossenbühl, Fritz, "Abwägung im Verfassungsrecht," *Deutsches Verwaltungsblatt*, 110 (1995), 904–12.

Otto, Volker, *Das Staatsverständnis des Parlamentarischen Rates. Ein Beitrag zur Entstehungsgeschichte des Grundgesetzes für die Bundesrepublik Deutschland* (Düsseldorf, 1971).

Papier, Hans-Jürgen, *Das Rechtsprechungsdreieck Karlsruhe—Luxemburg—Straßburg. Vortrag im Sommersemester 2006, 11. Juli 2006, Speyerer Vorträge, 89* (Speyer, 2006).

Papier, Hans-Jürgen, "Das Bundesverfassungsgericht als Hüter der Grundrechte," in D. Merten and H.-J. Papier, eds., *Handbuch der Grundrechte in Deutschland und Europa*, 3rd vol. (Heidelberg, 2009), 80.

Pasquino, Pasquale, "Constitutional Adjudication and Democracy. Comparative Perspectives: USA, France, Italy," *Ratio Juris*, 11 (1998), 38–50.

Patzelt, Werner, "Warum verachten die Deutschen ihr Parlament und lieben ihr Verfassungsgericht? Ergebnisse einer vergleichenden demoskopischen Studie," *Zeitschrift für Parlamentsfragen*, 36 (2005), 517–38.

Peilert, Andreas, "BVerfGE 65, 1—Volkszählung," in J. Menzel, ed., *Verfassungsrechtsprechung. Hundert Entscheidungen des Bundesverfassungsgerichts in Retrospektive* (Tübingen, 2000), 344–50.

Peters, Anne, *Elemente einer Theorie der Verfassung Europas* (Berlin, 2001).

Petersen, Niels, "Auf dem Weg zur zweckrationalen Relativität der Menschenwürde," *Kritische Justiz*, 37 (2004), 316–26.

Pildes, Richard, "The Supreme Court, 2003 Term—Foreword: Constitutionalization of Democratic Politics," *Harvard Law Review*, 118 (2004), 29–154.

Poscher, Ralf, *Grundrechte als Abwehrrechte. Reflexive Regelung rechtlich geordneter Freiheit* (Tübingen, 2003).

Poscher, Ralf, "Sicherheitsverfassungsrecht im Wandel," in T. Vesting and S. Korioth, eds., *Der Eigenwert des Verfassungsrechts. Was bleibt von der Verfassung nach der Globalisierung?* (Tübingen, 2011).

Post, Robert C., "Constitutional Scholarship in the United States," *International Journal of Constitutional Law*, 7 (2009), 416–23.

Postema, Gerald J., "Philosophy of the Common Law," in J. Coleman and S. Shapiro, eds., *The Oxford Handbook of Jurisprudence and Philosophy of Law* (Oxford, 2002), 588–622.

Preuß, Ulrich K., "Politik aus dem Geiste des Konsenses. Zur Rechtsprechung des Bundesverfassungsgerichts," *Merkur. Deutsche Zeitschrift für europäisches Denken*, 41 (1987), 1–12.

Preuß, Ulrich K., "Der Begriff der Verfassung und seine Beziehung zur Politik," in U. K. Preuß, ed., *Zum Begriff der Verfassung* (Frankfurt/Main, 1994), 7–33.

Raz, Joseph, *Practical Reasons and Norms* (London, 1975).

Riecken, Jörg, *Verfassungsgerichtsbarkeit in der Demokratie. Grenzen verfassungsgerichtlicher Kontrolle unter besonderer Berücksichtigung von John Hart Elys prozeduraler Theorie der Repräsentationsverstärkung* (Berlin, 2003).

Rixen, Stephan, "Was folgt aus der Folgerichtigkeit?," *Die Sozialgerichtsbarkeit* 57 (2010a), 240–5.

Rixen, Stephan, "Verfassungsrecht ersetzt Sozialpolitik? Hartz IV auf dem Prüfstand des BVerfG," *Sozialrecht aktuell* 14 (2010b), 81–7.

Robertson, David, *The Judge as Political Theorist. Contemporary Constitutional Review* (Princeton, 2010).

Roellecke, Gerd, "Aufgaben und Stellung des Bundesverfassungsgerichts im Verfassungsgefüge," in J. Isensee and P. Kirchhof, eds., *Handbuch des Staatsrechts der Bundesrepublik Deutschland*, 2nd vol. (Heidelberg, 1987), 53.

Roellecke, Gerd, "Karlsruhe," in E. François and H. Schulze, eds., *Deutsche Erinnerungsorte*, 2nd vol. (Munich, 2003), 549–64.

Roellecke, Gerd, "Aufgaben und Stellung des Bundesverfassungsgerichts im Verfassungsgefüge," in J. Isensee and P. Kirchhof, eds., *Handbuch des Staatsrechts der Bundesrepublik Deutschland*, 3rd vol. (3rd edn., Heidelberg, 2005a), 1201–19.

Roellecke, Gerd, "Aufgaben und Stellung des Bundesverfassungsgerichts in der Gerichtsbarkeit," in J. Isensee and P. Kirchhof, eds., *Handbuch des Staatsrechts der Bundesrepublik Deutschland*, 3rd vol. (3rd edn., Heidelberg, 2005b), 1221–32.

Roellecke, Gerd, "Institutionelle Gewähr der Verfassung," in O. Depenheuer and C. Grabenwarter, eds., *Verfassungstheorie* (Tübingen, 2010), 489–503.

Röhl, Hans Christian, "Verfassungsrecht als wissenschaftliche Strategie?," in H.-H. Trute, et al., eds., *Allgemeines Verwaltungsrecht—zur Tragfähigkeit eines Konzepts. Festschrift Eberhard Schmidt-Aßmann* (Tübingen, 2008), 821–38.

Roland, Sébastien, *Le triangle décisionnel communautaire à l'aune de la théorie de la séparation des pouvoirs. Recherches sur la distribution des pouvoirs législatif et exécutif dans la Communauté* (Brussels, 2008).

Roosevelt, Franklin D., "Address on Constitution Day, Washington D.C. (17.9.1937)," in F. D. Roosevelt and S. I. Rosenman, eds., *The Public Papers and Addresses of Franklin D. Roosevelt* (New York, 1938), 362.

Rorty, Richard, "The Priority of Democracy to Philosophy," in R. Rorty, ed., *Objectivity, Relativism, and Truth* (Cambridge, 1991), 175–96.

Rosen, Paul L., *The Supreme Court and Social Science* (Urbana, IL, 1972).

Rosenberg, Gerald N. (1991), *The Hollow Hope. Can Courts Bring About Social Change?* (Chicago, 1991).

Ruger, Theodore W., Pauline T. Kim, Andrew D. Martin, and Kevin M. Quinn, "The Supreme Court Forecasting Project: Legal and Political Science Approaches to Predicting Supreme Court Decisionmaking," *Columbia Law Review*, 104 (2004), 1150–209.

Rüthers, Bernd, *Die unbegrenzte Auslegung. Zum Wandel der Privatrechtsordnung im Nationalsozialismus* (6th edn., Tübingen, 2005).

Sadurski, Wojciech, *Equality and Legitimacy* (Oxford, 2008).

Sangmeister, Bernd, "'Der Krieg der Richter'– BVerfG, NJW 1998, 519," *Juristische Schulung*, 39 (1999), 21–8.

Schaal, Gary S., "Vertrauen in das Bundesverfassungsgericht und die Akzeptanz seiner Entscheidungen als Indikatoren der Geltung und Akzeptanz konstitutioneller Ordnungsvorstellungen," *Zeitschrift für Rechtssoziologie*, 21 (2000a), 419–46.

Schaal, Gary S., *Integration durch Verfassung und Verfassungsrechtsprechung? Über den Zusammenhang von Demokratie, Verfassung und Integration* (Berlin, 2000b).

Schäller Steven, "Präjudizien als selbstreferenzielle Geltungsressource des Bundesverfassungsgerichts," in H. Vorländer and A. Brodocz, eds., *Die Deutungsmacht der Verfassungsgerichtsbarkeit* (Wiesbaden, 2006), 205–34.

Schauer, Frederick, "Precedent," *Stanford Law Review*, 39 (1987), 571–605.

Schenke, Ralf, *Die Rechtsfindung im Steuerrecht. Konstitutionalisierung, Europäisierung, Methodengesetzgebung* (Tübingen, 2007).

Schenke, Ralf, "Methodenlehre und Grundgesetz," in H. Dreier, ed., *Macht und Ohnmacht des Grundgesetzes* (Berlin, 2009), 51–74.

Schenke, Wolf-Rüdiger, "Das "gefühlte" Misstrauen. Zur Verfassungsrechtslage nach der Entscheidung des Bundesverfassungsgerichts v. 25.8.2005 zur Vertrauensfrage nach Art. 68 GG," *Zeitschrift für Politik*, 53 (2006), 26–49.

Scheuner, Ulrich, "Probleme und Verantwortungen der Verfassungsgerichtsbarkeit in der Bundesrepublik," *Deutsches Verwaltungsblatt*, 67 (1952), 293–8.

Scheuner, Ulrich, "Die Überlieferung der deutschen Staatsgerichtsbarkeit im 19. und 20. Jahrhundert," in C. Starck, ed., *Bundesverfassungsgericht und Grundgesetz. Festgabe aus Anlaß des 25jährigen Bestehens des Bundesverfassungsgerichts*, 1st vol.: Verfassungsgerich tsbarkeit (Tübingen, 1976), 1–62.

Schiffers, Reinhard, *Grundlegung der Verfassungsgerichtsbarkeit. Das Gesetz über das Bundesverfassungsgericht vom 12. März 1951* (Düsseldorf, 1984).

Schlaich, Klaus, "Die Verfassungsgerichtsbarkeit im Gefüge der Staatsfunktionen," *Veröffentlichungen der Vereinigung der Deutschen Staatsrechtslehrer*, 39 (1981), 99–146.

Schlaich, Klaus and Stefan Korioth, *Das Bundesverfassungsgericht. Stellung, Verfahren, Entscheidungen* (8th edn., Munich, 2010).

Schlink, Bernhard, "Die Entthronung der Staatsrechtswissenschaft durch die Verfassungsgerichtsbarkeit," *Der Staat*, 28 (1981), 161–72.

Schlink, Bernhard, "Der Grundsatz der Verhältnismäßigkeit," in P. Badura and H. Dreier, eds., *Festschrift 50 Jahre Bundesverfassungsgericht*, 2nd vol. (Tübingen, 2001), 445–66.

Schlink, Bernhard, "Abschied von der Dogmatik. Verfassungsrechtsprechung und Verfassungsrechtwissenschaft im Wandel," *Juristenzeitung*, 62 (2007), 157–62.

Schmidt-Aßmann, Eberhard, *Das allgemeine Verwaltungsrecht als Ordnungsidee. Grundlagen und Aufgaben der verwaltungsrechtlichen Systembildung* (2nd edn., Berlin, 2006).

Schmitt, Carl, *Verfassungslehre* (Munich, 1928).

Schmitt, Carl, *Der Hüter der Verfassung* (Tübingen, 1931).

Schnapper, Dominique, *Une Sociologue au Conseil Constitutionnel* (Paris, 2010).

Schneider, Hans-Peter, "Acht an der Macht! Das Bundesverfassungsgericht als "Reparaturbetrieb" des Parlamentarismus?," *Neue Juristische Wochenschrift*, 52 (1999b), 1303–5.

Schneider, Hans-Peter, "Richter oder Schlichter? Das Bundesverfassungsgericht als Integrationsfaktor," *Aus Politik und Zeitgeschichte*, 16 (1999a), 9–19.

Schoch, Friedrich, "Der funktionale Zusammenhang zwischen der Vertrauensfrage des Bundeskanzlers und dem parlamentarischen Regierungssystem," *Zeitschrift für Staats- und Europawissenschaften*, 4 (2006), 88–102.

Scholz, Rupert, "Das Bundesverfassungsgericht: Hüter der Verfassung oder Ersatzgesetzgeber?," *Aus Politik und Zeitgeschichte*, 16 (1999), 3–8.

Schönberger, Christoph, "Die überholte Parlamentarisierung. Einflussgewinn und fehlende Herrschaftsfähigkeit des Reichstags im sich demokratisierenden Kaiserreich," *Historische Zeitschrift*, 272 (2001), 623–66.

Schönberger, Christoph, "'Verwaltungsrechtals konkretisiertes Verfassungsrecht'. Die Entstehung eines grundgesetzabhängigen Verwaltungsrechts in der frühen Bundesrepublik," in M. Stolleis, ed., *Das Bonner Grundgesetz. Altes Recht und neue Verfassung in den ersten Jahrzehnten der Bundesrepublik Deutschland (1949–1969)* (Berlin, 2006), 53–84.

Schönberger, Christoph, "Die Europäische Union zwischen 'Demokratiedefizit und Bundesstaatsverbot. Anmerkungen zum Lissabon-Urteil des Bundesverfassungsgerichts," *Der Staat*, 48 (2009), 535–59.

Schönberger, Christoph, "Der Aufstieg der Verfassung: Zweifel an einer geläufigen Triumphgeschichte," in T. Vesting and S. Korioth, eds., *Der Eigenwert des Verfassungsrechts. Was bleibt von der Verfassung nach der Globalisierung?* (Tübingen, 2011), 7–22.

Schönberger, Christoph, "Der Vorrang der Verfassung," in I. Appel, G. Hermes, and C. Schönberger, eds., *Öffentliches Recht im offenen Staat. Festschrift für Rainer Wahl* (Berlin, 2011c), 385–404.

Schönberger, Christoph, "Werte als Gefahr für das Recht? Carl Schmitt und die Karlsruher Republik," in C. Schmitt, ed., *Die Tyrannei der Werte* (3rd edn., Berlin, 2011d), 57–91.

Schorkopf, Frank, "Die prozessuale Steuerung des Verfassungsrechtsschutzes. Zum Verhältnis von materiellem Recht und Verfassungsprozessrecht," *Archiv des öffentlichen Rechts*, 130 (2005), 465–93.

Schorkopf, Frank, ed., *Der Europäische Haftbefehl vor dem Bundesverfassungsgericht* (Tübingen, 2006).

Schulze-Fielitz, Helmuth, "Das Bundesverfassungsgericht in der Krise des Zeitgeistes. Zur Metadogmatik der Verfassungsinterpretation," *Archiv des öffentlichen Rechts*, 122 (1997), 1–31.

Schulze-Fielitz, Helmuth, "Das Bundesverfassungsgericht und die öffentliche Meinung," in G. F. Schuppert and C. Bumke, eds., *Bundesverfassungsgericht und gesellschaftlicher Grundkonsens* (Baden-Baden, 2000), 111–44.

Schulze-Fielitz, Helmuth, "Schattenseiten des Grundgesetzes," in H. Dreier, ed., *Macht und Ohnmacht des Grundgesetzes* (Berlin, 2009), 9–50.

Schuppert, Gunnar Folke and Christian Bumke, *Die Konstitutionalisierung der Rechtsordnung. Überlegungen zum Verhältnis von verfassungsrechtlicher Ausstrahlungswirkung und Eigenständigkeit des "einfachen" Rechts* (Baden-Baden, 2000).

Schwarz, Hans-Peter, *Adenauer. Der Aufstieg: 1876–1952* (Stuttgart, 1986).

Segal, Jeffrey A. and Harold J. Spaeth, *The Supreme Court and the Attitudinal Model Revisited* (Cambridge, 2002).

Seyfarth, Georg, *Die Änderung der Rechtsprechung durch das Bundesverfassungsgericht* (Berlin, 1998).

Shapiro, Martin, *Courts. A Comparative and Political Analysis* (Chicago, 1981).

Sieberer, Ulrich, "Strategische Zurückhaltung von Verfassungsgerichten. Gewaltenteilungsvorstellungen und die Grenzen der Justizialisierung," *Zeitschrift für Politikwissenschaften*, 16 (2006), 1299–323.

Simmel, Georg, *Soziologie. Untersuchungen über die Formen der Vergesellschaftung* (3rd edn., Munich, 1923).

Simon, Helmut, "Verfassungsgerichtsbarkeit," in E. Benda, W. Maihofer, and H.-J. Vogel, eds., *Handbuch des Verfassungsrechts* (2nd edn., Berlin, 1995).

Slaughter, Anne-Marie, "A Global Community of Courts," *Harvard International Law Journal*, 44 (2003), 191–219.

Slaughter, Anne-Marie, *The New World Order* (Princeton, 2004).

Smend, Rudolf, "Das Bundesverfassungsgericht. Festvortrag zur Feier des zehnjährigen Bestehens des BVerfG am 26. Januar 1962," in R. Smend, ed., *Staatsrechtliche Abhandlungen und andere Aufsätze* (2nd edn., Berlin, 1968), 581–93.

Smend, Rudolf, "Festvortrag zur Feier des zehnjährigen Bestehens des Bundesverfassungsgerichts am 26. Januar 1962," in Bundesverfassungsgericht, ed., *Das Bundesverfassungsgericht 1951–1971* (Karlsruhe, 1971), 15–29.

Smend, Rudolf, "Verfassung und Verfassungsrecht," in R. Smend, ed., *Staatsrechtliche Abhandlungen und andere Aufsätze* (3rd edn., Berlin, 1994), 119–276.

Smith, Rogers, "Political Jurisprudence, the 'New Institutionalism,' and the Future of Public Law," *American Political Science Review*, 82 (1988), 89–108.

Sofsky, Wolfgang and Rainer Paris, *Figurationen sozialer Macht. Autorität—Stellvertretung—Koalition* (Frankfurt/Main, 1994).

Sörgel, Werner, *Konsensus und Interessen. Eine Studie zur Entstehung des Grundgesetzes für die Bundesrepublik Deutschland* (Stuttgart, 1969).

Spieker, Frank, *Hermann Höpker-Aschoff—Vater der Finanzverfassung* (Berlin, 2004).

Staupe, Jürgen, *Parlamentsvorbehalt und Delegationsbefugnis. Zur "Wesentlichkeitslehre" und zur Reichweite legislativer Regelungskompetenz, insbesondere im Schulrecht* (Berlin, 1986).

Stein, Erwin, "Zur staatskirchenrechtlichen Rechtsprechung des Bundesverfassungsgerichts," *Juristen-Jahrbuch*, 8 (1967), 120.

Steiner, Udo, "Zum Kooperationsverhältnis von Bundesverfassungsgericht und Europäischem Gerichtshof für Menschenrechte," in S. Detterbeck, ed., *Recht als Medium der Staatlichkeit. Festschrift für Herbert Bethge zum 70. Geburtstag* (Berlin, 2009), 653–68.

Stern, Klaus, "Zur Entstehung und Ableitung des Übermaßverbots," in P. Badura and R. Scholz, eds., *Wege und Verfahren des Verfassungslebens. Festschrift für Peter Lerche zum 65. Geburtstag* (Munich, 1993), 165–75.

Sternberger, Dolf, "Verfassungspatriotismus," in D. Sternberger, *Schriften*, 10th vol. (Frankfurt/Main, 1990), 3–16.

Stolleis, Michael, "Verwaltungsrechtswissenschaft in der Bundesrepublik Deutschland," in D. Simon, ed., *Rechtswissenschaft in der Bonner Republik. Studien zur Wissenschaftsgeschichte der Jurisprudenz* (Frankfurt/Main, 1994), 227–58.

Stone Sweet, Alec, *Governing with Judges. Constitutional Politics in Europe* (Oxford, 2000).

Stüwe, Klaus, "Das Bundesverfassungsgericht als verlängerter Arm der Opposition?," *Aus Politik und Zeitgeschichte*, 37/38 (2001), 34–44.

Sunstein, Cass R., *Legal Reasoning and Political Conflict* (New York, 1996).
Sunstein, Cass R., *One Case at a Time. Judicial Minimalism on the Supreme Court* (Cambridge, 1999).
Sunstein, Cass R., *A Constitution of Many Minds. Why the Founding Document Doesn"t Mean What It Meant Before* (Princeton, 2009).
Sunstein, Cass. R., "Legal Interference with Private Preferences," *University of Chicago Law Review*, 53 (1986), 1129–74.
Taylor, Charles, *Das Unbehagen an der Moderne* (Frankfurt/Main, 1995).
Thoma, Richard, "Rechtsgutachten betreffend die Stellung des Bundesverfassungsgerichts," Legal Opinion furnished in 1953 for the Federal Ministry of Justice, published in: *Jahrbuch des öffentlichen Rechts der Gegenwart*, 6 (1957), 161–94.
Treitschke, Heinrich von, "Bundesstaat und Einheitsstaat," in H. von Treitschke, *Historische und Politische Aufsätze*, 2nd vol. (8th edn., Leipzig, 1921), 74–235.
Tribe, Laurence H., *American Constitutional Law* (3rd edn., New York, 2000).
Troper, Michel, "The Logic of Justification of Judicial Review," *International Constitutional Law*, 1 (2003), 99–121.
Tushnet, Mark, "The Possibilities of Comparative Constitutional Law," *The Yale Law Journal*, 108 (1999), 1225–309.
Tushnet, Mark, *Weak Courts, Strong Rights. Judicial Review and Social Welfare Rights in Comparative Constitutional Law* (Princeton, 2008).
Van Ooyen, Robert C., *Der Begriff des Politischen des Bundesverfassungsgerichts* (Berlin, 2005).
Vanberg, Georg, *The Politics of Constitutional Review in Germany* (Cambridge, 2004).
Vogel, Hans-Jochen, "Videant Judices! Zur aktuellen Kritik am Bundesverfassungsgericht," *Die Öffentliche Verwaltung*, 31 (1978), 665–8.
Volkmann, Uwe, "Rechtsgewinnung aus Bildern. Beobachtungen über den Einfluss dirigierender Hintergrundvorstellungen auf die Auslegung des heutigen Verfassungsrechts," in J. Krüper, et al., eds., *An den Grenzen der Rechtsdogmatik* (Tübingen, 2010), 77–90.
Volkmann, Uwe, "Der Aufstieg der Verfassung. Beobachtungen zum grundlegenden Wandel des Verfassungsbegriffs," in T. Vesting and S. Korioth, eds., *Der Eigenwert des Verfassungsrechts. Was bleibt von der Verfassung nach der Globalisierung?* (Tübingen, 2011), 23–40.
Vorländer, Hans, "Integration durch Verfassung? Die symbolische Bedeutung der Verfassung im politischen Integrationsprozess," in H. Vorländer, ed., *Integration durch Verfassung* (Wiesbaden, 2002), 9–40.
Vorländer, Hans, "Deutungsmacht—Die Macht der Verfassungsgerichtsbarkeit," in H. Vorländer, ed., *Die Deutungsmacht der Verfassungsgerichtsbarkeit* (Wiesbaden, 2006), 9–33.
Vorländer, Hans and André Brodocz, "Das Vertrauen in das Bundesverfassungsgericht. Ergebnisse einer repräsentativen Bevölkerungsumfrage," in H. Vorländer, ed., *Die Deutungsmacht der Verfassungsgerichtsbarkeit* (Wiesbaden, 2006), 259–95.
Vorländer, Hans and Gary S. Schaal, "Integration durch Institutionenvertrauen? Das Bundesverfassungsgericht und die Akzeptanz seiner Rechtsprechung," in H. Vorländer, ed., *Integration durch Verfassung* (Opladen, 2002), 343–74.
Voßkuhle, Andreas, "Theorie und Praxis der verfassungskonformen Auslegung von Gesetzen durch Fachgerichte. Kritische Bestandsaufnahme und Versuch einer Neubestimmung," *Archiv des öffentlichen Rechts*, 125 (2000), 177–201.
Voßkuhle, Andreas, "Gibt es und wozu nutzt eine Lehre vom Verfassungswandel?," *Der Staat*, 43 (2004), 450–9.

Voßkuhle, Andreas, "Stabilität, Zukunftsoffenheit und Vielfaltssicherung—Die Pflege des verfassungsrechtlichen "Quellcodes" durch das BVerfG," *Juristenzeitung*, 64 (2009), 917–24.

Voßkuhle, Andreas, "Der europäische Verfassungsgerichtsverbund," *Neue Zeitschrift für Verwaltungsrecht*, 29 (2010a), 1–8.

Voßkuhle, Andreas, "Die Integrationsverantwortung des Bundesverfassungsgerichts," in P. Axer, et al., eds., *Das Europäische Verwaltungsrecht in der Konsolidierungsphase. Systembildung—Disziplinierung—Internationalisierung, Die Verwaltung*, supplement, 10 (Berlin, 2010b), 229–39.

Voßkuhle, Andreas, "Kommentierung Artikel 93 GG," in H. v. Mangoldt, F. Klein, and C. Starck, eds., *Kommentar zum Grundgesetz*, 3rd vol. (6th edn., Munich, 2010c), 665–787.

Wahl, Rainer, "Rechtliche Wirkungen und Funktionen der Grundrechte im deutschen Konstitutionalismus des 19. Jahrhunderts," *Der Staat*, 18 (1979), 321–48.

Wahl, Rainer, "Quo Vadis—Bundesverfassungsgericht? Zur Lage von Verfassungsgerichtsbarkeit, Verfassung und Staatsdenken," in B. Guggenberger and T. Würtenberger, eds., *Hüter der Verfassung oder Lenker der Politik? Das Bundesverfassungsgericht im Widerstreit* (Baden-Baden, 1998), 81–120.

Wahl, Rainer, "Der Vorrang der Verfassung," in R. Wahl, ed., *Verfassungsstaat, Europäisierung, Internationalisierung* (Frankfurt/Main, 2003), 121–60.

Wahl, Rainer, "Die objektiv-rechtliche Dimension der Grundrechte im internationalen Vergleich," in D. Merten and H.-J. Papier, eds., *Handbuch der Grundrechte in Deutschland und Europa*, 1st vol. (Heidelberg, 2004), 745–82.

Wahl, Rainer, "Lüth und die Folgen: Ein Urteil als Weichenstellung für die Rechtsentwicklung," in T. Henne and A. Riedlinger, eds., *Das Lüth-Urteil in (rechts-) historischer Sicht. Die Konflikte um Veit Harlan und die Grundrechtsjudikatur des Bundesverfassungsgerichts* (Berlin, 2005), 371–97.

Wahl, Rainer and Joachim Wieland, "Verfassungsrechtsprechung als knappes Gut," *Juristenzeitung*, 51 (1996), 1137–45.

Waldhoff, Christian, "Erna Scheffler—erste Richterin des Bundesverfassungsgerichts," *Jahrbuch des öffentlichen Rechts der Gegenwart*, 56 (2008a), 261–8.

Waldhoff, Christian, "Steuerrecht und Verfassungsrecht. Bericht über ausgewählte Entscheidungen zu verfassungsrechtlichen Vorgaben für die Besteuerung der Jahre 2002–2007," *Die Verwaltung*, 41 (2008b), 259–94.

Waldron, Jeremy, *Law and Disagreement* (Oxford, 1999).

Waldron, Jeremy, "The Core of the Case Against Judicial Review," *The Yale Law Journal*, 115 (2006), 1346–406.

Walter, Christian, "Hüter oder Wandler der Verfassung? Zur Rolle des Bundesverfassungsgerichts im Prozess des Verfassungswandels," *Archiv des öffentlichen Rechts*, 125 (2000), 517–50.

Weber, Max, "Die drei reinen Typen legitimer Herrschaft," in J. Winckelmann, ed., *Gesammelte Aufsätze zur Wissenschaftslehre* (7th edn., Tübingen, 1988 [1922]), 475–88.

Weber, Werner, *Spannungen und Kräfte im westdeutschen Verfassungssystem* (Stuttgart, 1951).

Weinkauff, Hermann, "Der Naturrechtsgedanke in der Rechtsprechung des Bundesgerichtshofs," *Neue Juristische Wochenschrift*, 13 (1960), 1689–96.

Wellmer, Albrecht, *Endgames—The Irreconcilable Nature of Modernity, Essays and Lectures* (translated by David Midgley), (Cambridge (MA) and London, 1998).

Wendenburg, Helge, *Die Debatte um die Verfassungsgerichtsbarkeit und der Methodenstreit der Staatsrechtslehre in der Weimarer Republik* (Göttingen, 1984).

Wengst, Udo, *Staatsaufbau und Regierungspraxis 1948–1953. Zur Geschichte der Verfassungsorgane der Bundesrepublik Deutschland* (Düsseldorf, 1984).

Werner, Fritz, "Verwaltungsrecht als konkretisiertes Verfassungsrecht," *Deutsches Verwaltungsblatt*, 74 (1959), 527–33.

Wesel, Uwe, *Der Gang nach Karlsruhe. Das Bundesverfassungsgericht in der Geschichte der Bundesrepublik Deutschland* (Munich, 2004).

Wiegandt, Manfred H., *Norm und Wirklichkeit. Gerhard Leibholz (1901–1982)—Leben, Werk und Richteramt* (Baden-Baden, 1995).

Wieland, Joachim, "Kommentierung Art. 14 GG," in H. Dreier, ed., *Grundgesetz Kommentar*, 1st vol. (2nd edn., Tübingen, 2004).

Wild, Michael, "BVerfGE 2, 79 - Wiederbewaffnung III. BVerfG und 'Hohe Politik,'" in J. Menzel and R. Müller-Terpitz, ed., *Verfassungsrechtsprechung. Hundert Entscheidungen des Bundesverfassungsgerichts in Retrospektive* (2nd edn., Tübingen: Mohr Siebeck, 2011) 69–73.

Wißmann, Hinnerk, "Wo kein Kläger, da kein Richter. Verfassungsprozessuale Anmerkungen zum Urteil des BVerfG v. 14.7.1998," *Die Öffentliche Verwaltung*, 52 (1999), 152–6.

Wißmann, Hinnerk, *Generalklauseln. Verwaltungsbefugnisse zwischen Gesetzmäßigkeit und offenen Normen* (Tübingen, 2008).

Wißmann, Hinnerk and David Heuer, "'Hirten der Verfassung'? Das Bundesverfassungsgericht, die Kirchen und der Sonntagsschutz," *Juristische Ausbildung*, 33 (2011), 214–22.

Wittig, Peter, "Politische Rücksichten in der Rechtsprechung des Bundesverfassungsgerichts," *Der Staat*, 8 (1969), 137–58.

Zuck, Rüdiger, "Die Wissenschaftlichen Mitarbeiter des Bundesverfassungsgerichts," in R. C. van Ooyen and M. H. W. Möllers, eds., *Das Bundesverfassungsgericht im politischen System* (Wiesbaden, 2006), 283–92.

Zweigert, Konrad, "Die Verfassungsbeschwerde," *Juristenzeitung*, 7 (1952), 321–9.

Zweigert, Konrad, "Duktus der Rechtsprechung des Ersten Senats des Bundesverfassungsgerichts und einige Erinnerungen an seine Anfangszeit," in Bundesverfassungsgericht, ed., *Das Bundesverfassungsgericht 1951–1971* (Karlsruhe, 1971), 95–120.

Zweigert, Konrad, "Einige rechtsvergleichende und kritische Bemerkungen zur Verfassungsgerichtsbarkeit," in C. Starck, ed., *Bundesverfassungsgericht und Grundgesetz. Festgabe aus Anlaß des 25jährigen Bestehens des Bundesverfassungsgerichts*, 1st vol.: Verfas sungsgerichtsbarkeit (Tübingen, 1976), 63–75.

Index

Note: *For the benefit of digital users, indexed terms that span two pages (e.g., 52–53) may, on occasion, appear on only one of those pages.*